THE TIEBOUT MODEL AT FIFTY

Charles Tiebout, circa 1950. Courtesy of Bruce Tiebout.

THE TIEBOUT MODEL

AT

FIFTY

Essays in
Public Economics
in Honor of Wallace Oates

EDITED BY

William A. Fischel

LINCOLN INSTITUTE
OF LAND POLICY
CAMBRIDGE, MASSACHUSETTS

Library of Congress Cataloging-in-Publication Data

The Tiebout Model at fifty : essays in public economics in honor of Wallace Oates / edited by William A. Fischel.
p. cm.
Includes bibliographical references and index.
ISBN 1-55844-165-4 (alk. paper)
1. Local finance—United States. 2. Property tax—United States. I. Fischel, William A.
II. Oates, Wallace E. III. Title.
HJ9777.A3T54 2006
336'.014—dc22   2006003713

Designed by Janis Owens, Books By Design, Inc.

Composed in Minion by SPI Publisher Services in Worcester, Massachusetts.
Printed and bound by Webcom Limited in Toronto, Ontario, Canada.
The paper is Legacy Offset, a 100% recycled, acid-free sheet.

MANUFACTURED IN CANADA

Contents

Foreword

This conference volume owes its conception and execution to the energy and entrepreneurial efforts of Bill Fischel, who obtained support for the papers, conference, and volume from the Lincoln Institute of Land Policy and the Rockefeller Center for Public Policy and the Social Sciences. The issues addressed here—related to local public finance and the taxation of land and property—are focal points for the Lincoln Institute's work program. The Institute is pleased to have supported and facilitated this work. It is also fitting that the volume honors the contributions of Wally Oates. He has played a critical role as expositor and popularizer of the Tiebout hypothesis. While Tiebout holds the patent on the hypothesis, Oates brought the product to market. In addition, the Lincoln Institute is fortunate to have Wally Oates as a member of its board of directors.

The papers in this volume mainly address empirical work on the Tiebout hypothesis in the United States, but related work has also been carried out in many other countries. For example, a paper recently authored for a Lincoln conference by Paul Cheshire and Stephen Sheppard, "Capitalising the Value of Free Schools: The Impact of Supply Characteristics and Uncertainty," addresses the relationship between school quality and housing prices in the United Kingdom.[1] There has been relatively little work in developing countries examining household choice of residences based on local services, because most metropolitan areas in developing countries have single, integrated metropolitan governments. However, a great deal of analysis covers a closely related topic—the use of betterment levies or value capture as a mechanism for financing provision of local services such as sidewalks, street lights, drainage, and road

---

[1] This paper, published in *The Economic Journal*, volume 114, issue 499 (November 2004), was selected by the Royal Economic Society as the best paper published in *The Economic Journal* in 2004.

paving.[2] In addition, in developing countries public services are also capitalized into land and property prices much as in the United States.

As work on the Tiebout hypothesis proceeds in the United States and elsewhere, a number of issues may deserve more empirical attention, including the following three. First, most work on the Tiebout hypothesis addresses the demand side, with little work addressing the implications of demand competition for the supply side. For example, is there any evidence that competition among local governments in a Tiebout setting affects the efficiency of local service production? Second, on the supply side, is there any evidence that local governments alter their existing bundles of services or innovate new products to attract households? Relatively little is known about sources of innovation in local public service provision, and the forces underlying the Tiebout hypothesis may play a role. Finally, zoning restrictions are often envisioned as keeping out the poor, but recent moves to limit the size of residences (through ordinances that regulate mansionization) seem aimed at limiting housing investment. It would be useful to analyze this new phenomenon from the perspective of the Tiebout hypothesis. This collection leads the way toward addressing some of these issues.

Gregory K. Ingram
President and CEO
Lincoln Institute of Land Policy

---

[2] The use of betterment levies in Colombia, termed *valorización*, is described in Roy Bahl and Johannes Linn, *Urban Public Finance in Developing Countries* (Oxford University Press, 1992).

Preface

Charles Tiebout's 1956 article, "A Pure Theory of Local Expenditures," is the most influential single article in the field of public economics, at least if one measures influence by citations in scholarly journals. Tiebout proposed an alternative to the political process for determining the demand for local public goods. Households would reveal their preferences by choosing their residence among local governments. People would "vote with their feet" (not Tiebout's term) instead of the ballot box, choosing the desired level of services among the many local governments that make up most American metropolitan areas. His approach has become the touchstone for the economic analysis of local government, and its influence in other areas of political economy continues to grow.

It occurred to me that the fiftieth anniversary of Tiebout's publication would be a good time to collect scholars who have been actively using its perspective in their work. They would present papers that both took stock of what had been done and illustrated the ongoing influence of this model. I contacted Joan Youngman at the Lincoln Institute of Land Policy in Cambridge, and she was enthusiastic and, even better, inclined to offer generous support for the conference and publication. Jim Brown, who was in his final year as president of the Institute, was as enthusiastic as Joan, and incoming president Greg Ingram continued his support and was an active participant in the conference. My Dartmouth colleague Andrew Samwick had recently become director of the Rockefeller Center for Social Sciences at Dartmouth, and he offered the services of the center in hosting the conference. Much of the organizing work was done by Judy Fothergill. I am grateful to all for their services and support.

The event itself came to pass in June 2005, in Hanover, New Hampshire. A special honor was the participation of the dean of public economics, Richard Musgrave, who had been Charles Tiebout's teacher at the University of Michigan. Richard and Peggy summer in Vermont at their house near Dartmouth, and

conference participants were appreciative of their insightful comments and rec-
ollections of a career that spanned more than half of the twentieth century.

The idea for the conference and volume was hardly original. I had long been
aware of the excellent and still-relevant volume that George Zodrow had put
together, *Local Provision of Public Services: The Tiebout Model After Twenty-Five
Years* (1983). Zodrow's conference was held on the twenty-fifth anniversary
year, 1981, which is why his date of publication was two years later. I held the
fiftieth-anniversary event a year early partly to ensure that publication would
actually occur on the fiftieth anniversary, but mostly because I wanted to get the
pick of the Tiebout scholars before someone else organized an event.

I should not have worried about the supply of scholars. The Tiebout model
has been worked into an even wider field of scholarship than it was in 1981.
Tiebout's is that rare paper whose influence rises with the passage of decades,
and my initial list of potential invitees was so large that I had serious problems
pruning it to a manageable number. I recruited Jon Sonstelie to help in the
selection and to sound out ideas, but those miffed at not attending have only
me to blame. I also thank the Department of Economics of the University of
California, Santa Barbara, which provided office support during my sabbatical
leave, when the editorial work for this volume was completed.

One definition of a classic is the article that everyone knows but no one reads.
To help remedy that deficiency, Tiebout's 1956 article is reprinted on the following
pages. Those who have not seen it may be pleasantly surprised by how readable it
is. Thanks to the University of Chicago Press for permission to reprint the article.

The conference and volume are also tributes to Wallace Oates, whose name
is inextricably linked with Tiebout's in local public economics. Oates's 1969
paper on capitalization gave empirical content to Tiebout's article. In his 1972
book, *Fiscal Federalism*, Oates wove the Tiebout model into this important area
of economics. Few economists would disagree that Oates put Tiebout on the
map, and this celebration of Tiebout's original paper must also be regarded as
a celebration of the work that Oates did to bring this idea into the realm of public economics. Besides his published works, Wally's thoughtfulness, personal
modesty, and friendliness have done much to make Tiebout's somewhat jarring
idea acceptable to skeptical economists.

William A. Fischel
Santa Barbara, California
December 2005

A Pure Theory of
Local Expenditures[1]

CHARLES M. TIEBOUT

One of the most important recent developments in the area of "applied economic theory" has been the work of Musgrave and Samuelson in public finance theory.[2] The two writers agree on what is probably the major point under investigation, namely, that no "market type" solution exists to determine the level of expenditures on public goods. Seemingly, we are faced with the problem of having a rather large portion of our national income allocated in a "non-optimal" way when compared with the private sector.

This discussion will show that the Musgrave-Samuelson analysis, which is valid for federal expenditures, need not apply to local expenditures. The plan of the discussion is first to restate the assumptions made by Musgrave and Samuelson and the central problems with which they deal. After looking at a key difference between the federal versus local cases, I shall present a simple model. This model yields a solution for the level of expenditures for local public goods which reflects the preferences of the population

Reproduced by permission from the University of Chicago Press from Charles M. Tiebout, "A Pure Theory of Local Expenditures," *Journal of Political Economy* 64:5 (Chicago: University of Chicago Press, 1956), 416–424, © 1956 by the University of Chicago.

[1] I am grateful for the comments of my colleagues Karl de Schweinitz, Robert Eisner, and Robert Strotz, and those of Martin Bailey, of the University of Chicago.

[2] Richard A. Musgrave, "The Voluntary Exchange Theory of Public Economy," *Quarterly Journal of Economics*, LII (February, 1939), 213–17; "A Multiple Theory of the Budget," paper read at the Econometric Society annual meeting (December, 1955); and his forthcoming book, *The Theory of Public Economy*; Paul A. Samuelson, "The Pure Theory of Public Expenditures," *Review of Economics and Statistics*, XXXVI, No. 4 (November, 1954), 387–89, and "Diagrammatic Exposition of a Pure Theory of Public Expenditures," *ibid.*, XXXVII, No. 4 (November, 1955), 350–56.

more adequately than they can be reflected at the national level. The assumptions of the model will then be relaxed to see what implications are involved. Finally, policy considerations will be discussed.

The Theoretical Issue

Samuelson has defined public goods as "*collective consumption goods* ($X_n + 1, \ldots, X_n + n$) which all enjoy in common in the sense that each individual's consumption of such a good leads to no subtraction from any other individual's consumption of that good, so that $X_n + j = X_n^i + j$ simultaneously for each and every *i*th individual and each collective good."[3] While definitions are a matter of choice, it is worth noting that "consumption" has a much broader meaning here than in the usual sense of the term. Not only does it imply that the

act of consumption by one person does not diminish the opportunities for consumption by another but it also allows this consumption to be in another form. For example, while the residents of a new government housing project are made better off, benefits also accrue to other residents of the community in the form of the external economies of slum clearance.[4] Thus many goods that appear to lack the attributes of public goods may properly be considered public if consumption is defined to include these external economies.[5]

A definition alternative to Samuelson's might be simply that a public good is one which should be produced, but for which there is no feasible method of charging the consumers. This is less elegant, but has the advantage that it allows for the objections of Enke and Margolis.[6] This definition,

---

[3] "The Pure Theory . . . ," *op. cit.*, p. 387.

[4] Samuelson allows for this when he states that "one man's circus may be another man's poison," referring, of course, to public goods ("Diagrammatic Exposition . . . ," *op. cit.*, p. 351).

[5] There seems to be a problem connected with the external-economies aspect of public goods. Surely a radio broadcast, like national defense, has the attribute that A's enjoyment leaves B no worse off; yet this does not imply that broadcasting should, in a normative sense, be a public good (the arbitrary manner in which the level of radio programs is determined aside). The difference between defense and broadcasting is subtle but important. In both cases there is a problem of determining the optimal level of outputs and the corresponding level of benefits taxes. In the broadcasting case, however, A may be quite willing to pay more taxes than B, even if both have the same "ability to pay" (assuming that the benefits are determinate). Defense is another question. Here A is not content that B should pay less. A makes the *social judgment* that B's preference *should* be the same. A's preference, expressed as an annual defense expenditure such as $42.7 billion and representing the majority view, thus determines the level of defense. Here the A's may feel that the B's *should pay* the same amount of benefits tax.

If it is argued that this case is typical of public goods, then, once the level is somehow set, the voluntary exchange approach and the benefit theory associated with it do not make sense. If the preceding analysis is correct, we are now back in the area of equity in terms of ability to pay.

[6] They argue that, for most of the goods supplied by governments, increased use by some consumer-voters leaves less available for other consumer-voters. Crowded highways and schools, as contrasted with national defense, may be cited as examples (see Stephen Enke, "More on the Misuse of Mathematics in Economics: A Rejoinder," *Review of Economics and Statistics*, XXXVII [May, 1955], 131–33; and Julius Margolis, "A Comment on the Pure Theory of Public Expenditure," *Review of Economics and Statistics*, XXXVII [November, 1955], 247–49).

unfortunately, does not remove any of the problems faced by Musgrave and Samuelson.

The core problem with which both Musgrave and Samuelson deal concerns the mechanism by which consumer-voters register their preferences for public goods. The consumer is, in a sense, surrounded by a government whose objective it is to ascertain his wants for public goods and tax him accordingly. To use Alchian's term, the government's revenue-expenditure pattern for goods and services is expected to "adapt to" consumers' preferences.[7] Both Musgrave and Samuelson have shown that, in the vertically additive nature of voluntary demand curves, this problem has only a conceptual solution. If all consumer-voters could somehow be forced to reveal their true preferences for public goods, then the amount of such goods to be produced and the appropriate benefits tax could be determined.[8] As things now stand, there is no mechanism to force the consumer-voter to state his true preferences; in fact, the "rational" consumer will understate his preferences and hope to enjoy the goods while avoiding the tax.

The current method of solving this problem operates, unsatisfactorily, through the political mechanism. The expenditure wants of a "typical voter" are somehow pictured. This objective on the expenditure side is then combined with an ability-to-pay principle on the revenue side, giving us our current budget. Yet in terms of a satisfactory theory of public finance, it would be desirable (1) to force the voter to reveal his preferences; (2) to be able to satisfy them in the same sense that a private goods market does; and (3) to tax him accordingly. The question arises whether there is any set of social institutions by which this goal can be approximated.

Local Expenditures

Musgrave and Samuelson implicitly assume that expenditures are handled at the central government level. However, the provision of such governmental services as police and fire protection, education, hospitals, and courts does not necessarily involve federal activity.[9] Many of these goods are provided by local governments. It is worthwhile to look briefly at the magnitude of these expenditures.[10]

---

[7] Armen A. Alchian, "Uncertainty, Evolution, and Economic Theory," *Journal of Political Economy*, LVIII (June, 1950), 211–21.

[8] The term "benefits tax" is used in contrast to the concept of taxation based on the "ability to pay," which really reduces to a notion that there is some "proper" distribution of income. Conceptually, this issue is separate from the problem of providing public goods and services (see Musgrave, "A Multiple Theory . . . ," *op. cit.*).

[9] The discussion that follows applies to local governments. It will be apparent as the argument proceeds that it also applies, with less force, to state governments.

[10] A question does arise as to just what are the proper expenditures to consider. Following Musgrave, I shall consider only expenditures on goods or services (his Branch I expenditures). Thus interest on the

Historically, local expenditures have exceeded those of the federal government. The thirties were the first peacetime years in which federal expenditures began to pull away from local expenditures. Even during the fiscal year 1954, federal expenditures on *goods and services exclusive of defense* amounted only to some 15 billions of dollars, while local expenditures during this same period amounted to some 17 billions of dollars. There is no need to quibble over which comparisons are relevant. The important point is that the often-neglected local expenditures are significant and, when viewed in terms of expenditures on goods and services only, take on even more significance. Hence an important question arises whether at this level of government any mechanism operates to insure that expenditures on these public goods approximate the proper level.

Consider for a moment the case of the city resident about to move to the suburbs. What variables will influence his choice of a municipality? If he has children, a high level of expenditures on schools may be important. Another person may prefer a community with a municipal golf course. The availability and quality of such facilities and services as beaches, parks, police protection, roads, and parking facilities will enter into the decision-making process. Of course, non-economic variables will also be considered, but this is of no concern at this point.

The consumer-voter may be viewed as picking that community which best satisfies his preference pattern for public goods. This is a major difference between central and local provision of public goods. At the central level the preferences of the consumer-voter are given, and the government tries to adjust to the pattern of these preferences, whereas at the local level various governments have their revenue and expenditure patterns more or less set.[11] Given these revenue and expenditure patterns, the consumer-voter moves to that community whose local government best satisfies his set of preferences. The greater the number of communities and the greater the variance among them, the closer the consumer will come to fully realizing his preference position.[12]

A Local Government Model

The implications of the preceding argument may be shown by postulating an extreme model. Here the following assumptions are made:

---

federal debt is not included. At the local level interest payments might be included, since they are considered payments for services currently used, such as those provided by roads and schools.

[11] This is an assumption about reality. In the extreme model that follows the patterns are assumed to be absolutely fixed.

[12] This is also true of many non-economic variables. Not only is the consumer-voter concerned with economic patterns, but he desires, for example, to associate with "nice" people. Again, the greater the number of communities, the closer he will come to satisfying his total preference function, which includes non-economic variables.

1. Consumer-voters are fully mobile and will move to that community where their preference patterns, which are set, are best satisfied.

2. Consumer-voters are assumed to have full knowledge of differences among revenue and expenditure patterns and to react to these differences.

3. There are a large number of communities in which the consumer-voters may choose to live.

4. Restrictions due to employment opportunities are not considered. It may be assumed that all persons are living on dividend income.

5. The public services supplied exhibit no external economies or diseconomies between communities.

Assumptions 6 and 7 to follow are less familiar and require brief explanations:

6. For every pattern of community services set by, say, a city manager who follows the preferences of the older residents of the community, there is an optimal community size. This optimum is defined in terms of the number of residents for which this bundle of services can be produced at the lowest average cost. This, of course, is closely analogous to the low point of a firm's average cost curve. Such a cost function implies that some factor or resource is fixed. If this were not so, there would be no logical reason to limit community size, given the preference patterns. In the same sense that the average cost curve has a minimum for one firm but can be reproduced by another there is seemingly no reason why a duplicate community cannot exist. The assumption that some factor is fixed explains why it is not possible for the community in question to double its size by growth. The factor may be the limited land area of a suburban community, combined with a set of zoning laws against apartment buildings. It may be the local beach, whose capacity is limited. Anything of this nature will provide a restraint.

In order to see how this restraint works, let us consider the beach problem. Suppose the preference patterns of the community are such that the optimum size population is 13,000. Within this set of preferences there is a certain demand per family for beach space. This demand is such that at 13,000 population a 500-yard beach is required. If the actual length of the beach is, say, 600 yards, then it is not possible to realize this preference pattern with twice the optimum population, since there would be too little beach space by 400 yards.

The assumption of a fixed factor is necessary, as will be shown later, in order to get a determinate number of communities. It also has the advantage of introducing a realistic restraint into the model.

7. The last assumption is that communities below the optimum size seek to attract new residents to lower average costs. Those above optimum size do just the opposite. Those at an optimum try to keep their populations constant.

This assumption needs to be amplified. Clearly, communities below the optimum size, through chambers of commerce or other agencies, seek to attract new residents. This is best exemplified by the housing developments in some suburban areas, such as Park Forest in the Chicago area and Levittown in the New York area, which need to reach an optimum size. The same is true of communities that try to attract manufacturing industries by setting up certain facilities and getting an optimum number of firms to move into the industrially zoned area.

The case of the city that is too large and tries to get rid of residents is more difficult to imagine. No alderman in his right political mind would ever admit that the city is too big. Nevertheless, economic forces are at work to push people out of it. Every resident who moves to the suburbs to find better schools, more parks, and so forth, is reacting, in part, against the pattern the city has to offer.

The case of the community which is at the optimum size and tries to remain so is not hard to visualize. Again proper zoning laws, implicit agreements among realtors, and the like are sufficient to keep the population stable.

Except when this system is in equilibrium, there will be a subset of consumer-voters who are discontented with the patterns of their community. Another set will be satisfied. Given the assumption about mobility and the other assumptions listed previously, movement will take place out of the communities of greater than optimal size into the communities of less than optimal size. The consumer-voter moves to the community that satisfies his preference pattern.

The act of moving or failing to move is crucial. Moving or failing to move replaces the usual market test of willingness to buy a good and reveals the consumer-voter's demand for public goods. Thus each locality has a revenue and expenditure pattern that reflects the desires of its residents. The next step is to see what this implies for the allocation of public goods at the local level.

Each city manager now has a certain demand for n local public goods. In supplying these goods, he and $m-1$ other city managers may be considered as going to a national market and bidding for the appropriate units of service of each kind: so many units of police for the ith community; twice that number for the jth community; and so on. The demand on the public goods market for each of the n commodities will be the sum of the demands of the m communities. In the limit, as shown in a less realistic model to be developed later, this total demand will approximate the demand that represents the true preferences of the consumer-voters—that is, the demand they would reveal, if they were forced, somehow, to state their true preferences.[13] In this model there is no attempt on the part of local gov-

---

[13] The word "approximate" is used in recognition of the limitations of this model, and of the more severe model to be developed shortly, with respect to the cost of mobility. This issue will be discussed later.

ernments to "adapt to" the preferences of consumer-voters. Instead, those local governments that attract the optimum number of residents may be viewed as being "adopted by" the economic system.[14]

A Comparison Model

It is interesting to contrast the results of the preceding model with those of an even more severe model in order to see how these results differ from the normal market result. It is convenient to look at this severe model by developing its private-market counterpart. First assume that there are no public goods, only private ones. The preferences for these goods can be expressed as one of n patterns. Let a law be passed that all persons living in any one of the communities shall spend their money in the particular pattern described for that community by law. Given our earlier assumptions 1 through 5, it follows that, if the consumers move to the community whose law happens to fit their preference pattern, they will be at their optimum. The n communities, in turn, will then send their buyers to market to purchase the goods for the consumer-voters in their community. Since this is simply a lumping together of all similar tastes for the purpose of making joint purchases, the allocation of resources will be the same as it would be if normal market forces

operated. This conceptual experiment is the equivalent of substituting the city manager for the broker or middleman.

Now turn the argument around and consider only public goods. Assume with Musgrave that the costs of additional services are constant.[15] Further, assume that a doubling of the population means doubling the amount of services required. Let the number of communities be infinite and let each announce a different pattern of expenditures on public goods. Define an empty community as one that fails to satisfy anybody's preference pattern. Given these assumptions, including the earlier assumptions 1 through 5, the consumer-voters will move to that community which *exactly* satisfies their preferences. This must be true, since a one-person community is allowed. The sum of the demands of the n communities reflects the demand for local public services. In this model the demand is exactly the same as it would be if it were determined by normal market forces.

However, this severe model does not make much sense. The number of communities is indeterminate. There is no reason why the number of communities will not be equal to the population, since each voter can find the one that exactly fits his preferences. Unless some sociological variable is introduced, this may reduce the solution of the problem of allocating

---

[14] See Alchian, *op. cit.*
[15] Musgrave, "Voluntary Exchange . . . ," *op. cit.*

public goods to the trite one of making each person his own municipal government. Hence this model is not even a first approximation of reality. It is presented to show the assumptions needed in a model of local government expenditures, which yields the same optimal allocation that a private market would.

The Local Government Model Re-examined

The first model, described by the first five assumptions together with assumptions 6 and 7, falls short of this optimum. An example will serve to show why this is the case.

Let us return to the community with the 500-yard beach. By assumption, its optimum population was set at 13,000, given its preference patterns. Suppose that some people in addition to the optimal 13,000 would choose this community if it were available. Since they cannot move into this area, they must accept the next best substitute.[16] If a perfect substitute is found, no problem exists. If one is not found, then the failure to reach the optimal preference position and the substitution of a lower position becomes a matter of degree. In so far as there are a number of communities with similar revenue and expenditure patterns, the solution will approximate the ideal "market" solution.

Two related points need to be mentioned to show the allocative results of this model: (1) changes in the costs of one of the public services will cause changes in the quantity produced; (2) the costs of moving from community to community should be recognized. Both points can be illustrated in one example.

Suppose lifeguards throughout the country organize and succeed in raising their wages. Total taxes in communities with beaches will rise. Now residents who are largely indifferent to beaches will be forced to make a decision. Is the saving of this added tax worth the cost of moving to a community with little or no beach? Obviously, this decision depends on many factors, among which the availability of and proximity to a suitable substitute community is important. If enough people leave communities with beaches and move to communities without beaches, the total amount of lifeguard services used will fall. These models then, unlike their private-market counterpart, have mobility as a cost of registering demand. The higher this cost, *ceteris paribus*, the less optimal the allocation of resources.

This distinction should not be blown out of proportion. Actually, the

---

[16] In the constant cost model with an infinite number of communities this problem does not arise, since the number of beaches can be doubled or a person can find another community that is a duplicate of his now filled first choice.

cost of registering demand comes through the introduction of space into the economy. Yet space affects the allocation not only of resources supplied by local governments but of those supplied by the private market as well. Every time available resources or production techniques change, a new location becomes optimal for the firm. Indeed, the very concept of the shopping trip shows that the consumer does pay a cost to register his demand for private goods. In fact, Koopmans has stated that the nature of the assignment problem is such that in a space economy with transport costs there is *no* general equilibrium solution as set by market forces.[17]

Thus the problems stated by this model are not unique; they have their counterpart in the private market. We are maximizing within the framework of the resources available. If production functions show constant returns to scale with generally diminishing factor returns, and if indifference curves are regularly convex, an optimal solution is possible. On the production side it is assumed that communities are forced to keep production costs at a minimum either through the efficiency of city managers or through competition from other communities.[18] Given this, on the demand side we may note with Samuelson that "each individual, in seeking as a competitive buyer to get to the highest level of indifference subject to given prices and *tax*, would be led as if by an Invisible Hand to the grand solution of the social maximum position."[19] Just as the consumer may be visualized as walking to a private market place to buy his goods, the prices of which are set, we place him in the position of walking to a community where the prices (taxes) of community services are set. Both trips take the consumer to market. There is no way in which the consumer can avoid revealing his preferences in a spatial economy. Spatial mobility provides the local public-goods counterpart to the private market's shopping trip.

External Economies and Mobility

Relaxing assumption 5 has some interesting implications. There are obvious external economies and diseconomies between communities. My community is better off if its neighbor sprays trees to prevent Dutch elm disease. On the other hand, my community is worse off if

---

[17] Tjalling Koopmans, "Mathematical Groundwork of Economic Optimization Theories," paper read at the annual meeting of the Econometric Society (December, 1954).

[18] In this model and in reality, the city manager or elected official who is not able to keep his costs (taxes) low compared with those of similar communities will find himself out of a job. As an institutional observation, it may well be that city managers are under greater pressure to minimize costs than their private-market counterparts—firm managers. This follows from (1) the reluctance of the public to pay taxes and, what may be more important, (2) the fact that the costs of competitors—other communities—are a matter of public record and may easily be compared.

[19] "The Pure Theory . . . ," *op. cit.*, p. 388. (Italics mine.)

the neighboring community has inadequate law enforcement.

In cases in which the external economies and diseconomies are of sufficient importance, some form of integration may be indicated.[20] Not all aspects of law enforcement are adequately handled at the local level. The function of the sheriff, state police, and the FBI—as contrasted with the local police—may be cited as resulting from a need for integration. In real life the diseconomies are minimized in so far as communities reflecting the same socioeconomic preferences are contiguous. Suburban agglomerations such as Westchester, the North Shore, and the Main Line are, in part, evidence of these external economies and diseconomies.

Assumptions 1 and 2 should be checked against reality. Consumer-voters do not have perfect knowledge and set preferences, nor are they perfectly mobile. The question is how do people actually react in choosing a community. There has been very little empirical study of the motivations of people in choosing a community. Such studies as have been undertaken seem to indicate a surprising awareness of differing revenue and expenditure patterns.[21] The general disdain with which proposals to integrate municipalities are met seems to reflect, in part, the fear that local revenue-expenditure patterns will be lost as communities are merged into a metropolitan area.

Policy Implications

The preceding analysis has policy implications for municipal integration, provision for mobility, and set local revenue and expenditure patterns. These implications are worth brief consideration.

On the usual economic welfare grounds, municipal integration is justified only if more of any service is forthcoming at the same total cost and without reduction of any other service. A general reduction of costs along with a reduction in one or more of the services provided cannot be justified on economic grounds unless the social welfare function is known. For example, those who argue for a metropolitan police force instead of local police cannot prove their case on purely economic grounds.[22] If one of the communities were to receive less police protection after integration than it received before, integration could be objected to as a violation of consumers' choice.

Policies that promote residential mobility and increase the knowledge

---

[20] I am grateful to Stanley Long and Donald Markwalder for suggesting this point.

[21] See Wendell Bell, "Familism and Suburbanization: One Test of the Choice Hypothesis," a paper read at the annual meeting of the American Sociological Society, Washington, D.C., August, 1955. Forthcoming in *Rural Sociology*, December, 1956.

[22] For example, in Cook County—the Chicago area—Sheriff Joseph Lohman argues for such a metropolitan police force.

of the consumer-voter will improve the allocation of government expenditures in the same sense that mobility among jobs and knowledge relevant to the location of industry and labor improve the allocation of private resources.

Finally, we may raise the normative question whether local governments *should*, to the extent possible, have a fixed revenue-expenditure pattern. In a large, dynamic metropolis this may be impossible. Perhaps it could more appropriately be considered by rural and suburban communities.

Conclusion

It is useful in closing to restate the problem as Samuelson sees it:

> However, no decentralized pricing system can serve to determine optimally these levels of collective consumption. Other kinds of "voting" or "signaling" would have to be tried. . . . Of course utopian voting and signaling schemes can be imagined. . . . The failure of market catallactics in no way denies the following truth: given sufficient knowledge the optimal decisions can always be found by scanning over all

the attainable states of the world and selecting the one which according to the postulated ethical welfare function is best. The solution "exists"; the problem is how to "find" it.[23]

It is the contention of this article that, for a substantial portion of collective or public goods, this problem *does have* a conceptual solution. If consumer-voters are fully mobile, the appropriate local governments, whose revenue-expenditure patterns are set, are adopted by the consumer-voters. While the solution may not be perfect because of institutional rigidities, this does not invalidate its importance. The solution, like a general equilibrium solution for a private spatial economy, is the best that can be obtained given preferences and resource endowments.

Those who are tempted to compare this model with the competitive private model may be disappointed. Those who compare the reality described by this model with the reality of the competitive model—given the degree of monopoly, friction, and so forth—*may* find that local government represents a sector where the allocation of public goods (as a reflection of the preferences of the population) need not take a back seat to the private sector.

---

[23] "The Pure Theory . . . ," *op. cit.*, pp. 388–89.

The Tiebout Model at Fifty

Footloose at Fifty:
An Introduction to the
Tiebout Anniversary Essays

WILLIAM A. FISCHEL

A conceit of scholars has it that only an author's writings, not his or her personal life, are worthy of study. I have nonetheless found that there is a ready audience for what I have been able to learn about the life of Charles Tiebout. This inquiry in turn spurred me to ask why Tiebout's article languished for 13 years until Wallace Oates published his 1969 empirical work. My answer is "external events." The 1950s were the low point for local government in the United States, and current interest in the Tiebout model reflects the growing influence of localism. The balance of this chapter attempts to put the rest of the articles in this volume in the context of the ever-growing literature on the Tiebout model.

Who Was Charles Tiebout?

Charles Mills Tiebout was born on October 12, 1924, and grew up in Greenwich, Connecticut. Despite his fame among social scientists, Charles is not the most famous Tiebout. His father, Harry, was a successful psychiatrist who treated, among other disorders, alcoholism. One of his patients was "Bill W.," a cofounder of Alcoholics Anonymous. Unlike other contemporary psychiatrists, Harry Tiebout thought there might be something worthwhile in the methods of AA, and after investigating them, he became a strong proponent of the method. Harry is revered in AA circles as one of the fathers of the movement for this reason.

Charles followed in the footsteps of his father and older brother when he entered Wesleyan University in 1941. According to his son Bruce, Tiebout was not initially happy there, and he dropped out in 1942 to join the Navy, in which he served until the end of World War II. In 1946 Charles returned to Wesleyan with his bride, the former Elizabeth Gray, and newfound motivation. He became an honors student of economics and a campus leader in a number of organizations. He began his graduate studies at the University of Michigan months after he received his Wesleyan B.A. in 1950. It is unclear why he sought an academic career, but the inspiration may have been his older brother, Harry Jr., who had obtained a Ph.D. in philosophy at Columbia and was beginning a long career at the University of Illinois as Charles was finishing Wesleyan.

At Michigan, Tiebout made public finance one of his fields of concentration. Richard Musgrave, who was then working on his canonical *The Theory of Public Finance* (1959), offered a seminar on the subject for graduate students. Tiebout took this seminar in 1951 or 1952. In a conversation in 1994, Musgrave told me that Tiebout had in this seminar orally responded to his proposition about preference revelation for public goods. The problem is that if consumers cannot be excluded from public goods, would-be providers cannot expect to be paid for them, and government inquiries about willingness to pay will be met with strategic evasiveness. Hence Musgrave concluded that the only mechanism for determining the level of public goods would have to be political. Tiebout proposed a nonpolitical alternative involving local public goods and consumers shopping around for the community that best fit their demands. Musgrave recalled, however, that Tiebout had proposed his alternative in a joking style, so it was not clear how seriously he meant it.

Tiebout's sense of humor was the first characteristic that almost all of his contemporaries recalled. Even his three children—Charlie, Bruce, and Carol—thought he was funny, an accomplishment any parent can envy. (Bruce, who minds the family history, has generously supplied me with details of his life as well as the photograph of his father in this volume.) He also enjoyed practical jokes. Several of his acquaintances related the story of Tiebout and a friend being stuck in a midwestern city because of airport delays. They went downtown to pass the time, and Tiebout convinced some local dignitaries that they were scouting for business locations, which earned them a luxurious bacchanal at Chamber of Commerce expense. Sad to say, the facts are less gaudy. Charles Leven was the friend who was with Tiebout on that occasion, and Leven told me that they had simply cadged some free drinks from a gullible local banker during a few hours' delay. It is likely, however, that Tiebout did little to discourage the more rewarding account.

Tiebout's Michigan doctoral thesis was not an elaboration of his vote-with-your-feet idea that he had first expressed in Musgrave's class, and Musgrave was not on his thesis committee. The thesis was an empirical inquiry into local multiplier effects. Tiebout estimated the influence on employment and spending of an exogenous increase in spending in small midwestern cities. This application of Keynesian multiplier theory was completed in 1957, three years after he had taken a job at Northwestern University. The unsurprising answer to Tiebout's question was that the local multiplier effect was vanishingly small (that is, hardly greater than unity), as most of the secondary spending leaked out beyond the borders of the locality. Daniel Suits, who chaired Tiebout's thesis committee at Michigan, told me a few years ago that it was not regarded as a strong dissertation.

Tiebout wrote "A Pure Theory of Local Expenditures" (1956) when he was at Northwestern. Charles Leven was a graduate student there and became a close friend of the new assistant professor. Leven recalled that a Northwestern colleague, Meyer Burstein, had complained to Tiebout about the excessive cost of the local services in Evanston, Illinois. Tiebout asked him why he didn't just move to another community. Whether this caused Tiebout to recall his Michigan idea was not clear, but shortly thereafter he told Leven that he was sending an article to the *Journal of Political Economy* at Chicago.[1] Leven reported that Tiebout thought that the Chicago-school editors, regarded by their uptown rivals as excessively fond of free markets, would just have to publish it, since he had shown that governments could be just as efficient as private firms. (Albert Rees, who was department chair when I was a graduate student at Princeton in the early 1970s, once mentioned to me that he was proud to have been the *JPE* editor who accepted the article in 1956.)

Leven's recollection struck me as significant because many critics of the Tiebout model regard it as a manifestation of a libertarian-conservative approach to government. Indeed, an important intention of Tiebout's model was to show that the political process could be dispensed with for a large class of government activity. But Tiebout's own politics were within the mainstream of the Democratic Party. Bruce Tiebout said that his father had been considered for President Kennedy's Council of Economic Advisors on the recommendation of Secretary of Defense Robert McNamara, who was acquainted with Tiebout through his work on the regional economic impacts of defense projects. The anticipated appointment fell through when Lyndon Johnson succeeded Kennedy.

---

[1] Leven told me this story in 1999, and he elaborated on it in a four-page reminiscence about Tiebout (Leven 2003). Musgrave first told me in 1994 how Tiebout came up with his idea in his Michigan seminar, circa 1951. Leven told me that he had never heard Musgrave's account. Musgrave's remarks on the history of public finance at the 2005 Tiebout conference made it clear that his memory of events in that era remains sharp. I surmise that both stories are true, and Tiebout simply did not mention to Leven that he had thought of this idea at Michigan four or five years earlier. Leven's recollection that Tiebout dashed off a draft in "four or five days" (2003, 236) suggests that Tiebout had been thinking about it well before their encounter with Burstein, the unhappy Evanston resident. I must point out, however, that Leven's statement (2003, 237) that Tiebout never published anything else on local public finance after his 1956 paper overlooks Tiebout (1960; 1961), Tiebout and Houston (1962), and Tiebout and Chinitz (1965), all of which concern local public finance.

Tiebout's friends recall him as progressive-minded on social and political issues, and Bruce Tiebout assured me that his father was a dyed-in-the-wool Democrat and had no use for right-wing politics or economics.

Tiebout left Northwestern for a position at UCLA in 1958, where he was promoted to associate professor of economics with tenure. At UCLA he wrote some articles that followed from his 1956 article. (Wallace Oates discusses three of them in the next chapter.) But these articles did not figure in the later Tiebout literature that followed from Oates's 1969 article, although Ostrom, Tiebout, and Warren (1961) remains influential in political science.

In 1962 Tiebout moved to Seattle for an appointment at the University of Washington as a professor of economics and business. From that time on, he published and consulted on regional-science topics that stemmed from his doctoral dissertation and his later study of input-output models. This work was unrelated to his now-famous 1956 article. He soon gravitated to the University of Washington's geography department, and his research on regional multiplier effects is still influential among geographers.[2] He was president of the Western Regional Science Association in 1965, and the Association has a dissertation prize in his memory.

In Seattle Tiebout became the recipient and disburser of numerous federal grants and contracts, and his government consulting thrived. His family lived in Laurelhurst, a prosperous section of Seattle near the university. His regional-science work was making him well known and well off, and his students and colleagues regarded him with affection and esteem. His life came to a sudden end on January 16, 1968, when he was 43 years old. He suffered a heart attack while he was teaching and died the same day. His widow lived 31 years longer in Seattle, and their children still live in the area. None has pursued an academic career.

Why Did the Tiebout Model Start So Slowly?

Tiebout's now-famous paper did not take the economics profession by storm. Neither Paul Samuelson nor Musgrave, whose work Tiebout specifically addressed, was especially impressed by it. Musgrave (1959, 132) continued throughout his career to think of the Tiebout model as an interesting but special case, one with only limited application to the world of public finance. Samuelson took note of the article in a 1958 comment in the *Review of Economics and Statistics*, but he dismissed it as being both unrealistic and normatively unattractive.

---

[2] A bibliography of Tiebout's works on economic geography and regional science can be found on a Web site maintained by Gunter Krumme, who was one of Tiebout's students and is now a professor at the University of Washington's Geography Department. http://faculty.washington.edu/~krumme/VIP/Tiebout.html.

Their reactions were similar to that of most other economists who cited the article through the 1950s and 1960s. It was not until Wallace Oates published his 1969 article that connected Tiebout's idea with property tax capitalization that the "Tiebout hypothesis" took off. The annual count of citations to Tiebout more than doubled in the decade after Oates's publication, and economists began using the Tiebout model as a foundation for both theoretical and empirical work in local government.[3]

Oates himself describes how he came upon his idea to test the Tiebout model in the next chapter, and so the question I will pose here concerns fashions in economic models: Why did it take so long for Tiebout's model to be taken seriously? Obscurity of style or excessive mathematics cannot be the cause of its slow start. Tiebout's writing is clear, and the article's mathematics is minimal. Perhaps the converse argument, that it lacked a mathematically expressed model, was the problem. But that, too, seems inadequate as an explanation. Other seminal papers with little or no mathematics have been adopted by the mathematically talented and quickly made their way into the economics mainstream. Coase (1960) and Stigler (1971) come to mind.

An obvious answer to the slow start is that Tiebout himself gave up writing on the subject after he left UCLA in 1962. But that was not without having done several papers that built on his original hypothesis. In one of them, Tiebout even suggests the principle of capitalization: "When you seek good schools for your children, you often find the rents and housing prices are high" (1961, 94). Yet, he did not advance any systematic evidence in support of his idea.

Tiebout probably stopped writing about local public finance for career reasons. Most economists develop more than one line of inquiry and gravitate toward that which is best received by the profession. It seems likely that the response Tiebout was getting to his 1956 article was not encouraging enough to keep him or his graduate students interested in it, especially when his regional-science research was doing quite well.

Why was the response so tepid? It is unlikely that Tiebout's model was dismissed as an "everyone knows this" story. It really was different and original. It was not simply a restatement of federalism, fiscal or otherwise. Tiebout gave

---

[3] The time lag between Tiebout and Oates, who never met, may explain why most economists pronounce his name as "tee-BOO," as it would be in French, while his family and friends insist on "TEE-boe," rhyming with oboe. I surmised that the name was Dutch, but Dutch friends tell me that the final *t* would be pronounced in that case. The proprietor of the Tiebout Tavern, just off Tiebout Avenue in the Bronx in New York City, answered the phone with the pronunciation favored by the Tiebout family. A treatise on street names in the Bronx offers this background: "An ancient Dutch family of Huguenot extraction, the Tiebout name is found in the 1689 and 1703 Lists of Inhabitants, with sometimes the spelling 'Thibaud'" (McNamara 1991). The name "Thibaud" is pronounced "TEE-boe" in French. Bruce Tiebout confirmed that his ancestors were Huguenots who left France for the Netherlands and then emigrated to New York in the 1600s.

little attention to government organization, and Oates's original theory of fiscal federalism did not require that people move around. Residential mobility was the critical force in Tiebout's model. Everyone knew that Americans were mobile, but no economist had previously connected mobility with demand for the services of local government. The only contemporary parallel to Tiebout's model was an informal paper by George Stigler (1957), who pointed out that taxpayer mobility undermined local government's ability to redistribute wealth. But neither Stigler nor any of his students developed this insight further. Stigler's writing remained more obscure than Tiebout's, with not a single journal citation until Oates noted it in a 1968 article.

The more likely reason for the Tiebout model's slow start is that it was not right for its time. As Oates (1999) and Wickwar (1970) have demonstrated, interest in local government is subject to long historical cycles. The peak of one cycle in the United States appears to have been the two decades before World War I, when cities were growing rapidly, most government spending was local, and important people took an interest in both the governance and study of local institutions.

The 1940s and 1950s were pretty much the nadir of regard for local government. When I mentioned to my colleague Andrew Samwick that Tiebout was known for his sense of humor, Andrew quipped that he would have *needed* one to have come up with his model in the 1950s. Political attention at the time was on the international problems entailed by the Cold War. The communist half of the world organized all economic activity from the center, and many in the noncommunist world regarded centralization as the wave of the future.[4] Macroeconomic issues were at the forefront of economics, and Keynesianism had little use for local government. (Keep in mind that it was not until 1959 that Musgrave established the independence of the stabilization, allocation, and redistributive functions of government, which economists—and apparently no other social scientists—now regard as second nature.)

Before Tiebout and Oates, the treatment of local public finance in American economics textbooks alternated between hostility and condescension (Hansen and Perloff 1944; Samuelson 1948). When local government was in the news, it was almost always in a bad light. Journalists decried local resistance to desegregation, incompetent city governments, and the complacent conformity of the

---

[4] One datum in evidence of the era's concern with the Cold War was the lead article in the issue of the *Journal of Political Economy* in which Tiebout's 1956 article appeared. "Iron and Steel in the Balance of World Power," by John B. Parrish, described with some alarm how the Soviet Union might soon exceed American steel-making capacity. (This turned out to be an astute projection, though one whose consequences were less dire than Parrish assumed.) Professor Parrish, hardly a proponent of national planning, was moved to editorialize: "In my opinion, the maintenance of the relative position of the United States as a steel power is not a matter that can be left solely up to private industry" (1956, 384).

suburbs. Most academics were contemptuous of municipalities if they thought about them at all, and consolidation of school districts was always regarded as progress.

The changes in American life since the 1960s have not so much elevated general regard for local government—the aforementioned complaints can be heard today, too—as they have diminished regard for the national government. By the 1970s, the Keynesian consensus fell apart, people who favored central planning found less and less to admire in countries that did it, and national defense consumed a decreasing fraction of the federal budget. Americans responding to opinion polls expressed much less trust in national leaders than they had in the two decades following World War II. Within this setting, a model that suggested that politics was unimportant as long as one could choose among various governments started to look more attractive to enterprising scholars.

One point of this perspective is to suggest that some of the conditions that have increased the Tiebout model's salience since the 1960s may be diminishing. Household mobility has decreased in recent decades (Jacoby and Finkin 2004), so there are fewer occasions for migrants to think about the quality of local public services. (I would, however, still remind Tiebout skeptics, who wonder why people would move just because the sidewalks are deteriorating, that it is nearly costless to inquire about the quality of public services once one has decided to relocate for other reasons.) Funding for public schools, once largely a local responsibility, has become more uniform and centralized (at the state level) as the result of widespread litigation. (See chapter 3 by Brunner and Sonstelie in this volume.) Federal involvement in public education—generated by the political quarter that once championed local autonomy—has become more extensive than at any other time since the nineteenth century, when land grant policies helped to establish schools and colleges. National defense has come back to the front page, and federal officials are being held accountable for local problems such as disaster preparedness and environmental quality, even in cases that have negligible spillover effects.

There are offsets to these trends, of course. Ownership of a home in a well-run community is an important goal for most Americans, and home equity is the chief form of savings for the great majority. Even as enrollments drop, school-district quality continues to be a robust determinant of home values. Land use regulation, a lynchpin of later versions of the Tiebout model, remains largely local and nearly impervious to intellectual carping about its shortcomings and excesses. Local governments are still well represented in American statehouses and in Congress—most legislators started with a local office and remain beholden to city and county organizations for support—so preemption of local powers is not undertaken lightly. Whether scholars in the next half-century will still find the Tiebout model interesting and useful remains to be seen.

The Current State of Tiebout Scholarship

While the political trends that underlie interest in the Tiebout model may not be clear, the scholarly trends are clearly expansive. Papers in George Zodrow's (1983) twenty-fifth anniversary conference focused almost exclusively on the Tiebout model as the touchstone of the economics of local government. It has remained that, but its influence has expanded beyond economics and beyond the local public sector. The chapters in this book may be taken as indicators of this expansionary trend.

As anticipated, the essays for the conference were a mix of overview and new research. **Wallace Oates** offers an overview in chapter 2, "The Many Faces of the Tiebout Model." When an article becomes so widely cited in various fields of social science, its original context is sometimes lost. Oates's essay closely reviews the original article.

Economists have been divided about Tiebout's intention. Was his article primarily a theoretical exercise whose objective was to solve the preference-revelation problem? Or did Tiebout propose his model as a useful description of how fragmented metropolitan governments work? Oates's answer to these questions is . . . yes. Tiebout had both a theoretical point in mind—his answer to Musgrave and Samuelson—and the practical point that American metropolitan areas met the conditions for this theory. (Robert Inman's commentary on the Oates chapter offers an excellent review of the empirical tests of Tiebout's model, and Inman concludes that the evidence for its applicability to actual local governments is reasonably strong.)

The other large issue that Oates addresses is how to characterize the Tiebout model in this century. There are two important distinctions. The easier one is between what Tiebout originally said and what later scholars added to the model. It is clear that Tiebout neglected property taxation and said little about the power that municipalities care most about: land use regulation. Oates and Hamilton added those two crucial dimensions to the original model that are widely agreed to be necessary for its operation. Others added a profit motive for Tiebout's shadowy municipal managers (Sonstelie and Portney 1978; Epple and Zelenitz 1981) and provided evidence that the managers were attentive to voters (Borcherding and Deacon 1972; Bergstrom and Goodman 1973).

Many critiques of the Tiebout model overlook these crucial additions or treat them as if they were not part of the real model. It seems essential for any kind of scientific progress, however, to deal with a properly amended model than simply to complain about omissions in the original paper. The Keynesian model did not spring full grown from the brow of John Maynard Keynes, and little credence would be given to a critique of the model that dwelt solely on what was written in *The General Theory* in 1936.

Oates's other issue is whether the Tiebout model can be grafted onto other areas of economic inquiry beyond local public finance. The mobility of firms and households among states, regions, and countries is an important phenomenon, and to some extent these moves can be said to be shopping for better public services. American tradition (and probably that of other nations) holds that immigrants came from other countries partly to get a better shake from the public sector, broadly conceived. But Oates warns that extending the efficiency findings of the Tiebout model to this larger stage may not be warranted. The choice set for migrants is smaller, the instruments of taxation and regulation are less easily targeted, and mobility is more limited by cultural and family ties. Choosing between Budapest and Berlin is quite different from choosing between Grosse Pointe Farms and Grosse Pointe Woods.

School Finance and School Choice

The next two chapters concern the local government service that people consider most important: public schools. It is no exaggeration to say that economic analysis of American public education has been transformed by the Tiebout-Oates approach. It is equally evident that American courts of law have been oblivious to this literature. In chapter 3, "California's School Finance Reform: An Experiment in Fiscal Federalism," **Eric Brunner** and **Jon Sonstelie** review the aftermath of the twentieth century's most dramatic local-government event: the California Supreme Court's *Serrano* decision and the tax-revolt initiative, Proposition 13. (I say "event" because I think that the two are causally linked [Fischel 2004], but one does not have to accept that to appreciate Brunner and Sonstelie's masterly essay.) Following the California Supreme Court's December 1976 ruling that local school expenditures must be equalized—thus eliminating the fiscal basis for Tiebout sorting—California voters, in June 1978, cut the property tax in half and imposed assessment constraints that have kept the effective rate well below 1 percent.

California overnight became an almost natural experiment on the Tiebout model. Prior to *Serrano* and Proposition 13, California schools were financed like those of most other states, with a mixture of locally controlled property taxes supplemented by state-generated revenues. A Tiebout household could, if it were dissatisfied with the schools and school-related taxes in one community, relocate to another that better fit its demands. (One such foot-voter was plaintiff John Serrano Jr., as I document in Fischel [2004].)

After the *Serrano*–Proposition 13 event(s), this system was no longer operative. Brunner and Sonstelie, who have authored a host of studies related to this topic, give a balanced and fairminded account of what happens when one of the foundations of the Tiebout model is overturned. One clear finding is that, although spending has been equalized to a degree greater than almost any other state, test scores have remained as unequal as before. Their most puzzling findings are that the state government has been unable to fully replace locally generated spending (as *Serrano* advocates had hoped) and California households still evidently care as much about their school districts now as they did before *Serrano* and Prop 13. One would have thought that California voters would be eager to embrace vouchers after school-funding equalization, but the two voter initiatives that proposed a voucher system were soundly rejected. Brunner and Sonstelie find that voters are unwilling to give up on their local public schools despite the loss of local fiscal control. The Tiebout model appears to work in ways that transcend its fiscal requirements.

The other Tiebout-inspired essay about schools is chapter 4 by **Jack Buckley** and **Mark Schneider**. "School Choice, Parental Information, and Tiebout Sorting: Evidence from Washington, DC" reports previously unpublished research based on surveys of Washington parents who chose charter schools over public schools. Buckley and Schneider are political scientists, and their work here reflects a dimension of the Tiebout model that economists often overlook: How much knowledge do people actually have about the local public sector?

Buckley and Schneider's survey of parents who recently chose charter schools suggests a pessimistic answer. Parents who made this choice actually had more erroneous information about the quality of their schools than those who did not. This reinforces a long line of research by political scientists that suggests that the term *informed voter* is an oxymoron. If this were all we knew about public-sector choices, the Tiebout model would have long ago been dismissed as laughably irrelevant.

Yet, it is *not* dismissed, just as Richard Lester's (1946) evidence that business executives are interested in almost anything but maximizing profits did not deter economists from using that vital assumption. The obvious reply to the political science critique is evidence from the housing market. Someone must know about intercommunity differences in schools, since they are priced pretty accurately in housing values. And most economic tests of the median-voter model support the idea that voters in all but the largest school districts can evaluate spending programs (Inman 1978; Romer, Rosenthal, and Munley 1992). Yet, the Buckley and Schneider evidence should be a useful irritant to economists. More research needs to be done to understand just how the public-sector market works.

Government Structure in Metropolitan Areas

Tiebout himself intended his model not to have a political sector. The whole idea was to show that an economic decision—choice of residence—could determine an efficient set of local services. This may be why the model is more highly regarded by economists than by political scientists and law professors, whose stock in trade is the political sector. (As the presence of representatives of those disciplines in this volume suggests, however, the Tiebout model cannot be conveniently ignored.) Most economic research since the 1970s, however, has conceded that some sort of political structure must be assumed in order to generate any supply of public goods. The structure most frequently imposed has been the median voter model, which assumes the majority of voters get their way, regardless of the political structure. Coupled with the assumptions that communities are numerous and residents are mobile, the efficiency conditions of the model continue to hold.

William Hoyt's chapter 5 reexamines this sanguine conclusion. In "Imperfect Competition Between Communities, Politics, and Capitalization," he points out that many American metropolitan areas are not characterized by numerous, small localities. Some areas have only a few local governments, and others have many small suburbs plus one or two large cities. Using the tools of public choice and microeconomic theory, Hoyt explores the implications of these imperfectly competitive local government structures. One important possibility is that very large local governments might not be responsive to the majority of voters. They may instead be captured by development interests or entrenched bureaucracies.

Hoyt's most provocative finding is that in large municipalities, in which bureaucrats are more likely to rule, the benefits and burdens of taxes and spending will not be fully capitalized in the city's housing prices. Some of the burdens will be exported to other jurisdictions. As a result, housing prices become less accurate as a measure of public service benefits throughout the metropolitan area. While his empirical evidence on this is not conclusive, Hoyt's theory may explain why the Tiebout model tests best in the suburbs rather than in central cities.

Zoning, Exclusion, and Segregation

Aside from education expenditures and property taxes, the Tiebout-relevant aspect of local government that most concerns social scientists is zoning. Tiebout mentioned zoning as a means of limiting population growth in a community in order to achieve optimal size. However, the modern application of zoning to the model did not arrive in economics until Bruce Hamilton (1975) introduced it. His modification of the Tiebout model required localities to use zoning not so much to limit population as to limit "free-riders" who would pay less in property tax than they consumed in services. This came to be known as "fiscal zoning." I have argued that American zoning is perfectly capable of doing what Hamilton assumed it could do (Fischel 1992), and the main reason municipalities do not use it to its full effect is because of state and federal constitutional constraints (Fischel 1995).

Chapters 6 and 7 address a more sophisticated—some would say "insidious"—role for zoning. In chapter 6, "Exclusion's Attraction: Land Use Controls in Tieboutian Perspective," **Lee Anne Fennell** surveys and analyzes the role of zoning as a means of excluding people. At one level, the term *exclusionary zoning* is redundant. Zoning necessarily excludes something if it has any effect at all, and excluding undesirable uses of property is at its foundation. But Fennell, a prolific legal scholar, explores how zoning can be used to shape the human personality of the community as well as its fiscal and environmental qualities.

One of the consistently applied constitutional constraints on zoning is that it cannot discriminate by race or by most other demographic characteristics, such as religion and income. But this does not eliminate the desire to do so. Fennell describes the many indirect ways by which constraints on the use of land could be motivated by their effect on the type of people who might live in the housing development that is subject to local zoning approval.

My own suspicion about zoning motives is that Fennell is often right: The object of NIMBYism is not necessarily the proposed apartment building's blockage of light and air, or even its smallish contribution to the tax base, but the possibility that poorer people will occupy it. And I must add that the super-rationality that Fennell imputes to zoning authorities is not so far from the truth. People motivated by the desire to protect and enhance their own property will think through the long-term implications of land use policies. (This truth, incidentally, undercuts most theories of the "race to the bottom" among local governments, which cast local governments as witless pursuers of industrial tax base, heedless of its adverse effect on community environments.) The difficulty for external overseers of the process, such as courts, is winnowing the legitimate from the illegitimate motives. Suburban officials have learned not to go on record as saying they opposed the development because they feared that minorities would occupy it. Talking only about preserving "small-town character" keeps these small-town characters out of court.

In an extended comment on Fennell's chapter, Robert Ellickson raises a contrarian point. If American suburbs are insufficiently diverse with respect to race, income, and ethnic origin, what is the optimal level of diversity? To use an example that he does not, American universities are almost all committed to "diversity," with the goal being to have the groups of American society proportionately represented in their student bodies and faculties. But if they were to accomplish that, all universities would look alike in this dimension. There would be no diversity from the point of view of those choosing to attend or work at any one of them. Among universities, that may be regarded as a good thing, but at the municipal level, Ellickson reminds us that it could mean no more Chinatowns, artist colonies, student ghettos, or gay neighborhoods. When Ellickson turns to proposed remedies for exclusionary zoning, however, he finds that few critics of the suburbs are willing to impose effective legal obligations on municipalities to become diverse. He concludes from this that, using Fennell's coinage, "we are all Tieboutians now."

Yet, Fennell's criticism of manipulative exclusion does not necessarily have to resolve Ellickson's concern about optimal diversity. The analogy that might be useful is that developed by William Baumol and Wallace Oates in *The Theory of Environmental Policy* (1975). Like most economists, they point out that one could go too far in pursuing environmental goals, which implies that there is some "optimal" level of pollution. But they acknowledge that neither they nor anyone else knows what that level is. Their recommendation, which was the innovative part of their argument, was to approach policy by increments. If you think you have too much pollution, try to reduce it in the most cost-effective way. After you've done that and you still think there is too much pollution, do it again.

Returning to Fennell's point, the remedy for exclusionary zoning might be similarly incremental. If the suburbs don't have enough diversity, leaning on them to allow some lower-cost housing is the right idea. The error to avoid—an error I think was made by the New Jersey Supreme Court's "regional fair-share" remedy for combating exclusionary zoning—is to adopt a grand solution and then wash one's hands of it.[5] Like environmental quality, the desirable mix of housing in a region is a moving target that must constantly be reevaluated.

The other chapter about zoning is that of **Stephen Calabrese, Dennis Epple,** and **Richard Romano**. The method of chapter 7, "Nonfiscal Residential Zoning," could hardly be more different from Fennell's institutional examination. Their article must be seen as a step in a career-long enterprise by Epple and his various coauthors to ground the Tiebout model in a formal economic theory. In particular, they have explored the role of zoning in shaping the character of communities. Among the more interesting is a model in which income-segregation can occur without zoning. The land market coupled with a plausible demand for public goods causes households to spontaneously sort themselves. This forestalls the endless chase of the poor following the rich in order to "free-ride" on public goods.

Building on this highly abstract model, Calabrese, Epple, and Romano explore the possibility that residents of already-sorted communities might want

---

[5] The *Mount Laurel II* language that exclusive New Jersey municipalities are fond of citing is this: "Finally, once a community has satisfied its fair share obligation, the *Mount Laurel* Doctrine will not restrict other measures, including large-lot and open area zoning, that would maintain its beauty and communal character." *Southern Burlington County NAACP v. Township of Mount Laurel*, 456 A.2d 390, 421 (N.J. 1983).

further sorting. The reason for this desire is that residents realize that there may be spillover benefits from having higher-income people live in their community. The spillover benefits are not directly fiscal in nature, as they would be in the Hamilton-inspired version of zoning. In the Calabrese-Epple-Romano world, residents get some direct benefits from living among the higher-income residents. (If this seems unappealing, the model could be motivated as well by living among the well educated.) In order to take advantage of this version of peer effects, the high-income suburb (or subdivision) has to effectively expel some of its lower-income (but hardly poor) residents. This cannot be done literally—almost all zoning changes "grandfather" previously existing uses—but one could think of a planner who goes through each stage of settlement on paper and then puts the final policy in place.

The interesting thing about this unsavory activity is that in the Calabrese et al. model, the "city" jurisdiction is actually in favor of the suburban expulsion of the not-rich-enough residents. This is because the excluded suburban residents must now live in the city, and they are richer than the other city residents. The involuntary immigrants create a spillover benefit for the city residents, who benefit from proximity to them. It's kind of like the jayvee basketball team benefiting because the varsity has cut some of the shorter players from its roster. Only those who lost their place are upset.

As abstract as this model is, it implicitly offers an explanation for why exclusionary zoning persists. State authorities can, in principle, override local zoning anytime they want. If cities were really that unhappy about suburban exclusion, they could get their state legislative representatives, who typically outnumber those from the most exclusive suburbs, to disallow the practice. In reality, though, exclusion from the suburbs of the rising middle class may be beneficial to the central city in that it stems the "flight to the suburbs" by their middle class.

Extensions of the Tiebout Framework

Chapters 8, 9, and 10 invoke the Tiebout model in settings that go beyond intrametropolitan choices of local services. Each chapter is distinctly different, but they share the expansive view of Tiebout's basic idea that has accounted for its growing influence in recent years. While I share Oates's skepticism about this expansion from the intrametropolitan setting, these chapters do illustrate the attraction of Tiebout's most basic idea: People can choose different locations, and when they do, public-sector considerations play a role in their choices.

Rick Hills is another law professor who has employed Tiebout-style arguments in his scholarship. The title of chapter 8, "Compared to What? Tiebout and the Comparative Merits of Congress and the States in Constitutional Federalism," plays on a theme that Oates raised in chapter 2: How should the

Tiebout model be evaluated normatively? Tiebout's original work sought to show that choosing among localities could mimic the private market. But in the real world, the choice is usually not between local government provision and private provision. The most pressing issues are local governments versus state and national governments. Only a few scholars seriously test the regulation of environmental quality by local governments against its provision by private firms. The environmental question is usually cast in terms of centralized versus local government regulation. Hills thus frames the question for legal scholars as one of federalism—the balance of authority among levels of government— not between government and private actors.

Hills notes in chapter 8 that the Tiebout model was initially disparaged by legal scholars, and he gives a thorough account of what they found wrong with it. Most economists would point out that their objections were based on distributive concerns about excluding the poor, while Tiebout's argument was about efficiency. Even in a society that everyone agreed was egalitarian, one would still expect sorting based on different preferences. And as chapters 2 and 4 by Oates and by Brunner and Sonstelie (in this volume) point out, the so-called homogenous suburbs and their school districts are in reality far more diverse than they are usually assumed to be.

The main efficiency problem that lawyers see in small governments is that they have so much perimeter relative to land area. This makes them likely to externalize costs on their neighbors; the paradigm is the municipal dump deliberately located on the downwind border. This is a problem more often invoked as a hypothetical example than examined empirically. My own investigation of an allegedly "beggar-thy-neighbor" landfill found that there was less to it than meets the nose, given the freight it is made to bear in the literature (Fischel 2001, ch. 8). However, Hills's rhetorical strategy is to concede the criticisms of Tiebout but then turn and ask whether centralization of local services does not have its own problems. The systematic error that Hills finds most relevant is that Congress is structurally inclined to make policies that are too uniform for a nation with as much diversity as the United States. Tiebout's legal critics should not get away with the implicit assumption that more centralized provision of public goods operates costlessly.

Despite a general mistrust of local government, legal scholarship has conceded to the Tiebout-style model in one particular area. The explicit reason for the federalization of environmental policy in the early 1970s was a story about the "race to the bottom" if regulation were left to the states. Borrowing freely from an article by Oates and Schwab (1988), Richard Revesz (1992) argued that the race-to-the-bottom scenario was founded on faulty analysis. States do like to attract businesses for employment and fiscal concerns, but those same citizens who want jobs and lower taxes also want better environments. As long as there is a reliable connection between state decision makers and their citizens—frequent elections would usually do it—it seems unlikely that states would foul their own nests.

Hills believes that Revesz won this argument. The race-to-the-bottom story is now confined to sniping about stateline spillovers and biased representation, not about chasing industry for fiscal gain. But the question here is whether this is a victory for the Tiebout model. The theater of operations is not a metropolitan area but the entire nation, among whose states people vote less often with their feet. Can the Tiebout model be stretched so far from its origins? It is tempting to say that Hills tells no more than a story about fiscal federalism, which does not inherently require mobility. Yet, there is mobility by firms among states; they do shop around for favored jurisdictions for tax reasons in the Oates-Schwab model. It might be best to refer to this class of models as "Tiebout-inspired."

Perhaps because it does stretch the model some, Hills draws a modest normative lesson from the merits of the Tiebout-among-the-states model. He uses it to make the case for judicial forbearance about interstate tax competition. Federal judges have been urged to use the "dormant commerce clause" (see Hills for a good explanation) to stop tax competition for business among the states. Hills suggests that having judges weigh in on this issue might have some unintended consequences. Lacking a Tiebout-inspired understanding of the role this competition plays in allocating industry, a decision to limit it could do more harm than good.

Chapter 9, by **Edward Cartwright, John Conley,** and **Myrna Wooders**, represents another branch of the Tiebout model. This offshoot was started by James Buchanan's economic theory of clubs (1965). Buchanan was aware of Tiebout's work (see his 1961 comment on Tiebout), though he did not cite Tiebout's original paper in his seminal article on clubs. In any case, club theory is more general than Tiebout's model. The clubs do not have to be set up to enjoy public services; their members can jointly consume any service, such as a swimming pool or Jerry Lewis movies. But club theory is also in a sense easier than Tiebout's theory because it does not necessarily involve geographic space. The problems of proximity are less imperative in clubs, since it is in principle easy for people to form their own club. The scarcity of land for housing, employment, and public facilities makes Tiebout models more difficult to solve.

The Cartwright-Conley-Wooders chapter, "The Law of Demand in Tiebout Economics," uses club theory to address a Tiebout-like problem. When potential clubs are scarce, as they are in a Tiebout world, members with different tastes and personal characteristics may be matched up less than perfectly. Starting from such a position, the authors ask what would happen to members' satisfaction (utility) if more members were added. In the conventional Tiebout model, adding more members to a community first lowers average costs to existing residents, but eventually the public service becomes congested, and additional members would reduce the satisfaction of preexisting residents. Cartwright et al. show that in their Tiebout-club model, it may be possible that this would not happen if the additional membership causes the matches of personal characteristics and tastes to improve. In some cases, crowding is offset by what might be called "the more, the merrier" principle.

This is a highly abstract and complicated model, and I would recommend reading Jan Brueckner's commentary as a guide to understanding it. The chapter demonstrates that economists have gone well beyond the issue of simple spatial crowding. They have begun to address the complexities of interactions among members of a group that engages in cooperative endeavors. I would speculate that the finding in chapter 9 suggests an interesting agglomeration economy that arises from club size. This could help in modeling the effects of urban size on productivity and consumer welfare.

Chapter 10, "Tiebout—Stability and Efficiency: The Examples of Australia and South Africa," by **Jeffrey Petchey** and **Perry Shapiro**, invokes yet another extension of the Tiebout model. The issue here is the use of central government fiscal aid to national regions to regulate the migration of population, usually to encourage people in poor regions to stay put. The seminal paper in this literature is Flatters, Henderson, and Mieszkowski (1974), which does not mention Tiebout at all, though subsequent literature has labeled this a Tiebout-style model.

The Flatters et al. model does invoke geographic migration and public goods. However, the jurisdictions are very large, so this might be called the regional-migration variant of the Tiebout model. The difference this makes is that relocation by migrants affects total labor supply and hence the productivity of labor in the region. In the traditional Tiebout model of local public finance, migrating from one community to another has no effect on employment. In Tiebout's original formulation, there is no labor income; in the more realistic variants on it, there are enough small communities within a labor market that community choice can be made without changing jobs.

When regional migration is considered, there is a potential conflict between private and public goods. A regional differential in the provision of public goods might draw labor to the region with the higher-quality services. But this immigration might cause labor productivity to fall in the place receiving the new workers. Petchey and Shapiro apply this model to a characterization of the history of Australia and, more loosely, to South Africa.

Australia, like many countries other than the United States, has long had a policy that transferred fiscal resources from some regions to others. Petchey and Shapiro describe the history of this policy as an attempt to prevent the breakup of the Australian confederation in the early twentieth century. The question they ask is why this policy has persisted long after the danger of secession has passed.

In principle, the Flatters et al. model could be used to justify some form of inter-regional fiscal transfers. The efficiency rationale would be that improving public goods in areas from which citizens might choose to migrate would dissuade them from migrating and thus maintain equal labor productivity among regions. It appears, however, that neither Australia nor South Africa meets the necessary conditions for the policies to improve the well-being of their citizens.

Conclusion

Like many influential models, Tiebout's has come a long way from its modest origins. It is now the accepted benchmark for local government in metropolitan areas. The economic analysis of American public schools, financed by thousands of local districts, has been transformed by it. Scholarly discussions of land use regulation do not go far before invoking the Tiebout model. Its influence has extended to political science and legal scholarship. It has been applied to nonmetropolitan settings such as club theory, regional fiscal transfers, and interstate competition for business.

Tiebout's influence does not stem from the rigorousness of the original article itself. As a model of local public finance, it is, as Oates points out, seriously incomplete. As a theoretical alternative to the ballot box, it works only under the most restrictive set of assumptions. What, then, explains its robustness? The answer appears to be that Tiebout saw a new way of looking at economic and political problems. Instead of assuming a stationary population in dealing with collective decisions, the world Tiebout envisioned is one of people in motion. His insight provided a new dimension in which economists, and now other social scientists, can rework familiar problems. The Tiebout perspective, rather than the original model, is what is so attractive.

How did he come up with this? Tiebout's theoretical methods were conventional, and his empirical evidence consisted of casual, though astute, observations. I once asked his boyhood friend Ross Worn (who married Tiebout's sister) if their Greenwich, Connecticut, background offered any clues. Mr. Worn could not recall anything, though he, like almost everyone else who knew Tiebout, remarked on his friend and brother-in-law's sense of humor. Maybe that was it. It could be that Charlie's irreverent sense of humor was what liberated him from conventional thinking and gave us the enduring and entirely serious Tiebout model.

References

Baumol, William J., and Wallace E. Oates. 1975. *The theory of environmental policy: Externalities, public outlays, and the quality of life.* Englewood Cliffs, NJ: Prentice-Hall.
Bergstrom, Theodore C., and Robert P. Goodman. 1973. Private demand for public goods. *American Economic Review* 63:280–296.

Borcherding, Thomas, and Robert Deacon. 1972. The demand for the services of non-federal governments. *American Economic Review* 62:891–901.

Buchanan, James M. 1961. Comment on Musgrave and Tiebout papers. In *Public finances: Needs, sources, and utilization.* Universities-National Bureau Committee for Economic Research. Princeton, NJ: Princeton University Press.

———. 1965. An economic theory of clubs. *Economica* 33:1–14.

Coase, Ronald H. 1960. The problem of social cost. *Journal of Law and Economics* 3:1–44.

Epple, Dennis, and Allan Zelenitz. 1981. The implications of competition among jurisdiction: Does Tiebout need politics? *Journal of Political Economy* 89:1197–1218.

Fischel, William A. 1992. Property taxation and the Tiebout model: Evidence for the benefit view from zoning and voting. *Journal of Economic Literature* 30:171–177.

———. 1995. *Regulatory takings: Law, economics, and politics.* Cambridge, MA: Harvard University Press.

———. 2001. *The Homevoter hypothesis.* Cambridge, MA: Harvard University Press.

———. 2004. Did John Serrano vote for Proposition 13? *UCLA Law Review* 51:887–932.

Flatters, Frank, J. Vernon Henderson, and Peter Mieszkowski. 1974. Public goods, efficiency, and regional fiscal equalization. *Journal of Public Economics* 3:99–112.

Hamilton, Bruce W. 1975. Zoning and property taxation in a system of local governments. *Urban Studies* 12:205–211.

Hansen, Alvin H., and Harvey S. Perloff. 1944. *State and local finance in the national economy.* New York: Norton.

Inman, Robert P. 1978. Testing political economy's "as if" proposition: Is the median income voter really decisive? *Public Choice* 33:45–65.

Jacoby, Sanford M., and Matthew W. Finkin. 2004. Labor mobility in a federal system: The United States in comparative perspective. *International Journal of Comparative Labour Law and Industrial Relations* 20:313–337.

Keynes, John Maynard. 1936. *The general theory of employment, interest and money.* London: Macmillan.

Lester, Richard A. 1946. Shortcomings of marginal analysis for wage-employment problems. *American Economic Review* 36:63–82.

Leven, Charles. 2003. Discovering "Voting with your feet." *Annals of Regional Science* 37:235–238.

McNamara, John. 1991. *History in asphalt: The origin of Bronx street and place names encyclopedia,* 3rd ed. New York: The Bronx County Historical Society.

Musgrave, Richard A. 1959. *The theory of public finance.* New York: McGraw-Hill.

Oates, Wallace E. 1968. The theory of public finance in a federal system. *Canadian Journal of Economics* 1:37–54.

———. 1969. The effects of property taxes and local public spending on property values: An empirical study of tax capitalization and the Tiebout hypothesis. *Journal of Political Economy* 77:957–971.

———. 1999. An essay on fiscal federalism. *Journal of Economic Literature* 37:1120–1149.

Oates, Wallace E., and Robert M. Schwab. 1988. Economic competition among jurisdictions: Efficiency enhancing or distortion inducing? *Journal of Public Economics* 35:333–354.

Ostrom, Vincent, Charles M. Tiebout, and Robert Warren. 1961. The organization of government in metropolitan areas: A theoretical inquiry. *American Political Science Review* 55:831–842.

Parrish, John B. 1956. Iron and steel in the balance of world power. *Journal of Political Economy* 64:369–388.

Revesz, Richard. 1992. Rehabilitating interstate competition: Rethinking the "race-to-the-bottom" rationale for federal environmental regulation. *NYU Law Review* 67:1210–1254.

Romer, Thomas, Howard Rosenthal, and Vincent G. Munley. 1992. Economic incentives and political institutions: Spending and voting in school budget referenda. *Journal of Public Economics* 49:1–33.

Samuelson, Paul A. 1948. *Economics: An introductory analysis.* New York: McGraw-Hill.

———. 1958. Aspects of public-expenditure theories. *Review of Economics and Statistics* 40:332–338.

Sonstelie, Jon C., and Paul R. Portney. 1978. Profit maximizing communities and the theory of local public expenditures. *Journal of Urban Economics* 5:263–277.

Stigler, George J. 1957. The tenable range of functions of local government. In *Federal expenditure policy for economic growth and stability.* Joint Economic Committee, Washington, DC (November 5).

———. 1971. The theory of economic regulation. *Bell Journal of Economics* 2:3–21.

Tiebout, Charles M. 1956. A pure theory of local expenditures. *Journal of Political Economy* 64:416–424.

———. 1957. The community income multiplier: An empirical study. Unpublished Ph.D. dissertation, Department of Economics, University of Michigan.

———. 1960. Economies of scale and metropolitan governments. *Review of Economics and Statistics* 42:442–444.

———. 1961. An economic theory of fiscal decentralization. In *Public finances: Needs, sources, and utilization.* Universities-National Bureau Committee for Economic Research. Princeton, NJ: Princeton University Press.

Tiebout, Charles M., and Benjamin Chinitz. 1965. The role of cost-benefit analysis in the public sector of metropolitan areas. In *The public economy of urban communities,* Julius Margolis, ed. Washington, DC: Resources for the Future.

Tiebout, Charles M., and David B. Houston. 1962. Metropolitan finance reconsidered: Budget functions and multi-level governments. *Review of Economics and Statistics* 44:412–417.

Wickwar, W. Hardy. 1970. *The political theory of local government.* Columbia: University of South Carolina Press.

Zodrow, George R., ed. 1983. *Local provision of public services: The Tiebout model after twenty-five years.* New York: Academic Press.

2

The Many Faces of the Tiebout Model

WALLACE E. OATES

Since its arrival on the public finance scene some 50 years ago, the Tiebout model has played a strikingly diverse range of roles. Indeed, it appears, in important ways, to mean different things to different people. The model has been employed as everything from an algorithm for the resolution of the basic preference-revelation problem in the theory of public goods to a descriptive theory of local public finance. There are thus several quite different literatures that draw on Tiebout's seminal contribution in fundamental ways. My purpose in this chapter is to lay out this range of applications and to explore each of them in turn. This provides an opportunity both to assess the contributions of the model and to offer some reflections on the literature itself. I begin with some thoughts on Tiebout's own view of his paper. From there, however, the model took on a life of its own, which I will examine in subsequent sections.

Tiebout's Intent and Presentation

Tiebout (1956) is quite clear about one of the basic objectives of his paper. He seeks to set the record straight on the fundamental problem of the revelation of preferences for public goods. In the introduction and the first section of the paper, he describes the "Musgrave-Samuelson" treatment of the free-rider problem, observing, "As things now stand, there is no mechanism to force the

For their many valuable comments on earlier drafts of this paper, I am most grateful to Spencer Banzhaf, John Conley, William Fischel, Robert Inman, Richard Musgrave, Fabio Padovano, and Robert Schwab.

consumer-voter to state his true preferences; in fact, the 'rational' consumer will understate his preferences and hope to enjoy the goods while avoiding the tax" (417). Tiebout's purpose in the paper is to show that, in principle at least, there exists a mechanism or solution to the free-rider problem for a specific class of public goods—namely, local public goods. And he proceeds in his terse nine-page paper to sketch out a model of local public expenditure in which individual households reveal their preferences for local public goods through choosing a jurisdiction in which to reside that provides their desired level of consumption of these goods. The model is a highly simplified and abstract formulation with little institutional content. He envisions a very spare world in which mobile households select a community of residence from a broad menu of alternatives on the basis solely of the levels of local public goods offered and their associated tax liability. In Tiebout's world, taxes function much like prices in private markets so that individuals, through "voting with their feet," are induced into making location decisions that reflect both their preferences for local public goods and the marginal cost of providing these goods—decisions that generate a Pareto-efficient outcome as would a system of competitive markets.

My earlier sense was that Tiebout never really intended to provide a descriptive or explanatory theory of local public-sector behavior. As he clearly states, he wants to take issue with the existing theory of public goods; he shows that the received wisdom (as embodied in the writings of two of the giants in the field, Richard Musgrave and Paul Samuelson) is off the mark in a fundamental way. There is, he argues, an important class of public goods for which there exists, in principle, a mechanism that induces an accurate revelation of preferences and that leads to efficient levels of public outputs. Paul Seabright (1996) argues for just such a reading of the paper; Seabright contends that "Tiebout's model is best seen as a pioneering contribution to the theory of mechanism design, rather than saying anything about the decentralization of power in government" (63).

However, after yet another rereading of the paper and further discussion, I think this is an overly restrictive view. There is clearly more here than just a formulation of a preference-revealing algorithm. Although Tiebout's treatment is seriously wanting as a theory of local public finance (in ways that I will mention shortly), he does at various points try to justify and explain his model in terms of "real" behavior. Early on in the paper, he provides motivation for his model with a discussion of the importance of local public finance. He enumerates the range of public services provided by local government in the United States and notes that in 1954 local expenditures on goods and services exceeded federal spending on nondefense public goods. And he goes on to argue, "The important point is that the often-neglected local expenditures are significant, and when viewed in terms of expenditures on goods and services only, take on even more significance. Hence an important question arises whether at this level of government any mechanism operates to insure that expenditures on these public goods approximate the proper level" (Tiebout 1956, 418).

Later in the paper, Tiebout points out the range of choice and the concern with local services (such as schools) of households moving from the city to the suburbs (418). He then examines the channels through which communities seek to attain and maintain their optimum size. He cites the actions by "chambers of commerce or other agencies" to attract local residents, offering specific examples of Park Forest in the Chicago area and Levittown in New York (419). And he concludes the paper with a section on "Policy Implications" in which he explores (albeit very briefly) the issue of municipal integration. Tiebout is clearly concerned with providing a theory that has some explanatory power.

At the same time, there is a puzzling failure to address certain of the most fundamental issues in local public finance. There is no real treatment, for example, of taxes. In fact, the word "tax" appears only a few times in the paper—and never is the form or nature of local taxation explored. Taxes (whatever form they take) are simply regarded as a "price" for local public goods. Likewise, there is no treatment of how local governments come into being or of local budgetary processes. It was these omissions that left me with the earlier impression that the paper did not represent a serious attempt to provide a real theory of local finance. At any rate, it is surely fair to say that it is seriously incomplete in this regard.

Tiebout's strategy in the paper is pretty clear, and it explains, I think, the selective way in which he puts together his highly simplified model of local finance. His purpose is to construct a model that is as closely related as possible to the structure of a competitive market; he tries to establish a kind of equivalence between the local public sector and a competitive market so that he can invoke the various properties of a competitive equilibrium to show that local finance induces individuals to reveal their preferences for local public goods and does so in such a way as to promote an efficient use of resources. As he puts it,

> Just as the consumer may be visualized as walking to a private market place to buy his goods, the prices of which are set, we place him in the position of walking to a community where the prices (taxes) of community services are set. Both trips take the consumer to market. (422)

He repeatedly makes the point that "the solution [to his model] will approximate the ideal 'market' solution" (421). And in his concluding sentence, he suggests that in comparing his model with the reality of the competitive model, we "*may* find that local government represents a sector where the allocation of public goods (as a reflection of the preferences of the population) need not take a back seat to the private sector" (424).

This focus of the paper, incidentally, explains his extended treatment of certain issues that are seemingly less central to local finance. He discusses at some length, for example, the issue of a fixed factor (his illustration is a local beach) so that he can define an optimal size for his communities in terms of the minimum point on an average cost curve to establish the needed parallel to a competitive firm. In short, Tiebout's purpose in this paper is to convince us that the local public sector is, in certain essential ways, very like a private, competitive market and, for this reason, is not subject to the usual problems afflicting the provision of public goods. Writing over three decades later, Bruce Hamilton (1987) sums up by noting that where the necessary conditions are satisfied, "the Tiebout model is a simple and elegant extension of the competitive model" (641).

At any rate, there is not a lot more to go on. Tiebout unfortunately did not follow up his seminal paper with much in the way of further work to flesh out his earlier treatment. There are only three later papers that address these issues at all. In the first, Tiebout (1961) explores some spatial issues in the provision of local public goods, including an interesting treatment of the optimal number and spacing of things like fire stations, where the benefits taper off with distance from the site of provision. The second (Tiebout and Houston 1962) examines metropolitan finance in the context of multilevel government; it addresses a series of matters, including merit goods and income redistribution, but it really does not (in my view) add much substance to the analysis. The third piece is an insightful and provocative joint paper with Vincent Ostrom and Robert Warren (1961) that explores the governance of metropolitan areas and suggests that a "polycentric political system" is not necessarily a recipe for chaos; it is rather a complex system of governments that can have some appealing properties. In the last years before his premature death in 1968 at age 43, he devoted his efforts primarily to developing a Keynesian framework for the analysis of regional economic development (complete with regional and local multipliers, etc.).[1] But the Tiebout model would live on. By presenting the profession with a powerful, but modestly developed, idea, the Tiebout paper became the point of departure for an extended research program.

The Reappearance of the Tiebout Model: The Issue of Capitalization

The Tiebout model (to the best of my knowledge at least) lay essentially dormant for over a decade. There is little reference to it in the literature. Even Musgrave (1959), who presided over the birth of the model in Ann Arbor, gives

---

[1] William Fischel has informed me that in this later work, he was returning to the subject of his doctoral dissertation, which ultimately proved less significant than his famous *JPE* paper.

it only a passing reference in his monumental treatise on *The Theory of Public Finance*, where he treats it in less than a page under the heading "A Special Problem of Local Finance" (132–133).[2] Here he simply notes that "the possibility of moving to other communities establishes something equivalent to a market mechanism in local finance" (133). In a quick and admittedly incomplete survey of existing public finance texts in the 1960s and early 1970s, I was able to find only one citation and discussion of Tiebout, that of James Buchanan (1965). The Tiebout model clearly had not become part of the corpus of the theory of public finance.[3]

When the Tiebout model did reappear, it took the form of a testable proposition concerning local fiscal behavior. In 1969 I published a paper that purported to be an empirical test of the Tiebout hypothesis. It had occurred to me that if mobile households were "shopping" for local public services at the lowest price, we should find that housing prices reflect both the quality of local services and the associated tax bill. I thus (perhaps somewhat naively) proposed, as a test of Tiebout, the capitalization of differentials in local public outputs and local tax liabilities into local property values.[4] And, indeed, this is what the results showed: the capitalization of fiscal differentials into house values. This I took as evidence in support of the Tiebout model.[5]

The capitalization issue has turned out to be much more complicated than I appreciated in my early paper. Following my piece, Matthew Edel and Elliott

---

[2] Fischel (2001), in his insightful and entertaining history of the Tiebout paper, points out that Tiebout first presented his idea around 1952 in Musgrave's seminar at the University of Michigan. Musgrave recalls that Tiebout "presented his ideas in a lighthearted, joking manner" (77), leading Fischel to raise the intriguing question "Why would someone come up with a good theory and not be serious about it?" (77).

[3] More recently, I have found one early treatment of Tiebout. Dick Netzer (1966), in his book on the property tax, describes the Tiebout model and suggests, as an empirical test, the absence of any correlation between tax rates and property values across local jurisdictions in a metropolitan area. His idea (like that expressed later in Edel and Sclar [1974]) is that in a Tiebout equilibrium, higher taxes would be offset by benefits from higher levels of local services.

[4] In truth, I must admit that I did not exactly set out to test the Tiebout model. I had assembled a small body of fiscal data on 52 New Jersey municipalities for a single year (a data set that by today's standards would be laughed out of court) that I was employing as an exercise to learn how to do multiple-regression analysis. In graduate school at Stanford, my course in econometrics had been a miserable failure; we were never asked, or shown how, to estimate a regression equation. And I was trying to learn the technique to remedy an embarrassing gap. I spent my time at the computer center learning how to punch cards, run them through the card reader, and interpret the output. While looking over the results, it occurred to me that the data could be used to address the interesting question of capitalization, since I had information both on the "median value of owner-occupied homes" and on tax rates and local expenditures for the communities in my data set. There is thus a real serendipitous element in the origins of this paper. I did not actually set out to test Tiebout!

[5] When, as a young assistant professor at Princeton, I first presented a draft of the paper at a conference to a group of eminent public-finance economists, one of the first responses I received was that it was "trivial." I was told that since we all know that such capitalization occurs, my paper was simply verifying the obvious. Fortunately, the other members of the seminar (and subsequently referees at the *Journal of Political Economy*) were more charitable.

Sclar (1974) claimed that I had misinterpreted the Tiebout model—that in full Tiebout equilibrium, there should be no capitalization at all. They pointed out that since Tiebout communities are fully replicable, there cannot be, in long-run equilibrium, any fiscally advantaged jurisdictions. The value of the higher level of public services in a particular community will be exactly offset by an increased tax liability. Thus, there can be no *net* benefits to be capitalized in a full Tiebout equilibrium. The presence of such capitalization can only take place as part of a short-run adjustment process (analogous to short-run profits in the competitive model). Edel and Sclar then presented evidence suggesting that over time the extent of capitalization tends to disappear, which they took to indicate a movement toward a long-run Tiebout equilibrium.

The capitalization issue, however, turns out to be yet more complicated. Indeed, there is now a large theoretical literature that explores the conditions under which capitalization will occur and under which such an outcome can be consistent with an efficient Tiebout equilibrium (see, for instance, Epple, Zelenitz, and Visscher [1978]; Yinger [1982]; Rubinfeld [1987]; Yinger et al. [1988]). Much, it turns out, depends on the setting in terms of the number of jurisdictions (whether they are expandable or not), the fixity of boundaries, and local decision-making processes. I shall not try here to recount what is a major literature in its own right. But I am sympathetic to Fischel's claim that since the local public sector is not characterized by the same ease of entry that typically exists in the private sector, there is a relative fixity of boundaries and jurisdictions resulting in a fairly inelastic supply of jurisdictions that allows fiscal advantages to persist over time (Fischel 2001, 64–65).[6]

In addition to the theoretical work on this matter, there have been dozens of empirical studies of capitalization—so many, in fact, that Fischel (2001) notes that "capitalization studies are now an undergraduate exercise, and it is difficult to interest journal editors in new studies without a major twist" (60). Nearly all these studies find significant degrees of capitalization of fiscal differentials. The trickier issue is whether capitalization is complete: Do fiscal differentials fully manifest themselves in variation in property values—or is capitalization less than complete? Fischel (2001, 39–71) provides a nice, nontechnical review and interpretation of this body of work and concludes persuasively "from these studies that persistent property tax differences among homes within the same housing market will be fully capitalized." Moreover, as Fischel (2001, 45) notes further, "Everything seems to be capitalized," including environmental amenities, crime rates, accessibility, and many other features of the local landscape.

---

[6] At the same time, one can't push this too hard. As Henderson (1985) points out, there has, in fact, been considerable growth in the number of communities and in the adjustment of boundaries through annexation in the United States.

Indeed, many studies now take full capitalization as a premise and use differentials in local property values to measure what people are willing to pay for a wide variety of local amenities. Such studies, for example, have been used extensively to measure the value of cleaner air in urban areas.

The Tiebout Model, Housing Markets, and Zoning

Since Tiebout's allocation mechanism depends on residential location decisions ("voting with your feet"), it seems clear that a full-blown model of local fiscal behavior must somehow integrate local housing markets: Such a model must address the interaction between the housing market and the provision of local public services. In particular, it must explain how the housing market allocates households among jurisdictions where local services and tax rates vary. The basic approach, which Stephen Ross and John Yinger (1999) call the "consensus bid-function" approach in their splendid review article, has two parts: bidding and sorting. In this framework, mobile, utility-maximizing households, divided into distinct income/preference classes, bid for places in the different jurisdictions, which offer a variety of local service-tax packages. The bid functions of the different groups generate an aggregate bid function (the envelope of the individual group functions), and the places in the various communities are filled by households with the highest bids. The approach has some interesting implications. It implies, first, that levels of local services and the associated tax liabilities are capitalized into housing prices. And second, the sorting outcomes are not, in general, characterized by perfect homogeneity. Jurisdictions can contain a range of different income classes. They tend to be more homogeneous than a pattern of random sorting, but they can encompass a substantial degree of heterogeneity in household income.

Early attempts to introduce housing into the Tiebout model revealed a basic problem. They showed that, in a model with housing and local property taxation (the primary form of local finance, at least in the United States), Tiebout sorting does not fully resolve the preference-revelation and free-rider problems. In a world in which local governments finance their budgets with property taxes, there exists a basic incentive for free-rider behavior. A household in such a world can purchase a house with a value substantially below those of other residents in the community and thereby consume public goods at a tax price below that of other households in the community (and presumably below marginal cost); such a household can effectively get a (partial) free ride on the higher tax payments of other residents of the community.

This problem was addressed by Bruce Hamilton (1975), who extended the Tiebout model to encompass a specific form of local zoning. In the Tiebout-Hamilton model, communities not only provide a specific level of output of the local public good, but they also invoke a zoning rule that effectively establishes a floor on local housing consumption. In a full equilibrium, communities in a Tiebout-Hamilton world are homogeneous not only in demands for local public outputs, but also in housing consumption. And this resolves the free-rider problem, since all households in a given community will have the same tax liability, which in turn is equal to the cost per household (the marginal cost) of providing local public goods.

An unsettling implication, however, of the Hamilton resolution of the problem is the apparent requirement of an enormous number of communities, a community with a level of local public services and a zoned level of housing consumption that satisfies the preferences of all the various households in the region. The Tiebout model, in its original form, seemed to place a heavy demand on the number of communities to provide the requisite menu of local services. But the Hamilton extension of Tiebout increases this number exponentially. Moreover, the extreme form of homogeneity envisioned in the Tiebout-Hamilton world doesn't seem to characterize the real world very well. Howard and Janet Pack (1978), for instance, found a substantial degree of heterogeneity of family income and housing consumption in their empirical study of suburban communities in Pennsylvania, evidence that they took to be inconsistent with the Tiebout model. However, in a subsequent paper, Hamilton (1976) addressed this issue by showing that the model can accommodate some heterogeneity in housing. So long as the distribution of types of housing is stable over time, the differentials in tax bills become capitalized into property values so that the basic Tiebout outcome is preserved. (See Fischel [2001, 68–69] for an interesting discussion of this point.)

Finally, let me return to the issue of local taxation, which is hardly mentioned by Tiebout. Local taxes in the Tiebout model are surrogate prices that indicate the costs to potential residents of the services provided in the jurisdiction. What form should these taxes take? In the United States, at least, local governments rely heavily on property taxation, and so the question naturally arises as to whether local property taxes can function as "prices" in a Tiebout world. This has been, and remains, an issue surrounded by some controversy. In the extended Tiebout-Hamilton model with a local zoning constraint, the local property tax is converted into a perfect Tiebout price: The tax is equal precisely to the marginal cost of the public services provided to residents. In full equilibrium, residents thus pay a tax equal at the margin to the benefits they receive; it's a perfect benefit tax. In other settings, however, the local property tax has been modeled as a tax on capital. This is the so-called "new view" of the incidence of the property tax, which dates back to the seminal paper by Peter Mieszkowski (1972). From this perspective, local property taxes result in some distortions in housing and local public-goods choices. The extent of these distortions is not altogether clear, but there remains yet an ongoing debate between those who see local property taxation as a benefit tax that sustains (at least roughly) a Tiebout equilibrium and those who see the tax having more serious distorting effects.[7]

The Supply Side of the Tiebout Model and Politics

Perhaps the most unsettling aspect of the original Tiebout model is its virtually complete omission both of a supply side and of a process of budget determination. It is not clear, first, where the communities in the model come from or, second, how the levels of local public outputs are determined. Tiebout simply waves his hands and invokes an elastic supply of communities offering the requisite variety of local outputs, leaving the reader with the sense that there are profit-maximizing entrepreneurs waiting in the wings to supply communities, much as there are potential firms ready to enter a competitive industry where the prospect of positive profits exists.[8]

Moreover, households in the model are limited to residential location decisions. They are completely passive once this choice is made; they play no role in the determination of local public outputs. In Hirschman's terminology (1970), the Tiebout model focuses exclusively on the "exit" option and ignores completely the "voice" alternative. Tiebout households "vote with their feet"; they don't use the ballot box.

There are basically two approaches to addressing these issues. The first, more in the spirit of the original Tiebout paper, is simply to omit politics. Jon Sonstelie and Paul Portney (1978) and J. Vernon Henderson (1985), to cite two such treatments, have shown that it is possible to get efficient outcomes in a world in which developers (or "entrepreneurs") create communities in which they set levels of local services so as to maximize their profits. This is done in the Sonstelie-Portney model by choosing levels of local outputs that maximize local property values. It is thus not essential that the Tiebout framework incorporate politics. This I will call the "entrepreneurial version" of Tiebout.

A number of theorists in public finance have taken up the challenge of formally integrating this entrepreneurial version of the Tiebout model into general equilibrium theory (e.g., Wooders 1980, 1989, 1999; Bewley 1981; and

---

[7] For a recent exchange on this issue, see the papers by Fischel, Zodrow, and Nechyba in Oates (2001).

[8] Tiebout does make some vague reference to Armen Alchain's (1950) Darwinian view of evolution and economic theory in suggesting that somehow "the government's revenue-expenditure pattern for goods and services is expected to 'adapt to' consumers' preferences" (417). This seems to take place through a "city manager" who decides on and purchases units of local public services for his jurisdiction. But Tiebout then asserts that "in this model there is no attempt on the part of local governments to 'adapt to' the preferences of consumer-voters. Instead those local governments that attract the optimum number of residents may be viewed as being 'adopted by' the economic system" (420).

Scotchmer 1994). This body of literature provides a variety of rigorous formulations of the model and then explores issues in the existence of equilibria and their optimality properties. A major concern here is the nature of the restrictions that are required to bring such a model under the umbrella of the Fundamental Theorems of Welfare Economics. As this body of work is not really in my bailiwick, I am not in a position to do it justice. But it is at least worth noting that the theorists have been able to specify Tiebout-type models for which equilibria exist and are in the core and that can satisfy (at least approximately) Pareto optimality conditions. Myrna Wooders (1989), for example, shows that in a model with potential entry of new firms (jurisdictions), "approximate" Tiebout equilibria exist and converge (i.e., become arbitrarily close) to "competitive" outcomes as the economy becomes large and the costs of forming jurisdictions become small.

In this context, I want to return briefly to one of the most prominent of the early theoretical treatments of the Tiebout model, one that a number of us found both puzzling and disturbing. Truman Bewley (1981) found that a Tiebout equilibrium "does not have the nice properties of general equilibrium, except under very restrictive assumptions" (713). He was troubled by the fact that these assumptions are so restrictive that the public goods in Tiebout's model "become essentially private" (713). Moreover, Bewley concludes that the model is ultimately unsatisfactory: "I find a model with homogeneous communities and profit maximizing governments startling and strikingly in conflict with my everyday experience" (735). In his final sentence, Bewley observes of Tiebout that "when one considers his idea critically, one finds that in order to solve his problem in the way he suggests, one is obliged to strip the problem of all its distinguishing characteristics and to reduce it to a problem already solved in general equilibrium theory" (736).

Several aspects of Bewley's critique seemed troubling. First, it had never especially bothered me that local public goods in the Tiebout framework bore some basic similarities to private goods. Indeed, Tiebout himself suggests just such an interpretation in a section of his paper he calls "A Comparison Model," where he describes a world with only private goods in which all persons in a specific community are required "to spend their money in a particular pattern described for that community by law" (420).[9] Second, I have found myself less concerned than Bewley with the restrictive assumptions needed to characterize

---

[9] In my classes, I have found an analogy helpful in explaining the nature of a Tiebout equilibrium in which the Tiebout outcome is explicitly a special case of private goods. My analogy begins by noting that in a private market, if I wish to buy six "shirts," I go to a clothing store and take six shirts out of the shirt bin. If I lived in a Tiebout world, there would be separate stores that sell packages of one, two, . . . , six shirts; I would simply go to a store selling packages that contain six shirts and make my purchase. The outcome is the same in the two cases.

a Tiebout equilibrium. The purpose of a good model is to cut away nonessential complexity and focus our attention on an important mechanism or process. The Tiebout model does just that: it describes a powerful set of forces that have helped to shape the urban scene and says something about its properties. An economic model is nearly always some ideal representation of a process that has only an imperfect counterpart in the real world. In this case, I tend to agree with Fischel (2001, 70–71) that, although it involves enormous simplification, the "Tiebout Model Works Okay" as a description of local public finance. And, third, the fact that the Tiebout model reduces the problem of local public goods to one "already solved in general equilibrium theory" is not, I think, so troubling; as I argued earlier, this was basically what Tiebout had in mind in arguing that the equilibrium in his model was essentially equivalent to a competitive equilibrium. At any rate, I have been somewhat reassured in all this by the work of some later theorists who also do not find Bewley fully convincing. As John Conley has pointed out to me, Bewley's treatment is limited to his specific analytical construct: he does not consider the universe of models. There are a variety of subsequent treatments which, using other settings that retain the essential features of a Tiebout economy, establish sufficient conditions for the "Tiebout Theorem" (namely that jurisdictional equilibria exist and are Pareto efficient) to be at least approximately valid.[10]

However, a model of local finance without local government surely seems incomplete. A second approach, responding to the Epple-Zelenitz (1981) call for "approaches which merge the role of collective choice institutions with that of jurisdictional competition" (91), integrates some form of local public decision making, a "voice" option, into the model. Much recent work has extended the Tiebout model in this direction by building into it some form of local budget determination. I will call this class of models the "collective choice version" of Tiebout.

In one of the early papers of this kind, Dennis Epple and Allen Zelenitz (1981) assume a bureaucratic form of local government with Niskanen-type officials who seek to maximize their rents. They show that competition among a large number of jurisdictions can limit the rent-taking capacity of local officials but not eliminate it altogether; inelastic supplies of land allow local officials some scope for exploitation. But most of the modeling of the collective choice version of Tiebout has used the workhorse median-voter model. It is not easy to characterize in a general way the findings that emerge from this body of work. As Ross and Yinger (1999) point out, outcomes are sensitive to the

---

[10] I am grateful to John Conley for his valuable comments and patience in working through this issue with me. For more on this, see chapter 9 in this book.

specific assumptions made about what voters know, the behavior of renters versus homeowners, the precise collective-decision rule, and the technology of public production. For example, it matters whether or not resident-voters are myopic in the sense that they do not realize that their budgetary decisions will influence housing prices and housing consumption in their jurisdictions. And the variety of possible outcomes have different implications, for example, for the presence of capitalization. This continues to be a very active area of research (e.g., Kessler and Lulfesmann 2005).

The normative implications of the collective choice versions of Tiebout are likewise somewhat problematic. Inasmuch as the median-voter outcome is perfectly efficient only under certain restrictive conditions, it is hardly surprising to find that this class of models typically generates outcomes that do not satisfy the Pareto-efficiency conditions (Wildasin 1986). Sources of inefficiencies in these models can include imperfect outcomes in housing markets, property-tax finance, and imperfect information among voters. As Yinger (1982) has pointed out, this forces the whole analysis into a second-best framework, which implies that the usual efficiency conditions for outputs of local public services must themselves be amended. But the more important (and harder) question, it seems to me, is the magnitude of these distortions relative to other ways of organizing the local public sector. It is hard to believe, for example, that a more centralized determination of local public outputs is likely to produce better results on grounds of economic efficiency (e.g., Bradford and Oates 1974).

At a more informal level, Fischel (2001) argues that supplementing Tiebout with politics (in this case, the median-voter model) provides a framework that both provides a reasonable description of local finance (at least in certain parts of the United States) and that encourages efficient local fiscal behavior. Under Fischel's "homevoter hypothesis," resident homeowners have a powerful incentive to select local programs for which the benefits exceed the costs, inasmuch as the net benefits will be capitalized into their property values. Fischel, moreover, provides an intriguing, informal conjecture on all this. He argues that "Tiebout's neglect of local government politics requires only modest amendment of his model. In most local governments one just has to replace Tiebout's invisible municipal managers with the median-voter model. The median voter will want to do most of the same things that an entrepreneurial private manager would want to do" (96).[11]

---

[11] My treatment here has been limited to residential property. For an early and interesting extension of the Tiebout model to encompass commercial-industrial property, see Fischel (1975). In a first-best setting, a mobile firm should face a "tax-price" in each jurisdiction that equals the marginal cost of the public services it consumes (e.g., refuse disposal, police and fire protection, etc.) plus any external costs (e.g., pollution or congestion) generated by its activities.

On Production Functions in the Local Public Sector

Some time ago, Bradford, Malt, and Oates (1969) argued that production functions for certain important local services, such as education and public safety, are likely to have a distinctive character with significant policy implications. Their claim was that, unlike most production functions in the private sector, the vector of inputs for these local services includes not only the usual "capital and labor" elements, but also the characteristics of the community's households. The quality of education in local schools, for example, depends not only on the teachers and facilities, but also on the pupils themselves. Children tend to get a better education if they attend schools populated by bright and highly motivated students. Such peer-group effects are widely documented and appreciated. Likewise, levels of public safety will tend to be higher in communities populated by law-abiding residents. The argument, in short, is that the characteristics of the residents of a community are themselves an important input into the production function for local services.[12]

This consideration introduces another layer of complexity into the Tiebout model, because it implies that the technology of producing public goods depends on the sorting process. In particular, it implies that individuals have a kind of "external effect" on the communities in which they choose to reside: They not only influence the local tax base, but they also have differentiated effects on the outputs of local services. As Jan Brueckner and Kangoh Lee (1989) show, this can, in principle, be accommodated in a framework in which competitive developers are in a position to charge differential prices to prospective residents (that effectively internalize the effects the individuals have on local outputs) and thereby provide the "intraclub transfers" required to sustain an equilibrium. However, Charles de Bartoleme (1990) shows that matters become more complicated in a setting with local governments in which local policy is constrained to treat all residents alike. Indeed, Schwab and Oates (1991) show that, in such a model with local government, optimal community composition can involve a tradeoff between the gains from homogeneity in demands among residents and the gains from heterogeneity in the production of local public goods. Their analysis provides a case on efficiency grounds for equalizing intergovernmental grants. But this is a complicated issue. For example, as Richard Arnott and John Rowse (1987) show in their work on peer-group effects, the normative implications of interactions among pupils in schooling depend in fundamental ways on the curvature properties of the

---

[12] Lee Anne Fennell (2001) provides an illuminating extension of this basic point in her treatment of "user participation" in the production of local public goods. She explores the many, and sometimes subtle, ways in which interactions among, and strategic decisions by, users influence the levels (and quality) of local public outputs.

educational production function. More specifically, they find that the desirability of "perfect streaming" (classes with students of the same ability) as compared to "mixing" (classes with students of different abilities) depends critically on *how much* students benefit from being in a class with students of a slightly higher ability or lose from being in a class with students of lesser ability.

The recognition of these kinds of interactions in the production functions for local services has both normative and positive implications. On the positive side, I (Oates 1977, 1981) have argued that it provides powerful incentives for local zoning ordinances. The usual rationale for economic zoning (as embodied, for example, in the expanded Tiebout-Hamilton model) is fiscal in nature. The community sets some kind of lower bound on the consumption of housing so as to prevent free-riding on the local tax base; this is so-called "fiscal zoning." But where there are interactions in the local production function, where higher income and housing consumption are positively correlated with "characteristics" that enhance local public outputs, there is another motive for what can be called "public-goods zoning." Such zoning seeks to influence the composition of the community in ways that are favorable to higher levels of local services. Indeed, I think this is a major reason why communities are often so jealous of their local zoning prerogatives. All this is admittedly not easy to disentangle at an empirical level, for public-goods zoning, in practice, may not be easily distinguishable from fiscal zoning (Bogart 1993).[13]

Empirical Testing of Tiebout

Since the early capitalization studies, there have been a wide variety of efforts to test the Tiebout hypothesis. They have taken diverse forms: Some are relatively informal looks at the world to see if it is Tiebout-like (or if the conditions are favorable to Tiebout-sorting processes), while others are formal econometric tests of various specifications of the Tiebout model and their implications. I shall not try here to provide a comprehensive review of this body of work; this would entail a major essay in its own right. But I would like to provide some sense of this research and my reading of its implications for the explanatory power of the Tiebout model.

One of the first issues that arises in thinking about the relevance of Tiebout to observed behavior is the matter of adequate choice. Tiebout households "shop" for a community in which to reside—and the question naturally poses

---

[13] Recognition of this kind of interaction also has important implications for the econometric estimation of peer-group effects. It suggests that there is a basic endogenous element in the formation of peer groups that needs to be taken into account when modeling interactions among individuals. Evans, Oates, and Schwab (1992) show that such endogeneity can have profound effects on the signs, significance, and magnitudes of estimated peer-group effects.

itself of whether there exists a sufficiently broad menu of alternative jurisdictions. The conventional wisdom is that Tiebout sorting is most likely in a metropolitan setting where an individual who works in the center city (or elsewhere in the area) will have a wide choice among communities in which to live. Fischel (1981) examined the reasonableness of this contention by looking at the number and structure of local governments in urban areas in the United States. And he found lots of choice in the larger Urbanized Areas (UAs). In most of the large UAs in the United States, Fischel finds dozens of alternative local governments with independent fiscal and zoning powers; in some, there are several hundred such jurisdictions. In addition, Fischel, after calculating concentration ratios for each area (i.e., the fraction of the land area in the metropolitan area occupied by the four largest local jurisdictions), concludes that the structure of these areas is typically "competitive" rather than "monopolistic." In short, there is evidence that a wide range of choice among jurisdictions exists in a large number of urban places: The ingredients for a Tiebout process seem present. Moreover, the evidence on commuting patterns suggests that job location (which is itself widely dispersed in most metropolitan areas) does not exert much of a constraint on residential choice; Hamilton (1982), for example, found that commuting patterns between residential and job locations were practically random as compared to the predictions of a standard urban economic model.

The second question is whether, within this wide distribution of communities, we actually observe Tiebout-sorting behavior. This is not an easy question to answer. One approach is to look directly at patterns of stratification in local communities. In a Tiebout world, we would find households with similar demands for local public services grouped together in communities. Moreover, local zoning ordinances (an element of the expanded Tiebout-Hamilton model) should result in tendencies toward homogeneity in local housing consumption. Thus, some studies have examined the extent of heterogeneity in income and housing in local communities. We cannot directly observe household demands for local services, but such demands are surely positively correlated with income so that a Tiebout world should exhibit tendencies toward income stratification. The tough question here is, how much stratification? Since demands are not perfectly correlated with income, we should not expect to see anything approaching perfect stratification by income. As mentioned earlier, Pack and Pack (1978), in an early study using Pennsylvania communities, looked at the variation in income and housing values within communities. And they found variation in excess of that which they deemed consistent with a Tiebout world. However, the question remains as to how much homogeneity Tiebout requires. As noted earlier, the "consensus bid function" approach to Tiebout sorting can accommodate a significant range of income heterogeneity. (See also Hamilton [1976] and Fischel's discussion [2001, 68–70].) One early study in this spirit by Bruce Hamilton, Edwin Mills, and David Puryear (1975) examined the variation in Gini coefficients measuring the distribution of income in central city and suburban census tracts. This study found that tracts in metropolitan areas with a greater range of school choice (as measured by the number of school districts) exhibited a higher degree of income stratification, a finding that they take to support the Tiebout hypothesis. However, this finding did not extend to stratification as measured by Gini coefficients for housing values. A later study of this sort by Randall Eberts and Timothy Gronberg (1981), using a Thiel measure of the degree of income inequality, found evidence in support of Tiebout. Looking across metropolitan areas in the United States, Eberts and Gronberg found that in areas with a greater number of school districts (i.e., with a wider scope for choice), there was a higher degree of homogeneity among households (i.e., less income inequality).[14]

More recently, Dennis Epple and Holger Sieg (1999) have derived some testable implications from a basic model of locational equilibrium. These take the form of predictions concerning the distribution of households by income across communities and of the relationships among income distributions, housing prices, and the provision of local public services. Using data from the Boston metropolitan area, they find that a simple correlation analysis produces results that are generally consistent with the predictions of the model. One test of the model, for example, is the prediction that the ranking of communities by level of income should be independent of whether the ranking is done according to median income or to the choice of any income quantile. The model performs fairly well on this (and other) tests. Of particular interest is a finding from the decomposition of intracommunity variation in income that suggests that the unobserved heterogeneity in preferences within communities is "quite substantial" (673).

Other work as well has tried to draw out testable implications of the Tiebout model and subject them to empirical testing. One such implication is efficiency in the provision of local services. As Jon Sonstelie and Paul Portney (1978) showed, profit-maximizing communities will provide efficient levels of public outputs—levels of outputs that satisfy the basic Samuelson condition for efficiency in the provision of public goods. Such a set of outputs will result in the maximization of local property values (as it does also in Fischel's [2001] more informal analysis of the homevoter hypothesis). In an early test that used these propositions, Jan Brueckner (1982) found, using a sample of Massachusetts communities, that he could not reject the null hypothesis of

---

[14] There are, however, some troublesome simultaneity issues here. As Alesina, Baqir, and Hoxby (2004) point out, the number of jurisdictions (here school districts) is itself likely to be an endogenous variable.

efficient local outputs. More specifically, Brueckner's test found "no systematic tendencies toward either under- or over-production of local services" (321).

More recently, Paul Rhode and Koleman Strumpf (2003) have proposed a different test of the Tiebout model that used a historical approach. In their model, we would expect the declining costs of mobility over time to result in greater heterogeneity across jurisdictions, since lower moving costs should encourage Tiebout sorting. However, using three different samples (a national sample of municipalities, counties, and the 92 municipalities in the Boston metropolitan area) and several measures of heterogeneity (including both fiscal and demographic variables), they find just the opposite. With data reaching back over decades (and, in some instances, over a century), they find a consistent tendency toward increased homogeneity across jurisdictions.

Thus, a body of widely differing kinds of evidence exists, much (but not all) of which seems favorable to Tiebout. Theoretical work since the original Tiebout paper has provided us with more rigorous formulations of the model from which scholars have ferreted out a number of testable propositions. And the model seems to be standing up reasonably well to these tests. The Tiebout perspective, in short, seems to have some explanatory power.

An Alternative Approach to Tiebout: "Incomplete Contract Theory"

An intriguing body of new literature has emerged, mostly from the field of industrial organization, that seeks to apply some of the new theory of the firm to issues in fiscal decentralization (e.g., Cremer, Estache, and Seabright 1996). Borrowing from the principle-agent framework in a setting of imperfect information, this literature attempts to transfer some of the insights from issues in the management of the firm to the operation of the local public sector. This can provide, I think, some interesting new ways to think about Tiebout.[15]

Carolyn Hoxby (1999) provides a nice application of this approach to local finance in a paper on productivity issues. The central problem in her paper is the limitation of rent-taking by the providers of local services in an incomplete-contracts setting, where it is not possible to write "verifiable contracts" (i.e., contracts under which legal enforcement is based on information concerning performance). Such a setting creates serious problems for a social planner, who is not in a position to observe agents' efforts or possibly jurisdiction-specific cost conditions. However, in a Tiebout world with local property taxation, agents (i.e., the providers of local services) may have incentives for investing more effort so as to increase local outputs. These incentives arise in the Hoxby framework

---

[15] For a survey and assessment of this literature in terms of the development of a new "second-generation theory of fiscal federalism," see Oates (2005).

because the higher levels of local services become capitalized into increased property values, which, given local tax rates, translate into larger budgets and higher rewards for the agents. Thus, a Tiebout world with local property taxation can create a set of incentives that enhances productivity.

While the Hoxby incentive mechanism is a very specific one that depends on certain (perhaps questionable) features of the local fiscal landscape (e.g., unchanging local tax rates when property values rise), it does suggest a further perspective on Tiebout.[16] In a world of imperfect information, Tiebout sorting can both generate valuable information for households and provide important incentives for performance. Fiscal performance manifests itself in local property values. As Hayek (1945) pointed out in a famous essay long ago, prices convey a lot of information that facilitates efficient decision making. In the local public-sector context, this can be part of a process of "yardstick competition" by which households can compare the relative performance of neighboring jurisdictions in the provision of local services (Besley and Case 1995). The general point here is simply that a Tiebout world may provide some incentive-enhancing mechanisms in addition to the standard efficiency gains from Tiebout sorting. This is a line of work that merits further investigation.

A Note on Two Close Cousins to Tiebout: The Theory of Clubs and the Regional Model

The Tiebout model has a close relative in the economic theory of clubs. Less than a decade following the publication of Tiebout's paper, James Buchanan (1965) published his famous piece on "An Economic Theory of Clubs." The Tiebout model and the theory of clubs are often addressed in the same breath as if they are virtually interchangeable. However, there are some important distinctions that put the two models in sharper relief.

As Suzanne Scotchmer (1994) and others have pointed out, the theory of clubs deals solely with joint consumption, with a "group of consumers sharing a common facility" (94). In this sense, it is somewhat less complicated than the Tiebout model; we do not have to deal with "space" (Rubinfeld 1994). In a Tiebout world, we must address the issue of household location in a geographically defined jurisdiction, which (as we have discussed) implies the presence of housing and land markets. What the two models have in common is the nature of the shared good. In both settings, individuals jointly consume an impure public good, a good that

---

[16] The evidence on the issue of unchanging tax rates is mixed. In an intriguing empirical study of Massachusetts cities and towns, Howard Bloom and Helen Ladd (1982) found that during years when property reassessments took place, tax levies in Massachusetts cities increased more than if revaluation had not occurred. However, the long-run effect is less clear. Moreover, no short-run or long-run effect of revaluation was found in towns in Massachusetts, suggesting some basic differences in the nature of fiscal decision making in cities and towns!

is subject to costs of congestion. This makes it possible to define in a similar way in both models an optimal-size group for the consumption of the shared good: For each level of output, there is a group size that minimizes costs per person— and this is the optimal-size group for that level of output (or size of facility).

In the theory of clubs, the presence of free entry drives profits to zero, and, as Scotchmer shows, this can produce a Pareto-efficient outcome in much the spirit of the usual competitive equilibrium. Free entry is a somewhat more complex concept in a Tiebout framework. It is relatively straightforward to envision entrepreneurs providing club goods such as movies and swimming pools, but the issue of the formation of local jurisdictions obviously presents a more complicated set of issues. The Tiebout problem is more extended and rich. The analysis of the existence and stability of equilibria and of their efficiency properties thus requires more structure and additional restrictions in a Tiebout-type model than in the theory of clubs.

One of the most striking of the simplifying assumptions in Tiebout's paper is that the sole source of income for all households is dividend income. This seems, on first glance, to be a highly restrictive and unrealistic condition. It is thus important to understand its important role in the model. What this assumption achieves is freeing households from any employment constraints in their choice of a community of residence. In particular, they need not reside in the same jurisdiction in which they work. This means that a household can choose the jurisdiction that best satisfies its preferences for local public outputs with no concern for the location of employment (including potential commuting costs). Recognition of this condition immediately suggests that the application of the Tiebout model really should not extend beyond a metropolitan area. Within a single urban complex, an individual can work in the central city (or elsewhere in the area) and still have access to a wide range of communities within which to reside. As mentioned earlier, Fischel (1981) explored the relevance of the Tiebout model by looking at the range of choice exhibited by the number and structure of local jurisdictions within urban areas. The Tiebout model is thus basically a model of metropolitan fiscal behavior.

However, there are other offshoots of Tiebout that drop the assumption of dividend income and require instead that individuals reside in the same jurisdiction in which they employed. The seminal paper by Frank Flatters, J. Vernon Henderson, and Peter Mieszkowski (1974) develops just such a model and finds that it differs in important ways from Tiebout. Most especially, unconstrained mobility in such a model does not lead, in general, to an efficient outcome. There are various sorts of costs of such mobility that are not internalized in individual decisions and that lead to inefficient location patterns. As the authors show, a set of equalizing grants is needed to induce efficient decisions. Requiring individuals to live and work in the same jurisdiction really suggests something larger than a single metropolitan area with its myriad of local communities. For this reason, I prefer to call this "the regional model" to distinguish it from Tiebout. The regional model has its valuable applications in terms of examining, for example, location decisions in settings where regions have differing endowments of natural resources that affect both wages and revenues of state or provincial governments. But all this goes beyond the scope of this paper. What is important here is to distinguish Tiebout from what is a much broader class of models that embody costless mobility of individuals (and capital).[17] Some writers, it seems to me, have been a little careless and misleading in identifying all models of mobile households with Tiebout.

Another Brief Note: Tiebout and the Theory of Fiscal Decentralization

Some of the more recent literature seems to regard the Tiebout model as virtually the centerpiece of the theory of fiscal decentralization (e.g., Cremer et al. 1996). I want simply to suggest that this represents an exaggeration of its role in the theory of fiscal federalism. The core of the Tiebout process involves mobile households that seek out jurisdictions that best satisfy their preferences for local public goods. But such mobility is not necessary to the case for fiscal decentralization. Indeed, even were there no mobility whatsoever, there is still a compelling case for decentralized public decision making. The point is that the efficiency gains for "local" fiscal choice have their source in differing demands for local public goods across jurisdictions. And we should expect such differences to exist even in the absence of mobile households. People across different localities are unlikely to be homogeneous. And this in itself (in addition to any interjurisdictional variation in costs of provision) will result in differences in the efficient levels of provision of local public goods. The Decentralization Theorem (Oates 1972, 35, 54–63), which lays out a set of sufficient conditions for fiscal decentralization to be welfare-enhancing, does not depend in any way on Tiebout-sorting behavior.

This is of some importance, since the case for fiscal decentralization applies as well to larger jurisdictions, such as regions, provinces, and states, where Tiebout behavior is surely less prevalent than in a local setting. The efficiency role of Tiebout sorting in a local context is to increase the gains from decentralization. By making jurisdictions more homogeneous in terms of their demands for local public goods, the Tiebout process can effectively increase the potential gains from local fiscal choice. But it is not the sole source of such gains. The case for fiscal decentralization does not rest on Tiebout.

---

[17] This broader class of mobility models has figured importantly in the huge (and still emerging) literature on fiscal competition and harmonization. For a comprehensive treatment, see, for example, Dietmar Wellisch (2000).

Conclusion: Efficiency and Equity Issues in a Tiebout World

The Tiebout paper has provided an invaluable point of departure for the theory of local public finance. First, it gives us a normative framework for thinking about the provision of local public goods. Tiebout sorting promotes an efficient use of scarce resources in a manner analogous to that of a competitive market. And, when augmented with some local politics, it offers further insights into how both exit and voice options for individual households can enhance the efficient operation of the local public sector. Second, the Tiebout vision provides the framework for a useful explanatory model of local finance. Indeed, the model focuses attention on a powerful set of forces that have helped shape the landscape of urban America.

Many observers, however, find themselves uncomfortable in a Tiebout world. While it is true that it promotes efficient resource use through the stratification of communities by demands for local services, this very stratification has some unappealing distributional consequences. A world composed of high-income communities walled off by zoning ordinances that effectively prevent entry by lower-income households is troubling. In particular, it precludes much in the way of local redistributive programs, since the wealthy and poor tend to live in different jurisdictions. The response of some economists is simply to note that redistributive measures are not really suitable to local government anyway. Aggressive measures by a local government to redistribute income from rich to poor will inevitably set in motion forces inducing the rich to exit and the poor to enter—forces that, in practice, will serve to limit efforts at the local level to devise and introduce redistributive measures (Brown and Oates 1987). Redistributive policies, in short, are really not the business of local government.

But this view does not sit well in some quarters. Equality of opportunity is a cherished principle in America, and the pursuit of this principle has focused much attention on primary and secondary education in the United States. A Tiebout world is seen by many as inimical to the achievement of this objective with its high-income communities with excellent schools juxtaposed to poorer school districts with inferior school systems. Indeed, this is the basis for the rejection of local property tax financing of schools and the associated reforms of school finance in many states over the past 30 years (Inman and Rubinfeld 1979). In some states, this has taken the form of a fundamental shift of responsibility for the structure and functioning of K–12 education to state government; in other states, the primary emphasis has been on instituting systems of equalizing grants to funnel more monies into relatively poor school districts.

This is a complicated issue. Fischel (2001 and elsewhere) has argued, for example, that the *Serrano* decision in California in 1971 effectively broke the link between local property taxation and the quality of local schools; the local electorate was deprived of its basic budgetary tool for improving local education. He contends further that this was instrumental in the enactment of Proposition 13 and the centralization of school finance in California—and with devastating results. More generally, Fischel believes that the loss of local tax prerogatives and the associated control of levels of local services has come at a high cost in terms of reduced levels of civic interest and engagement. In particular, this is why "the apparent quality of public education has declined nationwide as the states' share of funding for it has risen" (2001, 161). This is surely not to say that there is no room for substantial programs of equalizing grants to provide assistance to poor districts. But it is crucial that this be done in ways that maintain incentives for local efforts to improve public services.[18]

In sum, a Tiebout world (amended in certain ways to accommodate local politics) has much to commend it on efficiency grounds. It allows the local public sector to cater to a wide variety of preferences and to do so in a relatively efficient manner. Attempts to mute its force can come at a high cost in terms of impairing both local fiscal performance and involvement in civic affairs. At the same time, the stratification and the diversity that such a world fosters can come into conflict with other social values. There seems to be an inevitable tension here. But however we may feel about this tension between economic efficiency and other social objectives, the Tiebout model describes a powerful and pervasive set of social and economic forces that must be addressed in the design of public policy.

REFERENCES

Alchain, Armen A. 1950. Uncertainty, evolution, and economic theory. *Journal of Political Economy* 58:211–221.

Alesina, Alberto, Reza Baqir, and Caroline Hoxby. 2004. Political jurisdictions in heterogeneous communities. *Journal of Political Economy* 112:348–396.

Arnott, Richard, and John Rowse. 1987. Peer group effects and educational attainment. *Journal of Public Economics* 32:287–305.

Besley, Timothy, and Anne Case. 1995. Incumbent behavior: Vote seeking, tax setting and yardstick competition. *American Economic Review* 85:25–45.

Bewley, Truman F. 1981. A critique of Tiebout's theory of local public expenditures. *Econometrica* 49:713–740.

Bloom, Howard S., and Helen F. Ladd. 1982. Property tax revaluation and tax levy growth. *Journal of Urban Economics* 11:73–84.

---

[18] Many years ago, David Bradford and I (1974) conducted a conceptual experiment in which, having estimated a demand function for local school spending for a sample of New Jersey municipalities, we calculated the hypothetical welfare losses from moving from a system of decentralized school finance to a more centralized system in which spending per pupil is equalized. The welfare losses were quite large, reflecting the relatively price-inelastic demand function. See Oates (1997) for a more general treatment of the measurement of the welfare gains from fiscal decentralization.

Bogart, William T. 1993. What big teeth you have!: Identifying the motivations for exclusionary zoning. *Urban Studies* 30:1669–1681.

Bradford, David F., R. A. Malt, and Wallace E. Oates. 1969. The rising cost of local public services: Some evidence and reflections. *National Tax Journal* 22:185–202.

Bradford, David F., and Wallace E. Oates. 1974. Suburban exploitation of central cities and governmental structure. In *Redistribution through public choice*, H. Hochman and G. Peterson, eds. New York: Columbia University Press.

Brown, Charles C., and Wallace E. Oates. 1987. Assistance to the poor in a federal system. *Journal of Public Economics* 32:307–330.

Brueckner, Jan K. 1982. A test for allocative efficiency in the local public sector. *Journal of Public Economics* 14:311–332.

Brueckner, Jan K., and Kangoh Lee. 1989. Club theory with a peer-group effect. *Regional Science and Urban Economics* 19:399–420.

Buchanan, James. 1965. *The public finances.* Homewood, IL: Richard Irwin.

———. 1965. An economic theory of clubs. *Economica* 32:1–14.

Cremer, Jacques, Antonio Estache, and Paul Seabright. 1996. Decentralizing public services: What can we learn from the theory of the firm? *Revue d'Economie Politique* 106: 37–60.

de Bartoleme, Charles A. M. 1990. Equilibrium and inefficiency in a community model with peer group effects. *Journal of Political Economy* 98:110–133.

Eberts, Randall W., and Timothy J. Gronberg. 1981. Jurisdictional homogeneity and the Tiebout hypothesis. *Journal of Urban Economics* 10:227–239.

Edel, Matthew, and Elliott Sclar. 1974. Taxes, spending, and property values: Supply adjustment in a Tiebout-Oates model. *Journal of Political Economy* 82:941–954.

Epple, Dennis, and Holger Sieg. 1999. Estimating equilibrium models of local jurisdictions. *Journal of Political Economy* 107:645–681.

Epple, Dennis, and Allan Zelenitz. 1981. The implications of competition among jurisdictions: Does Tiebout need politics? *Journal of Political Economy* 89:1197–1218.

Epple, Dennis, Alan Zelenitz, and Michael Visscher. 1978. A search for testable implications of the Tiebout hypothesis. *Journal of Political Economy* 86:405–425.

Evans, William N., Wallace E. Oates, and Robert M. Schwab. 1992. Measuring peer group effects: A study of teenage behavior. *Journal of Political Economy* 100:966–991.

Fennell, Lee Anne. 2001. Beyond exit and voice: User participation in the production of local public goods. *Texas Law Review* 80:1–87.

Fischel, William A. 1975. Fiscal and environmental considerations in the location of firms in suburban communities. In *Fiscal zoning and land use controls*, E. Mills and W. Oates, eds. Lexington, MA: Heath-Lexington Books.

———. 1981. Is local government structure in large urbanized areas monopolistic or competitive? *National Tax Journal* 34:95–104.

———. 2001. *The homevoter hypothesis: How home values influence local government taxation, school finance, and land-use policies.* Cambridge, MA: Harvard University Press.

Flatters, Frank, J. Vernon Henderson, and Peter Mieszkowski. 1974. Public goods, efficiency, and regional fiscal equalization. *Journal of Public Economics* 3:99–112.

Hamilton, Bruce W. 1975. Zoning and property taxation in a system of local governments. *Urban Studies* 12:205–211.

———. 1976. Capitalization of intrajurisdictional differences in local tax prices. *American Economic Review* 66:743–753.

———. 1982. Wasteful commuting. *Journal of Political Economy* 90:1035–1053.

———. 1987. Tiebout hypothesis. In *The new Palgrave: A dictionary of economics, vol. 4*, J. Eatwell et al., eds., 640–642. London: Macmillan.

Hamilton, Bruce W., Edwin S. Mills, and David Puryear. 1975. The Tiebout hypothesis and residential income segregation. In *Fiscal zoning and land-use controls*, E. Mills and W. Oates, eds. Lexington, MA: Heath-Lexington Books.

Hayek, F. A. 1945. The use of knowledge in society. *American Economic Review* 35:19–30.

Henderson, J. Vernon. 1985. The Tiebout model: Bring back the entrepreneurs. *Journal of Political Economy* 93:248–264.

Hirschman, Albert O. 1970. *Exit, voice, and loyalty.* Cambridge, MA: Harvard University Press.

Hoxby, Caroline M. 1999. The productivity of schools and other local public goods producers. *Journal of Public Economics* 74:1–30.

Inman, Robert P., and Daniel L. Rubinfeld. 1979. The judicial pursuit of local fiscal equity. *Harvard Law Review* 92:1662–1750.

Kessler, Anke S., and Christoph Lulfesmann. 2005. Tiebout and redistribution in a model of residential and political choice. *Journal of Public Economics* 89:501–528.

Mieszkowski, Peter. 1972. The property tax: An excise tax or a profits tax? *Journal of Public Economics* 1:73–96.

Musgrave, Richard A. 1959. *The theory of public finance.* New York: McGraw-Hill.

Netzer, Dick. 1966. *Economics of the property tax.* Washington, DC: Brookings Institution.

Oates, Wallace E. 1969. The effects of property taxes and local public spending on property values: An empirical study of tax capitalization and the Tiebout hypothesis. *Journal of Political Economy* 77:957–971.

———. 1972. *Fiscal federalism.* New York: Harcourt Brace Jovanovich.

———. 1977. The use of local zoning ordinances to regulate population flows and the quality of local services. In *Essays in labor market analysis*, O. Ashenfelter and W. Oates, eds. New York: Wiley.

———. 1981. On local finance and the Tiebout model. *American Economic Review* 71:93–98.

———. 1997. On the welfare gains from fiscal decentralization. *Journal of Public Finance and Public Choice* 2–3:83–92.

———, ed. 2001. *Property taxation and local government finance: Essays in honor of C. Lowell Harriss.* Cambridge, MA: Lincoln Institute of Land Policy.

———. 2005. Toward a second-generation theory of fiscal federalism. *International Tax and Public Finance* 12:349–374.

Oates, Wallace E., and Robert M. Schwab. 1991. Community composition and the provision of local public goods: A normative analysis. *Journal of Public Economics* 44:217–237.

Ostrom, Vincent, Charles M. Tiebout, and Robert Warren. 1961. The organization of government in metropolitan areas: A theoretical inquiry. *American Political Science Review* 55:831–842.

Pack, Howard, and Janet Rothenberg Pack. 1978. Metropolitan fragmentation and local public expenditures. *National Tax Journal* 31:349–362.

Rhode, Paul W., and Koleman S. Strumpf. 2003. Assessing the importance of Tiebout sorting: Local heterogeneity from 1850 to 1990. *American Economic Review* 93:1648–1677.

Ross, Stephen, and John Yinger. 1999. Sorting and voting: A review of the literature on urban public finance. In *Handbook of urban and regional economics, vol. 3*, P. Cheshire and E. Mills, eds. Amsterdam: North-Holland.

Rubinfeld, Daniel L. 1987. The economics of the local public sector. In *Handbook of public economics*, A. Auerbach and M. Feldstein, eds. Amsterdam: North-Holland.

————. 1994. Comments on Chapter 4. In *Modern public finance*, J. Quigley and E. Smolensky, eds. Cambridge, MA: Harvard University Press.

Schwab, Robert M., and Wallace E. Oates. 1991. Community composition and the provision of local public goods: A normative analysis. *Journal of Public Economics* 44:217–237.

Scotchmer, Suzanne. 1994. Public goods and the invisible hand. In *Modern public finance*, J. Quigley and E. Smolensky, eds. Cambridge, MA: Harvard University Press.

Seabright, Paul. 1996. Accountability and decentralization in government: An incomplete contracts model. *European Economic Review* 40:61–89.

Sonstelie, Jon C., and Paul R. Portney. 1978. Profit maximizing communities and the theory of local public expenditures. *Journal of Urban Economics* 5:263–277.

Tiebout, Charles. 1956. A pure theory of local expenditures. *Journal of Political Economy* 64:416–424.

————. 1961. An economic theory of fiscal decentralization. In *Public finances: Needs, sources, and utilization*. Princeton, NJ: Princeton University Press.

Tiebout, Charles, and David B. Houston. 1962. Metropolitan finance reconsidered: Budget functions and multi-level governments. *Review of Economics and Statistics* 44:412–417.

Wellisch, Dietmar. 2000. *Theory of public finance in a federal state*. Cambridge, UK: Cambridge University Press.

Wildasin, David. 1986. *Urban public finance*. New York: Academic Press.

Wooders, Myrna Holtz. 1980. The Tiebout hypothesis: Near-optimality in local public good economies. *Econometrica* 48:1467–1485.

————. 1989. A Tiebout theorem. *Mathematical Social Sciences* 18:33–55.

————. 1999. Multijurisdictional economies, the Tiebout hypothesis, and sorting. *Proceedings of the National Academy of Science* 96:10585–10587.

Yinger, John. 1982. Capitalization and the theory of local public finance. *Journal of Political Economy* 90:917–943.

Yinger, John, Howard S. Bloom, Axel Boersch-Supan, and Helen F. Ladd. 1988. *Property taxes and house values: The theory and estimation of intrajurisdictional property tax capitalization*. Boston: Academic Press.

Commentary

Robert Inman

Wallace Oates has provided us with a valuable overview of the contributions of Charles Tiebout's (1956) model of local government finance. Like all of Wally's papers, this one is correct, clear, and insightful. My hope here is to build on Wally's summary with a brief review of efforts to test empirically the validity of the Tiebout framework and then, given our empirical understanding, comment on the importance of Tiebout's view of government finance for the design of fiscal policy generally. Simply put, Tiebout conjectured that for an important class of public services—in particular those whose technologies displayed significant congestion in service provision—competitive governments operating much like competitive firms would provide the service efficiently, not just at the lowest cost but also at a level that maximized resident welfare. The most natural setting for such competitive governments is in metropolitan areas populated by many small suburban jurisdictions. It is here that we typically test the validity of Tiebout's conjecture.

Wally's characteristic modesty leads him to downplay his own contribution to our empirical understanding of local public economies, but Oates (1969) was the first serious effort to formally test the structure and predictions of the Tiebout hypothesis. Oates's pathbreaking contribution reached two conclusions. First, both improvements (deterioration) in the quality of local public services, *holding tax rates constant*, or reductions (increases) in local taxes paying for those services, *holding service quality constant*, will be capitalized into higher (lower) local land values in any community with less than a perfectly elastic supply of land. Second, *tax-financed increases in local public service quality* may increase, decrease, or leave unchanged local land values, depending on whether new residents value the community's service improvement more than, less than, or equal to the taxes required to finance the increase. Oates found that for his sample of New Jersey local governments, tax-financed increases in public education led to higher local property values.

Oates's findings are exactly what we would expect if local government services are being provided in a market setting. The market structure is somewhat special, however, but the economic intuition is straightforward. Buying a residence (land) in a community is economically equivalent to buying an admission ticket to an amusement park. The purchase price of a residence includes, along with the value of the home's physical space, the initial entry fee of a two-part tariff, where the second part of the tariff consists of local taxes paid to cover the costs of local public services. If new residents value public services in a particular community more than their associated taxes, then they will pay a premium above the value of a home's housing attributes for the privilege of moving into that community. If, however, potential residents find a community's public services do not justify the taxes paid, then new residents will demand compensation before moving into that community—compensation that will be paid as a decline in housing prices. Finally, if potential residents are just indifferent between the value of extra services received and extra taxes paid, then no premium will be paid and no compensation will be required. In the Oates's market of northern New Jersey communities, high-quality schools were scarce, so the sample's average community could increase home values by spending more on public schools. Oates's capitalization results could plausibly occur only if a market for public services such as the one envisioned by Tiebout in fact existed.

Oates's now classic paper set the research agenda for the empirical analysis of Tiebout's conjecture. Our task is to understand exactly how this market works and to then evaluate the market's performance against the economist's usual standards of efficiency and equity. To do so, we must first understand individual demand for local public goods, then the cost of providing such goods, and finally, the process of market equilibrium. In this brief survey, I limit my comments to what I regard as the central contributions in this growing empirical literature.

After decades of expenditure "determinant" regressions, Henderson (1968) and Gramlich (1969) offered the first serious efforts to ground local fiscal choice in household demand theory. These papers implicitly assumed a single, politically stable decision maker across jurisdictions: the "decisive voter," who was identified as the voter with the average income in the community. This approach took an important step forward with the work of Bergstrom and Goodman (1973) when they detailed a set of sufficient conditions needed to identify the decisive decision maker as the median-income voter in each community. The Bergstrom-Goodman analysis implicitly assumed as a maintained hypothesis that local politics set budgets through an open-agenda majority rule process—for example, via a referendum or Downsian competitive politics. Inman (1978) provided a first statistical test of the Bergstrom-Goodman conditions for a sample of Long Island school districts, also assuming open-agenda, majority rule politics prevailed, and there I could not reject the null hypothesis that the median voter was indeed the voter with the median income. Filimon, Romer, and Rosenthal (1982) extended the analysis by providing a framework that allowed a formal test of the open-agenda majority rule assumption against an alternative hypothesis of a closed-agenda budget maximizer. For a sample of Oregon school districts, they rejected the open-agenda hypothesis in favor of their closed-agenda specification. For a sample of small New York State school districts, however, Romer, Rosenthal, and Munley (1992) could not reject the open-agenda hypothesis typically assumed in median voter politics.

While providing a valuable starting point for the study of the estimation of the demand for local public goods, these community demand studies are handicapped by the necessity of having to disentangle demand information from data jointly determined by resident preferences and political aggregation. Using community-level data, one must either assume a demand specification so as to identify the appropriate model of political choice or, alternatively, assume a model of political choice to identify the appropriate demand specification. Neither restriction seems particularly compelling. Bergstrom, Rubinfeld, and Shapiro (1982) provided an important advance when they showed us how to use survey information to directly estimate citizen preferences for local public goods. Resulting micro-estimates of price and income elasticities of demand for local services are typically much lower than estimates obtained from community demand studies: price and income elasticities of −.20 and .20, respectively, from micro-demand studies and −.50 and .50 or higher from community studies. The likely reasons for these differences are household sorting into communities by omitted demand characteristics (called "Tiebout bias") and, within any one community, higher voter turnout by voters with unmeasured high demand for local public services. Citizens with an unmeasured preference for local public goods tend to collect in communities with low tax prices and higher (median or mean) incomes and are more likely to vote. Both effects lead to estimates of price and income elasticities biased away from zero when using community data. Finally, micro-studies are also able to show that personal attributes such as having children in public school (+), being a college graduate (+), being a public employee (+), and being retired or unemployed (−) all impact on citizen demands in plausible ways. The Bergstrom-Rubinfeld-Shapiro analysis gave strong support to Tiebout's assumption that people demand local public goods in much the same way—utility maximization—as they do more familiar private goods and services.

The defining cost attribute of local public goods, and perhaps the single most important assumption in Tiebout's original argument, is that such goods exhaust all economies of scale in population with relatively few users (N) of a public facility (X). Economies of scale in population will be exhausted when the average cost per person of providing a given level of government services ($g = \hat{g}$) just equals the marginal costs of providing that level of service to one more person: $C(N; \hat{g})/N = \partial C(N; \hat{g})/\partial N$. When true, the community will be at the minimum average cost per person needed to provide $\hat{g}$. Tiebout's conjecture assumes this minimum can be achieved for relatively small populations, perhaps no more than 10,000 to 20,000 residents. In the simple but plausible case where service costs $C(N; \hat{g}) = w \cdot X(N; \hat{g})$ and w is constant—think wages (w), teachers (X), test scores (g), and students (N)—then, when economies of scale in population have been fully exploited, $w \cdot X/N = C(N; \hat{g})/N = \partial C(N; \hat{g})/\partial N = w \cdot \partial X(N; \hat{g})/\partial N$. Thus, at the minimum of the average cost per person curve, $wX/N = w \cdot [\partial X(N; \hat{g})/\partial N]$, or $\varepsilon_{X,N} = [(\partial X/\partial N)/(X/N)] = 1$. The condition that $\varepsilon_{X,N} = 1$ stands as a direct test that communities are cost efficient in their provision of their chosen level of public services. If, however, $\varepsilon_{X,N} = [(\partial X/\partial N)/(X/N)] > 1$ (< 1), then marginal costs exceed (are below) average costs, average costs are rising (falling) in N, and communities are too large (small) for the provision of their chosen level of $g = \hat{g}$. Bergstrom and Goodman (1973) were the first to suggest this indirect test of Tiebout cost efficiency; they found local communities were at the minimum or on the rising portion of their aggregate cost curve ($\varepsilon_{X,N} \geq 1$) for the provision of a standard bundle of local services. The community sizes in their sample ranged from 10,000 to 150,000 residents, confirming Tiebout's suspicion that small communities could efficiently provide most local public services: education, libraries, police (excluding courts and prisons), fire services, trash pickup (not waste disposal), road maintenance and snow removal, and parks and recreation.[1] Only if $\varepsilon_{X,N} < 1$ and local communities display significant economies of scale in population would Tiebout's conjecture be at risk. In that case we would be in a world with only a few, perhaps only one, efficient provider of public services: Samuelson's original public goods economy.

Tiebout's founding assumptions of rational, utility-maximizing consumers and efficient, small providers seem well supported by the data, but is there a

---

[1] Bergstrom and Goodman (1973) reached their conclusions from a reduced form specification imposing the identifying restrictions that factor costs (w) are independent of city size, and city size impacts household demand for public services only through its impact on public goods congestion. For samples of small suburban communities, these restrictions seem reasonable. Still, direct estimates of the public goods congestion technology are valuable—see, for example, Craig (1987) for police services; Getz (1979) for fire services; and Ehrenberg et al. (2001) for a survey of congestion (class size) in the provision of education. Those studies confirm the Tiebout assumption as well: These important local services can be efficiently provided in small communities.

market process that then efficiently matches consumers to providers as Tiebout assumed? Three tests, two indirect and one direct, have been offered in the empirical literature. If efficient sorting into communities holds, it must be part of an equilibrium process where no resident has an incentive to move into any other community given its own and all other communities' current provision of public services *and* where the politically decisive resident of each community has no incentive to change the level of service provision in her community. Epple and Sieg (1999) specify and estimate such an equilibrium model for a sample of communities in the Boston metropolitan area and find they cannot reject the model's key predictions as to income sorting or that communities with predicted higher demands for an index of local public goods (education and crime) also have higher housing prices. Epple, Romer, and Sieg (2001) extend the Epple-Sieg analysis of Boston area suburbs to explicitly include local fiscal choice. They use a median voter model, but, more important, they also allow residents' tastes for local services to vary along a dimension in addition to income. This added dimension of taste proves important and suggests the simple median-*income* voter specification to local choice may miss an important dimension of citizen preferences, an observation that follows directly from the micro-demand studies for local goods as well. These results also caution against "testing" the Tiebout framework by looking for plausible patterns in community demographic composition as, for example, in Rhode and Strumpf (2003). Tiebout conjectures that individuals will sort into communities according to their preferences for public goods; Epple and his colleagues find that a significant component of those preferences comes from heterogeneity in citizen tastes not well measured by obvious demographic attributes.

While finding that Tiebout's conjecture does a good job in explaining the location patterns of households across Boston suburbs is reassuring evidence in its favor, it tells us nothing about the efficiency performance of local governments in such a setting. Hoxby's (2000) study of the impact of local school competition on student test performance, spending per pupil, and teacher-pupil ratios provides a more direct, though not quite complete, test of the conjecture. Hoxby regresses individual student achievement on an index of school competition in the student's metropolitan statistical area (MSA) and finds that students in MSAs with many small public school districts have statistically and quantitatively significantly higher test scores than their counterparts in MSAs with few or only one public school district. Further, teacher-pupil ratios are higher in more competitive MSAs, consistent with the view that public service outputs (g) rise as public inputs rise (X/N). Finally, costs per student (C/N) are lower in more competitive MSAs. These three results are fully consistent with Tiebout's conjecture that competitive local governments foster public-sector efficiency. Students appear to learn more and at a lower cost in more competitive public economies.[2]

Though it is encouraging that the model creates cost efficiency in the provision of local public goods, what evidence is there that Tiebout competition leads to the overall welfare maximization either for community residents or for the local public goods market as a whole? Overall efficiency requires not only low costs, but also that citizens get what they want—where individual marginal benefits from more public services, $MB(g)$, are equal to an individual's share ($\approx 1/N$) of the marginal social costs, $MC(g)$, needed to produce that extra level of the public good, $MB(g) \approx (1/N) \cdot MC(g)$. Bergstrom et al. (1988) test whether this condition holds within a community based on their micro-econometric estimates of citizens' marginal benefits for public education for a sample of Michigan school districts. Setting $MB(g)$ equal to the average marginal benefit in each community, they find that for most school districts, $MB(g) < (1/N) \cdot MC(g)$, local public services are overprovided when average marginal benefits are compared to marginal social costs. Strikingly, however, when average marginal benefits are compared to marginal *private* costs, allowing for subsidization of residential services by commercial-industrial property or for federal deductibility of local taxation, community choices do equate average marginal benefits and (now) marginal private costs, $MB(g) \approx (1/N) \cdot MC(g) \cdot (1-\theta)$, where θ is the share of property tax base that is commercial or the share subsidized by federal deductibility. If there is an economic inefficiency in this Tiebout economy, it is not Tiebout's fault! Whether local school budgets are decided by open or closed agendas, each community's average resident appears to get what he or she wants.

But Tiebout wanted to do more than just make the average resident in each community happy. The Tiebout conjecture is that there will be a market equilibrium when no one's welfare can be improved by moving. Brueckner (1982)

---

[2] Hoxby's results have recently come under challenge from Rothstein (2004). The central issue is a technical one of how best to control for omitted factors that might jointly influence test performance and local costs and the number of local school districts in the MSA. One can imagine that MSAs that have poor test performance or high costs for some unmeasured taste or cost reason might also be MSAs where parents might also establish alternative educational opportunities. The omitted factor might imply low test scores, high costs, and many schools, biasing the observed correlation away from support for the Tiebout conjecture. Hoxby seeks to correct for this bias using an instrumental variable—the presence of many streams and rivers—to predict the number of school districts in the MSA. By conventional tests, the presence of rivers and streams is a valid statistical instrument, and Hoxby's results that school competition improves test scores and lowers school costs are confirmed. Rothstein questions the validity of Hoxby's statistical instrument, suggests an alternative, and finds no impact of increased competition on school test score performance, though he continues to find competition reduces per-pupil spending. Thus, even with Rothstein's approach, competition pushes local public schools to be more efficient, providing the same output at lower cost. Hoxby's (2005) reply to Rothstein addresses his concerns and reconfirms her primary conclusions that competition increases test scores and lower costs.

defines the condition necessary for evaluating the global welfare performance of a Tiebout marketplace, and it implies the very intuitive result that market efficiency obtains when no existing or new (free-entry) community can increase its land values—that is, charge a higher entry fee to join its public goods consumption "club"—for a small, tax-financed increase in its public goods. If an individual is not willing to pay extra to move to another community, he must be individually happy where he is. Absent significant moving costs or non-public-good amenities, individual marginal benefits from public goods must equal individual marginal costs. Brueckner performed his test for a sample of eastern Massachusetts communities and could not reject the null hypothesis of global efficiency for his sample of communities.

Though piecemeal, the econometric evidence is uniformly supportive of the Tiebout conjecture. Households demand local public goods in a manner consistent with utility maximization. Local governments supply local public goods in a manner consistent with cost minimization. Local fiscal competition within large metropolitan areas controls local government costs and appears to provide sufficient choice to households to ensure overall allocative efficiency. Why, then, have recent policy debates regarding the design of local fiscal policy seemed so resistant to embracing the lessons of the Tiebout argument?

Two reasons suggest themselves: political capture and fiscal fairness. Fiscal competition checks public employee wages and local costs, and in a competitive Tiebout economy the observed distribution of spending and taxation is regressive against income. It is no surprise, then, that public employee unions, public interest lawyers, and elderly homeowners often reject the Tiebout economy and embrace state policies to centralize the financing of local public services. To do so, however, threatens the potentially significant efficiency gains that follow from Tiebout fiscal competition. Advocates for fiscal centralization need not win this debate.

First, the rents earned from the monopoly position of public employees protected by state "duty-to-bargain" laws serve no economic purpose other than to redistribute resources from taxpayers and families to public employees. While high wages are needed to attract and retain talented public employees— teachers in particular—it is difficult to find a compelling argument to justify high compensation for *all* employees. The reform of state public employee bargaining rules to encourage, not undermine, local fiscal competition and then, in the new bargaining environment, the subsidization of local governments to adopt more flexible employee reward structures are policy alternatives that benefit families and talented public employees alike (see Lavy 2002). Tiebout's argument and the empirical evidence reviewed here provide the intellectual foundation for such reforms.

Second, advocates of fiscal fairness have rightly observed that richer families in a Tiebout market economy can provide better schools for their children than can lower-income families (see Inman and Rubinfeld 1979). Further, since tax payments for those schools are functionally equivalent to market purchases, and K–12 education is an economic necessity—a good whose estimated income elasticity of demand is less than 1—local taxes will appear regressive against income. Again, this is not the fault of Tiebout competition but simply a fact of economic life that can be addressed through subsidies for the consumption of the valued economic necessity. To combat hunger, we subsidize the needy's purchase of food; we do not shut down the marketplace and centralize food production and allocation. There is no logical reason why targeted subsidies cannot perform a similar function within a Tiebout market economy. In such a setting, Nechyba (1996) has shown that the appropriate price subsidy is an open-ended matching grant for the valued local public service and targeted tax relief for those unduly burdened by local taxation.

As Tiebout suggested and Oates first demonstrated empirically, competitive local governments, like competitive producers generally, have the potential to provide local public goods and services efficiently. While more empirical research formally testing the central efficiency conjecture of the Tiebout argument is surely needed—and here the new structural econometrics by Bayer and McMillan (2005) finding a strong positive effect on school competition on student performance is welcome—it is perhaps also time to publicly advocate the power of, and benefits from, the Tiebout conjecture to the wider public-policy community. As economists, it would be a waste to keep such a good idea to ourselves.

REFERENCES

Bayer, Patrick, and Robert McMillan. 2005. Choice and competition in local education markets. National Bureau of Economic Research. Working Paper 11802, Cambridge, MA.

Bergstrom, Theodore, and Robert Goodman. 1973. Private demand for public goods. *American Economic Review* 63:280–296.

Bergstrom, Theodore, Judith Roberts, Daniel Rubinfeld, and Perry Shapiro. 1988. A test for efficiency in the supply of public education. *Journal of Public Economics* 35:289–307.

Bergstrom, Theodore, Daniel Rubinfeld, and Perry Shapiro. 1982. Micro-based estimates of demand functions for local school expenditures. *Econometrica* 50:1183–1205.

Brueckner, Jan. 1982. A test for allocative efficiency in the local public sector. *Journal of Public Economics* 19:311–332.

Craig, Steven. 1987. The impact of congestion on local public good production. *Journal of Public Economics* 32:331–354.

Ehrenberg, Ronald, Dominic Brewer, Adam Gamoran, and J. Douglas Williams. 2001, November. Does class size matter? *Scientific American:* 79–85.

Epple, Dennis, Thomas Romer, and Holger Sieg. 2001. Interjurisdictional sorting and majority rule: An empirical analysis. *Econometrica* 69:1437–1465.

Epple, Dennis, and Holger Sieg. 1999. Estimating equilibrium models of local jurisdictions. *Journal of Political Economy* 107:645–681.

Filimon, Radu, Thomas Romer, and Howard Rosenthal. 1982. Asymmetric information and agenda control: The bases of monopoly power in public spending. *Journal of Public Economics* 17:51–70.

Getz, Malcolm. 1979. *The economics of the urban fire department.* Baltimore: Johns Hopkins University Press.

Gramlich, Edward. 1969. State and local governments and their budget constraint. *International Economic Review* 10:163–181.

Henderson, James. 1968. Local government expenditures: A social welfare analysis. *Review of Economics and Statistics* 50:156–163.

Hoxby, Caroline. 2000. Does competition among public schools benefit students and tax-payers? *American Economic Review* 90:1209–1238.

———. 2005. Competition among public schools: A reply to Rothstein (2004). National Bureau of Economic Research. Working Paper 11216, Cambridge, MA.

Inman, Robert. 1978. Testing political economy's "as if" proposition: Is the median income voter really decisive? *Public Choice* 33:45–65.

Inman, Robert, and Daniel Rubinfeld. 1979. The judicial pursuit of local fiscal equity. *Harvard Law Review* 92:1162–1750.

Lavy, Victor. 2002. Evaluating the effect of teachers' group performance incentives on pupil achievement. *Journal of Political Economy* 110:1286–1381.

Nechyba, Thomas. 1996. A computable general equilibrium model of intergovernmental aid. *Journal of Public Economics* 62:363–398.

Oates, Wallace. 1969. The effects of property taxes and local public spending on property values: An empirical study of tax capitalization and the Tiebout hypothesis. *Journal of Political Economy* 77:957–971.

Rhode, Paul, and Koleman Strumpf. 2003. Assessing the importance of Tiebout sorting: Local heterogeneity from 1850 to 1990. *American Economic Review* 93:1648–1677.

Romer, Thomas, Howard Rosenthal, and Vincent Munley. 1992. Economic incentives and political institutions: Spending and voting in school budget referenda. *Journal of Public Economics* 49:1–33.

Rothstein, Jesse. 2004. Does competition among public schools benefit students and taxpayers? A comment on Hoxby (2000), Education Research Section, Princeton University. Working Paper 10, Princeton, NJ.

Tiebout, Charles. 1956. A pure theory of local expenditure. *Journal of Political Economy* 64: 416–424.

3

California's School Finance Reform: An Experiment in Fiscal Federalism

Eric J. Brunner

Jon Sonstelie

Although public education is the largest category of local public expenditure, Tiebout (1956) didn't make public schools the primary example in his classic theory of those expenditures. Perhaps inspired by his locale, he chose to exemplify his theory by a community with a 500-yard beach. Whatever the motivation, his choice was a prudent one. It is one thing to argue for the efficiency of partitioning families among communities according to their demand for beach space; it is quite another to advance the same argument for partitioning families according to their demand for something as important as the education of their children.

Oates (1969) was more forthright. In his seminal paper on capitalization, he explicitly defined and estimated the price of public school quality. Families got good schools for their children if they were willing to pay for them. Moreover, in his theory of fiscal federalism, Oates (1972) had a ready answer for those who might object that the willingness to pay for good public schools is determined largely by a family's income. The equitable distribution of income is best addressed at a higher level of government, Oates argued; a public service should be provided by the lowest level of government consistent with economies of scale. Because economies of scale in education are achieved at very low populations (Kenny 1982), public education ought to be provided by many, small school districts; higher levels of government can deal with the inequities stemming from that system.

Legal theorists didn't see it that way. Looking at the local provision of public education through the lens of *Brown v. Board of Education*, 347 U.S. 483 (1954), they saw the wide disparities in spending per pupil across school districts as just another violation of the equal protection clause of the Fourteenth Amendment. This view had its first legal victory in California with the ruling of the state's Supreme Court in *Serrano v. Priest*, 96 Cal. Rptr. 601 (1971). The ruling initiated a chain of events that abruptly ended local financing of public schools in California. In seven short years, California transformed its school finance system from a decentralized one in which local communities chose how much to spend on their schools to a centralized one in which the state legislature determines the expenditures of every school district. The *Serrano* ruling led to similar rulings in other states, although no state reacted quite as radically as California.

It would be an exaggeration to claim that California's transformation was a natural experiment in fiscal federalism. The *Serrano* ruling could have led the state down many different paths, and the path California chose reflected its own complex politics. That qualification notwithstanding, California's story has many lessons for students of fiscal federalism. This article describes California's school finance system before *Serrano* and traces the transformation from local to state finance and delineates some consequences of that transformation. It concludes with lessons from California's experience.

School Finance in 1970 and the *Serrano* Ruling

California school districts differ considerably in size and grade span. In 1969–1970, there were 236 unified districts (kindergarten to grade 12), 723 elementary districts, and 120 high school districts. Sixty-four percent of students were enrolled in unified districts, with an average enrollment of 12,452. One of those districts, Los Angeles Unified, had over 650,000 students, 14 percent of the state's total. No other district was even remotely as large (San Diego was second with 130,000 students), though there were 12 districts with more than 35,000 students. All 12 were unified districts. In contrast, the average enrollment for the elementary districts was only 1,573. High school districts averaged 4,488 students. Though these smaller districts were numerous, it is important to remember that per-pupil statistics for California public schools are significantly influenced by a few large districts.

California school districts were larger on average than districts in other states. In California, the average was about 4,200 students; in the rest of the country, the average was less than 2,500. The larger average for California was partly due to the state's program to encourage the unification of elementary and high school districts. In 1935 the state had over 3,000 districts, none of them unified. By 1965 there were fewer than 1,500 districts, 191 of which were unified. In addition, during the same period in which the number of districts fell by half, the state's population tripled.

Before the *Serrano* decision, California's school finance system was similar to systems in other states. School districts levied their own property tax rates, and the state supplemented that revenue with apportionments from the state school fund. The state apportionments were based on a foundation formula with a minimum, called basic aid. The state imposed a maximum on each district's general purpose tax rate, and that maximum could only be exceeded if approved by a majority of a district's voters. In 1968–1969, all but 11 districts had rates in excess of this maximum, making school levy elections a regular occurrence. Districts could also impose of number of special tax rates without voter approval. The revenues from these special rates were earmarked for specific purposes. Property taxes were about 55 percent of the total revenue of school districts.

Assessed value per pupil differed widely across districts. In unified districts, 25 percent of students were enrolled in districts with assessed value per pupil above $13,456, and 25 percent were in districts with assessed value per pupil less than $7,946—a gap of 69 percent. The gap between the top 5 percent and the bottom 5 percent was 343 percent. Similar disparities existed for elementary and high school districts.

The disparities in assessed value per pupil were greater than the disparities in revenue per pupil. The state apportionment formula distributed more state aid to school districts with lower assessed value per pupil, and school districts with low assessed value tended to levy higher tax rates. For students in unified districts, the gap in revenue per pupil between the top 25 percent and the bottom 25 percent was only 14 percent. However, the gap between the top 5 percent and the bottom 5 percent was 70 percent.

Disparities in both revenue and assessed value caused the *Serrano* complaint. Specifically, the plaintiffs argued that those differences violated the equal protection clause of the Fourteenth Amendment. Under the legal framework that was developed from previous Supreme Court rulings, a state could classify people differently under the law if it had a reasonable rationale for doing so. Under certain circumstances, however, the state faced a higher hurdle in proving that its laws were reasonable. If a law affected a fundamental right, such as voting, and involved a suspect classification of people, such as race, the state's law would be subject to "strict scrutiny." The Warren Court expanded the definition of both fundamental rights and suspect classifications. In *Brown v. Board of Education,* it declared that segregated education violated the fundamental rights of black children. In *Harper v. Virginia Board of Elections,* 383 U.S. 663 (1966), it overturned Virginia's poll tax because it declared individual wealth a suspect classification. In *Baker v. Carr,* 369 U.S. 186 (1962), the Court declared that legislative districts had to have equal populations, making geography, in some respects, a suspect classification.

Reviewing those rulings, Wise (1967) argued that the local provision of education must also violate the Fourteenth Amendment. The Court had implied that education was a fundamental right and that wealth and geography were suspect classifications, so a system in which the quality of local public schools depends on geography and the wealth of families and their neighbors would not pass judicial scrutiny.

Similar theories were being advanced by Harold Horowitz (1966), a law professor at UCLA. Horowitz found a receptive audience in Derrick A. Bell Jr. Bell had worked with Thurgood Marshall in the NAACP Legal Defense and Education Fund and was head of the Western Center of Law and Poverty, a public interest law firm funded by the federal Office of Economic Opportunity. The two decided to test Horowitz's theories in court, making the *Serrano* suit the product of the "egalitarian revolution" spawned by the Warren Court (Kurland 1963) and the war on poverty initiated by President Lyndon Johnson. The plaintiffs were a number of schoolchildren and their parents, including John Serrano Jr., a parent. The defendants were a number of state and local government officials, including Ivy Baker Priest, state treasurer.

In their complaint, the *Serrano* lawyers made two specific claims. The two claims seem quite different, but they were connected by the plaintiffs' belief that assessed value per pupil was highly correlated with family income.[1] One claim was that, because assessed value per pupil varied across school districts, taxpayers in districts with low assessed value per pupil had to pay higher tax rates to achieve the same spending per pupil. The other claim was that students from disadvantaged families might require more educational resources than other students to have the same educational opportunities. The assumed correlation between income and assessed valuation implied that the taxpayers in districts with low assessed value per pupil were also low-income families who needed to spend more on their children's education. To provide the same educational opportunity for their children, low-income families would have to pay higher tax rates than other families. With regard to a fundamental right, education, the state treated individuals differently according to a suspect classification: wealth.

The *Serrano* complaint was filed in Los Angeles Superior Court, but the claims of the plaintiffs were not immediately tested in court. The defendants demurred, the plaintiffs appealed, and the case eventually reached the California Supreme Court. Because of two other events, the *Serrano* lawyers narrowed their argument to the fiscal inequities of the school finance system. The first event was the ruling of a federal court in *McInnis v. Shapiro*, 293 F.

---

[1] In their petition to the California Supreme Court, the *Serrano* lawyers wrote, "The relative wealth of school district residents correlates to a high degree with the relative wealth of school districts as measured by the assessed valuation per pupil."

Supp. 327 (N.D. Ill. 1968). In that case, the plaintiffs claimed a violation of equal protection because the school finance system in Illinois did not provide enough revenue to meet the educational needs of disadvantaged students. The federal court rejected that argument because educational need was too nebulous to adjudicate. *McInnis* was appealed to the U.S. Supreme Court, which affirmed the decision of the lower court (394 U.S. 322). As a consequence, in their appeal to the California Supreme Court, the *Serrano* lawyers downplayed their claim about the additional resource needs of disadvantaged students and focused more on the fiscal inequities arising from variations in assessed value per pupil. The *Serrano* lawyers were aided in this new focus by the second event: the 1970 publication of *Private Wealth and Public Education*, by Coons, Clune, and Sugarman. Coons and his coauthors took a more conservative approach than Horowitz in their legal critique of public school finance. They did not include differing educational needs as an element in their critique, taking revenue per pupil as the measure of educational quality. This measure put a spotlight on the fiscal inequities due to variations in assessed value per pupil.

The California Supreme Court accepted the logic of Coons and coauthors. It ruled that education was a fundamental right and school district wealth was a suspect classification. Differences in revenue per pupil due to differences in assessed value per pupil thus violated equal protection. In declaring district wealth a suspect classification, the court had entered new territory. The defendants argued that the concept of a suspect classification was meant to be applied to individuals, not to government entities. This argument would have required the plaintiffs to show that there was a correlation between the assessed value of a district and the income of families living in that district. The court rejected that argument, however, ruling that discrimination on the basis of district wealth is as invalid as discrimination based on individual wealth. The Supreme Court returned the case to the Superior Court for hearing, but its ground rules determined the outcome. The lower court was not required to examine evidence about the relationship between assessed value and family income or spending per pupil and family income. It could focus instead on variation in assessed value per pupil and whether school districts with lower assessed value per pupil had to levy higher tax rates to have the same spending per pupil. The answer to both questions was clearly affirmative, and the Superior Court ruled in favor of the plaintiffs.

If the Supreme Court had asked the Superior Court to examine the link between individual wealth and district wealth, the outcome may have been different. That examination would have been difficult at the time because Census data were not aggregated to the school district level. The Census Bureau completed that task in the late 1970s, however, allowing us now to examine the evidence.[2] Our framework for doing so is a simplified version of the median voter model due to Borcherding and Deacon (1972) and Bergstrom and Goodman (1973). A family's demand for school spending is a function of its income and its tax-price for school spending. The tax-price is the increase in the family's property taxes if the school district increases property tax revenue by one dollar per pupil. That tax-price equals the assessed value of the family's home divided by the district's assessed value per pupil. In logarithmic terms, this price is $p = h - v$, where h is the log of the family's assessed value and v is the log of the district's assessed value per pupil. Assume that the assessed value of a family's house is determined by its income, $h = h_0 + \theta y$, where y is the log of the family's income and θ is the income elasticity of housing demand. Assume further that a family's demand function for spending per pupil has constant price and income elasticities, $s = s_0 + \varepsilon p + \eta y$, where s is the log of the demand for spending per pupil, ε is the price elasticity of demand, and η is the income elasticity of demand. Combining the previous three equations, the demand for spending per pupil is $s = \beta_0 + \beta_1 v + \beta_2 y$, where $\beta_0 = s_0 + \varepsilon h_0$, $\beta_1 = -\varepsilon$, and $\beta_2 = (\varepsilon \theta + \eta)$. With the assumptions that spending per pupil in a district equals the demand of the median voter and that the median voter has median income, this demand function leads to the regression reported in table 3.1.

The model in table 3.1 excludes several important factors. For example, it ignores the fact that renters may face a different tax-price than homeowners (Oates 2005) and that parents with children in private school may have different demands for public school spending than parents with children in public schools (Sonstelie 1982). Yet, despite these omissions, the model explains more than 30 percent of the variation in spending per pupil for elementary districts and more than 50 percent for high school and unified districts. Moreover, the estimated coefficients are consistent with expectations. The coefficient β_1 should be positive because it is the negative of the price elasticity of demand. The coefficient is positive and more than 10 times its standard error in all three regressions. The coefficient β_2 is a function of the price elasticity of the demand for school spending, ε; the income elasticity of the demand for spending, η; and the income elasticity of housing demand, θ. Specifically, $\beta_2 = (\varepsilon \theta + \eta)$. Because both income elasticities should be positive and the price elasticity negative, β_2 could be positive or negative. In fact, as table 3.1 shows, the coefficient is positive for all three types of districts but not significantly different from zero for high school and unified districts.

The insignificant coefficients on median family income seem to suggest that income had little effect on spending per pupil, at least for high school and uni-

---

[2] The tabulation was done for only 739 of the 1,079 districts existing in 1969–1970, but those 739 districts enrolled 98 percent of students in 1969–1970.

TABLE 3.1

Coefficient Estimates for Median Voter Regressions, 1969–1970,
Dependent Variable: Log of Spending per Pupil
(Standard Errors in Parentheses)

Coefficient (variable)	Elementary Districts	High School Districts	Unified Districts
β_1 (log of assessed value per pupil)	0.171 (0.013)	0.265 (0.025)	0.267 (0.015)
β_2 (log of median family income)	0.137 (0.029)	0.002 (0.043)	0.035 (0.033)
Observations	401	110	228
Adjusted R-squared	0.346	0.508	0.569

Demand.

fied districts. That is, two districts with the same assessed value per pupil but different levels of median family income had roughly the same spending per pupil. While this is strictly true, the qualification about assessed value is important. Because housing is a normal good, the assessed value per pupil of residential property should rise with family income. If two districts had the same assessed values but different incomes, the lower-income district must therefore have had either more nonresidential property per pupil or fewer students per family. Either factor would lower the district's tax-price and thus offset the negative effect on demand of its lower income.

The critical relationship between income and assessed value is best illustrated with a simple example. Suppose that all property is residential and all districts have the same number of students per family. Then, assessed value per pupil would be roughly proportional to median family income, the tax-price of education would be approximately the same for all districts, and spending per pupil would primarily be a function of family income. The two variables in our median voter regressions would be nearly collinear, making it difficult to estimate their coefficients. A simple regression of spending per pupil on median family income would work very well, however. Most important, in this world, the complaint of the *Serrano* lawyers would have been exactly right. The quality of public schools, as measured by revenue per pupil, would have been determined almost solely by family income.

This example points to the critical role of the correlation between the log of median family income and the log of assessed value per pupil. In the example of the previous paragraph, that correlation is close to unity. Among California school districts in 1969–1970, the correlation was far short of unity. For elementary districts, it was .12. For unified districts, it was only .04, and for high school districts it was actually negative, −.05.

These low correlations of median family income and assessed value per pupil could be due to two basic factors. The first is variations in students per family. As Fischel (2004) pointed out in his analysis of voting patterns on Proposition 13, districts with many senior citizens had relatively high assessed value per pupil because they had fewer students per family. A second factor is the distribution of nonresidential property. While we do not know the value of nonresidential property in each school district, assessed values for California's largest school districts seem consistent with an uneven distribution of nonresidential property. Among the largest ten school districts, San Juan and Garden Grove, both middle-income suburban districts with little commercial or industrial property, had the lowest assessed value per pupil (less than $7,000 per pupil). Conversely, Oakland, Long Beach, and San Francisco, central cities with large amounts of industrial and commercial property, had assessed values greater than $15,000 per pupil.

Both factors, variations in nonresidential property and students per family, surely explain some of the variation in assessed value per pupil across districts. The question is whether they can explain the unexpectedly low correlation between median family income and assessed value per pupil. In particular, did the distributions of either variable across districts offset what we presume to be a strongly positive correlation between median family income and the average value of residences? In the case of students per family, the correlation with median family income would have had to have been strongly positive. In fact, the correlation between the logs of those two variables was very small for unified districts (.01) and negative for elementary and high school districts (−.21 and −.04). The distribution of students per family was not the explanation of the low correlation between median family income and assessed value per pupil.

This finding leaves the distribution of nonresidential property as a possible explanation. Evidence in favor of this explanation is the low correlation between median family income and assessed value per family. That is, when total assessed value, residential and nonresidential, is normalized by families instead of students, the correlation with median family income is low. For unified districts, the correlation was .05, for elementary districts −.21, and for high school districts −.04. If total assessed value per family is not correlated with median family income, a negative relationship between nonresidential property per family and family income must have offset the almost certainly positive relationship between assessed values of houses and the income of their residents.

Whatever the explanation, because assessed value per pupil was not strongly correlated with median family income in a district, high-income districts faced, on average, higher tax-prices for public school spending. The higher tax-price partially offset the direct effect of income on demand for public school spending, resulting in a weak relationship between spending per pupil and family income. In 1969–1970, the correlation of the log of spending per pupil to the log of median family income was .26 for elementary districts, .07 for unified districts, and −.05 for high school districts. In the Appendix, the correlation of median family income and spending per pupil is expressed as a function of the correlation of median family income and assessed value per pupil, providing a mathematical representation of the intuition we have presented for this result.

This focus on median income is revealing, and if California school districts were very homogeneous with respect to family income as the Tiebout model suggests, it would be all there is to say. In fact, however, districts were not homogeneous, and the variation in family income within school districts was also part of the story. To incorporate this variation, we determined the distribution of spending per pupil by income class. We took families in specific income ranges and attached to each the spending per pupil in the school district in which it lived. We then determined the percentage of families in each income class that lived in districts with less than a certain level of spending per pupil. By making these calculations, we trace out the distribution of spending per pupil for each income class. The results are displayed in table 3.2.

The distribution of spending per pupil is quite similar across income classes. For example, for families in unified districts with incomes over $25,000, 77.7 percent lived in districts with revenue per pupil less than $900. In comparison, for families with incomes between $10,000 and $12,000, 83 percent lived in districts with revenue per pupil below $900, a very slight difference. Similar comparisons hold true for other income groups and other types of districts. High-income families in elementary districts fare considerably better than other income groups in those districts, but the differences are still quite small.

Part of the explanation for the similarities displayed in table 3.2 is the low correlation between median family income and spending per pupil. Even if the distribution of income differed widely across districts, the distribution of spending per pupil by income group would be quite similar if higher-income districts did not tend to have significantly different levels of spending. But that is only part of the explanation. The second part is the similarity of the income distribution across communities. To take the extreme case, if the distribution of family income were the same in every district, the distribution of spending per pupil would be the same across income groups, regardless of the distribution of spending per pupil across districts. More generally, if there were more variation of family income within districts than across districts, the distribution of spending per pupil would be similar across income groups. In fact, most of the variation was within districts. For elementary school districts, 90 percent of the variance in family income was due to variance within districts. This portion was even larger for unified and high school districts.

TABLE 3.2

Distribution of Total Revenue per Pupil by Income Class, 1969–1970,
Percentage of Families in Income Class with Less Revenue per Pupil in
Their District

ELEMENTARY DISTRICTS

	Revenue per Pupil				
Family Income	**$600**	**$700**	**$800**	**$900**	**$1,000**
$0–$2,999	7.8%	50.8%	78.7%	91.3%	94.7%
$3,000–$5,999	8.0	50.7	79.0	91.1	94.8
$6,000–$7,999	6.9	50.4	79.4	91.1	94.5
$8,000–$9,999	5.7	50.1	78.4	91.0	94.3
$10,000–$11,999	4.9	49.4	77.5	90.8	94.3
$12,000–$14,999	4.3	48.6	76.2	90.1	94.0
$15,000–$24,999	4.0	45.0	71.7	87.4	92.6
$25,000 & above	4.8	37.7	61.6	79.1	87.8

HIGH SCHOOL DISTRICTS

	Revenue per Pupil				
Family Income	**$800**	**$900**	**$1,000**	**$1,100**	**$1,200**
$0–$2,999	11.6%	29.8%	70.5%	85.2%	89.6%
$3,000–$5,999	11.3	29.2	70.7	85.5	90.9
$6,000–$7,999	13.0	30.1	69.7	84.5	89.2
$8,000–$9,999	13.8	31.9	69.4	83.6	88.6
$10,000–$11,999	13.9	31.3	68.3	82.7	88.1
$12,000–$14,999	14.4	30.9	67.5	81.9	87.5
$15,000–$24,999	13.6	28.6	63.7	79.8	85.2
$25,000 & above	10.3	22.3	55.4	75.1	79.0

UNIFIED SCHOOL DISTRICTS

	Revenue per Pupil				
Family Income	**$700**	**$800**	**$900**	**$1,000**	**$1,100**
$0–$2,999	6.9%	34.3%	80.7%	89.8%	91.7%
$3,000–$5,999	7.4	36.7	82.2	90.8	92.7
$6,000–$7,999	7.9	37.5	82.2	90.8	92.6
$8,000–$9,999	9.4	39.7	82.6	91.5	93.1
$10,000–$11,999	10.2	40.5	83.0	91.6	93.2
$12,000–$14,999	9.9	40.1	83.0	91.5	93.2
$15,000–$24,999	9.0	37.0	81.9	90.6	92.5
$25,000 & above	5.4	26.9	77.7	86.8	89.6

Source: Controller's Annual Report and 1970 Census.

Revenue Limits, Proposition 13, and the Transformation from Local to State Finance

Though the facts about spending, assessed value, and income were never thoroughly examined by the courts, they began to come to light as the legislature attempted to fashion a response to the *Serrano* ruling. At first, the legislature focused on equalizing spending per pupil across districts by establishing a system of revenue limits for districts. A district's revenue limit was a cap of the sum of its local property taxes and its state noncategorical aid. Each district's revenue limit was based on its revenue per pupil in 1972–1973 and then increased annually from that base with the limits of low-spending districts increasing at a faster rate than the limits of high-spending districts. In addition, to encourage them to reach their limits, the legislature increased state aid to low-spending districts. Over time, this increase in state aid in combination with the convergence in revenue limits would cause revenue per pupil to converge across districts.

The limits on high-spending districts were politically unpopular, particularly because several large, urban districts were high-spending districts. Not only were these districts well represented in the legislature, but they also had large percentages of disadvantaged students and could thus argue that they required higher revenue to meet the educational needs of their students. In response to these arguments, the legislature established a categorical program, Education for Disadvantaged Youth, that directed additional state funds to large urban districts. The legislature has continued this pattern to the present, using categorical programs to address special needs and to respond to politically powerful districts. In fact, the school finance model crafted in response to the first *Serrano* ruling remains in place today. Revenue limits determine the bulk of district revenue, and categorical revenue is added to that base.

The legislature's response to the *Serrano* ruling did not satisfy the Los Angeles Superior Court. The equalization of revenue limits would take too long, and school districts constrained by the limits had a ready escape. They could override their limits with a simple majority vote of their residents. Because almost all California school districts had been regularly passing levy elections before *Serrano*, the override provision eviscerated the revenue limit system.

The Court's rejection of this system caused the legislature to attempt a more ambitious reform. It kept revenue limits and the override provision but subjected overrides to power equalization. For districts with low assessed value per pupil, the state would supplement their tax revenue from an override so that every school district would receive the same revenue from the same increase in property tax rates. This additional aid would be costly to the state, but it had a surplus at the time, which many legislators were earmarking for a solution to the *Serrano* ruling.

Power equalization was never implemented. Less than a month before it was slated to begin, the voters of California passed Proposition 13, which set a 1 percent limit on the property tax rate and gave to the legislature the authority to allocate the revenue from that rate among local governments. The legislature based its allocations on historical patterns, but because the 1 percent rate was less than half of the average rate before Proposition 13, those allocations fell far short of what governments had previously received. To compensate, the state increased aid to local governments, using the surplus it had accumulated. For school districts, state aid was determined by revenue limits. Each district's aid was the difference between its revenue limit and the property tax revenue it was allocated.[3] In other words, each district's revenue limit was the revenue per pupil it received from the property tax and state aid. In that sense, the state now determines each district's revenue.

Fischel (1989, 1996, 2001, 2004) has argued that the *Serrano* ruling caused Proposition 13. Faced with the prospect of losing control of their property tax revenue, homeowners voted to limit it. As evidence of his explanation, Fischel pointed out that voters had earlier rejected ballot initiatives to limit the property tax and to shift the financing of public schools toward the state. Only after the *Serrano* ruling placed the nexus between their taxes and their schools in jeopardy, Fischel argued, did voters change their minds and decide to limit property taxes. In any event, Proposition 13 did provide the legislature with a relatively straightforward response to the *Serrano* ruling. It made the property tax a state tax and ended what remained after *Serrano* of the local finance of public education.

Since Proposition 13, the legislature has gradually equalized revenue limits and thus revenue per pupil. In 1986 the Los Angeles Superior Court found that this equalization had gone far enough to satisfy the *Serrano* ruling. The legislature has continued to equalize revenue, however, by periodically bringing up the revenue limits of districts below the average. By 1999–2000, these differences were quite small. In unified districts, 25 percent of students were enrolled in districts with revenue limit funds greater than $3,901 per pupil, and 25 percent of students were enrolled in districts with revenue limit funds less than $3,806. The gap between the 75th and 25th percentiles was only 2 percent. For the 95th and 5th percentiles, the gap was 11 percent. In contrast, the equivalent gaps for 1969–1970 were 14 percent and 70 percent, respectively.

---

[3] A few districts receive more property tax revenue than their revenue limit. Under the current law, they keep that excess and also receive a small amount of basic aid from the state. The number of these districts changes as their enrollments and property tax revenues change. However, the number has never been large. Today there are only about 50 of these districts, enrolling less than 3 percent of the state's students.

State categorical programs have continued to grow. In 1999–2000, these programs constituted 25 percent of the revenue of unified districts, 22 percent of the revenue of elementary districts, and 18 percent of the revenue of high school districts. The legislature has also allowed districts to levy a tax on parcels of real property. We discuss this tax in more detail following.

State and federal categorical programs widen the disparities in revenue per pupil. In general, however, these disparities favor districts with high proportions of disadvantaged students. For example, for total revenue per pupil in unified districts in 1999–2000, the gap between the 75th and 25th percentiles is $962, much higher than the $95 gap in revenue limit funds. A simple regression of revenue per pupil on the percentage of low-income students (measured by eligibility for the free or reduced-price lunch program) reveals that most of that gap can be explained by categorical revenue favoring low-income students. For unified districts in 1999–2000, a low-income student yielded about $1,018 more revenue than other students. For an elementary school district, this increment was $451, and for a high school district, the increment was actually negative—specifically, –$301. There are large variations around these averages, however.

Though the finance of public schools has been centralized, the governance of those schools is still a local function. Local voters still elect school boards for their districts, and the school boards hire and fire top management, approve school district budgets, and set district policies. Each school district bargains with its employee unions over salaries, benefits, and working conditions, though the parameters for that bargaining are established by the budget decisions made in Sacramento. A key issue, of course, is the total revenue provided to schools. For collective bargaining, another important issue is the division of that total revenue between unrestricted revenue and categorical revenue. Unrestricted revenue funds salaries; categorical revenue is often protected from collective bargaining. For those reasons, the employee unions are active lobbyists in Sacramento, fighting to increase the flow of unrestricted revenue and thus the pool of money available for salary increases for their members. On the other hand, some categorical programs such as the large K–3 Class Size Reduction program were motivated at least partly by the desire to limit those salary increases. As a consequence, the legislature's decisions about how much district revenue to make unrestricted and how much to tie up in categorical programs are the first round of collective bargaining between districts and their employee unions.

The legislature has not been particularly generous with its public schools. From 1969–1970 to 1999–2000, spending per pupil in California fell about 22 percent relative to spending per pupil in all other states (figure 3.1). In 1969–1970, spending per pupil in California was 12 percent higher than in other states. It was actually 16 percent higher in 1977–1978, the year before

FIGURE 3.1   Real Spending per Pupil

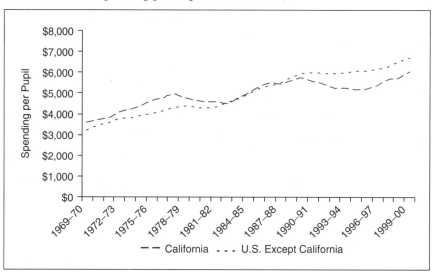

Proposition 13. This margin fell to 9 percent the next year and continued to decline in subsequent years. California's spending per pupil reached a relative low in 1994–1995, 15 percent below the level of other states. It recovered slightly to 10 percent below other states by 1999–2000.

This 10 percent gap understates the gap in resources. In 1999–2000, the teacher-pupil ratio in California was 26 percent lower than the ratio in other states. The gap in resources is larger than the gap in spending per pupil because California teachers were paid about 16 percent more than teachers in other states. The strong teachers' unions in California explain some of the difference in teachers' salaries, but the 16 percent premium is not far out of line with other salary differences. In 1999–2000, employees with bachelor's degrees earned about 14 percent more in California than in the rest of the country (Rose et al. 2003).

Since *Serrano*, courts have overturned school finance systems in several other states. California's relative decline in spending per pupil is not a general trend among these states. Manwaring and Sheffrin (1997) compare public school spending in states with court-ordered reform to spending in other states. Using a dynamic model that allows for lagged adjustment to reform and for the effect of reform to depend on a variety of state characteristics, they find that the expenditures of some states are higher than they would have been without reform, while expenditures in others are lower. Downes and Shah (1995) use a similar approach and reach a similar conclusion. Murray, Evans, and Schwab (1998) examine this issue at the school district level, revealing the effect of reform not just on average spending per pupil in a state but also on the distribution of spending per pupil across districts. They find that court-ordered reform tended to level up spending per pupil within a state. It raised expenditures in low-spending districts and had no effect on high-spending districts. Aware of the inconsistency of their results with California's experience, they reestimated their model without California districts and found that omitting these districts increased the positive effect of reform on expenditures. They attributed California's exceptional response to court-ordered reform to the strict revenue equality demanded by California's courts, though they did not explain why revenue equality necessarily leads to a leveling down.

One possible explanation of California's exceptional response is simply that it was first. Before the *Serrano* ruling, state legislatures could not have reasonably anticipated that the courts would overturn their school finance systems. After the *Serrano* ruling, however, many state legislatures began to examine their own liabilities and to reform their school finance systems. As a consequence, it is not quite as clear that the world can be neatly divided into states that reformed their systems after a court order and states that did not. Among both classes are surely some states that reformed their systems in an attempt to thwart a court order to do so.

Another possible explanation of California's exceptional response is that its school finance reform was accompanied by a property tax limitation. As we have just noted, Fischel has argued that *Serrano* caused Proposition 13, an argument that would disqualify property tax limitations as an independent explanation. But several states had tax limitations without court-ordered reform, providing an opportunity to separate the effects of tax limitations from the effects of court-ordered reform. Figlio (1997) demonstrated the promise of that explanation by showing that, after enacting limits, states increased student-teacher ratios and decreased teacher salaries. As further evidence of this negative effect, Figlio and Rueben (2001) showed that states with property tax limits experienced a reduction in the average quality of new public school teachers.

Though these studies do not identify the mechanism through which a property tax limitation affects public school quality, the mechanism seems obvious. The limit reduces property tax revenue, which reduces funds for public schools and thus public school quality. But lower property tax revenue can be replaced by other taxes or by increased aid to local governments from the state. In fact, California followed exactly this path. Despite the limit on the property tax rate, in 1999–2000 state and local governments in California spent 9 percent more per capita than governments in other states. Thus, California's relatively low public school spending cannot be explained by a generally low level of public expenditures. In an accounting sense, California's low public school spending is due to two factors. First, it had about 8 percent more pupils per capita than other states.

Second, despite the first factor, the state allocated a lower share of public funds to schools than other states. In California in 1999–2000, the expenditures of public schools constituted 22 percent of state and local public expenditures. In the rest of the country, this share was 24.6 percent. California's relative decline in spending per pupil does not reflect a general decline in the public sector but rather a choice about the allocation of a relatively abundant stream of state and local revenue.

Another explanation for California's relative decline in spending per pupil focuses on how school finance reform changed the tax-price of school spending. In response to court orders, other states implemented district power equalization and other financing schemes that alter the tax-price for school district spending but left districts with some authority over their own property tax rates. California took away from school districts the authority to tax property, which, from the perspective of school districts, made the property tax-price infinite. Hoxby (2001) determined how school finance reforms altered tax-prices for districts and then estimated how spending per pupil in districts responded to those changes in tax-prices. The tax-price in her analysis is the increase in district property tax revenue required to increase spending by one dollar. Before *Serrano* in California, this price was unity; after *Serrano*, it is infinite. Hoxby estimates than an increase in tax-price from unity to infinity decreases spending per pupil by 15 percent, thus explaining most of California's relative decline.[4]

This explanation is misleading, however, because it implicitly assumes that school spending decisions in California are made at the school district level. As we show in what follows, some limited school spending decisions are made at the school district level through parcel tax elections. However, the most important spending decisions are made by the legislature when it decides whether to increase revenue limit funding and categorical programs. At that level, the tax-price of school spending is certainly not infinite. School spending can be increased by increasing income or sales tax rates or by decreasing expenditures in other areas. Of course, legislatures in other states make similar decisions when they decide to increase foundation or equalization aid. What distinguishes California from those other states is the balance between state and local decisions. Almost all the spending decisions that count in California are made by the state legislature. Virtually none are made locally.

---

[4] Because a least squares regression is impossible when a regressor has an infinite value, Hoxby estimated spending per student as a function of the inverse of the tax-price. California's inverse tax-price is unity before *Serrano* and zero after *Serrano*. All school districts in New Mexico have inverse tax-prices of unity before reform and 0.05 after reform. In Oklahoma, some districts have inverse tax-prices as low as 0.15 after reform. In all other states, the lowest inverse tax-price after reform is 0.53, and inverse tax-prices are unity in 36 states after reform. Thus, the tax-price effect of school finance reform appears to be primarily identified by the postreform, relative decline in spending per pupil in California, New Mexico, and Oklahoma.

Picus (1991) focused directly on this issue, arguing that the indirect link between taxpayers and their local public schools has caused California's relative decline in school spending. Homeowners pay property, sales, and income taxes, which are then blended in Sacramento and returned to their local public schools. Compared to the days before *Serrano* in which they could simply vote to increase their property tax rates, taxpayers and families have no simple way to affect the funds of their local public schools. It is less clear why this should lead to lower spending on schools, however, because school districts and teachers' unions are very well represented in Sacramento.

Silva and Sonstelie (1995) propose another explanation that is also based on the change in the level of government at which educational spending decisions are made. If the demand for education is determined by family income and families are partitioned among school districts according to their income as the Tiebout model suggests, the statewide average of spending per pupil should approximately equal the average demand, which is then the demand of a family with average income. Under state finance, however, average spending per pupil, which will be the same in every district, should reflect the demands of the median voter, which is the demand of the family with median income. Because average income is greater than median income, the average of spending per pupil under local finance will be greater than spending per pupil under state finance. With this explanation, Silva and Sonstelie can explain about half of California's decline in spending per pupil. The difficulty with this explanation, however, is that school districts in California were not homogeneous with respect to family income. In 1970 there was much more variation of family income within school districts than across districts. Furthermore, nonresidential property was inversely correlated with median family income, and thus many school districts with low median income had high spending per pupil.

A related explanation was offered by Fernandez and Rogerson (1999), who incorporate the foundation aid system that California had in 1970. Under that system, low-income school districts find it cheaper to increase their spending by increasing the foundation than by increasing their own taxes. They thus support a relatively high foundation level, which higher-income districts supplement with their own taxes. The result is a higher level of spending than if all districts are required to have the same level of spending, as under state finance. Like Silva and Sonstelie, this explanation depends on the unrealistic assumption that school districts are homogeneous with respect to family income and that all property was residential. In addition, it has the unrealistic implication that many school districts do not supplement state foundation aid. In fact, as just related, all but 11 California school districts in 1970 voted in favor of property tax rates exceeding the statutory maximum, and every

California school in 1968–1969 supplemented its foundation aid by at least $130 per pupil.

A fourth explanation is directly related to the median voter model in table 3.1. In 1969–1970, the property tax was the source of marginal funds for school districts. For a homeowner, the tax-price of spending per pupil was its assessed value divided by the assessed value per pupil in its school district. For the state as a whole, nonresidential property made up 45 percent of that total (Sonstelie, Brunner, and Ardon 2000). Thus, on average, homeowners received a 45 percent subsidy for school spending. Proposition 13 put a strict lid on property tax revenue, and so the source of marginal funds for schools became the income and sales taxes. Both sources tax individuals directly, with very small percentages paid by business. Thus, Proposition 13 increased the tax-price of school spending by about 45 percent.

The effect of this price increase is determined by the price elasticity of demand, which is the negative of the coefficient on assessed value per pupil in the simple median voter model in table 3.1. That number is probably an underestimate, however. Spending per pupil was positively correlated with state aid, which was negatively correlated with assessed value per pupil. Thus, our estimate of the price elasticity is biased toward zero. Because of the flypaper effect (Hines and Thaler 1995), state aid may have had a relatively large effect on school district spending, making this bias quite large. In any event, our estimate of the price elasticity is $-.171$ for elementary districts, $-.265$ for high school districts, and $-.267$ for unified districts. Based on that evidence and the likelihood that the price elasticity is lower than our estimates, let us suppose that the price elasticity was $-.25$. A 45 percent increase in the tax-price of spending per pupil would then entail an 11 percent reduction in spending per pupil, which would explain about half the relative reduction California experienced.

If this explanation has validity, it only raises another question. Why doesn't California find another tax source to fund its schools, a source with the same subsidies from business? In fact, some school districts appear to be groping toward that solution as they refine their implementation of the parcel tax. These refinements are discussed below in the section on reform.

If school resources affect student achievement, California's relative decline in resources per pupil should be reflected in a relative decline in student achievement. This appears to have occurred. During the 1990s, California students performed poorly on the National Assessment of Educational Progress (NAEP), a standardized test in writing and mathematics administered to a sample of fourth- and eighth-graders throughout the country. This poor performance partly reflects the large percentage of immigrant students in the state, but even when corrections are made for family characteristics, California students are well below students in other states. As reported in Carroll et al. (2005), for the battery of NAEP tests administered between 1990 and 2003, California students scored .18 standard deviations below the national mean after adjusting for family characteristics. California's average adjusted score was the lowest of any state participating in the NAEP.

California students performed considerably better in the period before the transformation from local to state finance. The first piece of evidence comes from the National Longitudinal Study of the High School Class of 1972 (NLS). The study administered a standardized test to a sample of high school seniors in 1972 and also collected information about the characteristics of their families, including race, ethnicity, family income, and parental education. Using that data, Sonstelie et al. (2000) regressed test scores on family characteristics and a dummy variable indicating whether the student was a California resident. The coefficient on that dummy variable was not significantly different from zero. A similar regression produced the same result with data from High School and Beyond (HSB). The HSB test was administered to tenth- and twelfth-graders in 1980, two years after the transformation from local to state finance. However, the students taking the test would have received most of their education before the transformation.

This apparent decline in average performance would be less troubling if it were accompanied by an equalization of achievement across districts and income groups. There is little evidence of equalization across school districts, however. Downes (1992) examined district averages on a state-mandated achievement test. The distribution of district scores is very similar in 1976–1977 and 1985–1986. Moreover, in school districts with low spending per pupil in 1976–1977, and thus relatively large increases in spending from 1976–1977 to 1985–1986, student achievement did not rise faster than in other districts.

There is less evidence about the equalization of achievement across income groups. Because of the growing number of categorical programs, school districts with high proportions of low-income students do tend to receive more revenue per pupil. Yet, schools serving primarily low-income students have considerably lower scores on state-mandated achievement tests than do other schools. California now has a battery of achievement tests, which are aggregated into an Academic Performance Index (API) for each school. Figure 3.2 shows the API for California elementary schools plotted against the percentage of their students eligible for free or reduced-price lunch. This percentage and the API number are averages for the years 2001, 2002, and 2003. As figure 3.2 shows, the majority of schools in low-poverty neighborhoods achieved an 800 API, which is the state's goal for each school. However, very few achieved that goal in high-poverty neighborhoods. In fact, among the 752 elementary schools that have 90 percent or more of their students eligible for free or reduced-price lunch, none had an average API exceeding 800, and only 18 had an average exceeding 700. In contrast,

FIGURE 3.2   Elementary Schools, 2001–2003 Average

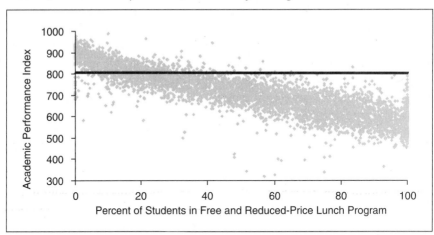

among the 584 elementary schools with 10 percent or fewer of their students eligible for free or reduced-price lunch, all but 36 had an API exceeding 800. We do not have comparable data for the period before California's school finance reform, so we cannot determine whether the data displayed in figure 3.2 represents an improvement. If it is indeed an improvement, it must be a modest one.

Three other studies put these California results in national perspective. Downes and Figlio (1997) examined student achievement on the NLS of 1972 and the National Educational Longitudinal Study (NELS) of 1992 and found that states that enacted tax or expenditure limitations experienced a significant drop in student achievement. However, court-ordered reform did not have a significant effect on student achievement, echoing the findings of Figlio (1997) concerning the effect on spending of tax limitations and finance reforms. Limitations have an effect, but reform by itself does not. These results suggest that California's decline in student achievement was due to its particular approach to school finance reform. Husted and Kenny (2000) focus on how different approaches to school finance reform affected student achievement. They measured reform by the extent to which a state has equalized spending per pupil across districts, the one measure by which California's reform ranks near the top. Using SAT scores from 1987 to 1992 as a measure of achievement, they found that average achievement was lower in states that had equalized spending. Furthermore, they also found that equalization had no effect on the disparity in student achievement within a state.

Card and Payne (2002) also investigate SAT scores but use a different measure of school finance reform. For each state, they estimate the relationship across school districts between median family income and spending per pupil. Court-ordered reform tends to flatten that gradient, and states that have flattened their gradients have also narrowed the gap between the SAT scores of students from highly and poorly educated families. The effects are relatively small, however. The estimated reductions are for SAT scores in 1990 through 1992 compared to scores in 1978 through 1980. For the 12 states that implemented a court-ordered reform during this period, the achievement gap was reduced by about 5 percent. California was not one of those states, and we do not know whether the SAT achievement gap in California narrowed in the 1980s.

Responses to Reform

The transformation described in the previous section affected the educational opportunities perceived by California families. After the transformation to state finance, public school resources were much more equally distributed across school districts but lower on average than districts in other states. As a consequence, for many California families, local public schools must have had fewer resources than they were willing to pay for. How have these families responded to this gap between their demand and the opportunities presented by the public sector? One possible response is private schooling. Another response is to supplement the public school resources provided by the state either through voluntary contributions or by enacting a local parcel tax. This section examines the magnitude of each of these responses.

Private School Enrollments

We examine trends in private school enrollment using data on families with school-age children from the 1970, 1980, 1990, and 2000 Public Use Microdata Samples (PUMS). For each year, we assigned families to deciles based on their annual income and then calculated the percentage of students enrolled in private school in each income decile. Table 3.3 shows the results of that exercise.[5]

Private school enrollment has increased among higher-income families. For example, among children from families in the highest-income decile, 13.1 percent attended private school in California in 1970, 17.2 percent in 1980, 20.8 percent in 1990, and 22.6 percent in 2000. A similar pattern of rising private school enrollments in California holds for children from families in the eighth and ninth deciles. Furthermore, among the top three income deciles, a considerably lower percentage of California students were enrolled in private schools

---

[5] For each year, table 3.A of the Appendix shows the maximum income for each decile measured in 2000 dollars.

TABLE 3.3

Percentage of Schoolchildren Enrolled in Private Schools,
by Family Income Deciles

Income Decile	1970		1980		1990		2000	
	CA	U.S. Except CA	CA	U.S. Except CA	CA	U.S. Except CA	CA	U.S. Except CA
Lowest	3.8%	4.8%	5.5%	5.4%	4.2%	3.6%	3.6%	4.8%
Second	4.4	6.0	6.7	6.3	3.7	5.1	4.0	5.6
Third	4.8	7.3	7.3	7.9	5.2	6.5	4.5	7.0
Fourth	5.5	10.3	7.7	9.1	6.3	8.2	5.9	7.9
Fifth	8.5	11.8	9.1	10.2	9.1	9.0	7.0	8.9
Sixth	9.2	12.9	10.6	10.8	8.5	9.5	8.6	9.7
Seventh	9.3	13.6	10.5	11.4	10.3	10.7	10.1	10.9
Eighth	10.3	14.7	13.7	12.8	13.5	12.4	12.2	12.3
Ninth	10.7	16.1	12.8	14.0	14.4	14.5	15.0	14.5
Highest	13.1	19.8	17.2	19.9	20.8	21.3	22.6	21.9

in 1970 than in the rest of the country. By 2000, however, private school enroll-ment rates among high-income families in California had reached the rate for similar families in other parts of the nation.

Factors other than school finance reform have undoubtedly contributed to the rise in private school enrollment among high-income families in California. For example, Betts and Fairlie (2003) use PUMS data from 132 metropolitan areas in 1980 and 1990 to examine the impact of immigration on propensity of native-born families to send their children to private school. Their results sug-gest that private school enrollment tended to rise in areas that experienced inflows of immigrant children. Over the last three decades, California has cer-tainly experienced large immigrant inflows, suggesting that some of the rise in private school enrollment is due to its effect. Nevertheless, it seems reasonable to conclude that at least part of the increase in private school enrollment was due to school finance reform.

Several recent studies provide evidence consistent with that notion. Using district-level data from California in 1970 and 1980, Downes and Schoeman (1998) found that private school enrollment rose in districts that experienced a decline in real spending per pupil over the same time period. They con-cluded that roughly half of the rise in private school enrollment in California between 1970 and 1980 could be directly attributed to school finance reform. Similarly, Husted and Kenny (2002) examined changes in private school enrollment in 159 metropolitan statistical areas (MSAs) in 1970, 1980, and 1990. They found that private school enrollments tended to rise in MSAs located in states that adopted policies designed to equalize spending per pupil. Furthermore, their results suggest that the leveling of school spending had a particularly large effect on private school enrollments in high-income MSAs.

These studies suggest that at least part of the rise in private school enrollment in California was a direct response to school finance reform. Nevertheless, it still seems surprising that more families did not opt out of the public sector. Nechyba (2003a, 2003b) provides an explanation for this moderate response. In his analysis, school finance centralization and spending equalization have two distinct effects on private school enrollment. First, while equalization causes spending per pupil to fall in some districts, it also causes spending per pupil to rise in other districts. As a result, while private school enrollment rates may rise in previously high-spending districts, they may fall in previously low-spending districts. Second, when public schools are financed at the local level with property tax revenues, families wishing to send their child to private school have an incentive to reside in low-quality/low-spending districts to take advantage of lower housing prices and to reduce their tax burdens. In contrast, when public schools are financed at the state level with statewide income tax revenues, families can no longer reduce their tax burdens by living in a low-quality/low-spending district. Consequently, school finance centralization increases the opportunity cost of living in a low-quality district and sending a child to private school. As a result, some families that previously chose to send their child to private school and live in a low-quality district may now choose to move to a high-quality district (those with high student peer quality) and send their child to public school. Simulations conducted by Nechyba suggest that this secondary effect of school finance centralization may be quite significant.

Voluntary Contributions

While school finance reform may not have engendered a dramatic increase in private school enrollments, it did provoke another response. In the aftermath of school finance reform, many districts established educational foundations to channel private contributions into public schools. Prior to 1970 there were fewer than 10 of these organizations operating in California. There are now more than 500. In addition, over the last several decades Parent Teacher Associations (PTAs) and booster clubs have become much more active in raising private contributions to supplement local school budgets. To examine how successful schools and school districts have been at raising voluntary contributions, we used data from the Internal Revenue Service's Master Business File to identify the contributions raised by all nonprofit organizations that supported either an individual school or a school district in California in 2001.[6] At the school level, contributions are raised primarily by PTAs and booster clubs. At the district level, contributions are raised primarily by local educational foundations.

As table 3.4 demonstrates, a number of schools and school districts have been quite successful in raising voluntary contributions. For example, 36 schools had contributions per pupil in excess of $500 in 2001, and among those schools the average contribution per pupil was $805. Similarly, 12 districts had contributions per pupil in excess of $500, and among those districts the average contribution per pupil was $1,776. As the fourth column demonstrates, the schools and school districts that were most successful in raising voluntary contributions were populated by the highest-income families.[7] Family income averaged $223,759 in the 12 districts with contributions per pupil in excess of $500. In contrast, it averaged only $68,690 in the 63 districts with contributions per pupil of less than $10.

Although several schools and school districts have been successful at raising voluntary contributions, overall the use of voluntary contributions is quite limited. In 2001, over 8,000 schools were operating in California, and only 36 of those schools managed to raise more than $500 per pupil. Similarly, of the 986 districts operating in California in 2001, only 12 managed to raise more than $500 per pupil. California's wealthiest communities have been the most active in raising voluntary contributions, but even in those communities, the use of voluntary contributions remains limited. Brunner and Imazeki (2005) find that even among the 1,425 elementary and middle schools with the highest average family incomes in 2000, fewer than a quarter of those schools raised more than $100 per pupil in 2001, and fewer than 2.5 percent raised more than $500 per pupil.

The final column of table 3.4, which shows how voluntary contributions varied with school or school district enrollment, provides a partial explanation for the limited use of voluntary contributions. At both the school and school district level, contributions per pupil tend to decline with enrollment. For example, the average

---

[6] While the IRS Master File includes all nonprofit organizations supporting K–12 schools in California, it only contains revenue data for those organizations with revenues of $25,000 or more. Thus, we are unable to identify the amount of revenue raised by organizations with revenues of less than $25,000. As a result, our data provide a lower bound on the actual amount raised by organizations supporting K–12 schools in California. For a detailed description of the methodology used to identify nonprofit organizations supporting K–12 schools and the revenue raised by those organizations, see Brunner and Sonstelie (1996) and Brunner and Imazeki (2005).

[7] District-level data on average family income in 2000 were obtained from school district demographic files prepared by the U.S. Census Bureau. Data on average family income by school attendance zone are not available. As a result, we used data on the location of each school in California to match schools to census tracts in 2000. We then used the average family income of the census tract in which the school was located as a proxy for the average income of families within a school attendance zone.

TABLE 3.4

Characteristics of Schools and Districts with Voluntary Contributions in 2001

Contributions per Pupil	Number of Schools/School Districts	Average Contribution per Pupil	Average Family Income	Average Enrollment
CONTRIBUTIONS TO SCHOOLS				
Less than $10	45	$5	$70,342	1,754
$10–$24	214	18	72,981	1,216
$25–$49	450	37	78,132	918
$50–$99	494	71	89,704	771
$100–$249	353	154	112,086	777
$250–$499	97	338	150,927	665
$500 and above	36	805	185,374	549
CONTRIBUTIONS TO DISTRICTS				
Less than $10	63	$5	$68,690	20,415
$10–$24	29	17	81,003	12,643
$25–$49	20	36	81,881	4,408
$50–$99	26	79	90,586	4,633
$100–$249	25	164	123,207	4,903
$250–$499	16	391	155,196	1,623
$500 and above	12	1,776	223,759	660

Note: Contributions to single-school districts are included as contributions to districts.

enrollment in schools with contributions per pupil in excess of $500 is only 549 students. In contrast, the average enrollment in schools with contributions of $10 or less is 1,754 students. The inverse relationship between school size and contributions per pupil alludes to an important limitation schools and school districts face when attempting to replace lost property tax revenue with voluntary contributions. Property tax payments are mandatory, whereas contributions are voluntary. That distinction is particularly important given the public good nature of voluntary contributions. Once a family contributes to their local public school, their contribution benefits not only their own child, but also the children of all other families who attend the same school. As a result, it is in the self-interest of any one family not to contribute and free ride off the contributions of other families. Furthermore, as noted by Sandler (1992), among others, the incentive to free ride tends to increase with the group size. Using data on voluntary contributions to California's public schools in 1994, Brunner and Sonstelie (2003a) find that a 1 percent increase in student enrollment leads to a .56 percent reduction in contributions per pupil. Thus, a doubling of school size would lead to a 56 percent decline in contributions per pupil. These results illustrate an important point: When the source of discretionary revenue is changed from the property tax to voluntary contributions, the price of school spending is likely to rise, since no enforcement mechanism exists to ensure each family contributes. Thus, even in California's highest-income communities, the ability to replace lost property tax revenue with voluntary contributions is likely to be quite limited.

Parcel Taxes

For taxpayers seeking to supplement the revenue of their local public schools, another option is the parcel tax. Unlike the property tax, the parcel tax is tax on real estate parcels, not the value of those parcels. Prior to the passage of Proposition 13, the state constitution explicitly prohibited the use of parcel taxes because it required property to be taxed in proportion to its full value. However, Section 4 of Proposition 13 gave local governments, including school districts, the authority to levy "special taxes" subject to the approval of two-thirds of the local electorate. Shortly after the passage of Proposition 13, the state legislature successfully argued that parcel taxes were special taxes as long as they were earmarked for a particular purpose (Doerr 1997). School districts in California first began placing parcel tax initiatives on their local ballots in 1983. As of 2005, there have been 369 parcel tax elections held by school districts, and of those elections, 189 were successful.[8]

Table 3.5 summarizes the size and distribution of parcel tax revenue per pupil in 2003–2004. As table 3.5 illustrates, the parcel tax has been used successfully by several districts to raise large sums of discretionary school revenue. For example, 14 districts managed to raise more than $1,000 per pupil through the parcel tax, and among those districts parcel tax revenue per pupil averaged $1,536. Two school districts, Kentfield Elementary and Bolinas-Stinson Union Elementary (both of which are located in Marin County), levy parcel taxes that raise over $2,000 per pupil. In those districts, parcel tax revenue accounts for over 20 percent of total school district revenue. Similar to districts that were most successful in raising voluntary contributions, districts that were most successful in raising revenue through the parcel tax were populated by families with the highest incomes. In the 14 districts that raised more than $1,000 per pupil through the parcel tax, the average income of families was $170,773. In

---

[8] Almost all school districts have imposed parcel taxes on a per-parcel basis (e.g., $100 per parcel) and for a relatively short time period (e.g., five years).

TABLE 3.5

Characteristics of Districts with Parcel Taxes in 2003–2004

Parcel Tax Revenue per Pupil	Number of School Districts	Average Revenue per Pupil	Average Family Income	Average Enrollment
Less than $250	17	$136	$79,319	7,221
$250–$499	15	364	133,674	4,289
$500–$749	9	600	179,553	3,300
$750–$999	3	909	168,426	1,801
$1,000 and above	14	1,536	170,773	2,034

contrast, in the 17 districts that raised less than $250 per pupil in parcel tax revenue, the average income of families was only $79,319.

The use of parcel taxes by school districts mirrors the use of voluntary contributions along another important dimension: Overall, usage of the parcel tax remains quite limited. Of the 989 school districts operating in California in 2004, only 58 levied a parcel tax. Furthermore, among those 58, only 26 managed to raise more than $500 per pupil in parcel tax revenue.

The use of the parcel tax has been limited by two factors. First, to enact a tax, a district must receive the approval of two-thirds of its voters, a high hurdle. Second, the tax-price of school spending is considerably higher for the parcel tax than for the property tax. As just discussed, when the source of discretionary tax revenue is the property tax, the tax-price of school spending is $H/(V/S)$, where S is the total number of students in a district, H is the assessed value of a family's home, and V is the total assessed value of all property in the district. In contrast, when the source of discretionary tax revenue is the parcel tax, the tax-price of school spending is $1/(N/S)$, where N is the total number of parcels within a district. A comparison of the two tax-prices reveals that, if V/N is greater than H, switching the source of discretionary tax revenue from the property tax to the parcel tax increases a family's tax-price. As it turns out, the tax-price of school spending does tend to be larger under the parcel tax. Brunner (2001) compares the tax-price of school spending under the property tax with the tax-price under the parcel tax for school districts located in Los Angeles County in 2000. His calculations suggest that switching the source of discretionary school revenue from the property tax to the parcel tax increases the tax-price of school spending for the average family by approximately 35 percent.

The primary reason for this sharp increase in the tax-price of school spending is related to the subsidy homeowners receive from nonresidential property.

With the property tax, the size of the subsidy depends on the *value* of nonresidential parcels as a percentage of total assessed value. With the parcel tax, the size of the subsidy depends on the *number* of nonresidential parcels as a percentage of the total number of parcels. Using data on the value and number of residential and nonresidential parcels in four California counties in 2000, Brunner (2001) found that the subsidy from nonresidential property is much higher under the property tax than it is under the parcel tax.[9] For example, homeowners in Los Angeles County would have received a 34 percent subsidy from nonresidential property if the source of discretionary school revenue were the property tax and only an 11 percent subsidy if the source of discretionary school revenue were the parcel tax.

For most districts in California, switching the source of discretionary school revenue from the property tax to the parcel tax led to a large increase in the tax-price of school spending, an increase that most likely made the parcel tax unappealing to all but the wealthiest districts. In support of that notion, nearly all districts that have managed to raise significant amounts of revenue through the parcel tax are located in suburbs and populated by high-income, highly educated, and white families. The one big exception is Emory Unified, a relatively small, urban school district located in Alameda County, with an average family income of only $43,582 and a student population that is over 98 percent non-white. Despite those facts, the school district raised $1,727 per pupil through the parcel tax in 2003–2004. Why has Emory been so successful in raising supplemental revenue through the parcel tax? The two most compelling answers to that question are related to the composition of Emory's property base and the type of parcel tax utilized by the district. In contrast to most other school districts with parcel taxes, Emory Unified contains a significant amount of commercial property. Furthermore, unlike most other school districts, which have imposed parcel taxes on a per-parcel basis, Emory imposes a parcel tax of $0.10 per square foot of improved property (i.e., structures such as homes, retail shops, and factories).[10] Because commercial and industrial property tends to be larger than residential property, under a square footage parcel tax, the owners of nonresidential property pay a larger share of any increase in school spending. As a result, such a parcel tax restores the subsidy from nonresidential property that existed under the property tax. In the case of Emory Unified, that subsidy was quite large: Approximately 75 percent of Emory's parcel tax revenue comes from nonresidential property (Smart Voter 2003).

---

[9] The four counties analyzed were Los Angeles, San Diego, San Mateo, and Marin.

[10] Two other districts, Albany Unified and Berkeley Unified, have imposed parcel taxes that are based on the square footage of property.

In addition to restoring the subsidy from nonresidential property, a parcel tax based on square footage has another advantage: Because parcel size tends to increase with homeowner income, a tax on the square footage of parcels is less regressive than a fixed-dollar tax per parcel of land. In light of these advantages, it seems natural to ask whether a square footage parcel tax might represent a viable source of discretionary tax revenue for other districts seeking to supplement their revenues. As noted by Brunner (2001), the answer to that question depends on whether such a tax would violate the guidelines set forth by the California Supreme Court in *Serrano v. Priest*. Recall that the court mandated the state to develop a school finance system that was fiscally neutral, implying that identical property tax rates should yield the same revenue per pupil. Unfortunately, a parcel tax based on square footage is unlikely to satisfy the court's definition of fiscal neutrality. To illustrate that point, consider two school districts, A and B, that are identical in every relevant respect (same number of students and the same number of parcels) except that in district A, each parcel is 1,000 square feet, and in district B, each parcel is 2,000 square feet. If both districts levied the same tax rate per square foot of property, district A would raise only half as much revenue as district B. As a result, such a tax would most likely violate the court's interpretation of fiscal neutrality—identical tax rates would not yield the same revenue per pupil. While the legality of square footage parcel taxes has not been challenged in court to date, it seems likely that broader use of the square footage parcel tax could lead to another *Serrano*-style lawsuit.[11]

School Finance Reform and Support for Private School Vouchers

Private schooling, voluntary contributions, and parcel taxes are local actions, options for individual families in the case of private schools or for groups of families connected to a school or school district in the case of contributions and parcel taxes. Californians have also had the opportunity to respond on a larger scale. In 1993 and then again in 2000, California voters placed private school voucher initiatives on the statewide ballot, initiatives that would have dramatically overhauled California's system of public school finance and increased the range of educational opportunities available to California families.[12] Did families in California view the voucher as a means of undoing school finance reform?

---

[11] As noted by Brunner (2001), if tax revenues from a square footage parcel tax were subject to district power equalization, a system of local school finance based on a square footage parcel tax would be fiscally neutral. As a result, the square footage parcel tax could be turned into a viable and flexible source of discretionary school revenue for school districts.

[12] In 1993, voters in California placed Proposition 174 on the statewide ballot, an initiative that would have provided parents with $2,600 for every child enrolled in a private school. In 2000, voters placed Proposition 38 on the statewide ballot. That initiative would have provided parents with a scholarship of approximately $4,000 for every child enrolled in private school.

On one level the answer to that question must surely be negative: Both the 1993 and the 2000 voucher initiative lost by approximately a 2 to 1 margin. On another level, however, the answer is less clear. Approximately two-thirds of all households in California have no school-age children. If those households tended to vote against the voucher (perhaps due to concern over the voucher plan's fiscal impact), it could still be that families with children were relatively supportive of the voucher. Furthermore, even among families with children, one would expect support for the voucher to vary with income. Because high-income families with children were the group most constrained by school finance reform, they should be the group most likely to support the voucher.

To examine those possibilities, we used the results of a survey conducted by the Public Policy Institute of California (PPIC) in the months just prior to California's 2000 voucher initiative. Between August and October of 2000, PPIC surveyed approximately 6,000 potential voters concerning issues related to the November 2000 ballot. The survey asked respondents to report their household income, whether or not they had children in public school, and how they intended to vote on the voucher initiative.[13] The results of that survey are shown in table 3.6, which illustrates how support for the voucher varied with a respondent's household income and whether the respondent had children enrolled in public school.[14]

The results of the PPIC survey reveal that voters with children in public school were indeed more likely to support the voucher than voters with no school-age children. For example, among voters with children in public school, 54.2 percent of those with income between $20,000 and $39,999 stated they would support the voucher initiative. In contrast, only 44.5 percent of voters with no school-age children in the same income range stated they would support the voucher. However, contrary to expectations, high-income voters with children were less likely to support the voucher than low-income voters with children. Voters with children in the highest-income groups were over 20 percentage points less likely to support the voucher than voters with children in the lowest-income group. In fact, voters with children in the highest-income group were no more likely to support the voucher than voters of similar income with no schoolchildren. Thus, despite the fact that high-income families with children were the group most constrained by school finance reform, they were also the group least likely to support the voucher.

What explains these puzzling reactions? Our answer to that question begins with a fundamental observation: School quality depends on more than just

---

[13] For a more detailed description of the PPIC survey, see Brunner and Sonstelie (2003b).

[14] Of the 6,006 survey respondents, a total of 1,343 reported having children enrolled in public school and also answered the questions about their household income and how they intended to vote on the voucher initiative. Similarly, a total of 2,923 respondents reported having no school-age children and answered the questions about household income and how they intended to vote on the voucher.

TABLE 3.6

Support for Private School Vouchers by Household Income

	PERCENTAGE VOTING YES ON VOUCHER INITIATIVE	
Household Income	Children in Public School (Obs = 1,343)	No Schoolchildren (Obs = 2,923)
Less than $20,000	62.2%	53.8%
$20,000–$39,999	54.2	44.5
$40,000–$59,999	50.8	40.3
$60,000–$79,999	51.2	40.5
$80,000–$99,999	50.9	44.3
$100,000 or more	41.5	42.6

spending per pupil; it also depends on factors such as the quality of a student's peer group and school efficiency. To the extent that these other factors are important determinants of school quality, equalizing spending will not equalize school quality. This point was demonstrated by Nechyba (2003b, 2004), using a computable, general equilibrium model. In the model, school quality depends on both spending per pupil and a vector of inputs correlated with parental income. Those inputs include student peer quality, parental monitoring, and voluntary contributions. His simulations suggest that centralization and the equalization of spending per pupil result in only a modest decline in residential income segregation. With state finance, school districts are still stratified by income, peer quality, and, thus, school quality. Epple and Romano (2003) reach a similar conclusion using a general equilibrium model that characterizes how families sort across neighborhood schools within a single school district. In their model, student achievement depends both on a student's own ability (which is assumed to be correlated with family income) and on the ability of the student's peer group. Because all neighborhood schools are assumed to have the same level of spending per pupil, variation in school quality arises solely from variation in average student peer quality across schools. Equilibrium in their model is characterized by income, peer quality, and school quality stratification, with the highest-income families living in neighborhoods with the highest-quality schools (schools with the highest-quality peer group), and the lowest-income families living in neighborhoods with the lowest-quality schools.

These studies suggest that even in California, where spending per pupil has been essentially equalized, there may still be significant income stratification across neighborhood schools and school districts, stratification that perpetuates

FIGURE 3.3   Distribution of Low-Income Students Across Elementary Schools
in 2003–2004

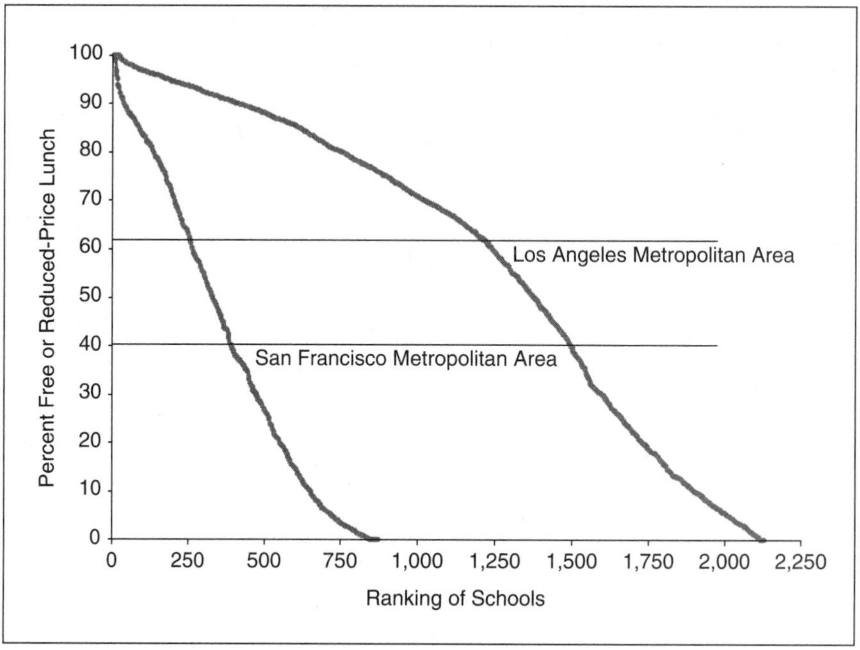

large differences in school quality. To examine that possibility we used data from
the California Department of Education on the percentage of free or reduced-
price lunch students (low-income students) in each elementary school in
2003–2004. Figure 3.3 illustrates how low-income students are distributed across
the 2,127 elementary schools in the Los Angeles metropolitan area and the 849
elementary schools in the San Francisco metropolitan area.[15] In the figure,
schools are ranked in descending order according to their percentage of free or
reduced-price lunch students. If low-income students were randomly distributed across schools, each school should contain roughly the same percentage of
these students. In the Los Angeles metropolitan area, this would imply that
roughly 62 percent of students in each school were eligible for a free or reduced-
price lunch (as illustrated by the horizontal dotted line). Similarly, in the San
Francisco metropolitan area, random assignment would imply that roughly 40
percent of students in each school were eligible for a free or reduced-price lunch.

---

[15] The Los Angeles metropolitan area includes the counties of Los Angeles, Orange, San Bernardino,
and Riverside, while the San Francisco metropolitan area includes the counties of San Francisco,
Alameda, Contra Costa, Marin, San Mateo, and Santa Clara.

As figure 3.3 makes clear, however, that is not the case: In both the Los Angeles and San Francisco metropolitan areas, there is a significant degree of income stratification across schools.[16]

The stratification of schools by family income is also a stratification of schools by student achievement. The relationship between student performance and family income is clearly represented in figure 3.2, a relationship that is consistent with the basic assumption underlying the model of Epple and Romano: School quality depends on both a student's own ability and the ability of his or her peers.

These differences in school quality may explain why high-income families were unwilling to support the voucher. Numerous studies have shown that houses located in neighborhoods with high-quality public schools sell at a significant premium. For example, using data on housing sales in the Los Angeles metropolitan area in 1992–1993, Brunner, Sonstelie, and Thayer (2001) find that homes located in the best school districts sell at a significant premium. Similarly, using 1990 block-level Census data on the value of homes located in the San Francisco Bay area, Bayer, Ferreira, and McMillan (2003, 2005) find that homes located in neighborhoods with high-quality schools command a significant premium.[17] Because the voucher would have decreased the price of private alternatives to good public schools, it also would have reduced the premium families would be willing to pay to live in such neighborhoods, causing property values in those neighborhoods to fall. As a result, high-income families located in neighborhoods with good public schools would have experienced significant capital losses had the voucher been implemented.

The threat of such losses clearly provided those families with an incentive to vote against the voucher. Brunner, Sonstelie, and Thayer (2001) find evidence consistent with that conclusion. Using precinct-level voting returns from California's 1993 voucher initiative, they find that homeowners located in school districts with high housing price premiums were significantly less likely to support the voucher than homeowners located in neighborhoods with low housing price premiums. They conclude that the most plausible explanation for their results is that homeowners located in good school districts voted against the voucher to protect their housing values. Brunner and Sonstelie (2003b)

---

[16] Epple and Romano (2003) present similar evidence of income stratification across high schools in the Los Angeles metropolitan area. Similarly, Bayer, Ferreira, and McMillan (2003, 2005) estimate an equilibrium model of residential sorting across neighborhood schools located in the San Francisco Bay area. Their results reveal substantial stratification along racial and socioeconomic lines across neighborhoods, with white, highly educated, and high-income households clustering in neighborhoods that contain the highest-quality schools.

[17] Note that the premiums found in these studies were not the result of higher spending per pupil, since school spending has been equalized in California. The premiums were primarily due to student peer quality and other determinants of school quality that still vary across schools.

reached the same conclusion based on their analysis of individual voting behavior on California's 2000 voucher initiative.

While the results of the preceding studies may explain why homeowners located in good school districts were unwilling to support the voucher, they cannot explain why both California's 1993 and 2000 voucher initiatives lost by a 2 to 1 margin. Does the overwhelming lack of support for school vouchers suggest that Californians were by and large satisfied with their public schools? Results from the PPIC's August 2000 survey suggest the answer to that question is clearly no. When asked to grade the quality of their local public schools on a scale of "A" to "F," less than 10 percent of voters gave their local public schools an "A," and more than 60 percent of voters gave their schools a grade of "C" or lower (Baldassare 2000). Evidently, even though the majority of California's voters are unsatisfied with the quality of their local public schools, that dissatisfaction has not engendered widespread support for school vouchers.

Conclusion

The lessons to be drawn from California's experience depend on the perspective one brings to it. For champions of decentralized government, the lessons are easy to draw. Since the centralization of school finance in California, school resources and student achievement have declined relative to other states. Families have attempted to circumvent the centralized system by opting out into the private sector and by using voluntary contributions and parcel taxes to supplement the inadequate public school resources provided by the state. Centralization has been a dubious achievement.

For fiscal conservatives, the lessons are very different. Under local finance, commercial and industrial property subsidized school spending. The subsidy was ended by Proposition 13, and now families are facing the true cost of public school spending. Given that cost, they have chosen to spend less, thus tempering the rapid rise in real spending per pupil over the last three decades (Hanushek and Rivkin 1997). The dismal performance of California students on achievement tests is a disappointment, but that performance is due more to the inefficiency with which funds are deployed than to the paucity of those funds.

For supporters of centralization, the lessons are more complicated. The centralization of school finance has permitted the state to direct more resources to school districts serving low-income students. Those students still do not perform at the level of other students, so there is more work to be done. Furthermore, families have done very little to circumvent the new system. Private school enrollment is not significantly higher than other states, voluntary contributions are not a major factor, parcel taxes have been enacted in only a few districts, and voters have overwhelmingly rejected the voucher. Centralized finance is politically stable, thus providing a platform for an even more progressive redistribution of educational resources.

Supporters of centralization might also add that their preferred system has not been given a fair test. California has centralized the finance of its public schools without centralizing the governance of those schools. This mismatch between finance and governance has undermined the effectiveness of the school system and made centralization less successful than it could be. For example, because school districts still engage in collective bargaining with their employees, the legislature feels obligated to tie up funds in categorical programs that may undermine the effectiveness of those funds. Furthermore, possibilities for addressing the needs of low-income students would likely increase if local governance were eliminated. In the current system, those needs are addressed through categorical programs that attempt to channel funds from the state to schools serving disadvantaged students. Those funds must pass through school districts, however, where local politics may frustrate the state's intention.

The transformation from local governance to state governance will not occur as rapidly as the transformation from local finance to state finance. Though they handed the property tax to the state legislature, the voters of California deeply distrust Sacramento, and it is impossible to imagine that they would favor an initiative to eliminate school districts and local school boards. Yet, there are clear signs that the institutions of local governance are crumbling. Schrag (1998) notes that because property tax rates are not determined at the local level, business in California has lost interest in local school districts, diminishing a traditional source of fiscal conservatism on local school boards. California's ambitious accountability system has also eroded local governance. The state has yet to take over a failing school, but it clearly has the power to do so, and it is only a matter of time before it does. Likewise, after an initial experiment with bonuses for teachers in high-performing schools, the state ran into fiscal difficulties and suspended the program. However, it seems only logical that an improved system of performance bonuses will be instituted as soon as the state's budget improves. Last, it is not impossible to imagine that the state's current bilevel system of collective bargaining—once with the state legislature and again with each school district—will yield to a more rational system of statewide collective bargaining. Any one of these changes would make the others more likely.

Champions of decentralized government will argue the folly of this trend. A school system that reports directly to Sacramento will become disconnected from the concerns of local residents, lose political support, and deteriorate even further. For these critics of the current direction, hope lies with the parcel tax. If the threshold for enacting the parcel tax were reduced to a simple majority, many more parcel taxes would be passed. Each such event would reconnect residents to their local school districts and reinvigorate local governance. A constitutional amendment is required to reduce the two-thirds requirement to a simple majority, but California's constitution must be the most pliable of any state's.

REFERENCES

Baldassare, Mark. 2000. *PPIC statewide survey: Californians and their government, August 2000*. San Francisco: Public Policy Institute of California.

Bayer, Patrick, Fernando Ferreira, and Robert McMillan. 2003. A unified framework for measuring preferences for schools and neighborhoods. Working paper. Department of Economics, Yale University.

———. 2005. Tiebout sorting, social multipliers and the demand for school quality. Working paper. Department of Economics, Yale University.

Bergstrom, Theodore C., and Robert P. Goodman. 1973. Private demands for public goods. *American Economic Review* 63:280–296.

Betts, Julian R., and Robert W. Fairlie. 2003. Does immigration induce "native flight" from public schools into private schools? *Journal of Public Economics* 87:987–1012.

Borcherding, Thomas E., and Robert T. Deacon. 1972. The demand for the services of non-federal governments. *American Economic Review* 62:891–906.

Brunner, Eric J. 2001. The parcel tax. In *Essays for the joint committee to develop a master plan for education—Kindergarten through university*, Jon Sonstelie and Peter Richardson, eds. San Francisco: Public Policy Institute of California.

Brunner, Eric J., and Jennifer Imazeki. 2005. Fiscal stress and voluntary contributions to public schools. In *Developments in school finance: 2004*, William J. Fowler, ed. Washington, DC: National Center for Educational Statistics.

Brunner, Eric J., and Jon C. Sonstelie. 1996. Coping with *Serrano*: Private contributions to California's public schools. *Proceedings of the Eighty-Ninth Annual Conference on Taxation, National Tax Association,* 372–381.

———. 2003a. School finance reform and voluntary fiscal federalism. *Journal of Public Economics* 87:2157–2185.

———. 2003b. Homeowners, property values, and the political economy of the school voucher. *Journal of Urban Economics* 54:239–257.

Brunner, Eric J., Jon C. Sonstelie, and Mark Thayer. 2001. Capitalization and the voucher. *Journal of Urban Economics* 50:517–536.

Card, David, and Abigail Payne. 2002. School finance reform, the distribution of school spending, and the distribution of student test scores. *Journal of Public Economics* 83:49–82.

Carroll, Stephen J., Cathy Krop, Jeremy Arkes, Peter A. Morrison, and Ann Flanagan. 2005. *California's K–12 public schools: How are they doing?* Santa Monica, CA: RAND Corporation.

Coons, John E., William D. Clune, and Stephen D. Sugarman. 1970. *Private wealth and public education.* Cambridge, MA: Harvard University Press.

Doerr, David R. 1997, February. The genesis of Proposition 218: A history of local taxing authority. *Cal-Tax Digest.*

Downes, Thomas A. 1992. Evaluating the impact of school finance reform on the provision of public education: The California case. *National Tax Journal* 45:405–419.

Downes, Thomas A., and David N. Figlio. 1997. School finance reform, tax limits, and student performance: Do reforms level-up or dumb down? Working paper. Department of Economics, Tufts University.

Downes, Thomas A., and David Schoeman. 1998. School finance reform and private school enrollment: Evidence from California. *Journal of Urban Economics* 43:443–481.

Downes, Thomas A., and Mona P. Shah. 1995. The effects of school finance reforms on the level and growth of per pupil expenditures. Working paper. Department of Economics, Tufts University.

Epple, Dennis, and Richard Romano. 2003. Neighborhood schools, choice, and the distribution of educational benefits. In *The Economics of School Choice*, Caroline M. Hoxby, ed. Chicago: University of Chicago Press.

Fernandez, Raquel, and Richard Rogerson. 1999. Education finance reform and investment in human capital: Lessons from California. *Journal of Public Economics* 74:327–350.

Figlio, David N. 1997. Did the tax revolt reduce school performance? *Journal of Public Economics* 65:245–269.

Figlio, David N., and Kim S. Rueben. 2001. Tax limits and the qualifications of new teachers. *Journal of Public Economics* 80:49–71.

Fischel, William A. 1989. Did *Serrano* cause Proposition 13? *National Tax Journal* 42: 465–473.

———. 1996. How *Serrano* caused Proposition 13. *Journal of Law and Politics* 12: 607–636.

———. 2001. *The homevoter hypothesis: How home values influence local government taxation, school finance, and land-use policies.* Cambridge, MA: Harvard University Press.

———. 2004. Did John Serrano vote for Proposition 13? *UCLA Law Review* 51:887–932.

Hanushek, Eric A., and Steven G. Rivkin. 1997. Understanding the 20th century growth in U.S. school spending. *Journal of Human Resources* 32:35–69.

Hines, James, and Richard Thaler. 1995. The flypaper effect. *Journal of Economic Perspectives* 9:217–226.

Horowitz, Harold W. 1966. Unseparate but unequal—The emerging Fourteenth Amendment issue in public school education. *UCLA Law Review* 13:1147–1172.

Hoxby, Caroline M. 2001. All school finance equalizations are not created equal. *Quarterly Journal of Economics* 116:1189–1231.

Husted, Thomas A., and Lawrence W. Kenny. 2000. Evidence on the impact of state government on primary and secondary education and the equity-efficiency trade-off. *Journal of Law and Economics* 43:285–308.

———. 2002. The legacy of *Serrano*: The impact of mandated equal spending on private school enrollment. *Southern Economic Journal* 68:566–583.

Kenny, Lawrence W. 1982. Economies of scale in schooling. *Economics of Education Review* 2:1–24.

Kurland, Philip B. 1963. The Supreme Court, 1963 term. Foreword: Equal in origin and equal in title to the legislative and executive branches of the government. *Harvard Law Review* 78:143–176.

Manwaring, Robert L., and Steven M. Sheffrin. 1997. Litigation, school finance reform and aggregate educational spending. *International Tax and Public Finance* 4:107–127.

Murray, Sheila E., William N. Evans, and Robert M. Schwab. 1998. Education finance reform and the distribution of education resources. *American Economic Review* 88:789–812.

Nechyba, Thomas J. 2003a. Centralization, fiscal federalism, and private school attendance. *International Economic Review* 44:179–204.

———. 2003b. School finance, spatial income segregation, and the nature of communities. *Journal of Urban Economics* 54:61–88.

———. 2004. Prospects for achieving equity or adequacy in education: The limits of state aid in general equilibrium. In *Helping children left behind*, J. Yinger, ed. Cambridge, MA: The MIT Press.

Oates, Wallace E. 1969. The effects of property taxes and local public spending on property values: An empirical study of tax capitalization and the Tiebout hypothesis. *Journal of Political Economy* 77:957–971.

———. 1972. *Fiscal federalism*. New York: Harcourt Brace Jovanovich.

———. 2005. Property taxation and local public spending: The renter effect. *Journal of Urban Economics* 57:419–431.

Picus, Lawrence O. 1991. Cadillacs or Chevrolets?: The evolution of state control over school finance in California. *Journal of Education Finance* 17:33–59.

Rose, Heather, Jon Sonstelie, Ray Reinhard, and Sharmaine Heng. 2003. *High expectations, modest means: The challenge facing California's public schools*. San Francisco: Public Policy Institute of California.

Sandler, Todd. 1992. *Collective action: Theory and applications*. Ann Arbor: University of Michigan Press.

Schrag, Peter. 1998. *Paradise lost: California's experience, America's future*. Berkeley: University of California Press.

Silva, Fabio, and Jon Sonstelie. 1995. Did *Serrano* cause a decline in school spending? *National Tax Journal* 48:199–215.

Smart Voter. 2003. Measure A, six-year parcel tax, Emery Unified School District. www.smartvoter.org.

Sonstelie, Jon. 1982. The welfare cost of free public schools. *Journal of Political Economy* 90:749–808.

Sonstelie, Jon, Eric Brunner, and Kenneth Ardon. 2000. *For better or for worse? School finance reform in California*. San Francisco: Public Policy Institute of California.

Tiebout, Charles M. 1956. A pure theory of local expenditures. *Journal of Political Economy* 64:416–424.

Wise, Arthur E. 1967. *Rich schools, poor schools: The promise of equal educational opportunity*. Chicago: University of Chicago Press.

APPENDIX

The median voter model is $s = \beta_0 + \beta_1 v + \beta_2 y$. Applying this linear relationship, the correlation between spending per pupil, s, and median family income, y, is

$$\rho_{sy} = \frac{\beta_1 \sigma_v \rho_{vy} + \beta_2 \sigma_y}{\left(\beta_1^2 \sigma_v^2 + 2\beta_1 \beta_2 \rho_{vy} \sigma_v \sigma_y + \beta_2^2 \sigma_y^2 \right)^{1/2}},$$

where σ_v and σ_y are the standard deviations of v and y across school districts, and ρ_{sy} and ρ_{vy} are the correlation coefficients of s and v with y across districts. When the correlation between assessed value and income (ρ_{vy}) is unity, the preceding equation also reduces to unity.

The partial derivative of ρ_{sy} with respect to ρ_{vy} is

$$\frac{\partial \rho_{sy}}{\partial \rho_{vy}} = \frac{\beta_1 \sigma_y \left(\beta_1^2 \sigma_v^2 + \beta_1 \beta_2 \rho_{vy} \sigma_v \sigma_y \right)}{\sigma_s^3}.$$

If $\beta_1 > 0$, $\beta_2 > 0$, and $\rho_{vy} > 0$, $\dfrac{\partial \rho_{sy}}{\partial \rho_{vy}} > 0$. Also, if $\rho_{vy} = 0$ and $\beta_2 > 0$, $\rho_{sy} > 0$. Thus, assuming $\beta_1 > 0$, $\beta_2 > 0$, and $\rho_{vy} > 0$, ρ_{sy} is a positive, increasing function of ρ_{vy}, which reaches a maximum of unity when ρ_{vy} is unity.

TABLE 3.A

Maximum Family Income for Family Income Deciles
in 1970, 1980, 1990, and 2000

Decile	1970	1980	1990	2000
Lowest	$17,752	$14,137	$12,973	$14,000
2	27,072	23,165	22,471	23,000
3	35,061	31,357	31,225	31,000
4	40,830	38,682	39,525	39,800
5	47,044	45,484	47,035	48,300
6	53,257	52,266	55,335	58,000
7	61,690	60,614	65,876	69,400
8	71,897	71,074	79,051	85,000
Highest	91,869	89,861	102,661	114,400

COMMENTARY

DAVID FIGLIO

California has experienced remarkable changes in its finance of schools over the last three decades, and countless scholars have discussed these major changes—the school finance reforms and their accompanying tax and expenditure limitations. This very thoughtful piece by Brunner and Sonstelie casts California's experiences in the light of fiscal federalism. Although the authors are careful not to overstate the degree to which California's school finance reform is an experiment in fiscal federalism (despite the title, which says just that), the authors do show some ways in which California's experiences could be seen as providing lessons for fiscal federalism.

The authors present a fascinating picture of California's school finance landscape prior to the *Serrano* ruling, and then describe the ways in which *Serrano* and other forces led California from a system of primarily local finance of education into a system of nearly pure state finance of education, and they identify some of the consequences of that massive change.

When looking back at California's experience, it is useful to begin—as the authors do—with California's experiment in school finance reform. When evaluating the pre-*Serrano* landscape in California, one is immediately struck by the lack of a strong relationship between the resources available to families and the resources allocated to their students. There existed a small, positive correlation between median family income and spending per pupil for elementary-only school districts and no apparent relationship whatsoever for high school or unified school districts. If this lack of a relationship between family income and school revenues was due to the fact that per-pupil revenues did not vary much across school districts, this finding would not be particularly striking. However, as the authors point out, there existed considerable variation in resources per pupil in pre-*Serrano* schools in California; this variation was just not highly linked to family incomes.

Following *Serrano* and the large-scale property tax and expenditure limit that accompanied it (Fischel 1989), California maintained its lack of a relationship between family incomes and per-pupil revenues and today has little variation in per-pupil revenues at all in schools. Following these policy changes, the revenue-per-pupil profile in California is nearly flat, and spending growth has been much slower in California than in the United States in general. Observers of California education today often consider California schools to be a "basket case"—with numerous pieces of supporting evidence: First and foremost is a widespread view of a test score crisis in California. California ranked near the top among states in test performance as reported in the National Longitudinal Study of the High School Class of 1972, but today it ranks among the very bottom states in the country, according to the National Assessment of Educational Progress. In 2005 only the District of Columbia averaged lower fourth- or eighth-grade reading scores than did California, and only a handful of states averaged lower than California on the mathematics examination.

This precipitous fall in relative test scores is viewed in some quarters as an ignominy. But observers of California telling stories of decline will also point to other bellwethers: The private school enrollment rate in California nearly doubled from 1970 to 2000, leading some to fear that the wealthy are "abandoning" public schools. And California school districts report difficulties in teacher recruitment, stoking concerns about a "teacher crisis" in California—a problem that only could have been exacerbated by California's widespread class-size reduction (Jepsen and Rivkin 2002).

Given the widespread concerns about the health of California's educational system, it is useful to evaluate the severity of the problems that many see in California's schools. When measured objectively, California's test score decline relative to the rest of the country looks less dire than it might at first glance. Studies that measure average changes in test scores will certainly overstate the decline in California student achievement, as the population of California students also changed dramatically over this time period, with a large increase in the proportion of the student body who are immigrants or nonimmigrant minorities. And these differences in observables mask the fact that California's student body differs on "difficult-to-observables" as well. For instance, California's immigrant population tends to be needier than are other states' immigrant populations, not only in terms of family characteristics, but also in terms of educational needs. In addition, while the population of children overall in California has become needier since *Serrano*, the population of public school children has become particularly so, since the rate of private school attendance among the less needy has increased considerably over this time period. In sum, California's test score decline would likely have been pronounced even in the absence of the school finance reforms and tax and expenditure limitations that occurred in the 1970s and thereafter. (This last line, however, is admittedly disingenuous, as arguably at least a portion of the private school increase in California was due to the policy changes [Downes and Greenstein 1996].)

While California's relative test score declines have almost assuredly been smaller than what many observers think, California's relative spending declines have been larger than what most observers report. A major source of revenue growth in California schools since *Serrano* has been categorical aid—much of which represents special education funds. In California, special education enrollment growth has outpaced growth in the United States as a whole over the last 30 years. Part of this is due to demographic factors, but even after adjusting for the demographic changes, California's relative special education growth is apparent. One potential explanation for this relative growth in special education is my previously mentioned point that California's student body has become needier over time along lines difficult to observe in general data: This trend could manifest itself both in lower test scores as well as in increased rates of special education. In addition, California schools may be responding to the fiscal incentives embedded within the categorical aid systems for financing special education (Cullen and Figlio 1998; Cullen 2003) and classifying more students as special needs in order to receive increased revenues.

At the same time, it has become relatively more expensive to provide "basic" education in California than in the country in general, as relative salaries for educated women in California have risen over this time period. As outside options become more appealing for potential teachers, fewer individuals are attracted into the teaching profession in California. This phenomenon could have resulted in a decline in teacher quality that is greater than might have been expected given the changes in school spending observed in California.

Putting these two patterns together, one observes that relative spending and relative test scores both fell in California following *Serrano*. When adjusted for changes in demographics and school populations, the relative test score decline is smaller than generally believed, and arguably the decline in school spending is larger than generally believed. It would be convenient to believe that the decline in school spending is responsible for the reduction in relative student performance in California, but this is highly unlikely. The test score declines in California are greater than what even the most "optimistic" estimates of the relationship between school spending and test scores would have indicated.

What, then, could be the culprit for the relative test score declines in California following *Serrano*? One possibility would be the reduced competition and local control that is attendant with the changes in school finance in the state. It is unlikely, however, that school finance reform per se led to this large change in California test scores. Other states had large school finance equalizations without large declines in test scores; Florida, for example, has a school finance profile that is just as flat as California's but without the large reduction in test scores. One difference between California and other states that could explain why California experienced particularly large reductions is the tax and expenditure limitation that occurred hand-in-hand with *Serrano*: Proposition 13 had a "lock-in effect" that could reduce schools' responsiveness to progressively less-footloose residents. Put differently, in California a loss of local control in school finance was coupled with an increasing inability for residents to shop for better options among other (constrained) communities.

Proposition 13—California's particularly restrictive tax and expenditure limitation—is likely to be responsible for a large fraction of the reduction in relative test scores in California. While tax and expenditure limitations often do not dramatically reduce school spending in the states that impose them, they are associated with substantially reduced student test scores (Figlio 1997; Downes and Figlio 1999) that far outstrip the levels that would be predicted by the spending declines. One possible explanation for this factor is a teacher–quality link: Figlio and Rueben (2001) find that states that enact tax and expenditure limitations experience large declines in relative teacher quality, as measured by the qualifications of entrants into the teaching profession. These declines are themselves larger than what might be expected based on (generally modest) changes in teacher salaries in a state, suggesting that there is a "zeitgeist effect" associated with tax and expenditure limitations: Potential teachers may view teaching as a less-desirable profession in states that impose these limitations, largely because of a change in the perceived environment of teaching.

The incidence of this teacher quality effect is borne by districts and schools that serve lower-income families. This finding is consistent with the perception that there has been less of a teacher quality "crisis" in middle-class California than there has been in the areas serving low-income families. (This could also be because middle-class school districts may "poach" quality teachers from schools serving low-income families.) In any account, this differential effect may also contribute to the test score decline in California if lower-income students' test scores are more responsive to school inputs than are higher-income students' scores (Betts 1995).

The comparison between California and Florida now becomes potentially more interesting. As just mentioned, Florida also experienced a large equalization in the 1970s, as well as a tax and expenditure limitation that is even more binding in some dimensions than was Proposition 13. However, Florida did not experience the same types of test score declines seen in California since *Serrano*.

What could be some reasons for the California-Florida difference in outcomes? One possible explanation is that Florida's tax and expenditure limitation was passed by the legislature and not directly by voters, so potential teachers in Florida may have viewed the tax cap as less of a referendum than did California's potential teachers. It may be the case that the "zeitgeist effect" found by Figlio and Rueben (2001) is less pronounced (or nonexistent) in the case of tax and expenditure limitations not passed by voters. Florida also already had extremely centralized school provision prior to the school finance reforms in the 1970s. Several large metropolitan areas already had only one school district prior to the changes in school funding; perhaps centralization matters less if jurisdictions are already centralized.

One lesson to be learned from both California's experience and its comparison with Florida is that not all school finance reforms are created equal. But this lesson goes beyond Hoxby's (2001) paper with that same title; two school finance reforms with very large changes in marginal tax prices can have very different consequences. It is not necessarily the case that large changes in school finance will lead to large reductions in student test scores; the devil is certainly in the details.

While the absolute magnitude of the effects of California's school finance reforms and accompanying tax and expenditure limitations on the level and distribution of spending, local control, and school performance can be debated, there is no question that these policies had large-scale consequences for schools in California. It is also apparent that similar-looking policies can and do have different effects in other settings, depending on the context of those settings. California schools and districts have sought alternative revenue sources—direct contributions and parcel taxes—in order to raise revenues that may have been locally raised in a different policy environment. The use of these alternative revenue streams in a serious way has been quite limited to date, partially because the parcel tax requires a high threshold of voter support for passing.

But while making it easier to enact parcel taxes would help to restore local governance over school revenues and spending, it will not come close to undoing the effects of *Serrano* and Proposition 13 in California. Much of this is due to the likelihood, described earlier, that the largest effects of *Serrano* and Proposition 13 have been due not to the direct financial impacts of the policies, but to the attendant changes in teacher labor markets and other factors associated with the policy changes. If the withdrawal of money per se is not the force primarily responsible for any degradation of education in California, then the reinstatement of money on a small-scale, local basis is also not likely to completely undo the estimated negative effects of *Serrano* and Proposition 13. Moreover, offering local voters the opportunity to override a tax and expenditure limitation could itself induce some new inefficiencies (Figlio and O'Sullivan 2001). In sum, while reducing the parcel tax threshold would allow more communities the opportunity to enact a more desired level of school spending, it is unlikely to be a panacea for schools.

Brunner and Sonstelie do a terrific job of describing the educational and political context in California on the eve of *Serrano*, as well as delineating the impacts on school revenue and spending. I have identified a number of additional consequences of these policies. It is clear that California's school finance reform has had far-reaching consequences for education in the state. And it is just as clear that it is difficult to conceive of these consequences as a result of "an experiment in fiscal federalism" as opposed to "a major policy overhaul that had the effect of centralizing school finance." These are different animals altogether, and the results of California-style policies enacted elsewhere may have different results, depending on the context and the particular mix of policies.

REFERENCES

Betts, Julian. 1995. Does school quality matter? Evidence from the National Longitudinal Survey of Youth. *Review of Economics and Statistics* 77:231–250.

Cullen, Julie. 2003. The impact of fiscal incentives on student disability rates. *Journal of Public Economics* 87:1557–1589.

Cullen, Julie, and David Figlio. 1998. Local gaming of state school finance policies: How effective are intergovernmental incentives? Working paper. University of Michigan.

Downes, Thomas, and David Figlio. 1999. Do tax and expenditure limits provide a free lunch? Evidence on the link between limits and public sector service quality. *National Tax Journal* 49:113–128.

Downes, Thomas, and Shane Greenstein. 1996. Understanding the supply of non-profits: Modeling the location of private schools. *Rand Journal of Economics* 27:365–390.

Figlio, David. 1997. Did the "tax revolt" reduce school performance? *Journal of Public Economics* 65:245–269.

Figlio, David, and Arthur O'Sullivan. 2001. The local response to tax limitation measures: Do local governments manipulate voters to increase revenues? *Journal of Law and Economics* 44:233–257.

Figlio, David, and Kim Rueben. 2001. Tax limits and the qualifications of new teachers. *Journal of Public Economics* 80:49–71.

Fischel, William. 1989. Did *Serrano* cause Proposition 13? *National Tax Journal* 42:465–473.

Hoxby, Caroline. 2001. All school finance reforms are not created equal. *Quarterly Journal of Economics* 116:1189–1231.

Jepsen, Christopher, and Steven Rivkin. 2002. *Class size reduction, teacher quality and academic achievement in California public elementary schools.* San Francisco: Public Policy Institute of California.

4

School Choice, Parental Information, and Tiebout Sorting: Evidence from Washington, DC

JACK BUCKLEY

MARK SCHNEIDER

Tiebout's (1956) seminal paper, "A Pure Theory of Local Expenditures," has shaped the academic discussion of political economy at the local level for almost 50 years. Tiebout provides a theory of economic competition among localities in which citizens function as consumers of the services of local government and may elect to "vote with their feet" if they are unsatisfied with the rate of property taxation or the mix of services provided. As is well known, the Tiebout model is based on a set of key assumptions, including unimpeded mobility of citizens, full information regarding the different packages of local public goods, a large number of communities among which consumer-voters can choose, and the absence of significant externalities. These are the central assumptions of the model and follow from the theory of ideal markets for private goods.

To these, Tiebout adds two other assumptions: There exists an optimal community size (there is some theoretical point at which communities are maximally efficient), and communities that are not of optimal size will try to attract or deter residents to reach that optimal size.[1]

The authors gratefully acknowledge the support of the Political Science Program at the National Science Foundation (grant number SES-0314656) for the conduct of this research. We also thank William Fischel, at the Lincoln Institute for Land Policy, and the Rockefeller Center for Public Policy and Social Sciences at Dartmouth for their support, as well, as the participants in the spring 2005 seminar series at the Department of Educational Research, Measurement, and Evaluation at Boston College's Lynch School of Education.

[1] This last assumption may conflict with a later statement that government policies are "more or less set." The issue of how active governments or government agencies are in setting policies is fundamental to much of the work that has followed the original Tiebout model, at least in political science (see, e.g., Peterson 1981; Schneider 1989).

Given these processes, Tiebout (1956) argues the following:

> The consumer-voter may be viewed as picking that community which best
> satisfies his preference[s]. . . . At the central level the preferences of the
> consumer-voter are given, and the government tries to adjust to the pat-
> tern of these preferences, whereas at the local level various governments
> have their revenue and expenditure patterns more or less set. Given these
> revenue and expenditure patterns, the consumer-voter moves to the com-
> munity whose local government best satisfies his set of preferences. The
> greater the number of communities and the greater the variance among
> them, the closer the consumer will come to fully realizing his preference
> position. (418)

Thus, the citizen or household becomes a "shopper" for a municipal
provider of a bundle of goods and services. And of these, clearly the most
salient is public education. Both parents of school-age children and homeowners concerned with the value of their real estate, to the extent that school quality remains capitalized in home values (Fischel 2001, 98–128), have been
empirically shown to pay particular attention to the schools when choosing a
new residence. And, as anyone who has bought a home can attest, real estate
agents often know as much about test scores, college placement rates, and other
measures of school accountability as educators and school district officials.

But how much do parents really know? In this chapter, we revisit Tiebout's
central assumption of full information on the part of consumer-voters. In particular, we examine this assumption given the widespread introduction of
another type of competition in local markets: school choice, particularly the
expansion of choice through the growth in the number of charter schools. The
plan of the chapter is straightforward. After a brief comparison of residential
mobility and school choice as Tiebout-like mechanisms for facilitating a local
market for public goods, we turn to a review of the literature on what (little)
parents know about the schools. We explain how theorists have introduced the
idea of the "marginal consumer" of education in an attempt to salvage the
Tiebout model. We then extend this idea to parents (consumer-voters) who
choose to "vote with their seat" by changing schools, as opposed to the more
traditional Tiebout model of "voting with their feet." That is, we examine the
knowledge and behavior of those parents who choose a new school without
moving their place of residence.

The theory of the marginal consumer holds that, even if global parental
knowledge levels are low, parents who are active shoppers should have, on average, higher levels of information. We test this prediction empirically, using data
from Washington, DC, gathered in 2001 as part of a larger study on charter
schools. We find that parents who are active shoppers for education, perhaps

particularly charter school parents, actually have a higher degree of error and that they are more prone to overestimate the academic quality of their child's school. We conclude by attempting to explain these findings and briefly exploring their policy implications.

Move for Schools—or Move Schools?

There is no doubt that the United States presents the numbers to support Tiebout-like market forces, for this is indeed a mobile society. According to the U.S. Census Bureau's Current Population Survey (CPS), about 14 percent of the population moved in 2002.[2] While this is a decrease from the approximately 20 percent who moved 10 years prior, it still represents a substantial number of people who are changing residences. Moreover, according to the CPS, about 60 percent of these moves are intracounty moves, and counties, one could argue, geographically define the limits of the local market for public goods.

Given this substantial intramarket mobility, even if the residential choices of only a fraction of movers are motivated by Tiebout's theorized shopping behavior, we could imagine that on the margin, they could be unleashing Tiebout-like forces for efficiency. This could be even more true if the movers are drawn from a population that is particularly attractive to the communities competing against one another—if, for example, movers are more affluent or somehow contributed disproportionately to the local tax base (see Peterson 1981; Schneider 1989; Teske et al. 1993).

However, there is debate about how important local bundles of taxes and services are in motivating locational choices—and hence whether mobility has enough of a Tiebout component in it to make the market work. Without doubt, most moves are motivated by personal factors and not by individuals shopping around for preferred public services or lower taxes. Again, according to the CPS, over 50 percent of moves in 2002 were motivated by housing factors (such as the search for a new or better house), and an additional 25 percent were family related (marriage, divorce, a new child). Given these factors, many argue that in the "real world," Tiebout forces may not be very powerful, or at least conditional on other life transitions.

Although this debate has focused on local taxes and services in general, even critics of the Tiebout model often suggest that the case for shopping around for schools may be stronger. Indeed, some data suggest that households expend more time and resources shopping for education than for other services. Residential mobility is the traditional way that parents vote with their feet in

---

[2] This information on mobility comes from the Census report "Geographic Mobility 2002–2003," available from http://www.census.gov/prod/2004pubs/p20-549.pdf.

searching for better schools. According to the National Center for Education Statistics (NCES), almost one-quarter of parents in the nation report that they have moved to their current neighborhood so that their child can enroll in the local school, and this proportion increases with levels of parents' educational attainment.[3] Thus, high-status parents, who in many ways have disproportionate leverage on school policies and on school performance, are more likely to actively shop for schools via residential mobility.

Additionally, in the last few decades the tight relationship between residential location and the choice of schools has eroded. Through a variety of school choice plans, the number of parents who can choose schools without moving is not trivial. According to the 2003–2004 NCES Schools and Staffing Survey (SASS), about 30 percent of the school districts in the nation have some form of within-district choice. In cities, that proportion more than doubles to 71 percent. And while only about 10 percent of school districts nationwide report magnet schools (which do not have geographic catchment zones), over 40 percent of central city school districts offer them. Although there are far fewer central city school districts than suburban ones, each of these central city districts is large in terms of pupil enrollment. Thus, this school district pattern, not surprisingly, translates into far more extensive choice at the household level. Again according to the NCES, the parents of over half of the students in the nation say that they have the opportunity to choose from among several public schools. It is thus possible that this form of choice produces the milieu in which competitive Tiebout-like forces might be observed even in the absence of extensive residential mobility.

Our empirical analysis here is based primarily on charter schools, one of the most popular forms of school choice in the nation. While our work was focused on Washington, DC, a city where charter school enrollment has grown to encompass over 20 percent of the children in public schools in the city, the charter school movement has been widespread throughout the nation. According to the Center for Education Reform, in the last decade charter school enrollment has grown from close to zero to over 1 million students in more than 3,600 schools. In many states, the number of students enrolled in charter schools is substantial. Florida and Arizona have close to 100,000 charter students each; Michigan and Texas over 85,000; and California tops the list with just short of 220,000.[4] In Washington, DC, 52 charter school campuses are providing schooling for over 20,000 students. And, since enrollment in charter schools is not restricted to the catchment zones used for most traditional public

---

[3] The source for this finding is the NCES report "Context of Elementary and Secondary Education: School Choice," available at http://nces.ed.gov/programs/coe/2004/section4/indicator25.asp.

[4] These data are from the Center for Education Reform as of January 20, 2006. The CER keeps a running total that can be downloaded from http://www.edreform.com/.

TABLE 4.1

Choosing a School in DC

In the Last Year, Did You:	Percent Agree (Standard Error)
Move your residence to get into a school?	7.3 (1.1)
Think about moving to get into a school?	23.3 (1.8)
Try to get into a DC charter school?	18.2 (1.4)
Try to get into a private school?	13.7 (1.4)
Try to get into a public school other than your neighborhood school?	20.4 (2.0)

Note: Data are from a telephone survey of 1,012 parents of school-age children in Washington, DC, conducted in 2001.

schools, parents can choose a different bundle of educational services without moving their residence.

In addition, table 4.1 presents other evidence of the prevalence of shopping for schools in our sample. In our survey we asked DC parents about voting with their feet. While many parents reported that they considered moving their residence, far more sought to exercise choice by trying to change schools. The most common forms of exercising choice by parents were to try to get their child into a DC charter school and to try to exercise intradistrict choice by moving their child to a different noncharter, traditional public school. Clearly, when it comes to education and the contemporary world of school choice, our concept of how Tiebout-like markets for local government services may work needs to be broadened. In the new world of school choice, it's not voting with your feet that matters—increasingly, it's voting with your seat.

Yet, even as school choice transforms the local market for education, the "information assumption" of the Tiebout model has also attracted considerable attention. A body of work by political scientists and others deals with the level of information that citizens in general have about politics and public policies, at both the national and the local level. Paralleling that body of research, a growing number of education researchers have studied how "perfect" parental information levels are with regard to schools.

School Choice, Information, and the Marginal Consumer

Social scientists have long documented that citizens have little information about either politics or a wide range of public policies. Dating back to at least Lazarsfeld, Berelson, and Gaudet's (1944) classic studies of elections, political scientists have shown that most citizens have poor information about their political choices. The data are so consistent that Bartels (1996, 194) suggests, "The political ignorance of the American voter is one of the best documented data of modern political science."

Since electoral politics are removed from the daily world of most citizens, some analysts have argued that the knowledge of candidates might be lower than their knowledge about the policies of government that may directly affect them. However, in several studies, Kuklinski and his colleagues find a citizenry woefully misinformed about basic aspects of public policies (see, for example, Kuklinski et al. 1996). More generally, Zaller and Feldman (1992) dismiss the suggestion that citizens are likely to learn more about matters important to them, arguing that the "tendency appears not to be very great or very wide-spread" (18; also see Price and Zaller 1993; Delli Carpini and Keeter 1996).

While a pattern of low information about politics and public policies is well known to social scientists, research on how much information consumers have about private goods points to a surprisingly similar pattern. According to Kardes (1994), "The typical consumer is exposed to a relatively small subset of available information about products and services, and the consumer attends to an even smaller subset of information to which he or she has been exposed. Not all information is encountered, and not all encountered information is attended to and processed" (400). Similarly, Bloch, Sherrell, and Ridgway (1986) argue that "consumers have surprisingly little enthusiasm for the pursuit [of information], even when buying expensive or socially risky goods" (119).

In short, even in markets for private goods, consumers typically spend little time gathering and analyzing information about the products and services they purchase (see, for example, Bettman 1986; Cohen and Chakravarti 1990; Fiske and Taylor 1991; Tybout and Artz 1994).

Lowery, Lyons, and DeHoog (1990) argue that Tiebout processes require high levels of information on the part of the individual consumer-voter—that for the Tiebout model to work, consumer-voters must have accurate knowledge of the alternative service-tax packages being offered elsewhere in their choice set. They further show that individual citizen-voters are unaware of alternative service-tax packages in other nearby jurisdictions, that a mismatch between preferences and existing service-tax practices has only inconsequential effects on the decision to leave a community, and that citizens misattribute which governments provide which services. In short, mobility decisions appear empirically to not be driven by service-tax issues.

Moreover, those respondents misattributing service provision or responsibility were found to be more positive about service quality. Lowery et al. (1990) attribute this to the incentive officials have to claim credit for quality services actually provided by other governments and to shift the blame for poor services they provide or fail to provide by only selectively correcting citizen-consumers' attribution errors. Given this high error rate, Lowery et al. question the extent to which Tiebout-like forces can be found.

One possibility is that the complexity of the total goods and packages offered by local governments in a metropolitan region makes it hard for the consumer-voter to gather information and that a high-salience, single-policy domain—such as education—may meet the requirements of the Tiebout model. However, even proponents of school choice recognize that the information requirements of fully formed competitive markets will likely not be met in the market for schools.

Education is a notoriously difficult product to describe, and people will continue to disagree about the outcomes by which to judge its quality: Is it test scores? Self-esteem? Graduation rates? Socialization into democratic norms? Lifetime earnings? The list goes on. Moreover, the level and quality of information about schools is often poorer than information about more traditional consumer goods (although the recent national trend toward high-stakes accountability may change the information environment), and there are few intermediaries or third parties (such as the Consumer Union) that independently test products and disseminate information about the quality and reliability of schools. In turn, most parents have very low levels of reliable information about the schools their children attend.

Empirical evidence about what parents know about schools, even in districts with choice, reflects this lack of information—a pattern that is more pronounced among parents with lower socioeconomic status. For example, data from the Alum Rock demonstration program showed that awareness of the voucher program was lower among parents with less formal education and those who had lower expectations for their children's educational attainment. In a survey of parents in Montgomery County, Maryland, Henig (1996) found that even among parents whose children attended magnet schools, many, especially minority parents, responded that they had never heard the terms "magnet school" or "magnet program." Schneider, Teske, and Marschall (2000) found that parents from lower socioeconomic status had poor information search strategies and were isolated from social networks, one of the most efficient ways in which parents with higher socioeconomic status learn about schools. Howell (2004) reports that only 29 percent of parents in underperforming schools in Massachusetts knew that their schools have failed to meet the NCLB standards of "annual yearly progress." Reflecting Schneider et al.'s (2000) finding regarding the effects of socioeconomic status on knowledge, Howell also finds that minority and disadvantaged parents have less information about their child's school than do white and more advantaged parents, and parents with limited English proficiency scored even worse.

In response, debate has often focused on the incentives for "rational" parents to learn more about the schooling options available to them due to the introduction of choice. From this perspective, a prime reason for such low information levels is a simple benefit/cost calculation: In a system without school choice, the costs of gathering information about schools are high relative to the benefits of such information—why invest time and resources in gathering information about schools when your "choice" of schools is determined by geographic attendance zones? Faced with this adverse calculation, most parents remain "rationally" ignorant. The next step in the argument is clear: If, through choice, we give parents a reason to know more about schools, they should become more informed.

This is one of the cornerstones for Chubb and Moe's (1988, 1990) argument for school choice: "In a system where virtually all the important choices are the responsibility of others, parents have little incentive to be informed or involved. In a market-based system, much of the responsibility would be shifted to parents (their choices would have consequences for their children's education), and their incentives to become informed and involved would be dramatically different" (1990, 564).

Other scholars exploring levels of information about public policies and politics have developed similar ideas. Lupia and McCubbins (2000) argue that the search for information is driven by a "calculus of decision" that is anchored by three fundamental points: "First, learning requires effort. Second, effort is a scarce resource for everyone. Third, and as a consequence of the first two facts, people choose what and when to learn. Thus, *learning is active*" (51; italics in original). Clearly, Lupia and McCubbins's calculus points in the same direction as Chubb and Moe's: Paying the cost of gathering and processing additional information makes sense only if the decision maker knows that the new information will help her avoid a mistake or help her make a better choice.

This calculus is evident in an ongoing conceptual shift among cognitive scientists and behavioral decision theorists in which humans are no longer viewed as "cognitive misers" (who invariably seek to reduce the effort needed to make good decisions), but are now viewed as "cognitive managers," individuals "who deploy mental resources strategically as a function of the perceived importance and tractability of the problem" (Tetlock 2000, 240). From this viewpoint, people "decide how to decide," choosing decision tools that reflect the benefits (decision accuracy) and costs (cognitive effort) of the particular decision task.

The ongoing shift in theoretical perspectives to situational decision making and humans as cognitive managers has not yet been widely incorporated into the debate over school choice. Rather, there is a long-standing argument made by critics of choice that education is a complex good that is difficult to describe in a way that people can understand. Also, less-educated parents (who probably stand to benefit most from any system of expanded choice) are the least able to access and analyze that information. A Twentieth-Century Fund report argued that parents are not "natural 'consumers' of education" and that "few parents of any social class appear willing to acquire the information necessary to make active and informed educational choices" (Ascher, Fruchter, and Berne 1996, 40–41). More colorfully, Bridge (1978) called the lack of information the "Achilles' heel" of choice. However, scholars studying school choice have suggested another mechanism by which Tiebout-like sorting and efficiency gains may still occur even given a consumer base with low average levels of information: the theory of the "marginal consumer."

Teske et al. (1993) extend the idea of "market mavens" popularized in the marketing literature to the local market for public goods, identifying a set of "marginal consumers" who are informed about schools and who exert pressure on local schools to be more efficient (see also Dowding, John, and Biggs 1994). Teske et al. apply this concept in their examination of households that gather extensive information about municipal services (especially education) prior to moving. They conclude the following:

> High-income movers have more accurate information about their schools and those who report they care about local schools are also more accurate about local public services and taxes. These important households gather accurate comparative information and they act upon this information when shopping around before entering a community. But even more important for understanding the local market for public goods, these citizens are the very people that communities have the strongest incentives to attract. As communities seek to attract these higher-income individuals, the resulting competition may benefit all citizens, including non-movers. (1993, 709)

The implications of the concept of the "marginal consumer" for a system of school choice is fundamental. While proponents such as Chubb and Moe (1990) and Coons and Sugarman (1978) imply that the full competitive benefits of choice at the systemic level require high levels of information across all parents, the idea of the marginal consumer suggests that the behavior of a smaller group of parents may be sufficient to produce significant benefits. If competitive markets require some but not all consumers to be sufficiently informed so as to pressure producers to deliver services efficiently, then the critiques of school choice based on the argument that on average parents have too little information to drive education reform are wrong.

For proponents of markets, there is clear appeal to this idea of local markets driven by a small number of mavens, given that, empirically, we know that most parents remain uninformed of much of what goes on in their children's schools. But it is also true that we can find a set of parents highly involved in and knowledgeable about schools. Thus, shifting the analytic focus from the average to the marginal consumer may avoid one of the most seemingly telling critiques of choice. However, there are also potential problems with the shift of focus to the marginal consumer—most fundamentally, the concept is under-specified.

For example, the number of marginal consumers necessary to drive the market is vague. While there seems to be a consensus that around 10 percent of the consumer population is enough to drive change, there is little or no scientific evidence underlying this estimate. The definition of who is a marginal consumer is also less than precise. In Teske et al. (1993), it is high-income movers; in Meier, Wrinkle, and Polinard's (2000) study of choice in Texas, it is Anglo parents; and in Schneider et al. (2000), it is all individuals who have chosen to exercise their right to choose in an option demand system. In each case, there are two shared ideas: that the individuals who have been characterized as the marginal consumer are seeking more information about schooling and educa-tion policy and that the marginal consumer is a more valuable "consumer" in the market (either because they are more affluent, more involved with the schools, or, in the case of charter schools, they carry with them substantial per-pupil funding). Clearly while the body of work on private markets and schools strongly suggests a theoretical mechanism by which the choices of a small num-ber of people can create pressure for more efficient outcomes, just as clearly, the concept of how exactly this may work in practice is still in its early stages of development.

In short, given the lack of good information among "consumer-parents," Tiebout-like mechanisms in school choice might not work. But this position does-n't address the argument that under certain circumstances enough parents—the marginal consumers of education—may be sufficiently motivated to become active learners and gather information to make reasonable choices. Moreover, we should note that in much of this debate there is some recognition that perhaps Tiebout shopping might be context specific—that is, these forces may be more observable in a high-salience domain compared to a low-salience one—and here education and schooling is most often singled out as the domain in which we should find Tiebout-like forces.

We now turn to an empirical examination of the accuracy of information about schools possessed by parents, both those who are active choosers and those who are not. If the active learning or marginal consumer theory is cor-rect, we should expect to find that, all else equal, parent-consumers who made a choice should, on average, possess more accurate information. We inspect the empirical foundation for this prediction using data from Washington, DC, a city where school choice is firmly entrenched.

FIGURE 4.1   Smoothed Density Plot of Parents' Error in Response When Asked About the Percent of Pupils in Their Child's School Reading at or Above the Basic Level (number of observations = 518)

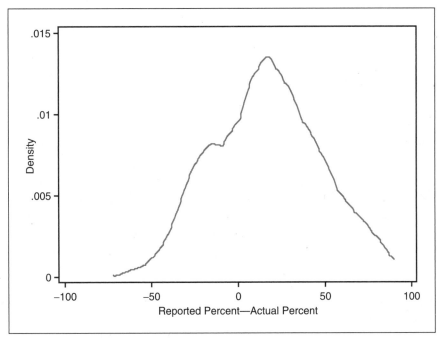

An Empirical Test

To examine the information accuracy of parent-consumers, we use original data from a random-digit dial telephone survey of more than 1,000 parents of school-aged children in Washington, DC, that we conducted in the fall and winter of 2001.[5] Our measure of information accuracy, the dependent variable in the subsequent analyses, was constructed by computing the difference between the response to the question "What do you think is the percentage of children in your child's school reading at or above the basic level?" and the actual percent at or above basic on the SAT-9 standardized test reported by the school in 2001. Only 652 parents provided an answer to this question (many reported that they could not answer it), and, after further losses due to inability to match their school or missing values in reported test scores from the schools, we were left with 518 observed values. In figure 4.1, we present a kernel-smoothed density plot of the parents' observed error, computed using the difference in

---

[5] The survey was conducted by the Center for Survey Research at the State University of New York at Stony Brook. Additional technical information about the survey instrument, response rates, and results is available upon request.

percentages just described. As figure 4.1 shows, the range of observed error is large (the standard deviation is approximately 30 percent), and the mean is about +18 percent, indicating a substantial positivity bias on the part of parents overall. That is, on average, parents are likely to overestimate the academic quality of their child's school.

Our first goal is to investigate the relationship between this observed error and the extent to which a parent is an active searcher or consumer of educational services. As our first measure of this key independent variable, we take the responses to the five questions reported in table 4.1 and reduce them to a single measure via principal components analysis on their covariance matrix. This procedure yields a single underlying dimension with eigenvalue greater than the average, which we retain as our single measure of active shopping for education.[6]

The next step is to regress our measure of error on the shopping measure and an additional number of control variables. However, as just noted, we are particularly concerned about missing data on the dependent variable, as it seems likely that at least some of the parents who did not respond to the information-accuracy item did so because of other measured or possibly unmeasured predictors (that is, the data are NMAR, or not missing at random, in Rubin's [1976] terminology). Since we suspect NMAR or, more commonly in econometrics, incidental truncation, we employ a Gronau-Heckman-type model of selection estimated by a probit model in addition to the outcome regression (Gronau 1974; Heckman 1976, 1979).

Because these models are known to be particularly sensitive to the normality assumption of the residuals, and since we are interested first in modeling the magnitude of parents' error independent of its direction, we first transform the observed error measures by taking their positive square root. We then estimate the following model:

$$y_{1i} = \mathbf{x}_i \beta + u_{1i} \qquad\qquad (4.1a)$$

$$y_{2i} = 1[\mathbf{z}_i \gamma + u_{2i} > 0] \qquad\qquad (4.1b)$$

where y_{1i} is parent i's root observed error; y_{2i} is an indicator variable coded 1 if the parent responds to the accuracy question from which y_{1i} is generated; $\mathbf{x}_i$ is a vector of covariates (including the active consumer principal component) predicting the error rate; $\mathbf{z}_i$ is a similar vector of predictors of whether or not

---

[6] Since there is significant listwise missing data on the fifth question, "In the last year, did you try to get into a public school other than your neighborhood school?," we estimate our principal components analysis using an expectation-maximization (EM) algorithm approach, which requires an additional assumption of multivariate normality (Roweis 1997; Weesie 1999). Additionally, since the component measures are dichotomous, we compute a second set of principal components using the matrix of interitem tetrachoric correlations. These second components are correlated to the first set at .9 or above. We retain the first set for subsequent analyses.

the parent responded; β and γ are the respective vectors of coefficients; and u_{1i} and u_{2i} are the residual or disturbance terms and are assumed to be distributed bivariate normal with zero means. As usual for models of this sort, we further assume $\text{Var}(u_1) = \sigma^2$, $\text{Var}(u_2) = 1$, and $\text{Cov}(u_1, u_2) = \rho$.

In addition to the summary active education consumer measure, we include in $\mathbf{x}_i$ the respondents' years of formal education and the square of this quantity; the number of discussants that they report talking with frequently about education; their response to a four-category ordinal item asking how often they talk to their child's teacher (treated here as a continuous regressor); a numerical conversion of the letter grade (A–F) that the parent assigns to their child's school; and how long (in years) the child has attended the school.

In $\mathbf{z}_i$ we include the active consumer measure; education and education squared again; the number of attempts that the telephone interviewer made before completing the interview (as a proxy for their general willingness to answer more complex, memory-based survey items); the respondent's employment status; and the actual percent of students reading at or above basic in the school (as a control for possible social desirability bias in non-response, induced if parents with children in underperforming schools are reluctant to report this).

After listwise deletion of units with missing values in $\mathbf{x}_i$ or $\mathbf{z}_i$, we are left with 664 observations, 404 of whom respond to the accuracy question and 260 who do not. We estimate the model using full-information maximum likelihood and present the results in table 4.2. The data are appropriately weighted given the survey design.[7]

Table 4.2 shows that, on average, and holding other covariates constant, as the measure of the respondent's shopping activity increases, his error increases as well; active education consumers appear to have *less* accurate information about their child's school. The active consumer measure does not, however, appear to be a statistically significant predictor of selection to respond to the survey item. Other statistically significant predictors include, in the outcome equation, the grade the parent assigns to the school (higher ratings predict lower error, $p < .01$, all reported p's two-tailed) and in the selection model, the parent's education (with more educated parents more likely to answer the knowledge question, although there may be some nonlinearity in this relationship, $p = .02$ for education, $.11$ for education squared) and parents being more likely to answer the question as the actual percentage of students scoring above basic or better increases ($p = .10$). We also estimate the error covariance between the two equations, ρ, at $-.723$.

---

[7] In particular, there is a designed oversample of charter school parents. We employ a poststratification weight (Little 1993) to account for this.

TABLE 4.2

Active Shoppers Are Less Accurate

Variable	Coefficient (Standard Error)
EQUATION 1: PARENT'S ERROR	
Active Shopper	12.270 (4.670)
Education	−0.343 (0.368)
Education^2	0.010 (0.014)
Number of Discussants	−0.014 (0.026)
Frequency Talk to Teacher	0.052 (0.106)
Parent's Grade for School	−0.459 (0.124)
Years in Present School	0.010 (0.076)
Intercept	9.811 (2.694)
EQUATION 2: SELECTION	
Active Shopper	−1.430 (2.209)
Education	0.217 (0.090)
Education^2	−0.006 (0.004)
Number of Interview Attempts	−0.013 (0.014)
Parent Employed	0.140 (0.123)
Percent Students at or Above Basic	0.006 (0.004)
Intercept	−2.037 (0.643)
ρ	−0.723 (0.138)
Number of Observations	664
Log-likelihood	−547.801
$\chi^2_{(7)}$	23.317

To facilitate interpretation of these results for the active consumer measure, we vary this measure between the observed mean −1 standard deviation and the observed mean +1 standard deviation, holding the other covariates constant at their sample means. We then generate predicted values of parent's error by simulating from the estimated covariance matrix of $\hat{\beta}$ and $\hat{\gamma}$ and reversing the square root transformation of y_1. We find that, on average, this increase in 2 standard deviations predicts a corresponding increase in error of about 8.2, measured in percent of students at or above basic in reading, with a 95 percent confidence interval of prediction of [2.0, 14.2].

Before considering the substantive significance of this result, we must first consider the possibility that the negative relationship between choice and accuracy is an artifact of our measurement of choice or shopping behavior. In particular, our measure is composed of several underlying survey responses (table 4.1), some of which are self-reports of considered behavior (e.g., "Did you think about moving your residence?" or "Did you try to get into a charter school?"), that may have been answered in the affirmative by too wide a range of parents. Accordingly, we duplicated the analysis just presented, but instead of the active consumer summary measure, we substituted only two direct measures of choice behavior: the parent's response to the "Did you move your residence?" question and another indicator for whether the child is in a charter school. With this exception, we estimate the same selection model as presented in equations 4.1 and 4.2, again using the positive square root of the respondent's error as the dependent variable. We report the results of this second model in table 4.3.

As table 4.3 illustrates, we find a positive and statistically significant effect for charter school enrollment ($p = .01$) on the parent's error but none for moving residence. Once again we simulate from the covariance matrix of estimated coefficients and find that, holding other covariates at their means (and for non-movers), charter school enrollment predicts an average increase in error of 4.5 (again measured in percent of students at or above basic in reading), with a 95 percent confidence interval of [0.86, 8.04], thus supporting our earlier result that active consumers of education appear to be less well informed about the academic quality of their schools.

Next, we examine the direction of the error. That is, we answer the question "Conditional on responding to the accuracy question, are active education consumers more likely to overestimate or underestimate the academic quality of their child's school compared to other parents?" To investigate this, we estimate the following model:

$$\Pr(y_i = 1 \mid \mathbf{x}_i) = \Phi(\mathbf{x}_i \beta) \tag{4.2}$$

where y_i is an indicator variable coded 1 if the parent's estimation of the percentage of students in the school reading at or above basic is an overestimate; and $\mathbf{x}_i$ is a vector of covariates that includes the active consumer measure, the respondents' years of formal education and the square of this quantity, the number of discussants that they report talking with frequently about education, their response to a four-category ordinal item asking how often they talk to their child's teacher (treated here as a continuous regressor), a numerical conversion of the letter grade (A–F) that the parent assigns to his or her child's school, and how long (in years) the child has attended the school. Φ denotes the normal cumulative distribution function. We estimate the vector of coefficients, β, using the standard maximum likelihood probit model and present the results in table 4.4.

As table 4.4 shows, even controlling for the other covariates, active consumers of education are more likely to exhibit positivity bias or overestimate

TABLE 4.3

Charter Parents Are Less Accurate

Variable	Coefficient (Standard Error)
EQUATION 1: PARENT'S ERROR	
Charter School	0.613 (0.245)
Moved Residence	0.383 (0.570)
Education	0.218 (0.388)
Education^2	−0.006 (0.014)
Number of Discussants	−0.008 (0.023)
Frequency Talk to Teacher	0.054 (0.100)
Parent's Grade for School	−0.475 (0.139)
Years in Present School	0.023 (0.089)
Intercept	2.931 (2.800)
EQUATION 2: SELECTION	
Charter School	−0.114 (0.096)
Moved Residence	−0.243 (0.199)
Education	0.216 (0.094)
Education^2	−0.005 (0.004)
Number of Interview Attempts	0.001 (0.014)
Parent Employed	−0.129 (0.139)
Percent Students at or Above Basic	−0.004 (0.003)
Intercept	−1.210 (0.649)
ρ	0.822 (0.100)
Number of Observations	664
Log-likelihood	−545.977
$\chi^2_{(8)}$	22.979

the academic performance of their child's school ($p = .05$). More precisely, the predicted probability of an average parent (holding all other covariates at their means) making an error in the positive direction increases from .51 (standard error = .06) to .66 (.05) as they vary from 1 standard deviation below the mean active consumer score to 1 standard deviation above. In addition, we find that education, parent's satisfaction (assigned grade), and the child's length of time in school all appear to be statistically significant predictors of positivity bias.

TABLE 4.4

Active Shoppers Overestimate Academic Quality

Variable	Coefficient (Standard Error)
Active Shopper	6.538 (3.381)
Education	−0.735 (0.342)
Education^2	0.026 (0.012)
Number of Discussants	0.005 (0.018)
Frequency Talk to Teacher	0.052 (0.075)
Parent's Grade for School	−0.353 (0.100)
Years in Present School	0.114 (0.060)
Intercept	6.217 (2.496)
Number of Observations	404
Log-likelihood	−228.258
$\chi^2_{(7)}$	21.804
Percent Correctly Predicted	70.3

As before, we reestimate the model using the behavior measures in place of the active consumer principal component. The results of this model are presented in table 4.5, and are substantively similar to those in table 4.4. We find that charter parents are more likely to overestimate ($p = .07$), but we find no effect for movers. Holding all else constant, the average predicted probability of positive error for a noncharter parent is .54 (standard error = .06) and for a charter parent, .65 (.05). Once again, we find parent's education, parent's school grade, and the child's length of time in school are statistically significant predictors.

Discussion

Our empirical analysis suggests that, even when controlling for other likely confounding variables, active shoppers or marginal consumers of education are more likely to incorrectly estimate the academic performance of their child's school and that this error is more likely to be an overestimate. That is, at least regarding academic achievement, parents who choose (perhaps particularly charter school parents) appear to be wearing what Erikson (1982, 1986) called "rose-colored glasses."[8] Why is this true? One answer comes from behavioral

---

[8] Elsewhere we investigate whether charter school parents wear "rose-colored glasses" when they evaluate the strength of their school community. In this case, we find the opposite effect: Charter parents are harder critics of their child's school. See Buckley and Schneider, forthcoming.

TABLE 4.5

Charter Parents Exhibit Positivity Bias

Variable	Coefficient (Standard Error)
Charter School	0.292 (0.161)
Moved Residence	0.348 (0.376)
Education	−0.751 (0.351)
Education^2	0.027 (0.012)
Number of Discussants	0.006 (0.018)
Frequency Talk to Teacher	0.051 (0.075)
Parent's Grade for School	−0.373 (0.101)
Years in Present School	0.121 (0.063)
Intercept	6.255 (2.554)
Number of Observations	404
Log-likelihood	−228.383
$\chi^2_{(8)}$	19.544
Percent Correctly Predicted	70.5

decision theory: motivated reasoning. The theory of motivated reasoning or biased processing involves a perversion of the model of rational decision making in which decision makers collect the facts that support an antecedent decision, rejecting or ignoring contrary evidence. Ironically, as Lodge and Taber (2000) argue, this effect may be more pronounced in those consumers who are actively involved in a public good or service:

> Biased processing is most likely among those whose general political knowledge and domain-specific political knowledge is rich, for it is sophisticates who typically hold the strongest attitudes, with the most confidence, and have the most facts at hand, thereby making them more able to assimilate supporting evidence and better equipped to discredit arguments that challenge their established beliefs or attitudes. (211)

Thus, a marginal consumer of education, as a more involved and possibly more cognitively complex decision maker, might process a greater quantity of information in a more thorough and efficient manner, but still perceive that information in an inaccurate (from a hypothetically objective perspective) fashion due to entrenched opinions or biases. Indeed, it does not require a stretch of the imagination to construct numerous examples of such motivated reasoning in a policy area as emotionally and ideologically charged as education.

Such errors of judgment are likely unintentional. One key lesson from the work of Lodge and his colleagues is that "hot cognition" may drive judgments and evaluations—that is, what people feel about their schools may reflect their choices and their behavior regardless of the reality of school performance. While parents will say that they value academic excellence as the most important attribute of schools, parents who choose may find more salient a different dimension of their child's school, such as safety, extracurricular offerings, or racial composition of the student body (Schneider and Buckley 2002). Assuming that the new school is an improvement in this other dimension, the parent's positive affect now generated toward the school could induce a sort of "spillover" into other attributes. For example, a parent pleased with the improved discipline in a charter school may unconsciously overestimate the school's reading performance.

It is also possible that the information available to parents may not be perfectly accurate. There is likely to be an information asymmetry between parents and schools, which almost certainly have more information about the true quality and nature of educational service provided. Levin and Belfield (2003, 15) note that "there has been considerable debate over whether school quality can be easily codified and quantified (or even manipulated), leading to the possibility that parents will be making choices based on false information." Schneider and various coauthors have shown that many parents know very little about the range of schooling available to them (Schneider et al. 1998). This asymmetry may be exacerbated by false advertising (Lubienski 2003; also see Kane and Staiger 2002) or through the spread of bad information through parents' social networks (Schneider et al. 1997). With regard to charter schools, these processes may be further exacerbated by the high level of hype generated by charter school proponents, who quite often refer to themselves as part of a "movement" and who extol the virtues (and dismiss the negatives) of charter schools (see Buckley and Schneider, forthcoming).

Moreover, both sources of error (biased or motivated reasoning and limited or incorrect information) are further compounded by strategic actors in the education bureaucracy. As Lowery et al. (1990) argue, government officials are often quick to claim credit for the successes of other branches of government—and deliberately slow to correct attribution errors by citizens regarding such successes. In the case of schools, what incentive does a principal or superintendent have to inform parents that her school's excellent reputation is unsupported by the last few years of test scores?

Whatever the causes of this bias, the consequence is the same: The conditions necessary for Tiebout-like sorting to lead to an efficient outcome may no longer be present. If the average parent has little information and the most active consumers of education have biased information, then it would seem unlikely that their decisions are jointly maximizing social welfare. What, then, is the solution? Since one possible cause of the problem is an information asymmetry, one answer may be to expand the quantity and quality of information available to parent-consumers. This policy goal can be met, in part, through the increases in systematic collection of accountability data mandated by the No Child Left Behind legislation that are prevalent throughout the nation. However, more and better data may not be enough. This information must get into the hands of parents in an easily interpretable format that allows for comparisons.

Like most market failures, the information asymmetry between schools and parents may require government action to remedy, although it is possible to envision a secondary market in K–12 education information such as that which exists for higher education, either electronically or in print form. However, in some of the areas where the need and support for market pressures to improve schools are greatest, further intervention may be required to ensure that low-income parents get the information they need for such a market to function. Here, the mass media may play an important role in the dissemination of accountability results and rankings, but getting this information into a form that is easy to both comprehend and use is no trivial matter.

Even if the quality and quantity of information available to parents are improved, however, it may remain difficult to overcome the effects of biased processing or motivated reasoning among the most active shoppers. If informed and actively choosing parents are more likely to erroneously judge their child's school, this could lead to adverse, systemic consequences beyond the utility or satisfaction of that individual. A key component of the marketlike mechanism in any school choice system is some form of accountability: Schools that are not meeting the demands of their customers must either change or close. If, however, the customers most likely to exit cannot accurately determine if their needs are being met, substandard schools may have little incentive to improve.

References

Ascher, Carol, Norm Fruchter, and Robert Berne. 1996. *Hard lessons: Public schools and privatization.* New York: Twentieth Century School Fund.

Bartels, Larry. 1996. Uninformed votes: Information effects in presidential elections. *American Journal of Political Science* 40:194–230.

Bettman, James R. 1986. Consumer psychology. *Annual Review of Psychology* 37:257–289.

Bloch, Peter, Daniel Sherrell, and Nancy Ridgway. 1986. Consumer search: An extended framework. *Journal of Consumer Research* 13:119–126.

Bridge, Gary. 1978. Information imperfections: The Achilles' heel of entitlement plans. *School Review* 86:504–529.

Buckley, Jack, and Mark Schneider. Forthcoming. *Charter schools: Hype or hope?*

Chubb, John E., and Terry M. Moe. 1988. Politics, markets and the organization of schools. *American Political Science Review* 82:1065–1089.

————. 1990. *Politics, markets, and America's schools.* Washington, DC: Brookings Institution.

Cohen, Jerry, and Dipankar Chakravarti. 1990. Consumer psychology. *Annual Review of Psychology* 41:243–288.

Coons, John E., and Stephen D. Sugarman. 1978. *Education by choice: The case for family control.* Berkeley: University of California Press.

Delli Carpini, Michael X., and Scott Keeter. 1996. *What Americans know about politics and why it matters.* New Haven, CT: Yale University Press.

Dowding, Keith, Peter John, and Stephen Biggs. 1994. Tiebout: A survey of the empirical literature. *Urban Studies* 31:767–797.

Erikson, Donald A. 1982. *The British Columbia story: Antecedents and consequences of aid to private schools.* Los Angeles: Institute for the Study of Private Schools.

————. 1986. Choice and private schools: Dynamics of supply and demand. In *Private education: Studies in choice and public policy,* D. C. Levy, ed. New York: Oxford University Press.

Fischel, William A. 2001. *The homevoter hypothesis.* Cambridge, MA: Harvard University Press.

Fiske, Susan T., and Shelley E. Taylor. 1991. *Social cognition.* New York: McGraw-Hill.

Gronau, Ruben. 1974. Wage comparisons—A selectivity bias. *Journal of Political Economy* 82:1119–1143.

Heckman, James J. 1976. The common structure of statistical models of truncation, sample selection, and limited dependent variables and a simple estimator for such models. *Annals of Economic and Social Measurement* 5:475–492.

————. 1979. Sample selection bias as a specification error. *Econometrica* 47:153–161.

Henig, Jeffrey. 1996. The local dynamics of choice: Ethnic preferences and institutional responses. In *Who chooses? Who loses?: Culture, institutions and the unequal effects of school choice,* B. Fuller, R. F. Elmore, and G. Orfield, eds. New York: Teachers College Press.

Howell, William G. 2004. *Parents, choice, and some foundations for education reform in Massachusetts.* Boston: Pioneer Institute for Public Policy Research.

John, Peter, Keith Dowding, and Stephen Biggs. 1995. Residential mobility in London: A micro-level test of the behavioural assumptions of the Tiebout model. *British Journal of Political Science* 25:379–397.

Kane, Thomas J., and Douglas O. Staiger. 2002. The promise and pitfalls of using imprecise school accountability measures. *Journal of Economic Perspectives* 16:91–114.

Kardes, Frank R. 1994. Consumer judgment and decision processes. In *Handbook of social cognition,* R. S. Wyer and T. K. Srull, eds. Hillsdale, NJ: Lawrence Erlbaum and Associates.

Kuklinski, James H., Paul J. Quirk, David Schwieder, and Robert E. Rich. 1996. Misinformation and the currency of citizenship. Paper presented at the Annual Meeting of the American Political Science Association, San Francisco.

Lazarsfeld, Paul F., Bernard Berelson, and Hazel Gaudet. 1944. *The people's choice: How the voter makes up his mind in a presidential campaign.* New York: Duell, Sloan and Pearce.

Levin, Henry M., and Clive R. Belfield. 2003. *The marketplace in education.* New York: Columbia University Teachers College, National Center for the Study of Privatization in Education.

Little, Roderick J. A. 1993. Post-stratification: A modeler's perspective. *Journal of the American Statistical Association* 88:1001–1012.

Lodge, Milton, and Charles Taber. 2000. Three steps toward a theory of motivated political reasoning. In *Elements of reason: Understanding and expanding the limits of political rationality,* Arthur Lupia, Matthew McCubbins, and Samuel Popkin, eds. New York: Cambridge University Press.

Lowery, David, William Lyons, and Ruth DeHoog. 1990. Institutionally-induced attribution errors: Their composition and impact on citizen satisfaction with local government. *American Politics Quarterly* 18:169–197.

Lubienski, Christopher. 2003. Innovation in education markets: Theory and evidence on the impact of competition and choice in charter schools. *American Educational Research Journal* 40:395–443.

Lupia, Arthur, and Matthew McCubbins. 2000. The institutional foundations of political competence. In *Elements of reason: Understanding and expanding the limits of political rationality,* Arthur Lupia, Matthew McCubbins, and Samuel Popkin, eds., 47–66. New York: Cambridge University Press.

Meier, Kenneth J., Robert D. Wrinkle, and J. L. Polinard. 2000. Bureaucracy and organizational performance: Causality arguments about public schools. *American Journal of Political Science* 44:590–603.

Peterson, Paul. 1981. *City limits.* Chicago: University of Chicago Press.

Price, Vincent, and John Zaller. 1993. Who gets the news? Alternative measures of news reception and their implications for research. *Public Opinion Quarterly* 57:133–164.

Roweis, Sam T. 1997. EM algorithms for PCA and SPCA. In *Proceedings from neural information processing systems* 10, 1997, Michael Jordan, Michael Kearns, and Sara Solla, eds., 626–632. Cambridge, MA: MIT Press.

Rubin, Donald B. 1976. Inference and missing data. *Biometrika* 63:581–592.

Schneider, Mark. 1989. *The competitive city.* Pittsburgh: University of Pittsburgh Press.

Schneider, Mark, and Jack Buckley. 2002. What do parents want from schools? Evidence from the Internet. *Educational Evaluation and Policy Analysis* 24:133–144.

Schneider, Mark, Paul Teske, and Melissa Marschall. 2000. *Choosing schools: Consumer choice and the quality of American schools.* Princeton, NJ: Princeton University Press.

Schneider, Mark, Paul Teske, Melissa Marschall, and Christine Roch. 1998. Shopping for schools: In the land of the blind, the one-eyed parent may be enough. *American Journal of Political Science* 42:769–793.

Schneider, Mark, Paul Teske, Christine Roch, and Melissa Marschall. 1997. Institutional arrangements and the creation of social capital: The effects of school choice. *American Political Science Review* 91:82–93.

Teske, Paul, Mark Schneider, Michael Mintrom, and Samuel Best. 1993. Establishing the micro foundations of a macro theory: Information, movers, and the competitive local market for public goods. *American Political Science Review* 87:702–713.

Tetlock, Philip E. 2000. Coping with trade-offs: Psychological constraints and political implications. In *Elements of reason: Understanding and exploring the limits of political rationality,* Arthur Lupia, Matthew McCubbins, and Samuel Popkin, eds. New York: Cambridge University Press.

Tiebout, Charles M. 1956. A pure theory of local expenditures. *Journal of Political Economy* 64:416–424.

Tybout, Alice, and Nancy Artz. 1994. Consumer psychology. *Annual Review of Psychology* 45:131–169.

Weesie, Jeroen. 1999. PCAMV: Stata module: Principal components with missing values. Accessed 25 April 2005 from http://econpapers.repec.org/software/bocbocode/sjw34.htm.

Zaller, John, and Stanley Feldman. 1992. A simple theory of the survey response: Answering questions versus revealing preferences. *American Journal of Political Science* 36:579–616.

COMMENTARY

THERESE McGUIRE

One of the key assumptions of the Tiebout model is that consumer/residents have perfect information about the set of service/tax packages offered by local governments. The authors of this chapter set out to test whether this assumption is valid in an important arena: the public provision of elementary and secondary education. They ask whether there is informed shopping in the market for K–12 education. If so, if parents have relevant information and use it in choosing schools, perhaps the Tiebout model is operative with respect to K–12 education, and we can be somewhat reassured that education is provided efficiently by the local public sector.

The authors take an interesting perspective on the question. They note that a fair bit of shopping for schools today can be done without having to move residence. Many public school districts have charter schools, magnet schools, open enrollment, and vouchers that allow parents to change schools without having to reside in the catchment area of the school. When Oates (1969) wrote his influential piece on the capitalization of education spending and taxes into property values, housing and (public) schooling choices were very much linked to one another. This is no longer true today, as parents can "vote with their seat" (a phrase coined by the authors). To test whether Tiebout forces are present, the authors examine whether active shoppers (defined following) have more or less accurate information (about test scores in their schools) than nonshoppers. They find less and conclude that "the conditions necessary for Tiebout-like sorting to lead to an efficient outcome may no longer be present."

This is a bleak conclusion for two reasons. If local education—the local good that people care the most about and invest the most time and effort in choosing—does not meet the Tiebout conditions, then what will? Also, the authors proposed remedy is to improve information flows through the implementation of accountability programs, but as Kane and Staiger (2002) have pointed out, accountability policies are fraught with their own set of problems. The authors could have taken their analysis further to buttress their findings and to explore related questions. I organize my suggestions around four questions that provide challenges to, as well as opportunities to enhance, the applicability and believability of the authors' model and results.

1. Have the authors devised an appropriate test for the presence of "Tiebout-like forces"?
2. Do the authors show what they purport to show?
3. Is "voting with your seat" (nonresidential-based choice) pervasive enough?
4. Are there alternative (and plausible) explanations for their results?

As to the first question, the authors' test for the presence of Tiebout-like forces is to examine whether active shoppers are better or worse informed than parents who are not actively looking at alternative schools. They identify active shoppers through a survey and through parents' choices. If survey respondents indicated that they had moved residence to get into a school, had thought about doing so, or had tried to get into a school other than their neighborhood public school, or if the parents had a child in a charter school, then the parents were designated as active shoppers. Survey respondents were also asked to give their estimate of the percentage of the children in their child's school who read at or above the basic level. The difference between this estimate and the actual percentage represents the level of accuracy of the parent's information. The key dependent variable is the measure of accuracy, and the key independent variable is an indicator variable for active shoppers. The authors find that active shoppers are less accurate in their estimate of the percentage of children in their child's school who read at or above the basic level.

This is an interesting finding, but the authors could have boosted our confidence in their result and its interpretation by providing additional evidence. One alternative, corroborative test would be to examine whether education is provided more efficiently—the hoped-for result of "Tiebout-like forces"—in markets with more active shoppers. For example, they could explore whether test scores are (output is) higher in schools with more active shoppers. Related, they could examine whether shoppers (movers) choose schools with higher test scores. (In general, the paper is lacking in descriptive information about the schools.) Additionally, it would be interesting to see evidence regarding another implication of the Tiebout model: that individuals sort by type. The prediction would be that there is greater sorting by type across schools in areas with more active shoppers. These further explorations would help to corroborate the presence or lack of "Tiebout-like forces."

What do the authors show and what do they purport to show? They show that active shoppers are less accurate in their guesses of the percentage of children at or above basic reading levels. This measure of "accuracy" or "informed consumer" is not necessarily the most relevant. The information sought by active shoppers might have more to do with the relative standing of a particular school rather than an absolute measure of performance. It would be useful to know if active shoppers know more or less about where their schools sit in the distribution or if they know more or less about the average level of test scores or the trend in scores in their schools compared to other schools. A shopper's school might be above some basic reading level, but still the school might be far below other readily available schools. My point is that, even if we stick to test scores (and do not branch into more nuanced measures of school quality), it is not clear that the results indicate that active shoppers are less well informed about the relative quality of their schools than parents who are not actively shopping.

The authors motivate their "voting with your seat" approach to education by noting that over one-third of school districts in the nation (and nearly two-thirds of school districts within cities) have some form of within-district choice. But we do not know from these facts how much effective choice is available. Many of the alternative schools within a given district have long waiting lists, capacity constraints, oversubscribed lotteries, and so on. As an example, in Chicago in AY2003-2004, 270,000 students were eligible to transfer under the No Child Left Behind legislation, but there were only 450 transfer slots available in the system. If, in reality, choice is limited by a shortage of slots, it would not be rational for parents to invest significant amounts of time and resources into gathering information. A finding that active shoppers are not better informed than nonshoppers would not be surprising because one of the conditions required for Tiebout-like shopping—that there be a sufficient number of options to choose among—may not be met.

The authors' primary finding is that more active shoppers are less informed about test scores, and they interpret this as a repudiation of the Tiebout model. An alternative explanation for or interpretation of this finding is what I will call the "Spanky and his gang" effect. Suppose active shoppers care more than others do about peer effects (including the benefits of bonding with friends), both in the classroom and, more important, in the neighborhood. Then they might invest time and effort in choosing a neighborhood in which to reside, and they would send their children to the local (neighborhood) public school with only vague knowledge of the school's test scores. For these parents, involvement in the social environment of the local neighborhood is enhanced by their children attending the local public school. By choosing a good neighborhood, the parents have chosen a school with good peer effects for their children. Detailed knowledge about test scores may not be needed if parents know the quality of the neighborhood and they know that neighborhood children attend the local public school. Note that this mechanism would again link housing choices to school choices, but through sorting by neighborhood peer effects.

This story would explain why active shoppers might be no more informed than nonactive shoppers. But is it consistent with their being less informed? The answer is yes, if active shoppers care more than others about peer effects. More plausibly, suppose active shoppers have greater means than nonactive shoppers to choose desirable neighborhoods. Then nonactive shoppers—whose means confine them to local schools in less desirable neighborhoods—would have a greater incentive to learn about test scores in their local schools so that they know when it is necessary to put pressure on the local school authorities.

REFERENCES

Kane, Thomas J., and Douglas O. Staiger. 2002. The promise and pitfalls of using imprecise school accountability measures. *Journal of Economic Perspectives* 16:91–114.
Oates, Wallace E. 1969. The effects of property taxes and local spending on property values: An empirical study of tax capitalization and the Tiebout hypothesis. *Journal of Political Economy* 77:957–971.

5

Imperfect Competition Between Communities, Politics, and Capitalization

WILLIAM H. HOYT

Although it has been discussed in many reviews since its publication in 1956, the Tiebout model is still difficult to pin down. The lack of a formal model within the paper as well as lack of clarity about what Tiebout set out to accomplish in the article has allowed for multiple interpretations. Most of the literature has treated the Tiebout model as consisting of a large number of clubs in which members must reside to obtain a jointly consumed good. One of the implications of this approach is the possibility of efficiency in provision of local public services. Another is efficient sorting of people, based on tastes. To obtain these conditions, it is usually assumed that more jurisdictions are better than fewer. If the number of municipalities in which members reside is large, service provision of a single club or municipality will not affect the utility of the mobile consumer-residents or property values in surrounding municipalities.

In contrast to much of the previous literature, this chapter analyzes local public service provision when jurisdictions are not perfectly competitive. While some of the contributions to "imperfect" competition in Tiebout models have been made in club models without residence decisions and land markets (e.g., Bewley 1981), the focus here is on studies in which housing markets are explicitly modeled. Some important predictions are only obtainable with inclusion of housing markets. These have implications for studies of

My special thanks to Robert Schwab and William Fischel for their helpful comments, as well as to other participants in the 50th Anniversary Tiebout Conference.

capitalization as well as the politics associated with the provision of local government services.

In a framework with mobile residents, multiple but finite jurisdictions, and a distorting property tax, we will see that the size of jurisdiction affects the rate of capitalization of public services and taxes within that jurisdiction. In addition, policies of large jurisdictions within the region will influence property values in the rest of the region. That a jurisdiction not only influences property values within its own borders but also in other jurisdictions has important implications for modeling the appropriate objective for the jurisdictional government.

Because of the potential importance for empirical analysis, we begin by examining two distinctions that are commonly found among studies examining imperfect competition among jurisdictions. The first concerns the objective of the local governments that is assumed by these studies. Brennan and Buchanan (1980), Epple and Zelenitz (1981), and Hoyt (1999) all model local governments as a "Leviathan" that maximizes some function of the difference between tax revenues and the actual costs of providing public services. This is called the "surplus" in the following text. In contrast, Hoyt (1991a, 1991b, 1992) considers the objectives of maximizing the utility of resident landowners and of maximizing land value.

The second distinction is more technical. Some models focus on how many equal-size jurisdictions there are in a region. These include Epple and Zelenitz (1981) and Hoyt (1991a, 1991b). In contrast, Hoyt (1992, 1999) considers differences in the size of jurisdictions within a region. The theoretical results from these two types of models are similar, but the empirical implications are different: What may appear to be differences in policies among jurisdictions due to differences in the *number* of jurisdictions within the metropolitan area may actually be differences due to the *size* (market share) that the jurisdiction possesses. Some simple numerical simulations that follow illustrate and quantify some of the theoretical results. These examples give some indication of the potential magnitude of differences in policies due to market share or the number of jurisdictions within a region (Hoyt 1992). They show how the *number* of jurisdictions, as opposed to their market shares, influences government policy.

The data in this chapter are for municipal governments located in metropolitan standard areas (MSAs) from the 2002 Census of Governments. This analysis provides an empirical examination of the relationship between local government expenditures and the population share of the metropolitan area within the municipality. Because these municipalities are located in several different MSAs rather than a single MSA, the impacts on the size (population) of the municipality and its market share are evident.

Capitalization, Imperfect Competition, and the Policy Choices of Local Governments

The capitalization of local public services and taxes found in Wallace Oates's study of municipal property values in northern New Jersey was the first empirical evidence in support of the Tiebout hypothesis (Oates 1969). His test found a positive coefficient on educational expenditures and a negative coefficient on the property tax rate in a hedonic regression of home values. However, Oates suggested another, stronger test of the Tiebout hypothesis, which holds that local public services are efficiently provided. Oates offered this test, albeit only informally and with caveats, by examining how a balanced-budget increase in the property tax rate for schools affects property values. He inferred that property values were maximized in his sample because additional value-increasing school expenditures would just offset the value-decreasing property taxes needed to pay for them.

While Oates's finding was much debated in the literature (Edel and Sclar 1974; Hamilton 1976; Epple, Zelenitz, and Visscher 1978; Yinger 1982), the notion that policies that maximized property value were efficient formed the basis of numerous empirical studies that followed. These included studies by Sonstelie and Portney (1980), Brueckner (1979, 1982), Bates and Santerre (2003), and Barrow and Rouse (2004). Sonstelie and Portney (1978) offer a theoretical proof of the link between property-value maximization and the efficient provision of local public services.

While a growing empirical literature examined the link between capitalization and public services, Epple and Zelenitz (1981) and Brennan and Buchanan (1980) addressed the issue of whether a large number of jurisdictions could guarantee the efficient provision of local public services. Brennan and Buchanan's Leviathan position suggests that that there should be an inverse relationship between the fiscal surplus (to be captured by the bureaucrats) and the number of jurisdictions. Their position suggests that increasing the number of jurisdictions should always reduce the appropriable surplus. Epple and Zelenitz, however, demonstrated that with limited land supply and therefore positive land rents, increasing the number of jurisdictions could reduce this surplus, but it will not eliminate it.

Following these two studies, a number of papers examined the relationship between the extent of competition among governments in a region and the level of government expenditures. Oates (1985) examined the relationship between state and local tax receipts (as a fraction of income) and how revenues and expenditures were allocated between state and local governments within the state. Oates argued that the Leviathan argument put forth by Brennan and Buchanan implied that more centralized governments would have higher taxes. Oates did not find evidence in support of this hypothesis.

Nelson (1987) extended and modified the work of Oates (1985) by including the number of residents per local government within a state as a measure of the extent of decentralization. He found limited evidence that increases in the number of residents per local government increased public expenditures. Zax (1989) performed a similar exercise to Nelson (1987) at the county rather than the state level. He found that more governments per capita reduced local government expenditures, which is generally consistent with Brennan and Buchanan's view. Finally, Forbes and Zampelli (1989) examined the relationship between local expenditures aggregated to the county and the number of counties within an MSA and found no evidence of any relationship.

The mixed results about the effect of local government competition on efficiency continued into the 1990s. A number of papers about competition among school districts, summarized and extended in Hoxby (2000), concluded that competition enhanced efficiency. The literature on tax competition for industry, however, often found that competition reduced welfare (Wilson 1986; Zodrow and Mieszkowski 1986). Hoyt (1991b) showed that increasing the number of governments would reduce both tax rates and welfare if governments are engaging in tax competition and choosing policies to maximize resident utility.

While numerous articles related to the Tiebout model have emphasized it as a constraint on the Leviathan governments, Fischel (2001) took a different, though not necessarily contrary, view. His contention is that homeowners in the local community are aware of how local policies affect their property values. Because of this, they seek to maximize these values through the local political process. It is possible that the relationship between the local government policies and the market power of localities is different when policies are dictated by homeowners than when Leviathan governments set policies and are constrained by the Tiebout market forces.

An Overview of the Imperfect-Competition Models

This chapter follows a literature that examines the impacts of imperfect competition among local governments on their policies. The "imperfection" is either a finite, inelastic number of jurisdictions, each of small size, or jurisdictions with a significant share of the regional population or land. In several papers, Hoyt (1991a, 1992, 1999) considered the implications of imperfect competition on both the level and mix of taxes. This work focuses on the relationship between the size or number of jurisdictions and the extent of capitalization of public services and taxes into property values. In a similar vein, Krelove (1993) and Henderson (1995) also examine how imperfect competition among governments affects the mix of taxes.

With imperfect competition, the objective of the municipal government becomes less clear—at least if it acts in the interest of its constituents. With imperfectly competitive governments, policies in one jurisdiction will affect the utility that households can obtain in other jurisdictions, since the policies can alter housing prices outside the jurisdiction as well as public services and tax rates. Three alternative constituencies can be affected differentially by local policies: absentee landowners not residing in the region; renters who own equal shares of land in all of the jurisdictions within the region; and resident-home-owners who, at least as modeled in Hoyt (1992, 1999), own land in a single jurisdiction but can reside in any of the jurisdictions within the region.

Absentee landowners would desire property-value maximization regardless of the relative size of the jurisdiction. With perfectly competitive jurisdictions and housing markets, in which taxes and services are completely capitalized, policy choices of a single jurisdiction do not affect other jurisdictions. With *incomplete* capitalization, however, aggregate changes in property values in the region do influence the income of renters (Krelove 1993). Thus, policies that increase property value in a single jurisdiction but reduce values in other jurisdictions do not increase utility for renters or those who own small amounts of land in all jurisdictions.

For homeowners, who own land in a single, specific jurisdiction, both the objectives and the appropriate model become even less clear. In a study examining the choice between property and land taxes, Henderson (1995) assumed that each household receives a share of land rent from the community in which it resides. However, that share of rent depends on the *endogenous* number of households in the community. In contrast, Hoyt (1991b) has each household receiving a share of rent in the community based on the *exogenous* (equilibrium) number of households in the community, which Henderson refers to as the *fixed shareholder* specification. The importance of this difference will be shown in the formal models in the next section.

Imperfect competition gives rise to interjurisdictional impacts on housing prices. The costs borne and benefits received by both residents and landowners from government policies now differ with the market share of the jurisdiction. Changes in policies in larger jurisdictions can cause residents to move in or out of the jurisdiction. As a result, housing prices in the regions must adjust to remain in equilibrium. Policies in a large jurisdiction may make it less desirable to live there. This leads to outflows of residents to the rest of the region, which raises housing prices there and reduces utility. Thus, the jurisdiction whose policies cause housing prices to change need not have as great a reduction in their own prices to enable residents there to obtain the same level of utility as obtained in the other jurisdictions in the region. That is to say, a large city can get away with inefficient policies because housing prices do not fully reflect the impact of those policies; some of the effects are reflected in *other* cities' housing prices. In general, then, imperfect competition moderates the impacts of the government policies on housing prices in the jurisdiction enacting the policy changes by increasing the impacts of these changes in housing prices in the rest of the region.

The moderation in the impacts of policies on housing prices means that increases in taxes in large cities bring about smaller decreases in property values there. By the same token, improvements in public services yield smaller increases in property values. Because of this, Hoyt (1999) argues that residents of large cities have less incentive to monitor taxes and services. Governments in larger cities can pass off more of their "inefficiency" as increases in property values in the rest of the region, and they thus face less stringent monitoring of their policies.

Next, we examine a simple model that generates differential capitalization of taxes and public services, depending on the jurisdiction's share of the market. Following this characterization of incomplete capitalization, we see how differences in capitalization yield differences in the choices of policies under alternative government objectives.

A Model of Incomplete Capitalization

To provide some context for the results found in this literature as well as to provide some additional results, a simple model of a metropolitan area with a single labor market is developed. (This follows, with slight modifications, Hoyt [1992].) Within the metropolitan area, assume that the N identical households (with N normalized to unity) can move among the J jurisdictions without cost. In addition their exogenous income ($\bar{y}$) is independent of the jurisdiction in which they choose to live.[1] Jurisdictions serve only as locations for homes and as providers of public services to their residents. Each jurisdiction j has land area L^j devoted exclusively to housing.

In addition to the exogenous labor income, each household obtains income from land rents. (Discussion of how this land rent is distributed is deferred for the moment.) Residents consume a private good (x), housing (h), and a publicly provided service (g). The private good, x, and the public service are each produced by one unit of capital income. Housing is produced using capital and land in a competitive industry. To keep the derivations and analysis relatively simple, assume that each household has the utility function, $U(x,h,g) = x + U^h(h) + U^g(g)$, with $U_h \equiv \frac{\partial U}{\partial h} > 0, U_{hh} \equiv \frac{\partial^2 U}{\partial h^2} < 0, U_g \equiv \frac{\partial U}{\partial g} > 0,$ and $U_g \equiv \frac{\partial^2 U}{\partial g^2} < 0.$[2] Letting p denote

---

[1] To fully close the model, the exogenous income should equal the value of the capital used to produce the three goods.

[2] The separable utility function that is linear in the private good makes the analysis simpler in two ways. First, the income elasticities for housing and the public service are zero, so increases in income,

the (net) price of a unit of housing and τ denote the ad valorem property tax on housing, let the indirect utility function for a resident of jurisdiction j be denoted by $V(y^j, p^j(1 + \tau^j), g^j)$.

Equilibrium Conditions

Although there are J jurisdictions in the region, it is convenient to reduce the number to two. One is a single jurisdiction (the central city) with a sizable share of the population and land in the region. The other is composed of a large number of suburbs. Since none of the jurisdictions in the suburban fringe have any sizable share of the region's population, they will, in equilibrium, all choose the same policies, and they can thus be treated as a single jurisdiction.

Costless mobility and identical incomes ensure that households will receive the same level of utility in the central city (jurisdiction 1) and the suburban fringe (jurisdiction 2) so that

$$V(p^1(1 + \tau^1), g^1) = V(p^2(1 + \tau^2), g^2). \tag{5.1}$$

In each type of jurisdiction the government budget constraints must be balanced:

$$\tau^j p^j h^j = g^j, j = 1, 2. \tag{5.2}$$

Clearing in the housing market requires interjurisdictional market clearing:

$$N^1 + N^2 = 1. \tag{5.3}$$

That is, the total population housed in the two types of regions equals the total population as well as intrajurisdictional market clearing:

$$N^j a(p^j) h\left(p^j(1 + \tau^j)\right) = L^j, j = 1, 2 \tag{5.4}$$

where $a(p^j)$ is land per unit of housing. Then, equation 5.4 is simply the condition that the demand for land in the jurisdiction equals the supply of land there.

Price Gradients with Market Power

Here, again following Hoyt (1992), we can contrast tax and public service capitalization in a jurisdiction with a sizable share of the market to capitalization in a jurisdiction that does not have a sizable share of the market. Rather than directly solving for the balanced-budget change in property values, we first examine the impacts of *independent* changes in the tax rate and public service

---

due to increases in the value of the household's endowment of land, do not affect the demand for housing. Second, this separability also means that the demand for housing is independent of the level of the public service.

in the central city. Consider first the impact of a change in the central city's tax rate on housing markets by differentiating equations 5.3 and 5.4 to find

$$N^2 \hat{p}_{\tau^1}^2 + N^1 \hat{p}_{\tau^1}^1 = -N^1 \frac{\varepsilon}{(\varepsilon + \theta)} \frac{1}{(1 + \tau^1)}. \tag{5.5a}$$

Differentiating equations 5.3 and 5.4 with respect to the central city's public service level gives

$$N^2 \hat{p}_{g^1}^2 + N^1 \hat{p}_{g^1}^1 = 0, \tag{5.5b}$$

where $\hat{p}_{\tau^i}^j \equiv \frac{dx}{x}$, the percentage change in the price of housing in jurisdiction j from the tax increase in jurisdiction i, with the change due to an increase in g_j analogously defined. The term $\varepsilon \equiv \frac{\partial h}{\partial p (1 + \tau)} \frac{p (1 + \tau)}{h}$ denotes the price elasticity of demand for housing; $\theta \equiv \frac{\partial a}{\partial p} \frac{p}{a}$, the price elasticity of land for housing; and $MRS^i \equiv \frac{\partial V^i}{\partial g^i}$. Equation 5.5a can be interpreted as stating that the population-weighted reduction in aggregate property values depends on the fraction of the population (or land) subject to the increase in the property tax. Equation 5.5b states that aggregate property values are unaffected by changes in the public services and only relative values change. To solve for the changes in property values as a result of the independent changes in the central city's tax policies, the equal utility condition, equation 5.1, is differentiated with respect to the central city's tax rate and used with equation 5.5a to obtain:

$$\hat{p}_{\tau^1}^1 = - \frac{N^2 p^1 h^1}{N^1 (1 + \tau^2) p^2 h^2 + N^2 (1 + \tau^1) p^1 h^1} -$$

$$\frac{N^1 p^2 h^2}{N^1 (1 + \tau^2) p^2 h^2 + N^2 (1 + \tau^1) p^1 h^1} \frac{\varepsilon}{(\varepsilon + \theta)} \frac{1}{(1 + \tau^1)}. \tag{5.6a}$$

Analogously, one can solve for the impact of a change in the central city's public services using equation 5.5b and differentiating equation 5.1 with respect to g^1 to obtain

$$\hat{p}_{g^1}^1 = - \frac{N^2 p^1 h^1}{N^1 (1 + \tau^2) p^2 h^2 + N^2 (1 + \tau^1) p^1 h^1} MRS^1. \tag{5.6b}$$

For cities of the suburban fringe, changes in policies are assumed to have no impact on the metropolitan-wide housing market. Determining the impacts of their policies involves only differentiating the equal utility condition, equation 5.1. Differentiating equation 5.1 with respect to τ^2 yields

$$\hat{p}_{\tau^1}^2 = - \frac{1}{(1 + \tau^2)} \tag{5.7a}$$

and differentiating equation 5.1 with respect to g^2 yields

$$\hat{p}^2_{g^2} = \frac{MRS^2}{\left(1 + \tau^2\right)h^2}. \tag{5.7b}$$

Figures 5.1 and 5.2 provide a graphical depiction of how the capitalization rates depend on the size or "market power" of the city. The four-quadrant diagram in figure 5.1 illustrates the equilibrium, with the northeast corner representing equilibrium in the housing market for the central city and the northwest corner representing the equal utility condition. The southwest corner gives the supply of housing (number of lots) in city 2 as a function of the price of housing there. The southeast corner translates N^2 into $1 - N^2$, which can be interpreted as the demand for lots in the central city. Figure 5.1 depicts an initial equilibrium (p^{1*}, N^{1*}, p^{2*}, N^{2*}) reflecting the initial taxes and public services (τ^{1*}, τ^{2*}, g^{1*}, g^{2*}), where it is assumed that $g^{1*} = g^{2*}$. Figure 5.2 illustrates an increase in the tax rate in the central city. This requires a shift in the equal utility condition of $dp^1 = -\dfrac{1}{\left(1 + \tau^{1*}\right)}d\tau^1$, which in turn shifts the housing supply curve. Then, as figure 5.2 shows, the decrease in price in the central city $p^{1*} - p^1$, is less than $\dfrac{1}{\left(1 + \tau^{1*}\right)}d\tau^1$, the shift in the equal utility condition, because, as the figure also shows, the price of housing in the suburban fringe increases as well.

Finally, the balanced budget impact of an increase in the central city's tax rate can be solved using equation 5.6 and differentiating the balanced-budget condition, equation 5.2. This gives

$$\hat{p}^1_1 = \frac{\left(1 - N^1\right)p^1h^1\left[MRS^1\left(1 + \dfrac{\tau^1}{\left(1 + \tau^1\right)}\varepsilon\right) - 1\right]}{\left[\left(1 - N^1\right)p^1h^1\left[1 - \tau^1\left[MRS^1(1 + \varepsilon) - 1\right]\right] + N^1p^2h^2\left[1 - \tau^2\left[MRS^2(1 + \varepsilon) - 1\right]\right]\right]}$$

(a)

$$- N^1\frac{\varepsilon}{\left(\varepsilon + \theta\right)}\frac{1}{\left(1 + \tau^1\right)} \times$$

$$\frac{p^2h^2\left[MRS^2\tau^2(1 + \varepsilon) - \left(1 + \tau^2\right)\right]}{\left[\left(1 - N^1\right)p^1h^1\left[1 - \tau^1\left[MRS^1(1 + \varepsilon) - 1\right]\right] + N^1p^2h^2\left[1 - \tau^2\left[MRS^2(1 + \varepsilon) - 1\right]\right]\right]}$$

(b)

$$\tag{5.8}$$

when we substitute $1 - N^1$ for N^2. Examination of equation 5.8 shows that we can view the impact on the price of housing as depending on two components. One

FIGURE 5.1   Equilibrium in the Housing Market

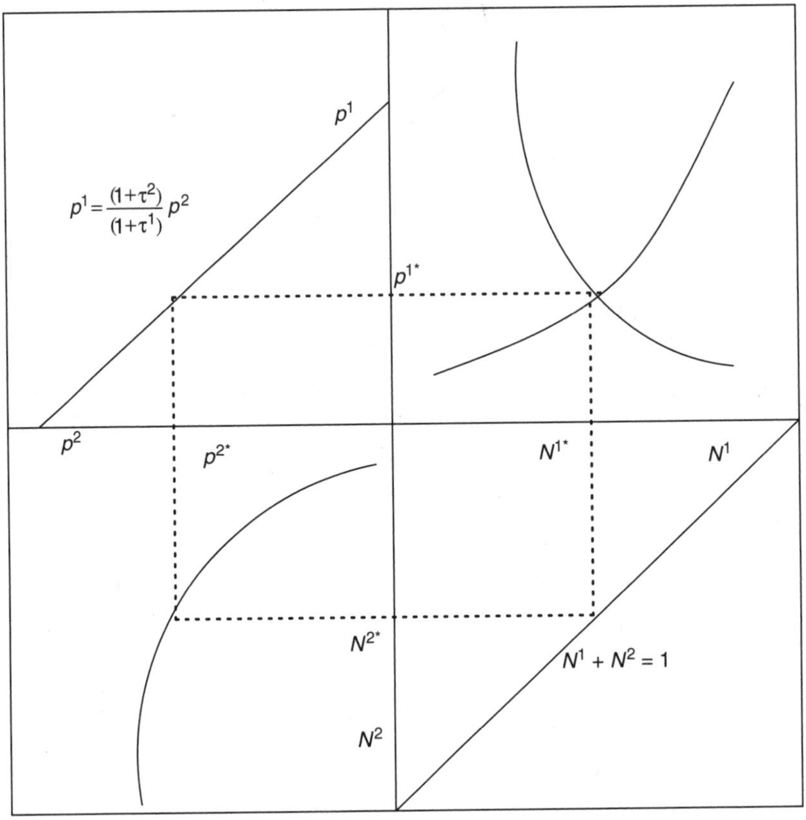

component decreases in importance as the market share of the jurisdiction increases the first term in equation 5.8, labeled (a). The other component increases the second term, (b). However, to understand the difference market share makes in the capitalization rate, it is helpful to evaluate $\hat{p}_1^1$ when both jurisdictions choose the same policies ($\tau^1 = \tau^2$, $g^1 = g^2$). In this case, equation 5.8 becomes

$$\hat{p}^1_{1_{\tau_1 = \tau_2 = \tau}} = \underbrace{\frac{\left(1 - N^1\right)\left[MRS\left(1 + \frac{\tau}{(1+\tau)}\varepsilon\right) - 1\right]}{\left[1 - \tau\left(MRS\left(1 + \varepsilon\right) - 1\right)\right]}}_{(a)} - \underbrace{N^1 \frac{\varepsilon}{(\varepsilon + \theta)} \frac{1}{(1 + \tau)}}_{(b)}. \quad (5.8')$$

Before discussing the price gradient for jurisdiction 1, we first determine the impact of a balanced-budget change in the tax policy for the suburban fringe.

Figure 5.2   A Change in the Tax Rate in the Central City

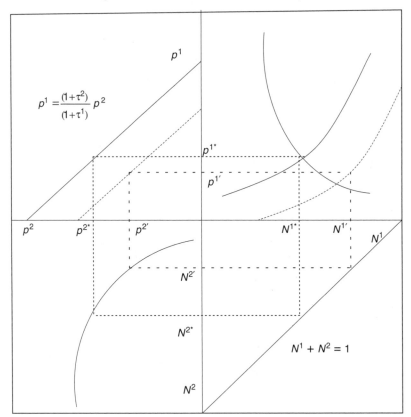

Then using equation 5.7 and, differentiating the budget constraint, equation 5.2, we obtain

$$\hat{p}_2^2 = \frac{\left[MRS^2 \left(1 + \dfrac{\tau^2}{\left(1+\tau^2\right)}\, \varepsilon \right) - 1 \right]}{\left[1 - \tau^2 \left(MRS^2 (1+\varepsilon) - 1 \right) \right]}. \tag{5.9}$$

Using equation 5.9, we can express equation 5.8 as

$$\hat{p}_1^1 \big|_{\tau_1 = \tau_2 = \tau} = \underbrace{\left(1 - N^1\right) \hat{p}_2^2 \big|_{\tau_1 = \tau_2 = \tau}}_{(a)} - \underbrace{N^1 \frac{\varepsilon}{(\varepsilon + \theta)} \frac{1}{(1+\tau)}}_{(b)}. \tag{5.10}$$

Then, for given policies, the difference in the price gradients for the central city and the suburban fringe depend on the market share of the central city (N^1) as well as the magnitude and sign of the gradient in the suburban fringe. We can also express this relationship by

$$\hat{p}^1_{1\,\tau_1=\,\tau_2=\,\tau} - \hat{p}^2_{1\,\tau_1=\,\tau_2=\,\tau} = \hat{p}^2_{2\,\tau_1=\,\tau_2=\,\tau} \tag{5.11}$$

To maintain equal utility across jurisdictions, the change in relative prices must equal $\hat{p}^2_{2\,\tau_1=\,\tau_2=\,\tau}$. For the competitive fringe, this reduction or increase in prices falls entirely on the jurisdiction imposing the tax. However, for a jurisdiction with market power, the change in prices is borne by both that jurisdiction and the fringe jurisdictions.

Policies with Property-Value Maximization

In Hoyt (1992), I demonstrated that in a metropolis consisting of a large city and a utility-taking competitive fringe, the central city should have lower tax rates. I demonstrated this result by considering the case in which all jurisdictions had the same tax rate (τ^*), with this tax rate maximizing property values for the competitive fringe—that is, $\hat{p}^2_{2\tau^2=\tau^*}=0$. Then from equation 5.10, it follows immediately that

$$\hat{p}^1_{1\,\tau_1=\,\tau_2=\,\tau^*} = -N^1 \frac{\varepsilon}{(\varepsilon+\theta)} \frac{1}{(1+\tau)} < 0 \tag{5.12}$$

so that the tax rate τ^* exceeds the property-value maximizing rate for the central city. With well-behaved reaction functions, the equilibrium must have $\tau^1 < \tau^2$. In addition to having lower tax rates, the central city will, in equilibrium, also have lower property values. The reasoning behind this result is simple. Any fringe jurisdiction could always have the same property value as the central city by merely choosing the same policy as the city, so the competitive fringe cannot have lower property values. However, the reverse is not true: The central city cannot replicate the outcome of the competitive fringe because its choices affect the metropolitan utility level.

Not discussed in Hoyt (1992) was the impact of the number of jurisdictions on tax rates (and property values) when there were identical jurisdictions. This situation would be similar to the analysis in Epple and Zelenitz (1981), with surplus maximization as the objective.[3] However, using equation 5.8, the price gradient with identical policies, and letting $N^1 = \frac{1}{J}$, we get

$$\hat{p}_\tau = \underbrace{\frac{\left(1-\frac{1}{J}\right)\left[MRS\left(1+\frac{\tau}{(1+\tau)}\varepsilon\right)-1\right]}{\left[1-\tau\left(MRS\left(1+\varepsilon\right)-1\right)\right]}}_{(a)} + \underbrace{\frac{-1}{J}\frac{\varepsilon}{(\varepsilon+\theta)}\frac{1}{(1+\tau)}}_{(b)}. \tag{5.13}$$

---

[3] In fact, an earlier version of Hoyt (1991a) used a model with explicit housing and land markets.

Since term (b) of equation 5.13 is negative, term (a) must be positive at the equilibrium tax rate τ^* when $\hat{p}_\tau = 0$. It is straightforward to determine the effect of an increase in the number of jurisdictions on equilibrium tax policies. By totally differentiating equation 5.13 with respect to the number of jurisdictions and evaluating at the equilibrium tax rate (where $\hat{p}_\tau = 0$), we find that $\frac{d\tau}{dJ} > 0$. Thus, the tax rate increases as the number of jurisdictions increases. While smaller jurisdictions in metropolitan areas should have higher property tax rates and property values than larger jurisdictions in those same areas, with equally sized jurisdictions, smaller jurisdictions and higher property tax rates will mean lower property values.

Policies with Utility Maximization

Modeling Homeownership

As discussed previously, imperfect competition and incomplete capitalization mean that maximizing the utility of the resident-landowner is not necessarily property-value maximizing. Two different views of the modeling of homeownership are the "corporate share" view of Henderson (1995) with endogenous land shares and the "fixed share" view of Hoyt (1991b, 1992, 1999) with exogenous land shares. These lead to distinctly different implications for local tax and service policies. Income in jurisdiction j with the corporate view of rents is $y_j = \bar{y} + \frac{r^j L^j}{N^j} = \bar{y} + r^j l^j$, where $\bar{y}$ is exogenous (labor) income; r^j is land rent; L^j is total land in the jurisdiction; and N^j is the population. In the *fixed shareholder* equation, $y_j = \bar{y} + \frac{r^j \bar{L}}{\bar{N}^j} = \bar{y} + r^j \bar{l}^j$, where $\bar{x}$ refers to an exogenous value for variable x, and l^j is land per resident.

One difficulty in trying to model homeownership is the dynamic aspect of property-value appreciation and ownership. To understand the approach in Hoyt (1991b, 1992, 1999), consider the impact of a change in the price of housing or, equivalently, land rent, on utility. As each household has the same share of land as they consume ($\bar{l} = a_l h$) in the jurisdiction in which they reside, utility of the resident-household is only affected by changes in taxes as a result of appreciation and the direct consumption of service g. Thus, their utility is unaffected by the appreciation or depreciation of their land in jurisdiction j as long as they continue to reside there, with the exception of its impact on their taxes. If the household chooses to move to jurisdiction 2, their utility there is affected by the policies in jurisdiction 1 as well. In this case, sale of their land changes their income, but in addition it will affect the cost of purchasing more land in jurisdiction 2. While the impact on the value of land that they own in their current jurisdiction affects the household's choice of policy, the interjurisdictional impacts on land rents mean that maximizing the value of current land ownership will not be utility-maximizing for households owning land in large jurisdictions.

In addition to having an endogenous allotment of land for each household that is a function of the number of residents in the jurisdiction, the equal utility condition in Henderson (1995) differs from that used by Hoyt as well. In Henderson (1995), the equal utility requirement is

$$V\left(\bar{y} + r^1 l^1, p^1(1 + \tau^1), g^1\right) \geq V\left(\bar{y} + r^2 l^2, p^2(1 + \tau^2), g^2\right). \tag{5.14}$$

In this view, the household purchases the land using exogenous income in each jurisdiction and receives a return (rent) based on it. This difference in the equal utility condition results in an additional impact on utility: additional income from purchases of additional shares of land. As discussed in Hoyt (1991b, 1992, 1999), if the household chooses not to move and land holdings equal land consumption ($\bar{l} = a_l h$), utility is only affected by changes in taxes associated with appreciation or depreciation of land holdings and changes in the public service level. In the present model, the additional impact on utility from changes in land holdings could increase or decrease utility. In Hoyt's modeling, the equal utility condition compares an individual with the same endowment of land— that is, an endowment of land in a single jurisdiction. For purposes of deriving price gradients, it could be an endowment in jurisdiction 1, the jurisdiction enacting the policy, or in jurisdiction 2, one of the other jurisdictions. In Henderson's model, the equal utility condition compares two different incomes, reflecting two different land holdings. An interpretation of Hoyt's rule is that utility in jurisdiction 2 for a household having land in jurisdiction 1 is based on the exogenous income and capital gain or loss associated with changes in the policies in jurisdiction 1. This is the income the household now has to purchase housing in jurisdiction 2. In Henderson's equation only the change in price and the increase or decrease in land purchases affect utility. The equal utility condition is not for the same individual holding land in a single jurisdiction but two individuals who have different land holdings.

The alternative modeling of income will yield different forms for the price gradients. In the limiting case of a single jurisdiction, both approaches give the same price change. This is because it depends only on the equilibrium in the housing market and not on the equal utility condition. For the other limiting case of competitive jurisdictions, ($N^1 = 1$ and $N^2 = 0$), the gradients are different. In the equation used by Hoyt, this limiting case yields the full capitalization result of no change in the gross price of housing $\left(d\left[p(1 + \tau)\right] = 0\right)$. In Henderson's model, however, full capitalization is not obtained. In fact, for plausible parameter values as well as the share of land in housing, it appears as if the price gradient may be positive, not negative.

Utility Maximizing Policies with Asymmetric Jurisdictions
As the preceding discussion suggests, conclusions about the policy choices made by governments maximizing the utility of resident-homeowners will

depend critically on how home ownership is modeled. Here we review the results obtained in Hoyt (1992), which assume exogenous land endowments.

A relatively simple way to see that the central city will not set the same policies as the competitive fringe is to work through the case with property-value maximization. This will consider the impact that a balanced-budget change in policy will have on the utility of the central-city household when the city sets its policies the same as the jurisdictions in the competitive fringe. Then the competitive fringe sets its policies so that $\hat{p}_2^2 = 0$. From equation 5.10, we find that this means that $\hat{p}_1^1 < 0$ and from equation 5.11 that $\hat{p}_1^1 = \hat{p}_1^2$. Then we can consider in jurisdiction 2 the change in the utility received by a landowner in jurisdiction 1:

$$\frac{dV_1^2}{d\tau_1} = ph\hat{p}_1^1 + \frac{\partial V^2}{\partial p(1+\tau)}(1+\tau)\,\hat{p}_1^2 = -\,\tau ph\hat{p}_1^1 > 0. \tag{5.15}$$

The loss in utility from the decrease in income due to a decrease in land rents $\left(ph\hat{p}_1^1\right)$ is more than offset by the gain in utility from the reduction in housing costs $ph(1+\tau)\,\hat{p}_1^2$. As in the case with property-value maximization with well-behaved reaction functions equilibrium must have $\tau^1 > \tau^2$.

From equation 5.15, it is interesting to note that in the absence of ad valorem property taxes and additional tax cost created by appreciation, maximizing property value would maximize utility. It is also worth noting that central city and suburban interests are aligned. Increases in the central city's tax rate above the property-value maximizing level benefit the resident-landowners in the central city, and they also cause the properties of landowners in other jurisdictions to appreciate.

As with the case of property-value maximization, Hoyt (1992) did not consider how the number of identical jurisdictions affected policies when governments maximized the utility of resident-landowners. However, from our analysis of the case for property-value maximization, we know that $\left.\frac{d\hat{p}_1^1}{dJ}\right|_{\tau^1=\tau^2=\tau^*} = \left.\frac{d\hat{p}_1^2}{dJ}\right|_{\tau^1=\tau^2=\tau^*} > 0.$ Then, given that utility is increasing in the tax rate as shown in equation 5.15, it follows that increases in the number of jurisdictions will reduce the property tax rate.

Leviathan Policies

Here we consider a third potential objective of governments: "surplus" maximization, which follows Epple and Zelenitz (1981) and Brennan and Buchanan (1980). Surplus is defined as the difference between revenues collected by the jurisdiction and the actual or true cost of providing the public services, $n(\tau ph - g)$. As discussed earlier, Epple and Zelenitz demonstrate that having more jurisdictions will reduce this surplus, but it will not be eliminated as long as positive land rents exist. The rents exist because of binding constraints on available land. For purposes of numerical examples in the next section, we essentially repeat the analysis done by Epple and Zelenitz. Consistent with our analysis of the property-value and utility maximizing policies, we also consider the case of an asymmetric equilibrium with a single jurisdiction with market power and a competitive fringe.[4]

Because the budget constraint is not binding in this case, it is necessary to determine price gradients with respect to the property tax and public services separately. With the objective of the government to maximize surplus, $N^1(\tau^1 p^1 h^1 - g^1)$, the first-order condition for the property tax can be expressed by

$$S^1_{\tau^1} = \hat{N}^1_{\tau^1}\left(\tau^1 p^1 h^1 - g^1\right) + p^1 h^1\left[1 + \tau^1\left((1+\varepsilon)\,\hat{p}^1_{\tau^1} + \varepsilon\,\frac{1}{(1+\tau^1)}\right)\right] = 0 \qquad (5.16a)$$

and the first-order condition for the public service is given by

$$S^1_{g^1} = \hat{N}^1_{g^1}\left(\tau^1 p^1 h^1 - g^1\right) + p^1 h^1\left(1 + \tau^1(1+\varepsilon)\,\hat{p}^1_{\tau^1}\right) - 1 = 0. \qquad (5.16b)$$

When the jurisdiction becomes small ($N^1 \to 0$), then $\hat{p}^1_{\tau^1} \to -\dfrac{1}{(1+\tau^1)}$ and $\hat{N}^1_{\tau^1} \to \dfrac{\theta}{(1+\tau^1)}$. Making these substitutions in equation 5.16 gives

$$\left(\tau^1 p^1 h^1 - g^1\right) = -\frac{p^1 h^1}{\theta} > 0. \qquad (5.17)$$

As Hoyt (1990) shows, θ, the price elasticity of demand for land, is equal to $\theta = \left(\dfrac{\partial l}{\partial r}\dfrac{r}{l}\right)\left(\dfrac{p}{rl}\right) = \dfrac{\eta}{\omega_l}$, where η is the elasticity of land (per unit of housing) with respect to land rent and ω_l is the share of land in the price of housing. Thus, the surplus that can be extracted is the share of land in housing divided by the price elasticity of land. If, for example, the elasticity of land is unity, surplus per resident is equal to land value ωph per home. If the demand for land is inelastic, the surplus will actually exceed the share of land in housing.

How Much Could Market Power Matter?

The case has been made in papers discussed earlier that size (market share) of jurisdictions may qualitatively affect their policies. Little has been done, however, to determine the *quantitative* differences in policies as a result of the size or number of jurisdictions within a market. This section offers some indication of the difference market share might make in determining municipal policies. Following the framework in the preceding section, we now consider three alternative government objectives: property-value maximization, utility maximization, and surplus maximization (Leviathan). For each of these three objectives,

---

[4] Epple and Zelenitz (1981) discuss asymmetric jurisdictions and heterogeneous population but do not provide any analysis of this case.

FIGURE 5.3   Market Share and Capitalization

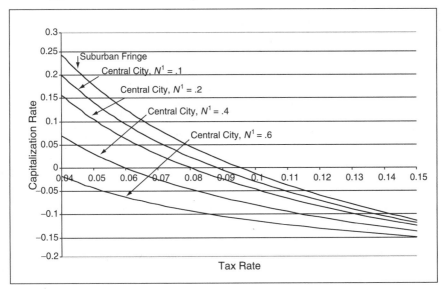

the results for the case of a single large jurisdiction and a competitive fringe, as well as the case for identically sized jurisdictions, are stated.

To abstract from concerns about income effects and to simplify programming, the utility function used is $U(x,h,g) = x + \alpha_h \ln(h) + \alpha_g \ln(g)$ with an income of $Y = 100$, $\alpha_h = 30$, and $\alpha_g = 10$. This means that the budget share of housing is 30 percent and that of public service is 10 percent. The demand for housing is $h(p(1 + \tau)) = \dfrac{\alpha_h}{p(1 + \tau)}$, making the price elasticity, $\varepsilon = -1$. The housing production function is Cobb-Douglas with $h = l^\beta k^{1-\beta}$, where we use $\beta = .25$, making $\theta = -4$.

Figure 5.3 illustrates the difference between the price gradients for the suburban fringe and for the central city, assuming alternative shares of population for the central city. As the figure illustrates, the greater the market share of the jurisdiction, the lower (less positive or more negative) the change in price. From equation 5.11, it follows that the vertical distance between the line for suburban fringe and that of the central city gives the increase in price in the suburban fringe as a result of the tax increase in the central city.

The Impact of Market Power on Tax Policy
Figure 5.4 illustrates the relationship between the tax rate set in the central city and the share of the population the city has when the government is either maximizing property value or utility. In these cases, the remainder of the metropolitan area, the suburban fringe, is setting policies as though they have no sizeable share of the population, with their price gradients described by

FIGURE 5.4   Tax Rates and Market Share

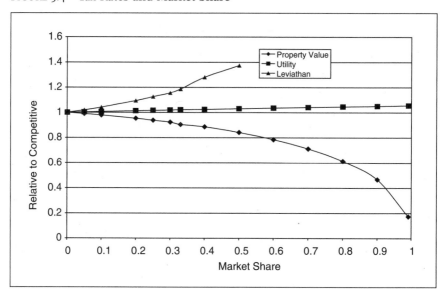

equation 5.6. For the Leviathan case we examine how the tax rate varies with the number of identical jurisdictions. For utility and property-value maximization, the results are similar to those reported here.

Property-Value Maximization
As figure 5.4 shows, in the case of property-value maximization, the tax rate in the central city decreases appreciably as the market share of the central city increases. A jurisdiction having 50 percent of the population of the metropolitan area will have a tax rate on the order of 15 percent lower than found in the competitive fringe, and with 80 percent of the population, a tax rate that is 40 percent lower than in the competitive fringe.[5]

Utility Maximization
As figure 5.4 shows, the impacts on the tax policy are much less pronounced than they are with property-value maximization. The tax rates in the central city are on the order of 3 percent higher than the rate in the competitive fringe for a central city with 50 percent of the population and 5 percent higher if the central city composed the entire metropolitan area.

---

[5] In fact, the market share figure is actually the percentage of land in the central city. But not surprisingly, this is close to the percentage of the metropolitan population in the central city.

TABLE 5.1

Tax Rates and Surplus with Leviathan Governments

Number of Jurisdictions	1,000	20	10	5	4	3	2
Market Share	.1%	5%	10%	20%	25%	33.3%	50%
Tax Rate	.667	.680	.694	.729	.750	.792	.917
Surplus as Percent of Tax Revenue	37.5%	38.7%	40.0%	42.9%	44.4%	47.4%	54.5%

Leviathan Policies

Here we follow Epple and Zelenitz (1981) and focus on the case with identical jurisdictions, not the case of a central city and the competitive fringe. With Leviathan or surplus-maximizing governments, the tax rate increases at a much faster rate than in the case of utility maximization: by 50 percent in the competitive case when there are two jurisdictions. While not shown in the figure, public service levels decrease by 10 percent. With substantial increases in the tax rate and reductions in public services, the Leviathan "surplus"—the difference between tax revenues and the cost of actually providing the public service—increases even more dramatically.

While it is useful to consider the relative changes in policies as market share increases for the Leviathan case, examination of the absolute levels offers some additional insights. Table 5.1 lists the relationship among the number of jurisdictions (or, equivalently, market share), the actual tax rate, and the surplus as a percentage of tax revenue. For perspective, the tax rate for the competitive jurisdiction maximizing property value is .333. Then, even with competitive jurisdictions, the tax rate with Leviathan governments is twice that which would be obtained with property-value maximizing governments.

The Impact of Market Power on Property Values

Figure 5.5 summarizes the changes in property values and market share for the three preceding cases. There is little change in property value with utility-maximizing governments as market share increases. With property-value maximizing governments, values increase modestly until the city has 50 percent or more of the market share, after which values grow considerably. Property values under Leviathan governments decrease steadily from even low levels of market power. Leviathan government is clearly worse for property owners.

An Empirical Examination of the Influence of City Share on Expenditures

With the exceptions discussed earlier, the impact of the number of municipalities within a metropolitan area on public service provision and tax rates has

FIGURE 5.5   Property Values and Market Share

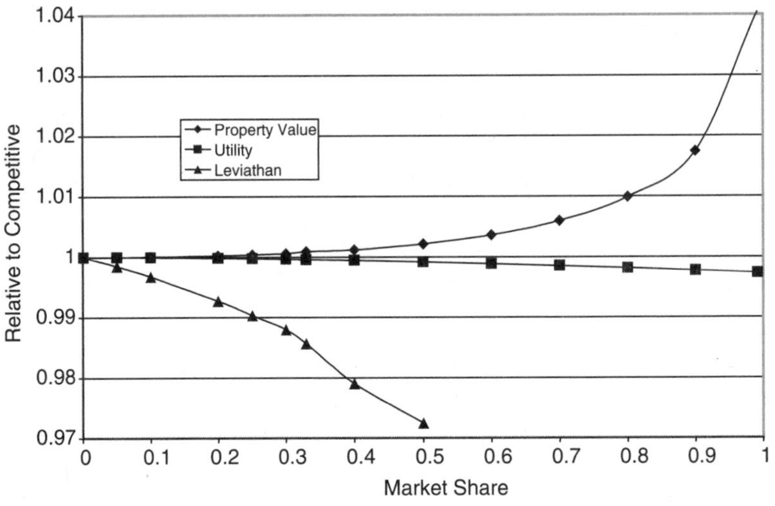

primarily been the focus of theoretical studies. This section tests the theory developed in the previous sections. Using a sample of metropolitan municipalities in 2002, we can examine the relationship between municipal expenditures[6] and the jurisdiction's share of the MSA's population. The sample is limited to MSAs having from 1 to 16 municipalities. Since we have a cross section of MSAs, separate identification of the impacts of population versus market share is possible. As tables 5.2A and B indicate, some of the cities with the greatest shares of metropolitan population are often relatively small in terms of absolute population, as they are frequently found in small MSAs. In table 5.3, we list the share of population in the single largest city for the fifteen largest MSAs in 2002. As the table shows, there is a great deal of variation in the market share of the central cities of these large MSAs. The Boston, Washington, and Miami MSAs have less than 10 percent of their population residing in the central city, while the MSAs of New York, Houston, and Phoenix have over 35 percent of their population residing in the central city. The number of municipalities in the MSA is also included as an explanatory variable to determine if this has an influence on expenditures beyond the influence of the market share of the municipality.

---

[6] Alternatively a measure of tax burden could be used. Municipal taxes per capita was also tried with qualitatively similar results.

TABLE 5.2A

The 10 MSAs with the Largest Share of Population in a Single City

MSA	City	City's Share of Population	City Population	MSA Population
Anchorage, AK	Anchorage, AK	100.0	257,808	257,808
Laredo, TX	Laredo, TX	94.8	183,160	193,180
Lincoln, NE	Lincoln, NE	90.9	215,928	237,657
Abilene, TX	Abilene, TX	88.2	108,024	122,478
El Paso, TX	El Paso, TX	87.3	612,770	701,908
San Angelo, TX	San Angelo, TX	86.3	88,244	102,300
Lubbock, TX	Lubbock, TX	83.4	190,002	227,890
Amarillo, TX	Amarillo, TX	82.4	171,959	208,691
Lawrence, KS	Lawrence, KS	80.2	78,911	98,343
Enid, OK	Enid, OK	79.4	45,196	56,954

The dependent variable in all estimates is current expenditures per capita. Explanatory variables are population, the number of municipalities in the MSA, and the share of the population. Other control variables are state and federal aid (per capita), median household income, the poverty rate, and other demographic measures intended to reflect characteristics that might affect both demand and costs of public services. Data on expenditures and intergovernmental aid as well as the population are for 2002. Data on demographic characteristics are for 2000. Summary statistics are found in table 5.4.

Results from OLS estimation are found in table 5.5. The coefficients of interest are those for population, the number of municipalities, and the share measures. In equation 5.1, which includes only *Population* and *Cities* (the number of municipalities in the MSA), the coefficients are positive and significant. In equation 5.2, in which we add *City Share*, the coefficients on *Population* and *Cities* remain positive and significant, while the coefficient on *City Share* is negative but insignificant. Equations 5.3–5.5 have quadratic specifications for *Population*, *Cities*, and *City Share*. Equation 5.4 includes measures of federal and state aid. Equation 5.5 includes the foregoing variables as well as sociodemographic variables that might affect expenditure levels. When we include quadratic terms, none of the coefficients on *Population*, *Cities*, or *City Share* — with the exception of the coefficient on *Cities* in equation 5.4 — are significant.

Because of concerns regarding the endogeneity of population and the city's share of the population as well as the endogeneity of federal and state aid, equa-

TABLE 5.2B

The 10 MSAs with the Smallest Share of Population in a Single City

MSA	City	City's Share of Population	City Population	MSA Population
Punta Gorda, FL	Punta Gorda, FL	10.0	13,711	136,992
Miami–Fort Lauderdale, FL	Miami, FL	9.9	369,253	3,711,102
Boston-Worcester-Lawrence, MA-NH-ME-CT	Boston, MA	9.8	555,249	5,667,225
Naples, FL	Naples, FL	9.5	19,604	207,029
Sarasota-Bradenton, FL	Sarasota, FL	9.2	50,763	550,077
Harrisburg-Lebanon-Carlisle, PA	Harrisburg, PA	7.9	48,619	618,375
Benton Harbor, MI	Benton Harbor, MI	7.3	11,719	159,709
Washington-Baltimore, DC-MD-VA-WV	Washington, DC	7.1	519,000	7,359,044
West Palm Beach–Boca Raton, FL	Boca Raton, FL	7.0	72,967	1,049,420
Greenville-Spartanburg-Anderson, SC	Greenville, SC	6.1	56,873	929,565

tions 5.3–5.5 are estimated using an instrumental variables approach. Instruments for population and the city's share of population (as well as the quadratic terms) are the land area of the city, the number of housing units in the city, the share of metropolitan land in the city, and the share of the metropolitan housing stock in the city. Instruments for the aid measures are the state median income, poverty rate, and political composition (party of governor, percentage of lower and upper house who are Democrats). Results from this estimation are found in table 5.6. The coefficients on the population, the number of municipalities, and share measures again are not significant, though the signs and magnitude of the coefficients on these variables in some cases are very different from the OLS results, particularly the coefficient on *Population* and that on *Cities*. As in OLS, however, these effects are not generally significant.

TABLE 5.3

The Share of Population in a Single City for 15 Largest MSA/CMSAs

MSA	City	City's Share of Population	City Population	MSA Population
New York–Northern NJ-LI, NY-NJ-CT-PA	New York, NY	36.8	7,428,162	20,196,649
Los Angeles–Riverside–Orange County, CA	Los Angeles, CA	22.7	3,633,591	16,036,587
Chicago-Gary-Kenosha, IL-IN-WI	Chicago, IL	31.5	2,799,050	8,885,919
Washington-Baltimore, DC-MD-VA-WV	Washington, DC	7.1	519,000	7,359,044
San Francisco–Oakland–San Jose, CA	San Jose, CA	12.6	867,675	6,873,645
Philadelphia-Wilm.–Atl. City, PA-NJ-DE-MD	Philadelphia, PA	23.6	1,417,601	5,999,034
Boston-Worcester-Lawrence, MA-NH-ME-CT	Boston, MA	9.8	555,249	5,667,225
Detroit–Ann Arbor–Flint, MI	Detroit, MI	17.6	965,084	5,469,312
Dallas–Fort Worth, TX	Dallas, TX	21.9	1,076,214	4,909,523
Houston-Galveston-Brazoria, TX	Houston, TX	41.1	1,845,967	4,493,741
Atlanta, GA	Atlanta, GA	10.4	401,726	3,857,097
Miami–Fort Lauderdale, FL	Miami, FL	9.9	369,253	3,711,102
Seattle-Tacoma-Bremerton, WA	Seattle, WA	15.5	537,150	3,465,760
Phoenix-Mesa, AZ	Phoenix, AZ	40.2	1,211,466	3,013,696
Cleveland-Akron, OH	Cleveland, OH	17.2	501,662	2,910,616

Because of the quadratic specification for *Population, Cities,* and *City Share,* it is difficult to directly interpret the coefficients. In addition, the marginal impact of both variables on expenditures and the statistical significance of this impact will vary with the magnitude of the variable. Table 5.7 reports the marginal impact of increase in population (1,000), the share of the population,

TABLE 5.4

Summary Statistics

Variable	Mean	Standard Error	Description
Expenditures	659	596	Current Municipal Expenditures per Capita
Population	339	1006	Population, 1,000s
City Share	21.7	21.5	Municipal Share of MSA Population
Cities	4.57	4.96	Number of Cities and Towns in MSA
Federal Aid	40.8	102.0	Federal Intergovernmental Aid per Capita
State Aid	185	319	State Intergovernmental Aid per Capita
Income	36,894	9239	Median Household Income (2000)
Urban	0.986	0.0287	Fraction of Population, Urban
African American	0.170	0.1778	Fraction of Population, African American
Native American	0.007	0.0099	Fraction of Population, Native American
Other Minority	0.035	0.0562	Fraction of Population, Other Minority
Hispanic	0.132	0.1612	Fraction of Population, Hispanic
Children	0.308	0.0675	Fraction of Household with Children < 18
Female Headed	0.088	0.0310	Fraction of Households with Children, No Adult Male Present
Over 65	0.133	0.0451	Fraction of Population > 65
Poverty	0.122	0.0529	Fraction of Households in Poverty

and the number of municipalities using the coefficients from the OLS estimation. Table 5.8 contains the marginal impacts using the IV results. For all equations with both OLS and IV estimation, increases in population have almost no impact on costs.

The impact of the city's share of MSA population seems to be influenced by the city's (relative) size for the OLS results. While results are mixed, they sug-

TABLE 5.5

OLS Results for Current per Capita Expenditures

	(1)	(2)	(3)	(4)	(5)
Population	0.067	0.075	0.026	0.01	−0.036
	(2.32)*	(2.53)*	(−0.33)	(−0.29)	(−1.01)
Population Squared			3.32E-06	6.51E-07	3.14E-06
			(−0.61)	(−0.26)	(−1.28)
Cities	34.523	29.894	40.471	−34.371	−17.764
	(5.89)**	(4.21)**	(−0.99)	(−1.84)	(−0.95)
Cities Squared			−0.382	1.97	0.786
			(−0.18)	(2.00)*	(−0.8)
City Share		−1.872	2.237	−0.936	0.418
		(−1.15)	(−0.4)	(−0.37)	(−0.17)
City Share Squared			−0.049	−0.018	−0.022
			(−0.78)	(−0.62)	(−0.81)
Federal Aid				2.233	2.116
				(16.82)**	(16.53)**
State Aid				1.37	1.45
				(30.70)**	(31.53)**
Income					0.011
					(81)**
Urban					−384.378
					(−0.86)
African American					288.69
					(2.05)*
Native American					−558.159
					(−0.42)
Other Minority					−114.98
					(−0.41)
Hispanic					−21.952
					(−0.17)
Children					−772.537
					(2.37)*
Female Headed					−3672.08
					(34)**

Continued

TABLE 5.5—Cont'd

OLS Results for Current per Capita Expenditures

	(1)	(2)	(3)	(4)	(5)
Over 65					−187.25
					(−0.54)
Poverty					2047.137
					(2.99)**
Observations	391	391	391	391	391
R-squared	0.11	0.11	0.11	0.82	0.85

Absolute value of *t* statistics in parentheses
*significant at 5%
**significant at 1%

TABLE 5.6

Instrumental Variable Results for Current per Capita Expenditures

	(4)	(5)	(6)
Population	0.7917	−0.1486	−0.2787
	(0.93)	(−0.76)	(−1.47)
Population Squared	−0.000058	.0000109	.00002
	(−1.45)	(0.78)	(1.46)
Cities	−95.576	26.0979	72.7846
	(−0.40)	(0.75)	(1.68)
Cities Squared	7.0653	−0.7805	−3.8002
	(0.62)	(−0.43)	(−1.71)
City Share	16.0039	3.9144	2.6348
	(0.44)	(0.61)	(0.30)
City Share Squared	−0.3905	−0.01307	0.0498
	(−0.88)	(−0.11)	(0.38)
Federal Aid		3.1591	2.4956
		(1.85)	(1.79)
State Aid		1.2372	1.3884
		(8.69)**	(10.03)**
Income			0.0134
			(3.87)**
Urban			−93.0862
			(−0.17)

Table 5.6—Cont'd

Instrumental Variable Results for Current per Capita Expenditures

	(4)	(5)	(6)
African American			226.0482
			(1.38)
Native American			−1938.342
			(−1.13)
Other Minority			174.8177
			(0.51)
Hispanic			−49.0709
			(−0.25)
Children			−1049.364
			(−1.74)
Female Headed			−3318.778
			(−1.83)
Over 65			83.06561
			(0.24)
Poverty			2618.315
			(2.53)**
Observations	391	391	391
R-squared	—	0.76	0.79

Absolute value of t statistics in parentheses
*significant at 5%
**significant at 1%

gest that when a city's share of the population is greater than 50 percent of the MSA population, an increase in market share of 1 percent will decrease per capita expenditures in a range from −1.6 to −3.8. Using the mean per capita expenditures of $659, this converts to an elasticity approximately ranging from −.12 to −.29 for a city with a population share of 50 percent and −.18 to −.43 for a city with a population share of 75 percent. For the IV results, there seems to be no significant impact of the population share.

The results for the number of cities are also mixed and sensitive to both the specification of the equation and the number of cities in the MSA. With fewer municipalities in the MSA, it appears that increases in the number of municipalities will decrease expenditures, though these results are not significant. As the number of municipalities in the MSA grows, additional municipalities may actually lead to increased expenditures, though this result is only significant in two equations.

TABLE 5.7

Marginal Impacts of Population, Market Share, and Number of Cities, OLS Results

		(3)	(4)	(5)
Population				
	50	0.02635	0.01048	−0.03611
	100	0.02668	0.01055	−0.03579
	200	0.02734	0.01068	−0.03516
	500	0.02933	0.01107	−0.03328
	1,000	0.03265	0.01172	−0.03014
Market Share				
	10	1.25	−1.29	−0.03
	25	−0.22	−1.82	−0.70
	50	−2.68	−2.70***	−1.83*
	75	−5.14	−3.58*	−2.95
Number of Cities				
	2	38.94	−26.49*	−14.62
	5	36.65*	−14.67	−9.90
	10	32.82***	5.04	−2.04
	15	29.00	24.74**	5.83

*significant at 10%
**significant at 5%
***significant at 1%

Conclusion

While much of the literature following Tiebout (1956) has been focused on considering the hypothesis in its most favorable setting, in which numerous jurisdictional choices are available to households, few metropolitan areas seem to satisfy these conditions. There are several extensions to the small amount of literature that considers the Tiebout hypothesis in a setting with imperfect competition, in which there are a finite number of jurisdictions, some of which may be substantially larger than others. Jurisdictional size will affect how local government policies are capitalized into housing prices and, depending on the objective of local governments, the level of government services.

This study has examined predictions about jurisdictional size, market share, and government expenditures for three government objectives: utility maximization, property-value maximization, and surplus maximization.

TABLE 5.8

Marginal Impacts of Population, Market Share, and Number of Cities, IV Results

		(4)	(5)	(6)
Population				
	50	0.789	−0.148	−0.278
	100	0.786	−0.148	−0.277
	200	0.780	−0.146	−0.275
	500	0.763	−0.143	−0.269
	1,000	0.735	−0.138	−0.259
Market Share				
	10	12.099	3.784	7.620
	25	6.241	3.588	15.097
	50	−3.522	3.261	27.559
	75	−13.285	2.934	40.021
Number of Cities				
	2	−81.446	24.537	65.184*
	5	−60.250	22.195	53.784*
	10	−24.923**	18.292*	34.783
	15	10.404	14.390	15.782*

*significant at 10%
**significant at 5%
***significant at 1%

To provide stronger predictions of the potential impact of the number of jurisdictions on government policies and housing prices, several numerical examples were offered. The simulations suggest strong impacts of market share on both property values and government policies when governments maximize either property value or surplus. For utility maximization, the relationship is much weaker. These simulations also indicate that the policies chosen by a jurisdiction are primarily influenced by its share of the market; the share of the market held by alternative jurisdictions has little influence on its policies. This is in stark contrast to the results for property-value maximization, where housing prices in a jurisdiction are apt to be strongly influenced by the existence of a neighboring jurisdiction with significant market share.

The last section was an empirical examination of the relationship between market share and government expenditures and the relationship between government expenditures and the number of jurisdictions. The empirical work focused on the expenditures of individual government units, in contrast to earlier studies' use of aggregate or average expenditures within a metropolitan area. The empirical findings are consistent with our expectation that the policies of the suburban fringe are not significantly affected by how much market power a central city might have. My findings suggest little relationship between government expenditures and the population of a jurisdiction, the number of jurisdictions in the MSA, or the fraction of the MSA population in it. The evidence suggests a slightly negative relationship between market share and government expenditures. These results do not support the view that governments are attempting to maximize either surplus or property values.

References

Barrow, Lisa, and Cecilia Elena Rouse. 2004. Using market valuation to assess public school spending. *Journal of Public Economics* 88:1747–1769.

Bates, Laurie J., and Rexford E. Santerre. 2003. The impact of a state mandated expenditure floor on aggregate property values. *Journal of Urban Economics* 53:531–540.

Bewley, Truman F. 1981. A critique of Tiebout's theory of local public expenditures. *Econometrica* 49:713–740.

Brennan, Geoffrey, and James M. Buchanan. 1980. *The power to tax.* London: Cambridge University Press.

Brueckner, Jan. 1979. Property values, local public expenditure, and economic efficiency. *Journal of Public Economics* 11:223–245.

———. 1982. A test for allocative efficiency in the local public sector. *Journal of Public Economics* 19:311–331.

Edel, Matthew, and Elliott Sclar. 1974. Taxes, spending, and property values: Supply adjustment in a Tiebout model. *Journal of Political Economy* 82:941–954.

Epple, Dennis, and Alan Zelenitz. 1981. The implications of competition among jurisdictions: Does Tiebout need politics? *Journal of Political Economy* 89:1197–1217.

Epple, Dennis, Alan Zelenitz, and Michael Visscher. 1978. A search for testable implications of the Tiebout hypothesis. *Journal of Political Economy* 86:405–425.

Fischel, William A. 2001. *The homevoter hypothesis.* Cambridge, MA: Harvard University Press.

Forbes, Kevin F., and Ernest M. Zampelli. 1989. Is Leviathan a mythical beast? *American Economic Review* 79:568–576.

Hamilton, Bruce. 1976. The effects of property taxes and local public spending on property values: A theoretical comment. *Journal of Political Economy* 84:647–650.

Henderson, J. Vernon. 1995. Will homeowners impose property taxes? *Regional Science and Urban Economics* 25:153–181.

Hoxby, Caroline. 2000. Does competition among public schools benefit students and taxpayers? *American Economic Review* 90:1209–1238.

Hoyt, William H. 1990. Local government inefficiency and the Tiebout hypothesis: Does competition among municipalities limit local government inefficiency? *Southern Economic Journal* 57:481–496.

———. 1991a. Property taxation, Nash equilibrium, and market power. *Journal of Urban Economics* 30:123–131.

————. 1991b. Competitive jurisdictions, congestion, and the Henry George theorem: When should property be taxed instead of land? *Regional Science and Urban Economics* 21:351–370.

————. 1992. Market power of large cities and policy differences in metropolitan areas. *Regional Science and Urban Economics* 22:539–558.

————. 1999. Leviathan, local government expenditures, and capitalization. *Regional Science and Urban Economics* 29:155–171.

Krelove, Russell. 1993. The persistence and inefficiency of property tax finance of local public expenditures. *Journal of Public Economics* 51:415–435.

Nelson, Michael. 1987. Searching for Leviathan: Comment and extension. *American Economic Review* 77:198–204.

Oates, Wallace. 1969. The effects of property taxes and local public spending on property values: An empirical study of tax capitalization and the Tiebout hypothesis. *Journal of Political Economy* 77:957–971.

————. 1985. Searching for Leviathan: An empirical study. *American Economic Review* 75:748–757.

Sonstelie, Jon, and Paul Portney. 1978. Profit maximizing communities and the theory of local public expenditures. *Journal of Urban Economics* 5:263–277.

————. 1980. Gross rents and market values: Testing the implications of Tiebout's hypothesis. *Journal of Urban Economics* 7:102–118.

Tiebout, Charles M. 1956. A pure theory of local expenditures. *Journal of Political Economy* 65:416–424.

Wilson, John D. 1986. A theory of interregional tax competition. *Journal of Urban Economics* 19:296–315.

Yinger, John. 1982. Capitalization and the theory of local public finance. *Journal of Political Economy* 90:917–943.

Zax, Jeffrey. 1989. Is there a Leviathan in your neighborhood? *American Economic Review* 79:560–567.

Zodrow, George, and Peter Mieszkowski. 1986. The new view of the property tax: A reformulation. *Regional Science and Urban Economics* 16:309–327.

COMMENTARY

ROBERT M. SCHWAB

Bill Hoyt's chapter is a valuable contribution to the literature on the Tiebout model. It addresses an important set of interrelated questions and offers valuable insights on all of them. Hoyt has written several excellent papers on the Tiebout model, and this chapter pulls together both his own work and the work of others.

Tiebout offered a very stylized view of the world. By now, virtually everyone who has studied public economics is familiar with the essential elements of that model. So, for example, in the Tiebout model consumers are perfectly mobile, all of their income is "dividend income" (that is, their income is independent of where they live), and many communities offer different combinations of taxes and public goods.

In the nearly 50 years since Tiebout published his paper, people have looked closely at some of these assumptions and have asked several questions that are missing in the original Tiebout formulation of the problem, including the following:

- How are communities formed? What role do entrepreneurial land developers play?
- How are publicly provided goods funded? Tiebout assumes local governments rely on head taxes. But, of course, local governments rarely use head taxes; instead, they rely heavily on property taxes and intergovernmental transfers.
- What is the appropriate public choice model? How are taxes and public spending chosen? What is the government's objective?
- Is the number of communities important? Does it matter if we consider a world that looks more like an oligopoly with a small number of communities instead of the perfectly competitive world that Tiebout describes?

Hoyt's chapter focuses on the last three of these issues: property taxes, the government's objective function, and the number of communities. These are clearly interesting and important questions. Roughly 80 percent of the U.S. population lives in metropolitan areas. On average, 38 percent of the population of a metropolitan area lives in the central city, and the remaining 62 percent lives in the suburbs. There is enormous variation, however, across metropolitan areas in the way the population is distributed. In some metropolitan areas nearly everyone lives in the central city. So, for example, more than 90 percent of the people in the Lincoln, Nebraska, metropolitan area live in Lincoln. In other metropolitan areas the central city is small relative to the suburbs; in the Boston and Washington, DC, metropolitan areas, for example, less than 10 percent of the population lives in the central city. This chapter examines the implications of these differences in the distribution of the population.

The chapter considers three plausible alternative objective functions for local governments:

• Property value maximization
• Maximization of consumer welfare
• Maximization of government welfare (measured in terms of the difference between tax revenue and the cost of providing government service)

The chapter then offers a way to choose among these alternative objective functions, which is its major contribution, since discerning government's objectives is a central issue in public economics. If the government is interested in maximizing its own welfare, then we need to constrain government choices. We might, for example, favor spending and tax limitations and term limits. If we can trust the government to act on our behalf, then such policies make little sense. This chapter weaves together theory, simulations, and empirical work on this issue; I look at each in turn.

The theory section considers a number of alternative models. The government's objective is the key difference among these models. Hoyt points out that if governments attempt to maximize aggregate property values, "then the tax rate increases as the number of jurisdictions increases." It is very hard to imagine a result along these lines emerging from a Niskanen or Brennan and Buchanan model. The result impacts much of what follows.

The simulations certainly drive home the central point that the relationship between government behavior and the level of competition among communities depends crucially on the government's objective function. Figure 5.4 shows the relationship between tax rates and market share (i.e., the fraction of the regional population living in the central city). The Leviathan (triangle-studded) line shows the results for a model where the government seeks to maximize its surplus, offering the standard Leviathan result: Less competition implies higher tax rates. As more people move to the central city of a metropolitan area, competition has less control over politicians, and politicians respond by raising the public budget.

Figure 5.4, however, suggests that the relationship between city size and public budgets is not straightforward. If we believe government wants to maximize our welfare (the square-studded utility line), then tax rates are essentially independent of market share. If we believe government attempts to maximize aggregate property values (the diamond-studded property value line), then we expect tax rates to fall as market share rises.

The empirical section of the chapter is motivated by the theory and simulations. It draws on 2002 data for a cross section of U.S. cities. The data set includes measures of tax rates and market share (i.e., the share of the metropolitan area's population). If we find that market share and tax rates are positively related, then we would interpret this as evidence in support of the Leviathan hypothesis. This empirical test is thus similar in spirit to the Oates 1985 *American Economic Review* paper (cited in Hoyt's chapter). We can also think of the empirical section as the public economics equivalent of the literature in industrial organization on the link between industry structure and firm performance.

This empirical work is much less straightforward than it might first appear to be. In particular, it is not clear that we can safely treat market share or population as exogenous determinants of tax rates. The theory tells us that tax rates and market share are determined simultaneously and that both are endogenous variables in a very rich, general equilibrium model. This implies that straightforward OLS estimation is inappropriate and that we need to use an approach such as instrumental variables to address simultaneity.

Bill Hoyt is well aware of this problem. He suggests the land area of the city, the number of housing units in the city, the share of the metropolitan land in the city, and the share of the metropolitan housing stock in the city as instruments for population and the city's share of population. I am not entirely convinced that these instruments are appropriate. For example, if the number of people in a city is endogenous, then the number of housing units these people live in must also be endogenous. I cannot offer a set of alternative instruments that are better candidates. This problem does suggest, however, that the empirical results need to be interpreted cautiously.

The main results from the empirical work are presented in tables 5.5 and 5.6. Those results suggest that the relationship between city size and public expenditures is, at best, tenuous. Most of the important coefficients are statistically insignificant in both the OLS and instrumental variables specifications.

There are at least two ways to interpret these results. It is always tempting to be discouraged by negative results. When we find little or no relationship between variables of interest, our first thoughts often turn to explanations as to why the study has "failed." In this case, it is very possible that these negative results are telling us something very important. The simulations suggest that if local governments are trying to maximize our welfare, then the relationship between city size and tax rates will be very weak. Perhaps the empirical results should be interpreted as evidence against the Leviathan view of the world and in favor of a much more optimistic view of the public sector.

Again, I consider Hoyt's chapter to be an excellent contribution to the literature on the Tiebout model. One does not often encounter a presentation that so deftly brings together so many different tools: theory, simulations, and econometrics. Perhaps by the time our grandchildren gather to celebrate the one hundredth anniversary of the publication of Charles Tiebout's seminal paper, we will have a clear understanding of what motivates public officials. If so, I believe Bill Hoyt's contribution will prove to be a valuable step in that direction.

6

Exclusion's Attraction: Land Use Controls in Tieboutian Perspective

LEE ANNE FENNELL

The Tiebout hypothesis transformed the scholarly understanding of local government by casting citizens as consumers who "vote with their feet" for preferred communities within a metropolitan area (Tiebout 1956). The idea that citizens shop for governmental bundles of services and amenities, just as they might shop for other products, is now a familiar element in local government discourse. But the contributions of Tiebout's ideas to land use policy have been limited by an insufficient specification of the products that the consumer-voters select with their feet. This chapter examines a key element that drives the choices of Tiebout's consumer-voters—exclusion. Exclusionary land use controls attract some consumer-voters even as they repel other consumer-voters. To understand why and how exclusion matters to the Tiebout hypothesis, it is necessary to parse both sides of the jurisdictional choice equation: the reasons that exclusion is such an attractive part of the bundles selected through residential choice and the limits on residential choice that result from such exclusion.

Land use controls have, of course, received significant attention from scholars working within Tiebout's framework. Bruce Hamilton (1975, 1976) established that, as a fiscal matter, zoning stabilizes the choice sets open to residents. Other work has studied the way that zoning addresses uncertainty for those choosing a place to live (e.g., Henderson 1980; Epple, Romer, and Filimon

For helpful comments and questions, I am grateful to Bob Ellickson, Bill Fischel, Daria Roithmayr, and participants in the conference on the Tiebout model held by the Rockefeller Center of Dartmouth College in Hanover, New Hampshire, in June 2005.

1988). Moreover, the significance of neighbors' characteristics—a potential product of exclusion—has not gone unrecognized in the literature on local public goods (e.g., Downs 1973; Oates 1981). But the literature lacks a synthesized account of the way that the various strains of exclusion factor into the consumer-voter's shopping experience and fit together to inform and qualify the Tiebout model's contributions to the law of land use. This chapter fills that void.

What's in the Foot-Shopper's Basket?

In Tiebout's (1956) model, local governments offer different bundles of services and amenities catering to different tastes, and individuals select among them, revealing their preferences in the process. In this account, the choice process focuses on governmentally supplied goods. However, a number of other items that come bundled with these local public goods also influence the consumer-voter's choice. To see how exclusion fits into the Tieboutian landscape, it is first necessary to clarify the nature of the bundled choice that consumer-voters make when they select a residential location.

The Bundled Residential Decision

To begin, consider the highly simplified version of Tieboutian choice depicted in figure 6.1.

Here, each letter represents a different political jurisdiction within a metropolitan area. The oval boundary represents the entire metropolitan area, within which our protagonist must locate if she is to enjoy the agglomeration benefits associated with metropolitan life. If we suppose that each jurisdiction provides a specific bundle of local public goods, then we might say that the foot-shopper's task is simply to select a local government from the metropolitan array much as a grocery shopper chooses a product from the shelf. Instead of pulling an item from the shelf, however, the foot-shopper makes her purchase by actually entering the selected jurisdiction through residential choice. Here, the square represents the consumer-voter's choice to locate in jurisdiction G.

But one cannot select a local government à la carte. It is physically impossible to put a desired jurisdiction's local public goods into one's shopping cart without also bringing along a physical structure (the residence one chooses), a place in a specific neighborhood, and a set of neighbors (e.g., Schelling 1971; Yinger 1981). The location of the selected residence has implications that far transcend the bare fact that the structure lies within one political jurisdiction rather than another (Hamilton 1983, 101), including its proximity to workplaces and to other jurisdictions that may provide benefits to or impose costs on the homeowner. Figure 6.2, which captures the influence of location and

FIGURE 6.1   Choosing a Jurisdiction

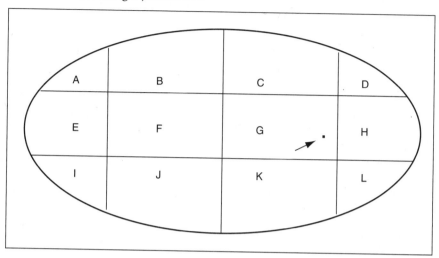

spillovers at several scales (cf. Ellickson 1993, 1325, fig. 2), provides a closer approximation of the consumer-voter's choice.

One of the small squares within the innermost oval represents the home that is selected by the consumer-voter. As before, we could say that she is "voting with her feet" in selecting jurisdiction G and that she is thereby choosing the local public goods offered by G. But she is choosing more than that in selecting a home. Most obviously, she is purchasing a property interest in the physical

FIGURE 6.2   The Bundled Residential Choice

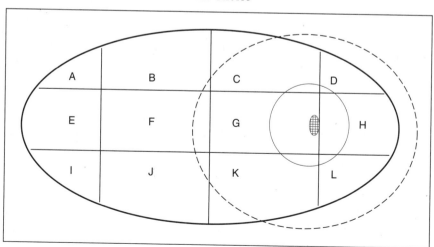

structure itself and the site on which it is located.[1] She is also purchasing a set of spillovers from very close neighbors that will directly impact her use and enjoyment of her home. This "direct spillover zone" is represented in figure 6.2 by the small oval grid area.

In addition, she is buying a daily living environment in a particular neighborhood and section of the metro area, represented by the circle with the solid line in figure 6.2. The daily living environment will contain not only many physical elements that may be significant to the homebuyer's quality of life (stores, parks, traffic, schools, and so on), but also many sets of people with whom she will interact, including those who attend the same schools, clubs, gyms, and places of worship as members of her household, as well as those who make use of nearby shops, parks, libraries, walking paths, museums, and so on (e.g., The Kaiser Committee 1972, 186; Rothenberg 1972; Jackson 1975). As indicated, part of this daily living environment lies beyond her jurisdiction's boundaries; the homebuyer's quality of life will therefore be influenced by the spending patterns and policies of the neighboring jurisdictions, as well as those of the jurisdiction in which she chose to reside. Both the daily living environment and the direct spillover zone will be directly influenced by the behavioral characteristics of neighbors who occupy those respective areas.

The homebuyer is also buying a set of commuting options for various points of interest in the metropolitan area, notably her current or potential workplace and those of other working members of her household. The people in Tiebout's stylized model live off dividend income and do not have workplaces to which they must commute, nor do they have any desire to consume extrajurisdictional amenities such as the educational, recreational, or cultural opportunities that might be available in neighboring towns or cities. If those simplifying assumptions are relaxed, it begins to matter not only what the local government can offer, but also where the jurisdiction is relative to other sites.

The outer dashed circle in figure 6.2 represents the homeowner's feasible commuting range from the selected home. In this case, her commuting range covers about half of the metropolitan area. The commuting range, like the daily living environment, is sensitive not only to the jurisdiction selected, but also to the location selected within the jurisdiction. The depiction of a single feasible range of commuting options is an obvious simplification; in fact, it would be possible to attach specific exercise prices (including the opportunity cost of time) to hundreds or thousands of different door-to-door trips from the selected home, including some that are far outside the given range. The radius of the dashed circle should

---

[1] I will focus here on the purchase of a home, as leaseholds present a somewhat different set of incentives (see, e.g., Ross and Yinger 1999, 2020).

be understood as an approximation of the maximum distance that the average homeowner could afford to travel round trip on a daily or near-daily basis.

As Tiebout suggested, the homebuyer is also selecting a bundle of local public goods; these will be paid for (in whole or in part) by property taxes. The local public goods that the homebuyer receives are not entirely produced by jurisdiction G, however. First, the homebuyer will consume local public goods not only in her home jurisdiction, G, but also in a number of other jurisdictions. She will frequently consume local public goods in jurisdictions H, C, D, K, and L, in which portions of her daily living environment are located. She may also take advantage of some of the local public goods offered by jurisdictions B, F, and J, portions of which lie within her commuting range (Heilbrun 1972, 538). In some cases, jurisdictions will be able to exclude nonresidents from consuming the jurisdiction's local public goods, but some benefit spillovers from adjacent jurisdictions are likely to occur (Musgrave 1969, 300).

Additionally, even those goods that are produced and consumed within jurisdiction G may not be exogenously provided by the local government. The cost and quality of many local public goods, such as public safety and education, depend on the behavioral characteristics of the other people consuming those goods (e.g., Schwab and Oates 1991). Hence, part of what the homebuyer is purchasing along with the house is a set of coproducers who will be responsible collectively for much of the value that she will receive from many of the local public goods offered in G.

Finally, the homebuyer is obtaining a political and social address when she selects a home. Politically, the homebuyer is becoming a member of not only the selected local government, but also any other local or regional political jurisdictions that encompass the home in question (such as special assessment districts, school districts, or regional governments) (e.g., Ladd and Yinger 1989, 145–166). The political goings-on in adjacent jurisdictions may also have the power to influence the homebuyer's experience, and the homebuyer in turn may be able to have some influence on the political process in the adjoining jurisdictions even though she cannot vote in them. She might, for example, join a rally, become involved in an interest group coalition that has power across jurisdictional lines, or pressure her own government to engage in formal or informal interlocal arrangements with the neighboring jurisdiction (e.g., Gillette 2001).

The purchased home also comes with a "social address": the place name with which the home is most closely identified. This place name represents a local public good for the households that share it and can be understood as performing a branding function that communicates quality levels to acquaintances, business associates, and potential purchasers. In central cities, neighborhoods often carry their own familiar brand names, such as the Castro in San Francisco, Hyde Park in Chicago, and Georgetown in Washington, DC (Gillette 2001, 203–204). In suburbs, the jurisdiction name is more likely to be the "brand name" identifier, although smaller subsets of the jurisdiction, such as private neighborhood developments, may become known by their own names.

Hence, what one purchases when choosing a home can be understood in shorthand form as comprising five bundles of attributes:[2] (1) the home's physical attributes ("the house"); (2) the home's "environmental" or atmospheric attributes, both in the direct spillover range and in the larger daily environment ("the living environment"); (3) the home's locational attributes relative to other sites of interest ("the commute options"); (4) the services and amenities offered by the local jurisdiction, including those partially produced by other residents, as well as services and amenities in neighboring or overlapping jurisdictions to which one has access ("local public goods"); and (5) the home's political and social address. Under conditions of full capitalization, differences in these attributes are priced into the home itself (e.g., Stiglitz 1983, 41–42; Fischel 2001).

Special Characteristics of the Product

Tieboutian choice involves a complicated product, to be sure, but can it nonetheless be usefully captured with the shopping metaphor that Tiebout introduced? Here it is helpful to consider five ways in which the product the homebuyer selects through residential choice is different from most ordinary consumer products. Some of these differences suggest that a more useful analogy to Tieboutian choice is that of a diner choosing a restaurant. In both cases one buys a particular item (a house or a meal) into which have been capitalized many attributes of interest that will unfold over time, that are subject to interdependencies and congestion, and that are not fully under the control of the management one has chosen (the local government or the restaurant owner). Although the restaurant metaphor is not perfect, it helps to highlight the features that give exclusion a central role in jurisdictional choice.

It is possible to have too many customers. For producers of ordinary consumer goods, attracting more customers is usually considered unambiguously desirable. Communities are different in this respect, a fact that Tiebout makes explicit in his discussion of optimum community size (1956, 419–420). At some point, communities will not be interested in attracting residents and will seek to dissuade additional entry. As in a restaurant setting, the potential for congestion limits the number of new entrants that can be accommodated without an

---

[2] This is just one of many ways that the components of the bundled housing choice could be delineated. The bundled nature of the choice, as well as the elements in the bundle, have been well noted in the literature (e.g., Jackson 1975, 6; Rose-Ackerman 1983, 74; Pozdena 1988, 43–44, 82).

increase in the average cost or a decrease in the average quality of the services and amenities (Oates 1981, 95). Given the inability to charge each entrant at a level that would equate to the marginal cost of extending service to him (id. at 93), it is possible to have "too many" customers.

Some parts of the bundle are not priced explicitly. When one purchases a bundled consumer product, such as a laptop computer with software already installed, the breakdown of the various components in the total price may or may not be transparent. Regardless, every piece of the package is part of an explicitly priced bundle, and no piece of the package can be consumed without buying the full bundle.

Restaurants, like jurisdictions, consist of priced and unpriced elements. One ostensibly pays "for a meal," but one buys more than just the meal: One receives waitservice, an eating environment, and a particular restaurant location. The tax and the tip capture some of these additional elements, but they are priced based on the cost of the meal itself, rather than on a pro rata share of the other elements consumed. Likewise, one pays for a house and pays property taxes based on that house purchase; one does not pay à la carte for the local public goods one uses.

The use of priced items to allocate the cost of unpriced items opens up the possibility that customers will attempt to consume the unpriced items without paying for a "fair share" of them via the priced items. For example, one could enjoy a fine restaurant's wonderful ambience, gorgeous views, and delightful service at a bargain price if one could occupy a choice table for hours while consuming nothing but coffee. Likewise, because local public goods are funded with property taxes rather than head taxes, one could obtain a local public good at a bargain by occupying an inexpensive home in a high-service area (Hamilton 1975, 205). The bargain would not be a permanent one, to the extent that the fiscal difference is capitalized into the home's price (Hamilton 1976, 744; Rubinfeld 1985, 592 n. 22), but the initial entrant could obtain the benefit of cheaper public services at the expense of those occupying more expensive homes.

A similar point can be made about local public goods produced by nearby jurisdictions within one's daily living environment or commuting range. While these goods are not priced into one's tax burden in one's home jurisdiction, they may be capitalized into the value of the home itself.

Customers and noncustomers generate spillovers. When one purchases a consumer good such as a toaster, the value of the product is typically unaffected by the actions or characteristics of other consumers of the product. Likewise, local spillovers in one's general environment do not usually have a large impact on the value of a product; most products can be transported and used in another location instead. Residential housing, like a restaurant meal, must be consumed on-site and in the immediate presence of other consumers (e.g., Diamond and Tolley 1982, 6; Hamilton 1983, 101). Often, the consumption will also occur within range of spillovers generated by noncustomers—that is, the acts of people or governments in adjacent jurisdictions. These spillovers, which may be positive or negative, can dramatically affect the value of the good one is consuming.

Consumers are also producers. Perhaps the most important difference between ordinary products and communities is that the consumers are themselves also coproducers of many of the most important local public goods (e.g., Schwab and Oates 1991). Residents of a local jurisdiction often directly influence the cost and quality of local services (e.g., id.; Oates 1977; Ross and Yinger 1999, 2038). It has been well noted that goods like education and public safety depend not just on exogenous inputs (teachers, school buildings, police officers, patrol cars), but also in large part on the characteristics and behavior of people who are ostensibly "receiving" the services: an elementary school's students or a neighborhood's residents (e.g., Oates 1977; Dynarski, Schwab, and Zampelli 1989; Schwab and Oates 1991; Manski 1992).

A school attended by well-prepared, well-nourished, motivated students will produce a better education for the same dollars, and a neighborhood populated by concerned, law-abiding, safety-minded citizens who watch out for each other will produce higher-quality public safety. Other local public goods are affected to a greater or lesser degree by characteristics or behavior of one's co-consumers (Diamond and Tolley 1982, 30). As just noted, one important local public good that the consumers produce is the social meaning of one's residence in a particular jurisdiction or neighborhood. The stock of a particular place name will rise or fall depending on the perceived characteristics of the people with whom it is associated.

Customers shape the product by voting. Finally, as the Tiebout model emphasizes, residents in a municipality are both market and political actors—consumers and voters (Rose-Ackerman 1983). As consumers, they choose a product, but as voters, they participate in shaping the product (Ross and Yinger 1999, 2003). This element of political control makes the residential choice different in kind from other market choices. Although the relationship between political choice and choice through mobility is not entirely clear cut (e.g., Epple and Zelenitz 1981; Yinger 1981), the fact that both processes occur simultaneously has some interesting implications (Ellickson 1971; Ross and Yinger 1999, 2022).

In the local government context—at least outside of the central city—political incentives can be understood by reference to the median voter model (e.g., Ross and Yinger 1999, 2019). Fischel (2001) maintains that the median voter will produce results that resemble those that might be produced through private market activity responsive to consumer demand (Oates 2006). Because the composition of the political body determines the position of the median voter, and thus the ultimate shape of the products that are provided by local government (Bogart 1993), the political preferences of one's co-consumers become important.

Time, Interdependence, and Uncertainty

The preceding discussion provides a rough inventory of the items comprising the bundled residential choice, as well as a catalogue of the bundle's special characteristics. But to fully understand the nature of the product, and the place of exclusionary land use policies within it, two additional factors bear emphasis. First, a home will be held over time for eventual resale. Second, the values of many of the bundled items turn on interdependent decisions made by other homebuyers.

The housing bundle ultimately produces two things for the buyer: a stream of consumption that continues for as long as she owns the house and a gain or loss on resale (e.g., Walters 1975, 41; Pozdena 1988, 82). Hence, the homebuyer's choice is only partly about consumption preferences; the purchase is also an investment. The buyer must not only select a package that she finds attractive, but she must also select a bundle that will continue to prove attractive to others on the resale market. She must worry not only about her own preferences in neighbors and her own predictions about the impacts of particular neighbors on local public goods, spillovers, the fisc, social reputation, and so on, but also about what potential homebuyers will think about all these factors (e.g., Fennell 2002, 646–648). As a result, even a homeowner who thinks of herself as quite progressive and enlightened may support exclusionary measures, telling herself that she must defer to the beliefs and preferences of members of the less-enlightened target audience to whom she will someday need to sell her home (id.; see also Massey and Denton 1993, 94–95).

The condition of the house itself—its maintenance and any renovations or improvements made to it—is the only strand of the bundle that the homeowner can personally control over time. Even then she will be subject to the regulatory regime in which the home is located, as well as to external factors such as weather patterns and vandalism rates. The other components of the housing bundle, such as the aesthetics of the living environment, are out of the individual homeowner's control (e.g., Jackson 1975, 4; Diamond and Tolley 1982, 8). Examining the components as they exist at the time of the purchase provides only a snapshot that is already on its way to becoming outdated by the time of the closing.

Closely related is the fact that each resident's home purchase exhibits important interdependencies with those of other residents. Where interdependent locational choices are distributed over time, early choices can influence or constrain later choices. While uncertainty is a pervasive feature of temporally distributed interdependent choices, early entrants in a community face particularly high levels of uncertainty and are likely to be eager to employ devices that will control the trajectory of future development—even when it means constraining their own land use options (Epple et al. 1988, 133). Later entrants have the advantage of being able to observe the results of the earlier choices; however, they face a smaller choice set. Not only do early decisions create path dependencies in overall spatial arrangements, but some of those decisions have the power to systematically restrict entry.

These dynamics will be explored in more detail below. For now, it is sufficient to emphasize that the selection of a home from among the available possibilities means choosing not a static product but a dynamic bundle of expectations that will unfold over time as interdependent choices are made. In this context, exclusionary policies act as "product stabilizers" that have the potential to lower the uncertainty associated with time and interdependence; this decreased uncertainty holds positive value for many homebuyers (Delafons 1969, 28–29; Poindexter 1995, 12). Because residential bundles that have not been stabilized in this way will have difficulty competing with those that have been so stabilized, exclusionary land use policies play a central role in Tieboutian choice.

The Role of Exclusion in Jurisdictional Choice

Land use controls can be viewed as collective property rights that are held by the community (Nelson 1977, 15–18). By limiting the uses to which land may be put, such controls can and do serve purposes apart from exclusion. For example, zoning restrictions can enable communities to overcome tragedies of the commons and to produce aesthetic and environmental results that could not be achieved without some form of centralized coordination and enforcement. As a result, it would not be unusual for a community with a stably fixed population to adopt land use controls designed to prevent individuals from engaging in self-interested behaviors that would generate harmful spillovers for neighbors. Such controls would have traction quite apart from any desire to alter or stabilize the community's composition.

However, the control of land use often has the predictable effect, and sometimes the conscious motive, of controlling the number, concentration, or characteristics of residents. In assessing the degree to which a land use control is exclusionary in this sense, one might look at the effects of the control, at the motivations of the voters responsible for the political result, or at some combination of the two. These are ultimately empirical questions. Significantly, a given policy may directly affect the consumption and behavior patterns of residents rather than—or in addition to—altering the composition of residents (Pogodzinski and Sass 1990). For example, a zoning restriction that specifies a particular minimum lot size could have one of two effects on a household that would prefer to consume a smaller lot size in that jurisdiction. The household might choose a different jurisdiction with a lower minimum lot size or might go ahead and consume the required additional housing in the subject jurisdiction. While either choice may involve distortions, a land use control that generated only decisions of the latter sort would not be exclusionary.[3]

Where a land use control has the effect of excluding segments of the population, we might define it as exclusionary, at least where motives exist for the kind of exclusion at issue. Of course, identifying interests that are served by the adoption of exclusionary land use controls does not establish that any particular land use policy was so motivated. Nonetheless, it is useful to consider the array of motives that residents might have for constricting entry into a jurisdiction.

Exclusionary Motives

There are a number of distinct motives for exclusionary land use controls, encompassing fiscal, spillover-related, public goods, political, and monopolistic considerations (Bogart 1993; Dietderich 1996, 31; Ellickson and Been, 2005, 769–770). These motives, which closely track the special product characteristics just highlighted, can explain why exclusionary land use controls are generated through the political process and why they prove attractive to those making choices among jurisdictions. The broad array of motives suggests that exclusion through land use controls is often intentional and overdetermined.

To be sure, it may be impossible to tell from the content of an exclusionary measure what motivated it (Bogart 1993, 1670). For example, a large minimum lot size might represent either "fiscal zoning" or "public-goods zoning," or it might, indeed, contain elements of both or derive from yet another motive for exclusion (Mills and Oates 1975, 8; Bogart 1993). This difficulty would be significant if different normative implications flowed from exclusion prompted by

---

[3] If the land use control is tailored to overcome spillovers within the jurisdiction that would otherwise be generated by self-interested behavior on the part of residents, the "distortions" in consumption it induces may be viewed as desirable adjustments in incentives (e.g., Lenon, Chattopadhyay, and Heffley 1996, 222).

different motives (Bogart 1993). Yet, some of the most troublesome implications of exclusion are generated regardless of the precise motive involved, as we shall see.

Fiscal Motives

Because it is not possible to charge each incoming member of the community a tax rate that matches the marginal cost of extending local public goods to her, two problems may result. First, as suggested by the discussion of optimum community size, people may enter the community beyond the efficient point. Second, as suggested by the discussion of unpriced elements, people may contribute too little to the tax base relative to the goods and services they consume.[4]

Hence, one motivation for exclusionary land use controls is purely fiscal. As Bruce Hamilton (1975) has explained, setting a minimum housing purchase through zoning forces payment of a minimum share of property tax. Pressure for fiscal zoning comes not just through the political process, but also, potentially, through the mechanism of Tieboutian choice. A homebuyer selecting a residence must factor into the housing choice the projected impact of taxes and local public goods over time on the value of the house. The chance that newcomers will come in and consume less-expensive housing (or otherwise increase costs relative to tax payments) will be part of that calculation.

An influx of lower-income households that increases service costs without proportionately increasing tax revenues would shift larger tax burdens onto those caught owning more expensive homes at the time of the influx (Fischel 2001, 69). The resulting property tax disadvantage would be capitalized as a reduction in the value of the more costly houses. As a result, a homebuyer will be attracted to jurisdictions that place limits on any future expansions of housing that would upset the relationship between taxes and benefits existing at the time of her entry into the community.

Spillover-Related Motives

The desire to limit negative externalities and to gain the benefit of positive externalities within a neighborhood or larger living environment can also drive exclusionary decisions (Bogart 1993, 1671–1672). Some land use controls attack spillovers directly (for example, by controlling the aesthetics of a residential area), while others are designed to screen residents based on their perceived propensities to generate negative or positive spillovers.

The problem is complicated by the possibility that those harboring prejudices may view the mere existence of certain resident characteristics as produc-

---

[4] The first problem is really a subset of the second. Once the optimum community size has been reached, further additions raise the cost of services to a point that will not be covered by the new entrant.

ing negative spillovers. So racism and classism may trigger exclusionary efforts (e.g., Ford 1994). To the extent these prejudices are widely shared, property values may be affected through capitalization. The fear of such impacts on property values may cause current homeowners to support exclusionary decisions even in the absence of personal prejudice.

Public Goods Motives

The fact that the consumers of local public goods also coproduce those goods provides another motive for exclusion. As already noted, the consumers of some of the most important local public goods—education and public safety—contribute directly to the production and cost of these goods through peer and neighborhood effects. Suppose that some co-consumers—call them "quality-enhancing users"—will make positive contributions, whereas others—"quality-detracting users"—will do the opposite (Fennell 2001; Schwab and Oates 1991, 220–230; Ross and Yinger 1999, 2044; see also Becker and Murphy 2000, 12). Jurisdictions have an incentive to attract the former and exclude the latter. Because the propensity to be a quality-enhancing user is not observable, some proxy must be used instead. If there is a perceived correlation between the quality of local public goods achievable at a particular cost and the socioeconomic backgrounds of the residents, land use controls may be consciously employed to limit entry to households in a certain income or wealth stratum (Ross and Yinger 1999, 2015).

One of the local public goods that the populace may produce is exclusivity itself (Dietderich 1996, 55). Consider the special local public good inhering in the status (or lack thereof) that comes with a residential place name. Some exclusion may be motivated by an effort to avoid dilution or tarnishing of the place "brand." For example, wealthy homeowners might fear that the entry of lower-income residents would produce a "down at the heels" image for the community.

Political Motives

As voters, residents determine the levels and types of local public goods that the jurisdiction will produce. To the extent that residence within the jurisdiction is both a necessary and sufficient condition for contributing to political outcomes, controlling the entry and exit of residents also means controlling the political apparatus through which decisions are made about local public goods.[5] Local governments may be viewed as placing central control in the hands of that abstraction known as "the median voter" (e.g., Fischel 2001,

---

[5] I am grateful to Bill Fischel for a discussion that led me to consider this point. For a brief overview of some of the literature on such "political economic zoning," see Bogart (1993) at 1672.

87–89). If current and potential voters within the jurisdiction occupy a range of positions with regard to local public goods, entry and exit can change the identity of the decisive voters in the median voter model, hence the political outcomes (e.g., Rose-Ackerman 1983, 65).

Thus, where the entry of residents cannot be decoupled from their participation in the political system, decisions about entry and exit necessarily implicate the decision-making apparatus. Land use policies that stem entry into the jurisdiction freeze in place a political apparatus for deciding about local public goods (Poindexter 1995, 15). Jurisdictions that would like to grow without feeling threatened politically may resort to land use policies that screen the population that enters the jurisdiction. The voters who control political outcomes would wish to select entrants that replicate as closely as possible the prevailing preferences within the jurisdiction. The resort to exclusionary devices that would make a jurisdiction "self-replicating" creates a feedback loop in which the political process produces zoning regulations that perpetuate the political processes that continue to maintain the zoning regulations, and so on (Ford 1994, 1871).

It is also possible that new entry will alter the distribution of social status or other relational goods within a jurisdiction (Frank 1985; Jencks and Mayer 1990, 116–117). Having gone to the trouble to "choose the right pond" (Frank 1985), current residents may be deeply invested in making sure that the pond remains "right." Interestingly, these political and social considerations could create pressures to exclude not only lower-income households, but also higher-income people whose entrance would otherwise appear desirable on fiscal and public goods grounds.

Monopolistic Motives

The fact that the bundled residential choice is an investment destined for eventual resale in a spatially sensitive market provides another possible motive for exclusionary land use controls. Constriction of the housing supply carries the potential to increase the home's resale value (e.g., White 1975, 73–74). Thus, a homeowner might wish to work through the political system to limit the supply of housing in her jurisdiction and thereby make her resale home relatively more scarce. Anything that helps to make the bundle of housing services in a given jurisdiction (or portion of a jurisdiction) uniquely valuable—whether an innovative local government, a choice location, access to natural resources, or any other factor—reduces the degree to which housing elsewhere offers a close substitute. The more unique a jurisdiction is, the more plausible exclusionary zoning becomes as a strategy for obtaining monopoly profits (Ellickson 1977, 400–403).

A countervailing factor involves the positive spillovers that the homeowner might enjoy as a result of the contributions to agglomeration effects that the new development would bring. Perhaps the influx of new residents on the edge of town will support the introduction of shops or services that the homeowner desires or that her future buyers might desire. Or perhaps the new entrants will add more to the tax base than they will consume in services (or will attract businesses that will do so). Even in such cases, however, the homeowner might demand land use controls that keep such entry in distant quarters of the jurisdiction to reduce the degree of substitutability.

Exclusion's Place in the Tiebout Model

Exclusion, put simply, is attractive. It promises stable or increasing home values, and thereby induces homeowners to enter the jurisdiction. At the same time, exclusion is choice-inhibiting; the excluded have fewer alternatives open to them as a result. Tiebout's ideas cannot be fully appreciated without taking into account the place of exclusion both as an attractive item in the bundles available to consumer-voters and as a constraint on the choice sets that consumer-voters encounter. Specifically, it is important to consider how the Tieboutian focus on exit and sorting is conditioned or qualified by an emphasis on the role of exclusion in jurisdictional choice.

Exclusion Versus Exit

The Tiebout hypothesis proceeds on the assumption of perfect mobility—the ability to costlessly exit when conditions prove unsatisfying (e.g., Been 1991, 508). One reaction to the previous discussion might be to ask whether exclusion is really all that important if exit remains available. That exit is not an acceptable substitute for zoning was established by Hamilton (1975), who raised the specter of the poor endlessly chasing the wealthy from jurisdiction to jurisdiction. If mobility is costless, being "chased" would itself impose no costs; the well-off would move frictionlessly from place to place, one step ahead of the poor. But the problems run deeper. Under conditions of full capitalization, all of the negative factors that trigger the consumer-voter's desire to flee the jurisdiction, including expectations about future value drops, have already been incorporated into her home's (now-lowered) value. She may still choose to exit, but doing so will not help her recoup her loss.

Will her departure nonetheless punish the jurisdiction that she exits? Not directly. Unlike a purchaser of a low-stakes consumer product who can walk away from a bad experience, a departing homeowner must find someone willing to buy her property before she can stop purchasing the local government's package through her tax payments—that is, she is responsible for recruiting a "replacement customer" (Oakerson 1999, 110–111). To find a replacement requires dropping her asking price to compensate the new buyer for the suboptimal portions of the package (Yinger 1981, 101). Because of this dynamic, Tieboutian choice may not produce efficient outcomes on its own where capitalization exists; voting with hands as well as with feet is required (e.g., Epple and Zelenitz 1981; Yinger 1981).

Moreover, moving is itself costly (Ladd and Yinger 1989, 293–294). In addition to the out-of-pocket and opportunity costs of moving one's household, movers lose whatever site-specific investments they have made in the home and neighborhood, including social capital. The prospect that one will have to move devalues the package one purchases upon entry into the neighborhood and deters socially valuable investments in the local community. From a homeowner's perspective, then, exit is an imperfect response mechanism. The standard alternative to exit is political action, or voice (Hirschman 1970). Residents who face falling home values might be expected to agitate for changes that will restore their home's value or at least arrest its fall. Exits and failures to enter that negatively impact home values will lead politically powerful homeowners to place pressure on the political apparatus—not by threatening to leave, but by threatening to withhold votes from the incumbents if the factors inducing a value-eroding exodus are not corrected (Fischel 2001). Tiebout-style choice generates responsiveness in this story through the mediation of politics. Yet, political responses become vulnerable and unstable once population changes are underway. Where exit generates entry that fails to replicate the existing political composition, power can shift to a contingent holding different preferences.

Consider how exclusion, a prophylactic alternative to both exit and voice, addresses these concerns. Land use policies that stabilize home values through exclusionary mechanisms are self-executing political products that make voice less necessary; they are also entry-inducing features designed to make future exit less necessary. Exclusion might be understood as a form of preemptive exit that operates prospectively to prevent drops in one's home value. Entering a jurisdiction with land use policies that limit entry makes one's exit from the previous jurisdiction (or choice not to enter other jurisdictions) meaningful: The people and politics that one has left behind (or chosen not to join) cannot follow along to the chosen jurisdiction. If the factors that would potentially make one want to exit are fundamentally bound up in the people with whom one might be grouped or the political decisions that might be made by the local jurisdiction, then exit could be made unnecessary by finding ways to control or foreclose entry.

Jurisdictions will rarely wish to engage in complete and categorical exclusion, however. Instead, municipalities will fine-tune the kind and degree of exclusion to make themselves as attractive as possible to the citizens that they wish to attract and retain. The typical result will be selective land use policies that operate as screens or filters, not as impenetrable barriers to all growth.

Sorting, Screening, Matching

The notion of sorting is also central to the Tiebout hypothesis. Yet, the term *sorting* is ambiguous—both as to the persons or things doing the sorting and as to the dimensions along which sorting occurs or ought to occur. The usual image of Tieboutian jurisdictional choice posits self-sorting based on attractions arrayed before the shopping consumer-voters by the local governments. People "sort with their feet," on this account; the individuals being sorted are also the ones doing the sorting. But the process is more complicated than that.[6] For the reasons just detailed, many jurisdictions do not stand ready to welcome all comers; rather, the intake valves of many jurisdictions feature screens that constrain entry. Such limiting devices hamper the free-form self-sorting in which households might otherwise engage. Making matters more interesting, the shape and size of the intake screens—that is, the content of land use controls—serve to attract those who are capable of making it through the screen.

Under these conditions, each exclusionary device concretely limits the alternatives open to those who are shut out, even as it helps to attract those who wish to avoid being grouped with those who are excluded. Of course, screening devices are not given by nature but rather are political products that are designed to keep current residents happy while attracting the preferred mix of new residents. When active screening is added to self-sorting, the picture is less one of open-ended shopping and more a dynamic process of matching households to jurisdictions based on some mix of the preferences of homebuyers and the preferences of other residents.

In Tiebout's account, self-sorting among jurisdictions is important because it reveals citizens' demand for local public goods, leading to the efficient provision of those goods. For jurisdictional choice to be revelatory, the decision to locate or stay within the jurisdiction must be both voluntary and driven at least in part by the local public goods offerings. As the number of jurisdictions is limited (either by exogenous factors or by the installation of "intake screens" in the form of land use restrictions), one's locational decision becomes less and less revelatory. At the limit, an individual facing a single jurisdictional choice within a given metropolitan area would reveal little about her demand for local public goods by "choosing" to reside within the jurisdiction (Frug 1998, 31). More generally, strong preferences about other parts of the residential bundle, especially location, may lead homebuyers to enter or remain in jurisdictions despite suboptimal local public goods provision.

---

[6] For one take on the dynamics involved, see Ross and Yinger (1999).

That the Tieboutian sorting process involves elements of screening and exclusion should not be surprising given Tiebout's discussion of congestion and optimum community size and given Hamilton's recognition of the limits of the property tax as a device for enforcing public goods contributions. But the point bears emphasis. Coercive governmental action in the form of land use controls structures Tiebout-style choice; matters are not simply left up to the market (e.g., Miller 1981, 185; Dietderich 1996, 42; Donohue 1997). This is important, because Tiebout-inspired normative arguments gain much of their appeal by suggesting that jurisdictional choice represents a marketlike exercise of consumer sovereignty (Donohue 1997).

Legal and Policy Implications

The balance of the chapter considers the legal and policy implications of the foregoing analysis from two perspectives. First, we examine mechanisms for exclusion in light of the multiple motivations detailed earlier. Second, we preview a theory of associational entitlement that would take seriously the collective action problem presented by residential grouping patterns.

Exclusionary Mechanisms

The shape that exclusion takes (who is excluded and how) depends in part on the relative strength of each of the several motives for exclusion and in part on legal restrictions that place off limits certain alternatives. The federal Fair Housing Act and other antidiscrimination laws preclude any overt exclusion based on protected characteristics, such as race, and outright income or wealth requirements to enter a jurisdiction also appear to be outside of the feasible policy space (Stiglitz 1983, 46). Widespread exclusionary devices include limits by housing type (for example, limiting an area to single-family homes) and minimum lot size requirements (Span 2001, 8–9; Ellickson and Been 2005, 788). Inside common interest communities, additional controls typically limit aspects of homes' design, color scheme, and building materials (Nelson 2005). Other exclusionary devices include moratoria, quotas, or other limits on the amount or speed of growth (Ellickson 1977, 390–391).

Goals, Proxies, and Unintended Consequences

Exclusionary mechanisms can be understood in light of the various goals that they serve. If the motivation for exclusion is fiscal, the goal is to collect sufficient property taxes for the services that the household will consume (and to exclude any household that cannot pay its share of taxes). Requiring consumption of a certain amount and kind of housing, such as a single-family home on a large lot, works to keep the property value, and so the property tax contribution, sufficiently high.[7] A simple head tax per household would more directly achieve the fiscal objective but would present other difficulties (Ellickson 1977, 398). Jurisdictions may also go beyond efforts to enforce "fair" tax payments and engage in what Michelle White (1975) has termed "fiscal squeeze zoning"—applying land use controls designed to extract a more than proportionate share of revenues from newcomers. Assuming existing homes would be exempt from the new zoning restrictions (Cribbet et al. 2002, 721), voters would be expected to support zoning restrictions that force the incoming residents to consume larger amounts of housing than they themselves consume (Ross and Yinger 1999, 2015).

Another form of fiscal zoning would involve consciously keeping out those who are likely to be costly to serve or who are going to consume large amounts of services. The usual targets of such efforts are families with children. While overt discrimination against families with children is prohibited (with some exceptions) by fair housing laws, local governments might attempt to steer development toward exempted housing for older persons or otherwise shape the housing menu in ways that would be expected to attract fewer families with children (Strahilevitz 2005). It should be noted, however, that political concerns would be expected to limit resort to both "fiscal squeeze" zoning and zoning for "low-service" demographic groups. Voters may be wary of population shifts that could change the political center of gravity and lead to unwanted changes in the types or levels of local public goods.

Exclusionary mechanisms may also be targeted at population characteristics or behaviors. Because there is no way to directly screen for the propensity to generate spillovers or make useful contributions to local public goods, a highly imperfect proxy is typically employed: the wherewithal to consume a home of the type and size required on a lot of the specified size. Similarly, a community that wishes to grow while keeping the same political balance may zone for similar housing types and sizes in the hopes that doing so will lead to replication of existing political characteristics.

---

[7] Given capitalization, a property tax can work as a head tax as long as the housing supply is fixed; the housing need not be homogeneous (Hamilton 1976; Fischel 2001). However, if heterogeneous housing cannot be created (or planned) in fixed quantities at the time the jurisdiction is created, political pressures may prevent the later introduction of less-expensive housing units. Even though the residents of the new, smaller housing will end up paying as much for the local public goods as the current residents (because the "bargain" associated with paying a smaller amount of property tax will be capitalized into the home's price), those left owning larger homes at the time the new housing is permitted will suffer a loss that represents a windfall for the developer of the new housing (or whoever owns the land at the time the new housing is allowed in), assuming that its introduction could not have been anticipated (Fischel 2001, 69). This potential loss represents a fiscal motivation to oppose the introduction of less-expensive housing units (Ellickson 1971, 337–338).

Where monopolistic motives for exclusion are in play, the goal is to reduce the supply of good substitutes for existing homes. If it is impossible, legally or politically, to keep out new entrants entirely, existing homeowners might attempt to limit development to distant parts of the jurisdiction or to dissimilar homes. Interestingly, the desire to keep out homes that will be good substitutes may be in tension with the desire to replicate the existing population for fiscal, political, public goods, or spillover-related reasons. Homes that serve an entirely different market may compete less directly with existing homes but may introduce different income levels that will undercut other goals of exclusion.

To the extent that exclusion by housing type is used as a proxy rather than because of the spillovers directly produced by different housing types, the menu of available housing choices is artificially constricted. Where not all housing types are represented in all jurisdictions, consumers must choose a package that includes a home type that they are willing and able to buy. Tiebout did not discuss the house itself as part of the consumer-voter's choice—an omission that would be consistent with the assumption that any physical structure and lot size can exist in any jurisdiction. The home and surrounding land might on this account be viewed as fungible "wrappers" in which the relatively unique local governmental bundles are delivered. If land use controls limit the type and style of housing in some jurisdictions, however, foot-shoppers would be unable to find a right-sized wrapper for their consumption of local government in all jurisdictions. This fact has implications for Tiebout's claim that jurisdictional choice reveals demand for local public goods.

Exclusion by lot size or housing type not only keeps out people who might otherwise prefer the mix of local public goods being provided in the jurisdiction, but it also distorts the housing choices of those who locate within the exclusive jurisdiction. A deadweight loss is produced if people consume more or different housing than they would prefer merely to win admission into the jurisdiction (Ellickson 1977, 397; Dietderich 1996, 32; Ross and Yinger 1999, 2015). Large lot zoning may lead people to consume more land or live at lower densities than they would otherwise choose (Pozdena 1988, 53). The overconsumption of space pushes the footprint of the metropolitan area outward, so people who need to aggregate together must come from further-flung suburbs and exurbs and will have larger distances to traverse (id. at 71). This cost increase is, of course, only partially internalized by the residents of the jurisdictions restricting density. The result may well be a tragedy of the spatial commons.

It is worth being precise about the resource that is overharvested in this story. It is not land as such but rather space that is instrumental in delivering the benefits of metropolitan agglomeration. If we assume that agglomeration benefits require some reasonable degree of physical proximity, then there is some distance between the component collaborative elements beyond which the benefits of collaboration are outweighed by what Melvin Webber (1963) has termed "communication costs." While this distance will vary depending on technological advances and the magnitude of the agglomeration benefits at issue, it is clear that "prime collaboration space" is a valuable commodity that jurisdictions do not bear the full costs of appropriating when they carry out exclusionary land use policies.

Scale of Exclusion

A jurisdiction can exclude on a whole-jurisdiction basis or can, instead, create internal zoning classifications that exclude only from portions of the jurisdiction (e.g., Vatter 2005; Calabrese, Epple, and Romano 2006). The scale of exclusion employed is important from two perspectives. First, from the point of view of homeowners or potential homeowners, the scale should be large enough to "get the job done," which in turn will depend on what is motivating the exclusion. Second, from society's point of view, exclusion should take place at a scale that prevents other jurisdictions from drawing benefits from (or offloading costs onto) the subject jurisdiction, but also at a scale that does not offload costs onto (or draw benefits from) other jurisdictions.

If enough simplifying assumptions are made, these two perspectives are not in conflict. A stylized vision of local public goods posits that everyone residing within the jurisdiction enjoys full levels of each local public good and that nobody outside of the jurisdiction enjoys any of the local public goods (Stiglitz 1983, 19). Such local public goods would fit a "club goods" or "limited access commons" model. They would be experienced as pure public goods inside the jurisdiction but would so successfully exclude outsiders as to look like private goods from the outside (e.g., id., 19; Ostrom, Tiebout, and Warren 1961, 834; Rose 1998, 155). In this setting, exclusion merely serves to separate those who are part of the "club" or limited-access commons from those who are not (Buchanan 1965, 13). The jurisdiction acts as a fully self-contained unit; by assumption, the jurisdiction is not expelling any externalities onto (or receiving any externalities from) its neighbors.

Where these simplifying assumptions do not hold, finding the right exclusion scale becomes problematic and contested. To take one obvious point of conflict, residents of a jurisdiction may want to push the costs of serving low-income people onto other jurisdictions. However, if low-income people must be served by *some* jurisdiction, their exclusion from the subject jurisdiction imposes an externality on other jurisdictions (e.g., Schragger 2001, 422). Likewise, the fact that other jurisdictions are bearing the costs of serving, protecting, and educating low-income people generates positive spillovers for the subject jurisdiction that it is not having to pay for. The flip side of this proposition is that jurisdictions that accept costly-to-serve residents may be the subject of cost-shifting by others. Collective action problems may keep jurisdictions acting independently from taking on an appropriate share of regional costs without bearing more than their share (Fischel 1985, 138–39; Gillette 1994, 1437; Lenon, Chattopadhyay, and Heffley 1996, 231). Faced with a choice between bearing too much and too little of the cost, jurisdictions are likely to choose the latter.

Left to their own devices, what scale of exclusion would jurisdictions choose? Or to put it slightly differently, what kinds of exclusion would be attractive in the Tieboutian sense? The desired scale of exclusion will depend on the motive animating the exclusion. For example, fiscal zoning works best on a jurisdiction-wide basis. If taxes are collected and spent throughout the municipality, then zoning classifications that apply to only a portion of the municipality will not serve the head tax equivalency function attributed to zoning (Hamilton 1975). However, if the benefits derived from local public goods are unevenly spread throughout the jurisdiction, then intrajurisdictional zoning could conceivably serve fiscal purposes.[8]

For spillover-related zoning, the operative concern is the size of the spillover range (Ostrom et al. 1961, 835; cf. Ellickson 1993, 1325). In some cases, spillovers are quite localized and could be adequately addressed by within-jurisdiction zoning. To take a simple case, low-income housing that is thought to generate negative aesthetic spillovers for high-income residences could be placed on the opposite side of the jurisdiction, with parks, government buildings, or other neutral uses serving as a buffer. Of course, spillovers—even relatively localized ones—can easily cross jurisdictional boundaries; in such instances, even whole-jurisdiction zoning would be inadequate absent arrangements with the neighboring jurisdiction. If these cross-boundary spillovers are limited in scope (say, affecting only the first two blocks beyond the border), intrajurisdictional zoning could dedicate the spillover zone to a use that would not suffer from the spillover.

Public-goods zoning presents a more complicated case. Here, the question depends on the scale of production and consumption of the local public goods for which consumers serve as important inputs. This is an interesting, and ultimately empirical, question. Consider the example of public schools in Jurisdiction G, for which the quality of students and characteristics of their families serve as inputs. It is true that excluding all "quality-detracting" or difficult-to-serve students from Jurisdiction G may help to enhance the educational product provided throughout Jurisdiction G. However, height-

---

[8] Musgrave (1969) makes a similar point when he observes that "if benefit intensity declines in successive rings around the [service] center, so should cost assessments" (296). Where a property tax makes contributions dependent on the amount of housing consumed, intrajurisdictional zoning in concentric circles could be used to calibrate payments to benefit levels. This would achieve the result suggested by Musgrave, in which "residents of the inner ring with a given taste and income will be called upon to contribute more than similar residents in the outer ring" (296).

ened production and consumption as a result of client inputs could occur at a micro level—say, at one high school's attendance zone within G. If this were so, then zoning *within* the jurisdiction could serve to attract and retain on public goods grounds. A homebuyer may care a bit less about the overall quality of the public school system in a given jurisdiction than she cares about the quality of the specific schools whose attendance zones contain her selected home.[9] Likewise, the overall crime levels in a city may be of less concern to a homebuyer than the safety in the area surrounding her home and in the areas that surround her frequent paths of travel.

The local public good of place name reputation may animate exclusion at either intrajurisdictional or whole-jurisdiction levels, depending on the extent of the area with which a given place name is identified. A profusion of smaller-scale place names coupled with intrajurisdictional zoning would reduce the incentive to exclude entrants from the entire jurisdiction. For example, existing residents of the "Old Town" district would not see a threat to the cachet of their place name if increased density were permitted in another area within the same jurisdiction known by a distinct place name, such as "New Frontier." Dilution of the "Old Town" name will only be avoided, however, if it is possible to enforce a common understanding of where, precisely, the boundaries of "Old Town" fall. Herein lies an explanation for the astonishing degree of vigilance with which some neighborhood residents and realtors police the use of place names by those just beyond the approved neighborhood boundaries.

Political motivations seem at first blush to imply whole-jurisdiction zoning; because every entrant becomes part of the same political apparatus, the only failsafe way to control the political apparatus is to control all entry. However, political or legal limits may make whole-jurisdiction zoning infeasible, or the greater political stability that comes with whole-jurisdiction zoning may be outweighed by the risk that litigation or legislation at the state level will ultimately generate more volatility in land use patterns. Political motives on their own would not imply any preference for a particular spatial pattern of residential housing within the jurisdiction. But intrajurisdictional zoning might be used to limit the total amount of housing stock open to people of different classes. Hence, intrajurisdictional zoning could be consistent with retaining political control among upper and upper-middle classes, especially if only small areas are zoned for lower-income housing and densities are controlled carefully (cf. Downs 1976, 198–199).

---

[9] In places where a school choice plan is in force, the homebuyer will treat the various possible schools as options that come with various commutes from the location of her selected home. In this case, the schools become part of the commuting option pack that she purchases with a given home's location.

Finally, monopolistic motivations would be expected to generate attempts to suppress as much potential housing competition as possible. The broader the scope of exclusion, the more potential competition will be blocked. Where it is not possible to block all new development (or is not desirable for other reasons, such as the loss of potential agglomeration benefits), the rational monopolist will attempt to allow in only housing that is not a very good substitute for her own. Intrajurisdictional zoning would provide a way to control the location and type of development.

In sum, although Tiebout-style choice is usually associated with whole-jurisdiction zoning, zoning *within* jurisdictions can also serve as an important element in inter-jurisdictional choice. Municipalities can gain a competitive edge not only by altering the overall quantity of different types of housing, but also by controlling spatial arrangements of housing within the jurisdiction (Ford 1994, 1854). A jurisdiction that tries to produce a blending of income classes by eschewing internal residential zoning classifications (Vatter 2005, 7–11) will find its efforts undermined if competing jurisdictions continue to offer stratified living arrangements that prove attractive to higher-income classes. If income mixing produces societal gains, intervention into zoning prerogatives at a higher governmental level might seem to be indicated. But would even a coordinated regional response rolling back exclusionary zoning produce the desired results? Answering this question requires the consideration of covenants as an alternative form of land use control.

Zoning Versus Covenants

Covenants have long been essential to the land use patterns of the only major unzoned American city—Houston—but they are becoming an increasingly pervasive alternative mechanism of land use control nationwide as private communities continue to proliferate. Covenants operating within private communities usually regulate residential housing to a greater extent, and at a higher level of specificity, than traditional zoning. As such, they represent attempts to fine-tune the living environment within the community and to prevent negative spillovers among residents while fostering positive ones. While some private communities are larger than some municipalities, the typical scale of a private community is smaller than that of a typical municipality. Taken together, these facts suggest that covenants can substitute for fine-grained intrajurisdictional zoning designed to address localized spillovers and to enhance the quality of small-scale local public goods. Covenants work much less well as substitutes for whole-jurisdiction or larger-scale intrajurisdictional zoning, although they could achieve some of the effects associated with such zoning, if exclusionary zoning were dramatically limited.

Consider fiscal motivations for exclusion. Limiting entry into the private community to those who will pay the established share of homeowners association dues allocates the costs of the local public goods offered within the community in a manner akin to fiscal zoning. However, if residents of private communities must still pay property taxes to support local public goods provided by the jurisdiction of which their community is a part, the inability to exclude smaller housing units from the municipality as a whole could lead to tax base slippage. But private communities may be able to work through the political system to obtain some relief from local property taxes (e.g., Rosenblum 1998, 153) or influence the funding and service levels of the municipality's local public goods. Moreover, if private communities are in a position to substitute private versions of most public goods, homeowners within these communities would likely vote to cut service levels at the municipality level (Stiglitz 1983, 46). Whether or not these tactics will be successful depends on the political power of those within private communities throughout the jurisdiction.

Political motives for exclusion seem unlikely to trigger covenants. Exclusion at the private community level would have little effect on the political balance that prevails in the jurisdiction as a whole, unless the private community makes up a large share of the jurisdiction. The development's internal political system—the homeowners' association—would not be expected to generate politically motivated exclusion, for two reasons. First, the developer decides at the outset on the precise amount and type of housing and retains political control over the development long enough to see that plan built out and most of the units sold (Henderson 1985, 262–263). As a result, the homeowners' association is not in a position to make decisions about the addition of new housing or different housing types.

Second, unlike municipal zoning, which can be altered politically at any time, covenants provide a way to make binding commitments regarding land use in period 1 that cannot be easily undone in period 2 (e.g., Henderson 1985). Such commitments, to the extent they are harder to undo than political commitments, valuably remove uncertainty for initial entrants and make them less vulnerable to political shifts (id.; Henderson 1980, 899–900).[10] This binding commitment to a planned pattern of development also curbs monopolistic tendencies or other exclusionary tendencies that early entrants might otherwise be tempted to exhibit (Henderson 1980, 894; cf. White, 1975).

Another important difference between covenants and zoning inheres in the public—and publicly enforceable—nature of the latter. While the rise of the private community governed by a homeowners' association has greatly simplified

---

[10] Of course, most private communities do allow changes on less than unanimous consent in order to avoid holdout problems. Nonetheless, typical supermajority requirements for major changes in land use provide greater protection than does a majoritarian political process.

covenant enforcement and has eliminated the free-rider problem that would otherwise exist with regard to addressing violations, it remains the case that the costs of enforcing covenants fall on homeowners within the private community rather than on the jurisdiction at large. Of course, this allocation of costs can be altered by law. Indeed, Texas state law provides for public enforcement of private covenants in Houston (Berry 2001).

The most important limitation on private covenants as a substitute for zoning is the fact that each household bound by a covenant regime must have consented to it, either expressly or by purchasing a home already bound by a covenant. This works easily and well in new developments; the developer simply drafts a master deed or declaration containing the applicable covenants, and every member of the community to whom she sells becomes thereby bound by the covenants. Matters are much more difficult in the case of an existing neighborhood. Without the central coordinating figure of a developer, hundreds or thousands of individual pairwise covenants would be required to reciprocally bind a community of even modest size (Epstein 1988, 914–915).

Administrative difficulties aside, holdouts would be able to inflict negative externalities on the rest of the community because they would not be bound by covenants to which they had not agreed. Moreover, the holdouts would not be required to contribute financially to local public goods and so could free-ride on any such goods that lacked cost-effective exclusion technologies. At least in the absence of a legal change that would overcome the holdout difficulty (Nelson 2005, 265–267), few existing neighborhoods are in a position to substitute covenants for zoning. This fact has important implications for zoning reform.

To illustrate, imagine that all zoning classifications that distinguished between different kinds of housing were prohibited. Because holdout problems thwart the establishment of new covenant-bound communities in existing neighborhoods, households wishing to use covenants as exclusion devices would be attracted to existing covenant-bound communities or to new developments that can readily set up covenant regimes. New developments require significant contiguous land and thus will be built predominantly in outlying areas where undeveloped land exists (Fischel 1999, 902). If existing covenant-bound communities are also predominantly located in newer portions of the metropolitan area, the stage would be set for outmigration from the older, core areas of the city.

To the extent that sprawling development patterns generate traffic and other externalities, creating pressures in the direction of outward movement from the metropolitan core would make matters worse. The resulting impacts on stratification and concentrated poverty could undo the gains from our hypothetical zoning reform. If something is to be done about exclusionary residential patterns, the remedy should address private exclusionary devices as well as public ones. Next, we will see how a system of land use control that takes seriously the gains and losses produced by different patterns of association supports such a comprehensive approach to exclusion.

Association Matters

Opponents of exclusionary zoning often focus their attention on fiscal arguments. The fiscal motivation for jurisdictional exclusion is easy to identify, and a proposed fix that promises to remove that incentive—say, statewide funding of education—is easy to propose. Differences in the tax base or unequal spending by different jurisdictions are also easy to spot, although a closer examination reveals complications that largely defuse the force of normative arguments based on these factors (Fischel 2001, 133–135). Nonetheless, the same fiscal arguments are made over and over—perhaps because financial arguments carry the cachet of hard numbers. But this approach misses the most important insight about residential choice: that association matters.

To be sure, it is unclear precisely *how much* association matters—for example, how much user production influences outcomes relative to other interventions—although the contribution appears to be substantial (see, e.g., Oates 1977, 213; Bénabou 1996). The mechanisms by which peer and neighborhood effects are produced are also opaque (Jencks and Mayer 1990, 113–115). Moreover, it is empirically unknown how much stratification might be reduced if the fiscal motivation for exclusion were entirely removed (Bogart 1993, 1679). While more study on these points is necessary, it seems likely that too much attention has been given to the fiscal side of local government and too little to the associational side. If peer and neighborhood effects are tremendously important to quality of life and to educational and safety outcomes, changes in associational patterns, not financial patterns, may be necessary.[11]

Gains from Different Grouping Patterns

The efficiency argument for paying attention to residential group formation across a metropolitan area stems from the observation that grouping may not be a zero-sum game (see, e.g., Fischel 2001, 69–70; Fennell 2001, 21 and n. 69; Ross and Yinger 1999, 2044). This is true in two respects. First, it is likely that the contributions that quality-enhancing individuals make to local public goods are not constant but rather depend on how many other quality-enhancing users are

---

[11] As discussed in Fennell (2001, 53–60, 71–73), groups and individuals can become more (or less) "quality enhancing." Hence, addressing exclusion is only one possible way to improve troubled groupings, but it may be an essential way if assembling a cooperative "critical mass" is needed to trigger community transformation (see, e.g., Schelling, 1978, 91–110; Oliver, 1985). By the same token, forcible reassignment or other effects of entering a new grouping might negatively influence someone's willingness to be a "quality-enhancing" participant (Fennell 2001, 71–73).

FIGURE 6.3   S-Shaped Production Function for a Local Public Good

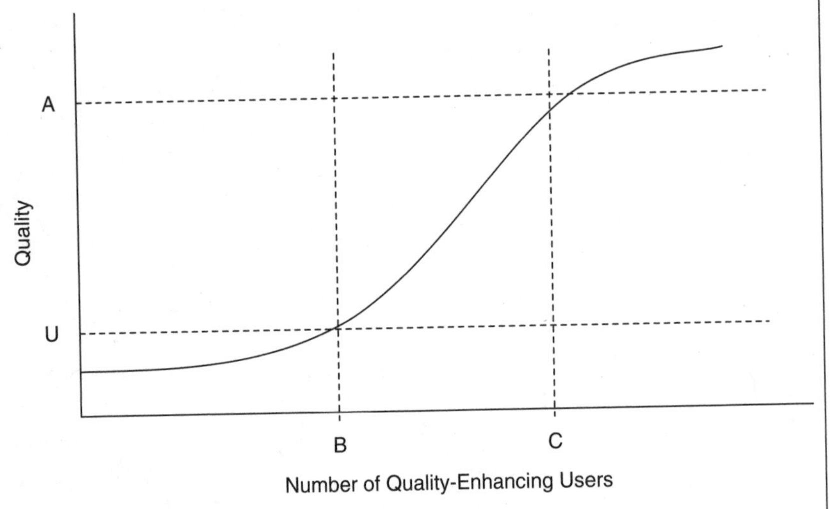

already in the pool. Second, different sets of groupings may produce varying amounts of negative or positive externalities.

The first issue relates to the production function for local public goods (Oates 1981, 95). If local public goods had a perfectly linear production function relative to the inputs of quality-enhancing individuals, then the movement of a quality-enhancing individual from one place to another would be a wash: The gaining jurisdiction would gain exactly what the losing jurisdiction lost (Jencks and Mayer 1990, 122). However, the production function for local public goods like education or public safety may be significantly nonlinear. While the true shape of the production function is an empirical question, one possibility is an S-shaped curve like that shown in figure 6.3 (Oliver et al. 1985, 527–528, fig. 1(a); Fennell 2001, 18, fig. 1).

The horizontal axis in figure 6.3 tracks the number of quality-enhancing users in a community, and the vertical axis tracks quality. The region below the lower horizontal dashed line marked U represents an unacceptable quality level, while the area above the top dashed line marked A represents an unambiguously acceptable quality level. If quality-enhancing users are distributed unequally throughout the various jurisdictions in a metropolitan area, then some of the jurisdictions will be in the area left of the vertical line marked B; others will be between B and C; and yet others will be to the right of C. It is evident that one quality-enhancing user moving from a jurisdiction that is in the range to the right of C to a jurisdiction between B and C will generate a net gain, bringing more to the community he joins than he will cost the community he leaves.

In addition to these changes, which are internal to the various gaining and losing groups, groupings of some kinds will generate spillovers that will affect quality of life in surrounding jurisdictions or communities. For example, when education or safety falls into the unacceptable region for a given community, the surrounding communities will suffer. Likewise, stellar local public goods may produce positive spillovers in the surrounding community. The magnitude of these spillovers is of course an empirical question, although it seems plausible that the negative spillovers associated with extremely inadequate local public goods would far outweigh positive spillovers associated with extremely high-quality local public goods. Hence it is possible that moving from a tighter distribution among groups in terms of the quality of their local public goods to one that is more dispersed would yield a set of spillovers that would be on balance more costly (or less beneficial) to the surrounding community.

These efficiency considerations provide reasons, in addition to social justice rationales, for caring about the pattern of residential groupings produced in a metropolitan area. Moreover, these considerations apply with equal force regardless of whether stratified groupings are produced through zoning, covenants, or some combination of the two. To address the associational issue comprehensively, however, it is necessary to confront what has become a red herring in discussions about residential exclusion generally: the invocation of "free association."

Free and Unfree Association

Tieboutian sorting is often conflated with notions of associational freedom. Invoking Tiebout, scholars pointedly ask: Why shouldn't people be able to freely choose the kinds of communities in which they wish to live? Why must every community be internally diverse? Why, indeed, can't dozens of distinct specialized communities exist side by side in our metropolitan areas, offering a rich smorgasbord of choices to all? The answers to these questions come back to exclusion. If exclusion and its motivations are taken seriously, the flaws in the associational freedom argument become apparent.

In the case of residential housing, one must live with some set of neighbors if one is going to take advantage of the agglomeration benefits of the metropolitan area. The sorting of households into jurisdictions within a metropolitan area can be understood as the exhaustive partitioning of a set into subsets. This fact makes forced exclusion (from one or more subsets) a form of forced inclusion (in one of the remaining subsets). The popular version of the Tiebout hypothesis sidesteps this associational difficulty with the handy notion that different people want different things. Some people like art and culture, the story runs, while others want athletic fields and sports stadiums, while still others want excellent schools and libraries.

The unstated premise of this "differing tastes" model is that preferences are nonconflicting, so that everyone is happy with their grouping. This seems implausible (Frug 1998). We might suppose that many people would prefer to group up with those who are best positioned to achieve important goals, like producing high-quality education and public safety at low cost.[12] Some choosing protocol must determine who gets into the more-preferred groupings and who is effectively relegated to some less-attractive grouping.

Residential exclusion—whether government-produced through zoning or government-sponsored through the enforcement of private covenants—establishes a protocol that privileges certain associational choices over others and determines the currency in which bids may be made for associational primacy. Whatever the efficiency-based arguments for the choosing protocols established through land use controls, it is wrong to characterize them as facilitating or vindicating "free association" across the board. It is impossible, however, to avoid setting *some* protocol for groupings that will frustrate some people's associational objectives (Wechsler 1959, 34), whether that protocol is "chase the rich" or "first in time rules the game" or "switch on the Waring blender."[13] "Free association" does not constitute a normative argument in favor of land use policies that have the purpose and effect of excluding some segment of the population from residential areas that they would otherwise choose to enter.

Toward a Theory of Associational Entitlements

Legal scholarship on land use controls has understandably focused on legal entitlements to do or not do various things with or on the land. But what goes under the head of "land use control" is in substantial part directed at controlling association (see, e.g., Mills 1979, 536). Controlling who will be one's neighbors means controlling living environments, controlling politics, and controlling the quality of local public goods for which consumers are signifi-

---

[12] To be sure, concerns about relative standing in the community could create pressures in the other direction (Frank 1985; Jencks and Mayer 1990, 116–117). It is also true that the pervasive existence of land use restrictions does not provide conclusive proof that conflicting preferences are being suppressed; the restrictions might be superfluous, merely reproducing what market processes would produce in any event (see Ross and Yinger 1999, 2015). But given the tremendous social harm associated with concentrated poverty, and especially its devastating effects on the life chances of young children, the assumption that the present exclusionary arrangements are what "everyone wants" does not seem convincing.

[13] Ellickson and Been (2005) refer to a land use regime that "would call for all land uses and all types of households to be represented in each neighborhood in proportion to their representation in the entire metropolitan area" as the "Waring blender model" (771).

cant inputs. To confront the reality of land use controls as they impact residential choice requires a theory of associational entitlements.

One of the unstated assumptions underlying efficient sorting into jurisdictions is that the jurisdictions are offering bundles of services and amenities that they have a right to offer. If some of the offerings are stolen from others, then the resulting competition will be unfair and the resulting allocation will not be efficient. For example, suppose that a jurisdiction attracts residents by offering an unlimited, free supply of water. It is able to supply this local public good only because it diverts water from another community, which it thereby deprives of adequate water. There is little question that this is not the sort of jurisdictional competition that will produce efficient results.

The associational interests infringed by exclusion should be analyzed similarly. Of course, the sorts of entitlements that are infringed through sorting are not as well defined as those to water. However, if one accepts the notion of an underlying entitlement not to have costs off-loaded from (or benefits diverted to) another jurisdiction, then exclusion that produces such off-loading (or diversion) is illegitimate. At present, we lack a vocabulary for such an entitlement.

As a starting point, we might conceptualize associational possibilities within a metropolitan area as a common resource susceptible to the same sorts of dilemmas as other common pool resources. Groups form out of a background population, carrying with them various amounts of associational surplus or deficit. As privileged groups set up land use mechanisms designed to skim out as much associational surplus as possible, excluded households become more concentrated. These groups left behind may suffer associational deficits that far outweigh the cumulative benefits enjoyed by the prioritized groupings and may also emit externalities harmful to the larger community. Significantly, the logic of associational entitlements would extend beyond traditional zoning to encompass land use controls in private developments. Working out the parameters of such an entitlement will not be easy or uncontroversial. But work in that direction should begin.

Advancing the notion of an associational entitlement does not imply summarily forcing higher-income people into lower-income neighborhoods against their will. Recognizing an entitlement is only half the task—and perhaps not even the most interesting half. A legal system must then decide how that entitlement is to be protected—whether through property rules, liability rules, or perhaps even a hybrid arrangement that uses options to serve a demand-revealing function (Calabresi and Melamed 1972; Ellickson 1977; Fennell 2005). For example, the notion of compensation schemes (liability rules) to redress harm caused by land use controls (see, e.g., Ellickson 1977, 506) could provide a starting point for thinking about associational entitlements.

Conclusion

The contributions of Tiebout's ideas to the analysis of land use controls have remained largely untapped to date. The version of the Tiebout hypothesis popularized in law schools tells a free-market or free-association story that does not capture the constraints that exclusion places on jurisdictional choice. This normative spin has alienated many of those who are most concerned about the problems of exclusion, even as it has led others to accept stratification induced by land use controls on the grounds that it is an efficient product of jurisdictional competition.

A closer look at Tiebout's work reveals its relevance to the critical analysis of land use controls. Most significantly, Tiebout reminds us to focus on the aspects of the jurisdictional bundle that attract residents. If exclusion is the prize in the cereal box that drives jurisdictional choice, then it makes sense to look closely at how—and why—jurisdictions use exclusion competitively. Likewise, we cannot understand jurisdictional choice without examining the choice-constraining effects of such attractive exclusion. This chapter is just an initial step toward a more fully articulated discussion of the connections between the Tiebout hypothesis, exclusion, and land use policy, but I hope that it will encourage legal scholars to take a closer look at Tiebout's remarkable work—both to plumb its depths and to confront its limits.

REFERENCES

Becker, Gary S., and Kevin M. Murphy. 2000. *Social economics: Market behavior in a social environment.* Cambridge, MA: Belknap Press of Harvard University Press.

Been, Vicki. 1991. "Exit" as a constraint on land use exactions: Rethinking the unconstitutional conditions doctrine. *Columbia Law Review* 91:473–545.

Bénabou, Roland. 1996. Equity and efficiency in human capital investment: The local connection. *Review of Economic Studies* 63:237–264.

Berry, Christopher. 2001. Land use regulation and residential segregation: Does zoning matter? *American Law and Economics Review* 3:251–274.

Bogart, William T. 1993. "What big teeth you have!": Identifying the motivations for exclusionary zoning. *Urban Studies* 30:1669–1681.

Buchanan, James M. 1965. An economic theory of clubs. *Economica* 32 (new series): 1–14.

Calabrese, Stephen, Dennis Epple, and Richard Romano. 2006. Non-fiscal residential zoning. In *The Tiebout Model at Fifty,* William A. Fischel, ed. Cambridge, MA: Lincoln Institute of Land Policy.

Calabresi, Guido, and Douglas Melamed. 1972. Property rules, liability rules, and inalienability: One view of the cathedral. *Harvard Law Review* 85:1089–1128.

Cribbet, John E., Corwin W. Johnson, Roger W. Findley, and Ernest E. Smith. 2002. *Property: Cases and materials.* 8th ed. Westbury, NY: Foundation Press.

Delafons, John. 1969. *Land-use controls in the United States.* 2nd ed. Cambridge, MA: MIT Press.

Diamond, Douglas B. Jr., and George S. Tolley. 1982. The economic roles of urban amenities. In *The economics of urban amenities*, Douglas B. Diamond Jr. and George S. Tolley, eds. New York: Academic Press.

Dietderich, Andrew G. 1996. An egalitarian's market: The economics of inclusionary zoning reclaimed. *Fordham Urban Law Journal* 43:23–104.

Donohue, John D. 1997. Tiebout? Or not Tiebout? The market metaphor and America's devolution debate. *Journal of Economic Perspectives* 11:73–81.

Downs, Anthony. 1973. *Opening up the suburbs: An urban strategy for America*. New Haven: Yale University Press.

———. 1976. The future of American ghettos. In *The urban economy*, Harold M. Hochman, ed. New York: Norton.

Dynarski, Mark, Robert Schwab, and Ernest Zampelli. 1989. Local characteristics and public production: The case of education. *Journal of Urban Economics* 26:250–263.

Ellickson, Bryan. 1971. Jurisdictional fragmentation and residential choice. *American Economic Review* (papers and proceedings) 61:334–339.

Ellickson, Robert C. 1977. Suburban growth controls: An economic and legal analysis. *Yale Law Journal* 86:385–511.

———. 1993. Property in land. *Yale Law Journal* 102:1315–1400.

Ellickson, Robert C., and Vicki L. Been. 2005. *Land use controls: Cases and materials*. 3rd ed. New York: Aspen Publishers.

Epple, Dennis, Thomas Romer, and Radu Filimon. 1988. Community development with endogenous land use controls. *Journal of Public Economics* 35:133–162.

Epple, Dennis, and Alan Zelenitz. 1981. The implications of competition among jurisdictions: Does Tiebout need politics? *Journal of Political Economy* 89:1197–1217.

Epstein, Richard A. 1988. Covenants and constitutions. *Cornell Law Review* 73:906–927.

Fair Housing Act, 42 U.S.C. §§ 3601 et seq.

Fennell, Lee Anne. 2001. Beyond exit and voice: User participation in the production of local public goods. *Texas Law Review* 80:1–87.

———. 2002. Homes rule. *Yale Law Journal* 112:617–664 (book review of Fischel 2001).

———. 2005. Revealing options. *Harvard Law Review* 118:1399–1488.

Fischel, William A. 1985. *The economics of zoning laws: A property rights approach to American land use controls*. Baltimore: Johns Hopkins University Press.

———. 1999. Voting, risk aversion, and the NIMBY syndrome: A comment on Robert Nelson's "Privatizing the Neighborhood." *George Mason Law Review* 7:881–903.

———. 2001. *The homevoter hypothesis: How home values influence local government taxation, school finance, and land-use policies*. Cambridge, MA: Harvard University Press.

Ford, Richard Thompson. 1994. The boundaries of race: Political geography in legal analysis. *Harvard Law Review* 107:1843–1921.

Frank, Robert H. 1985. *Choosing the right pond: Human behavior and the quest for status*. New York; Oxford [Oxfordshire]: Oxford University Press.

Frug, Gerald E. 1998. City services. *NYU Law Review* 73:23–96.

Gillette, Clayton P. 1994. Courts, covenants, and communities. *University of Chicago Law Review* 61:1375–1441.

———. 2001. Regionalization and interlocal bargains. *NYU Law Review* 76:190–271.

Hamilton, Bruce W. 1975. Zoning and property taxation in a system of local governments. *Urban Studies* 12:205–211.

————. 1976. Capitalization of intrajurisdictional differences in local tax prices. *American Economic Review* 66:742–753.

————. 1983. A review: Is the property tax a benefit tax? In *Local provision of public services: The Tiebout model after twenty-five years*, George R. Zodrow, ed. New York: Academic Press.

Heilbrun, James. 1972. Poverty and public finance in the older central cities. In *Readings in urban economics*, Matthew Edel and Jerome Rothenberg, eds. New York: Macmillan.

Henderson, J. Vernon. 1980. Community development: The effects of growth and uncertainty. *American Economic Review* 70:894–910.

————. 1985. The Tiebout model: Bring back the entrepreneurs. *Journal of Political Economy* 93:248–264.

Hirschman, Albert O. 1970. *Exit, voice, and loyalty: Responses to declines in firms, organizations, and states*. Cambridge, MA: Harvard University Press.

Jackson, John E. 1975. Public needs, private behavior, and metropolitan governance: A summary essay. In *Public needs and private behavior in metropolitan areas*, John E. Jackson, ed. Cambridge, MA: Ballinger Publishing.

Jencks, Christopher, and Susan E. Mayer. 1990. The social consequences of growing up in a poor neighborhood. In *Inner-city poverty in the United States*, Laurence E. Lynn Jr. and Michael G. H. McGeary, eds. Washington, DC: National Academy Press.

The Kaiser Committee. 1972. *A decent home: Report of the president's committee on urban housing* (Washington, DC: U.S. Government Printing Office, 1969). Reprinted in *Readings in urban economics*, Matthew Edel and Jerome Rothenberg, eds. New York: Macmillan.

Ladd, Helen F., and John Yinger. 1989. *America's ailing cities: Fiscal health and the design of urban policy*. Baltimore: Johns Hopkins University Press.

Lenon, Maryjane, Sajal K. Chattopadhyay, and Dennis R. Heffley. 1996. Zoning and fiscal interdependencies. *Journal of Real Estate Finance and Economics* 12:221–234.

Manski, Charles F. 1992. Educational choice (vouchers) and social mobility. *Economics of Education Review* 11:351–369.

Massey, Douglas S., and Nancy A. Denton. 1993. *American apartheid: Segregation and the making of the underclass*. Cambridge, MA: Harvard University Press.

Miller, Gary J. 1981. *Cities by contract: The politics of municipal incorporation*. Cambridge, MA: MIT Press.

Mills, Edwin S. 1979. Economic analysis of urban land-use controls. In *Current issues in urban economics*, Peter Mieszkowski and Mahlon Straszheim, eds. Baltimore: Johns Hopkins University Press.

Mills, Edwin S., and Wallace E. Oates. 1975. The theory of local public services and finance: Its relevance to urban fiscal and zoning behavior. In *Fiscal zoning and land use controls*, Edwin S. Mills and Wallace E. Oates, eds. Lexington, MA: Lexington Books.

Musgrave, Richard A. 1969. *Fiscal systems*. New Haven: Yale University Press.

Nelson, Robert H. 1977. *Zoning and property rights: An analysis of the American system of land-use regulation*. Cambridge, MA: MIT Press.

————. 2005. *Private neighborhoods and the transformation of local government*. Washington, DC: Urban Institute Press.

Oakerson, Ronald J. 1999. *Governing local public economies: Creating the civic metropolis*. Oakland, CA: ICS Press.

Oates, Wallace E. 1977. The use of local zoning ordinances to regulate population flows and the quality of local services. In *Essays in labor market analysis*, Orley C. Ashenfelter and Wallace E. Oates, eds. New York: Wiley.

———. 1981. On local finance and the Tiebout model. *American Economic Review* (papers and proceedings) 71:93–98.

———. 2006. The many faces of the Tiebout model. In *The Tiebout model at fifty*, William A. Fischel, ed. Cambridge, MA: Lincoln Institute of Land Policy.

Oliver, Pamela, Gerald Marwell, and Ruy Teixeira. 1985. A theory of the critical mass I: Interdependence, group heterogeneity, and the production of collective action. *American Journal of Sociology* 91:522–556.

Ostrom, Vincent, Charles M. Tiebout, and Robert Warren. 1961. The organization of government in metropolitan areas: A theoretical inquiry. *American Political Science Review* 55:831–842.

Pogodzinski, J. Michael, and Tim R. Sass. 1990. The economic theory of zoning: A critical review. *Land Economics* 66:294–314.

Poindexter, Georgette C. 1995. Towards a legal framework for regional redistribution of poverty-related expenses. *Washington University Journal of Urban and Contemporary Law* 47:3–50.

Pozdena, Randall Johnston. 1988. *The modern economics of housing: A guide to theory and policy for finance and real estate professionals.* New York: Quorum Books.

Rose, Carol M. 1998. The several futures of property: Of cyberspace and folk tales, emission trades and ecosystems. *Minnesota Law Review* 83:129–182.

Rose-Ackerman, Susan. 1983. Beyond Tiebout: Modeling the political economy of local government. In *Local provision of public services: The Tiebout model after twenty-five years*, George R. Zodrow, ed. New York: Academic Press.

Rosenblum, Nancy L. 1998. *Membership and morals: The personal uses of pluralism in America.* Princeton, NJ: Princeton University Press.

Ross, Stephen, and John Yinger. 1999. Sorting and voting: A review of the literature on urban public finance. In *Handbook of regional and urban economics, vol. 3*, Paul Cheshire and Edwin S. Mills, eds. Amsterdam: North-Holland.

Rothenberg, Jerome. 1972. The nature of redevelopment benefits. In *Readings in urban economics*, Matthew Edel and Jerome Rothenberg, eds. New York: Macmillan.

Rubinfeld, Daniel L. 1985. The economics of the local public sector. In *Handbook of public economics, vol. 2*, Alan J. Auerbach and Martin Feldstein, eds. Amsterdam: North-Holland.

Schelling, Thomas C. 1971. Dynamic models of segregation. *Journal of Mathematical Sociology* 1:143–186.

Schragger, Richard C. 2001. The limits of localism. *Michigan Law Review* 100:371–472.

Schwab, Robert M., and Wallace E. Oates. 1991. Community composition and the provision of local public goods: A normative analysis. *Journal of Public Economics* 44:217–237.

Span, Henry A. 2001. How the courts should fight exclusionary zoning. *Seton Hall Law Review* 32:1–107.

Stiglitz, Joseph E. 1983. The theory of local public goods twenty-five years after Tiebout: A perspective. In *Local provision of public services: The Tiebout model after twenty-five years*, George R. Zodrow, ed. New York: Academic Press.

Strahilevitz, Lior. 2005. Exclusionary amenities in residential communities. University of Chicago, Law and Economics Working Paper No. 250; and University of Chicago, Public Law Working Paper No. 98. Available at http://ssrn.com/abstract=757388.

Tiebout, Charles M. 1956. A pure theory of local expenditures. *Journal of Political Economy* 64:416–424.

Vatter, Marc H. 2005. A welfare analysis of residential zoning within a jurisdiction. Available at http://ssrn.com/abstract=636962.

Walters, Alan A. 1975. *Noise and prices.* Oxford [UK]: Clarendon Press.

Webber, Melvin M. 1963. Order in diversity: Community without propinquity. In *Cities and space: The future use of urban land,* Lowdon Wingo Jr., ed. Baltimore: Johns Hopkins Press.

Wechsler, Herbert. 1959. Toward neutral principles of constitutional law. *Harvard Law Review* 73:1–35.

White, Michelle J. 1975. Fiscal zoning in fragmented metropolitan areas. In *Fiscal zoning and land use controls,* Edwin S. Mills and Wallace E. Oates, eds. Lexington, MA: Lexington Books.

Yinger, John. 1981. Capitalization and the median voter. *American Economic Review* (papers and proceedings) 71:99–103.

The Puzzle of the Optimal Social Composition of Neighborhoods

ROBERT C. ELLICKSON

The papers by Charles Tiebout (1956) and Lee Anne Fennell (2006) both serve as handy springboards for exploring a central and controversial issue of urban policy: the optimal sorting of people among residential neighborhoods. It is plain that many households seek to reside in environments inhabited mostly by people like themselves and also that many developers and local politicians cater to these tastes. The familiar result, in metropolitan areas of the United States and elsewhere, is a sharp differentiation of suburbs and central-city neighborhoods by social class and race. Professor Fennell is concerned about how exclusionary measures adopted by localities and developers may contribute to this pattern. To what extent is the pattern worrisome and what, if anything, should be done about it?

Before offering some brief thoughts on these dauntingly difficult questions, I highlight several of the significant contributions that Lee Fennell makes in her paper. Tiebout's analysis might be misconstrued to imply that households "shopping with their feet" for a new residence are apt to focus mainly on the identities of governing localities. Fennell elegantly demonstrates that would-be movers, while indeed much concerned about location, commonly give more weight to the features of, say, a residence's immediate block-front, local shopping opportunities, and daily commuting ranges, than to the basket of local government policies tied to that residence. In addition, while Tiebout envisioned that suburbs would compete primarily by offering different packages of taxation and spending policies, Fennell emphasizes that suburbanites also are highly likely to be interested in the social characteristics and political inclinations of their neighbors. They therefore may be tempted to use zoning and other regulatory policies to exclude "undesirables." (Of course, they rarely admit this openly but instead

I thank Jan Brueckner for references and William Baude for research assistance.

mask their efforts behind a fog of rhetoric about unwanted environmental and fiscal impacts.) As Fennell cogently notes, even homeowners who personally favor having diverse neighbors may end up supporting exclusionary policies in order to maximize the market value of their homes. She convincingly argues that many scholars present too sunny a picture of the Tiebout model. Tiebout himself started his analysis by explicitly assuming that local political choices have no external consequences. If exclusionary policies are costly to those excluded, however, as plainly is often the case (Cutler and Glaeser 1997; Denton 2001), Fennell demonstrates that Tiebout-style competition among suburbs can turn out to be a negative-sum game. In a volume that mostly celebrates Tiebout, this is a highly appropriate cautionary note.

The Shortcomings of a Metropolitan Area with Undifferentiated Neighborhoods

This brings us to the substantive issue that is the focus of this comment: the ideal level of residential integration. Like most others who address this issue, I focus mainly on the extent of black-white segregation in urban areas. This is appropriate not only on account of the baneful roles of slavery, Jim Crow policies, and antiblack prejudice in American history, but also because African Americans live in more segregated circumstances than do the members of any other racial group. In light of these facts, most commentators understandably assert, without expectation of challenge, that greater degrees of racial integration in housing (and hence schooling) are unquestionably normatively desirable. When new U.S. Census data appear, researchers pore over them to calculate the rate of progress, if any, toward the goal of a more integrated society. But such a normative perspective, although generally sound, is too simple.

For many decades, scholars have relied mainly on Karl Taeuber's dissimilarity index to measure segregation. The dissimilarity index is a measure of the percentage of the persons in the group under consideration that would have to move in order for the members of that group to be randomly distributed in the pertinent territory.[1] According to this metric, black-white segregation in U.S. metropolitan areas increased markedly from about 44.0 in 1890 to about 79.0 in 1970, but thereafter declined steadily to 65.2 in 2000.[2] Depending on the eye of the observer, the rate of black-white desegregation in the 1990s can be regarded as either "very slow" (Logan 2003, 254) or, at least in some ways, "remarkable" (Glaeser and Vigdor 2003, 226).

---

[1] Glaeser and Vigdor (2003) provide more technical definitions of this and other indexes of segregation.

[2] Glaeser and Vigdor (2003, 217–218, 234). The first two numbers are visual estimates based on the authors' graph on p. 218. Segregation indexes, it should be noted, are substantially higher when calculated at the block level (Massey and Denton 1993, 47).

The extreme level of segregation in the Detroit metropolitan area, where the dissimilarity index in 2000 was 84.0 (Glaeser and Vigdor 2003, 228), is rightly regarded as disturbingly high. But consider whether a metropolitan area's index also could be troublingly low. If reductions in the dissimilarity index were always to be applauded, the optimal index reading would be 00.0. Under that condition—what might be called a "Waring blender" distribution of the population (Ellickson and Been 2005, 771)—all demographic groups would be randomly distributed throughout a metropolitan area. There would be great demographic diversity *within* each neighborhood but no diversity at all *among* them. There would not only be no distinctively black or white neighborhoods, but also no Chinatowns, no blue-collar neighborhoods, no gay neighborhoods, no graduate-student ghettos, no clusters of struggling artists. When teaching various law school courses, I ask students to assess this Waring blender model of metropolitan population distribution. Respondents invariably are negative. They regard the absence of specialized communities as boring and too restrictive on freedom of association.

There is evidence that most African Americans similarly would object to a Waring blender distribution of metropolitan population. The most-cited of the relevant studies were conducted by Reynolds Farley and associates (1993). The Farley team surveyed black households in the Detroit metropolitan area to ascertain their preferences about the black-white racial distribution of households living on their immediate block. In Farley's most recent survey in 1992, the great majority of black respondents favored a block that was at least half black, and their most popular choice was a block more than two-thirds black (Farley et al. 1993, 23). If the Detroit metropolitan area were to have had a dissimilarity index of 00.0 at the time of this survey, 22 percent of the residents on each of its blocks would have been black. Few of Farley's black respondents gave high ratings to a block of that sort (although 87 percent did state that they would be willing to move into it).

Although Farley's results are hardly definitive,[3] other evidence suggests widespread black support for at least the option of living in a mostly black neighborhood. Although few African American scholars have abandoned integrationist ideals, many increasingly note the political and social advantages of the existence of some predominantly black neighborhoods (Cashin 2001; Powell and Spencer 2003). It is increasingly noted that observed black

---

[3] For many reasons, Farley et al.'s results should be interpreted with caution. Detroit is one of the most segregated metropolitan areas in the United States. Their survey explored attitudes only about the racial composition of block-fronts, not of neighborhoods. Farley's black respondents frequently stated that their preferences derived mainly from fears that whites wouldn't welcome them (Ellen 2000, 136). Finally, there is evidence that black households actually put little weight on the racial makeup of neighborhoods when they move (Ellen 2000, 131–151).

clusterings are at least partly voluntary (Tein 1992; Patterson 1997, 46–48). And there have long been black separatists who reject integrationist aspirations altogether (Hall 1977).

If Detroit's current dissimilarity index of 84.0 is too high, but an index of 00.0 also would be too low, the knotty normative question is how to identify an optimal, or at least acceptable, degree of integration.[4] Consider Los Angeles County, which in 2000 had a black-white dissimilarity index of 68.0. The average black household in Los Angeles then lived in a census tract that was 34 percent black (Logan 2003, 245).[5] Can African Americans in most areas of Los Angeles now be regarded as acceptably integrated? In light of the results of surveys such as Farley's, should Los Angeles policy makers conceivably consider initiatives to increase the concentration of black households in some neighborhoods?

Two Contrasting Scholarly Views

The Unbending Integrationist Perspective

Perhaps the most-cited recent publication on racial segregation in the United States is *American Apartheid* by sociologists Douglas Massey and Nancy Denton (1993). The authors' title nicely captures their normative outlook. They regard the current degree of racial segregation in American neighborhoods as thoroughly pernicious and deem government policy still to be at the root of it. (But compare Ellen [2000], which offers a more temperate assessment.) In their most unguarded moments, Massey and Denton endorse, to reduce black poverty, the "dismantling" or "eradication" of the ghetto (1993, 15, 218). These statements imply that governments should adopt affirmative policies to both break up existing poor black neighborhoods and also prevent their future formation. Massey and Denton's normative ideal surely isn't a dissimilarity index of 00.0, a pattern that appeals to virtually no one. But their stance is unclear because at no point do they explicitly discuss the optimal level of racial integration.

Most legal scholars who analyze issues of housing segregation also implicitly favor ever greater racial diversity within neighborhoods. (See Fiss [2003, 28–43, but compare 29]; Sander [1998]; and Schuck [2003, 203–260], which offers a more complex assessment.) In general, this position is understandable and defensible. Many current demographic clusterings have resulted from the persistence of negative racial stereotypes and also from exclusionary zoning prac-

---

[4] Ellen (2000, 15–16) provides a concise review of the literature on the issue.
[5] This result is partly attributable to the relatively low percentage of blacks (about 10 percent) in Los Angeles County in 2000.

tices and other government efforts to promote segregation. In addition, the perverse dynamics of tipping can lead to a greater degree of neighborhood segregation than most people desire (Schelling 1978, 140–155). Breaking up underclass subcultures possibly also may have major social benefits (Ellen 2000, 157–160).[6] But what if some largely middle-class African American neighborhoods have come into being mainly on account of the residents' preferences to congregate mostly with people like themselves? Then confident policy prescriptions are not as easy to make.

Tiebout and Other Devotees of Municipal Specialization

Urban economists generally are more likely than scholars in other disciplines to appreciate the advantages of diverse neighborhoods. Expanding consumer choice, after all, is one of the holy grails of economics. But urban economists at times are insensitive to the possibly negative social consequences of municipal differentiation. In his landmark article, Tiebout mainly foresaw households sorting themselves out according to preferences for government taxation and service policies, not according to preferences concerning the social characteristics of their neighbors.[7] Economists building on the Tiebout model, of course, have added social factors to the mix. Hamilton (1975) described how a municipality could use zoning to prevent fiscal free-riding by the less wealthy. Applying notions of "club goods" and "peer effects," other economists have given weight to the fact that people can care deeply about who their neighbors are (see, e.g., Brueckner and Lee 1989; Schwab and Oates 1991). In general, however, urban economists in the Tieboutian tradition pay more attention to the benefits that like-minded people can obtain from clustering together than they do to Fennell's principal concern: the costs this clustering can impose on those excluded from the club. (But see, for example, Cutler and Glaeser [1997] and Calabrese, Epple, and Romano [2006], two works that explicitly consider effects on both insiders and outsiders.)

Analyzing the Issue of the Optimal Degree of Integration

In sum, unbending integrationists and devotees of suburban specialization both typically avoid tackling the issue of the optimal degree of integration. Nor does Fennell's chapter discuss the issue at any length. In this brief comment, I put forward a few conceptual tools that may help provide purchase on the question.

---

[6] Findings from the ongoing Moving to Opportunity experiment, available on its Web site (see References), should shed more light on these questions.

[7] But see Tiebout's brief recognition that consumers also desire to associate with "nice" people (1956, 418, n. 12). Especially since he was writing before the civil rights revolution, it is notable that Tiebout in

The Tradeoff Between Bonding and Bridging Social Capital

An exclusionary policy commonly is likely *both* to benefit insiders *and* to harm outsiders. This makes normative assessment difficult (see Stolzenberg [1993], an empathetic inquiry into the issue of group boundaries). As mentioned, urban economists sometimes are insensitive to the external-harm portion of the equation. Fennell, for her part, at times downplays the internal-benefit portion—for example, when she refers to "rights of association" as a "red herring."[8] Although associational rights surely should not be permitted to automatically trump all other considerations, they plainly are entitled to some weight (Span 2001, 9–14).

Robert Putnam's (2000) distinction between two forms of valuable social capital is conceptually fruitful in this context. Social capital consists of relational ties between people that give rise to trust and cooperative interaction. Putnam distinguishes between "bonding" social capital—that which exists among the insiders of a group—and "bridging" social capital—that between members of different groups (22–24). Entitling members of a group to exclude commonly will enhance their bonding social capital—a good thing as far as it goes. Putnam nevertheless puts particular stress on the value, in a diverse and pluralistic society, of bridging social capital. Because bridging between groups tends to make each group less closely knit, however, the production of more bridging social capital typically results in the sacrifice of some bonding social capital. To an economist the problem is like the familiar tradeoff between guns and butter. In both contexts, the optimal outcome likely calls for production of some of each. In the case of the two forms of social capital, one practical difficulty is that little if anything is known about the shape of the production-possibilities frontier.

The Normative Relevance of the Size of an Excluding Group

It is plausible that associational rights (including exclusionary rights) usually are more important for members of a small group than for members of a large group. ("Size" turns mainly on the headcount of a group's members but perhaps also partly on the territorial area that the group controls.) Enabling small groups to form strong internal bonds helps individuals find havens of relative intimacy in a mass society of strangers. A university thus is likely to segregate

---

his landmark article makes no mention of either race or social class. Fennell rightly chides him for this omission.

[8] Fennell shows sensitivity to insiders' concerns, however, when she suggests that the "associational entitlements" that she proposes might only be protected by means of liability rules.

its faculty offices by department in part to foster within-department bonding. This policy is likely to lead to the evolution of quite different cultures in the campus buildings that house, say, the economics and French departments. As group size increases, however, a group's exclusionary policy tends both to contribute less to bonding social capital and to interfere more with the production of bridging social capital. For example, if the professors in a university's science departments were to request the establishment of a special dining room solely for their use, university administrators probably would be wise to reject their plea. While the dining room might contribute to bonding among the scientists, it also likely would seriously impede bridging between science and nonscience professors.

If one conceives of a social group as a granule, one can imagine policy makers pursuing integrationist policies in a residential setting at a variety of different grains.[9] Here is a list of grains of urban social environments, which become coarser the lower they appear in the list:

1. household[10]
2. block-front
3. cluster of several residential blocks
4. neighborhood (roughly, an elementary school attendance area)
5. submunicipality (roughly, a high school attendance area)
6. entire municipality (situated within a much larger metropolitan area)

Proponents of integrationist policies should specify at what grain they desire to achieve more social diversity. Should policy makers, for example, make efforts to integrate residents at the block-front level or only much more coarsely—say, at the municipality-wide level? Anthony Downs, in his book *Opening Up the Suburbs* (1973), implies that he is mainly interested in achieving integration at the neighborhood and submunicipality levels, policies that would diversify student bodies in local schools.

The tangled history of the much-discussed Mount Laurel litigation in New Jersey illustrates the risks of erratic thinking about the grain of desired social integration. The New Jersey Supreme Court's *Mount Laurel I* decision,[11] which cast into doubt exclusionary zoning practices throughout the state, prohibited a developing municipality from practicing social exclusion at the citywide level and arguably also at the submunicipality level. The *Mount Laurel I* court,

---

[9] Compare Fennell's discussion of the "scale of exclusion."

[10] The Supreme Court has been particularly protective of family households, whose associational rights commonly do serve as trumps. See, for example, *Moore v. City of East Cleveland*, 431 U.S. 494 (1977).

[11] *Southern Burlington County NAACP v. Township of Mount Laurel*, 336 A.2d 713 (N.J. 1975).

however, explicitly stated that a New Jersey municipality was entitled to establish exclusive zones for certain of its areas (probably as large as an entire neighborhood) as long as it made the construction of lower-cost housing "reasonably possible somewhere." By contrast, eight years later, *Mount Laurel II*,[12] a decision handed down by a mostly revamped set of New Jersey Supreme Court justices, shifted emphasis to a much finer grain of integration. This second decision in effect ordered New Jersey municipalities to favor development projects within each of which at least 20 percent of the units would be heavily subsidized. The *Mount Laurel II* court thus sought to achieve economic integration within each new subdivision—in practice, a grain as fine as the cluster of blocks and, in some instances, the block-front. If, in a relatively intimate setting, bonding social capital indeed warrants more nurturing than does bridging social capital, *Mount Laurel I* seems the more socially sensitive of the two decisions.[13]

Fennell is greatly concerned about developers' possible use of covenants as exclusionary devices. But covenants, as she herself notes at places, usually operate at a much finer grain than zoning classifications do. When a real estate firm develops a large new community, it may have a degree of monopoly power vis-à-vis a Tieboutian shopper. In these relatively rare cases, Fennell's concerns about covenants are justified. Most housing construction projects, however, involve no more than several dozen units. A survey of California residential community associations found that the median number of units per association was 43 (Ellickson and Been 2005, 584), the equivalent of no more than a block-front or a cluster of blocks. A municipality's exclusionary policies, by contrast, commonly operate more coarsely (usually somewhere between numbers 4 and 6 on the list), a grain more likely to suppress the production of bridging social capital. In general, exclusionary covenants are far less worrisome than exclusionary zoning.

Anticipating Changes in Preferences About Neighborhood Composition

Economists traditionally have taken individuals' preferences as givens. For example, if it is true (as Farley asserts) that most blacks prefer to live in neighborhoods that are at least half black, some economists might be reluctant to question either the stability or source of that taste. Preferences about neighborhood makeup, however, are hardly immutable. An ambitious policy maker therefore might attempt to satisfy not extant tastes about the identity of neighbors but rather such tastes as they might evolve. Numerous studies indicate, for

---

[12] *Southern Burlington County NAACP v. Township of Mount Laurel*, 456 A.2d 390 (N.J. 1983).

[13] Ellickson (1981) provides more detailed criticisms of the "inclusionary zoning" approach that *Mount Laurel II* embraced. But compare Dietderich (1996).

example, that antiblack prejudice on the part of whites has declined during the past half-century, partly on account of increasing contact with blacks (Ellen 2000, 104–130, 159). In addition, in surveys many blacks indicate that they are averse to living near whites partly because they fear whites will not welcome their presence (Ellen 2000, 136). Policy makers therefore plausibly can antici-pate continuing weakening among members of both racial groups of tastes for segregated neighborhoods.

The Merits of Modest Interventions to Facilitate Tiebout-Style Shopping

Because Fennell leaves policy particulars for another occasion, it is difficult to assess the merits of the "associational entitlements" she proposes. She appar-ently would grant these entitlements to individuals and households. If so, she is a Tieboutian in the sense that she is willing to leave the process of pairing households with neighborhoods mostly in the hands of the households them-selves, as opposed to placing it in the hands of government officials empowered to dictate residential patterns from on high.

It is striking that even integrationists as staunch as Massey and Denton also turn out to be Tieboutians in the same sense. Massey and Denton's occasional call for "dismantling the ghetto" ultimately proves to be merely rhetorical. There once was a federally funded effort to dismantle ghettos: the urban renewal program of 1949–1974. Many cities used urban renewal funds to raze poor, black neighborhoods, thereby destroying much bonding social capital. Advocates for the poor applauded the eventual demise of the program. A gov-ernment bent on achieving a Taeuber dissimilarity index of 00.0 likely would have to be similarly coercive, perhaps even to the point of forcibly evicting members of demographic groups overrepresented in a particular neighbor-hood. No one—and certainly neither Massey nor Denton—favors anything of the sort.

When Massey and Denton get down to specifics, they put forward a two-pronged program principally designed to better enable poor and minority households to vote with their feet (1993, 223–233). First, the authors urge enactment and vigorous enforcement of strict fair housing statutes prohibit-ing racial and other discrimination by housing providers. Second, they advo-cate that governments offer housing vouchers and similar financial carrots to induce poor and minority households to voluntarily choose greater racial and class integration. Other staunch integrationists similarly eschew more coercive measures and instead favor enhancing the ability of poor households to shop among neighborhoods (Fiss 2003). We are all, it appears, Tieboutians now.

REFERENCES

Brueckner, Jan K., and Kanogh Lee. 1989. Club theory with peer group effect. *Regional Science and Urban Economics* 19:399–420.

Calabrese, Stephen, Dennis Epple, and Richard Romano. 2006. Non-fiscal residential zoning. In *The Tiebout model at fifty*, William A. Fischel, ed. Cambridge, MA: Lincoln Institute of Land Policy.

Cashin, Sheryll D. 2001. Middle-class black suburbs and the state of integration: A post-integrationist vision for metropolitan areas. *Cornell Law Review* 86:729–776.

Cutler, David M., and Edward L. Glaeser. 1997. Are ghettos good or bad? *Quarterly Journal of Economics* 112:827–872.

Denton, Nancy A. 2001. The role of residential segregation in promoting and maintaining inequality in wealth and property. *Indiana Law Review* 34:1199–1209.

Dietderich, Andrew G. 1996. An egalitarian's market: The economics of inclusionary zoning reclaimed. *Fordham Urban Law Journal* 24:23–104.

Downs, Anthony. 1973. *Opening up the suburbs: An urban strategy for America.* New Haven, CT: Yale University Press.

Ellen, Ingrid Gould. 2000. *Sharing America's neighborhoods: The prospects for stable racial integration.* Cambridge, MA: Harvard University Press.

Ellickson, Robert C. 1981. The irony of "inclusionary" zoning. *Southern California Law Review* 54:1167–1216.

Ellickson, Robert C., and Vicki L. Been. 2005. *Land use controls.* 3rd ed. New York: Aspen Publishers.

Farley, Reynolds, Charlotte Steeh, Tara Jackson, Maria Krysan, and Keith Reeves. 1993. Continued racial segregation in Detroit: "Chocolate city, vanilla suburbs" revisited. *Journal of Housing Research* 4:1–38.

Fennell, Lee Anne. 2006. Exclusion's attraction: Land use controls in Tieboutian perspective. In *The Tiebout model at fifty*, William A. Fischel, ed. Cambridge, MA: Lincoln Institute of Land Policy.

Fiss, Owen M. 2003. What should be done for those who have been left behind? In *A way out: America's ghettos and the legacy of racism*, Joshua Cohen, Jefferson Decker, and Joel Rogers, eds., 3–43. Princeton, NJ: Princeton University Press.

Glaeser, Edward L., and Jacob L. Vigdor. 2003. Racial segregation: Promising news. In *Redefining urban and suburban America: Evidence from Census 2000, vol. 1*, Bruce Katz and Robert E. Lang, eds., 211–234. Washington, DC: Brookings Institution Press.

Hall, Raymond L., ed. 1977. *Black separatism and social reality: Rhetoric and reason.* New York: Pergamon Press.

Hamilton, Bruce W. 1975. Zoning and property taxation in a system of local governments. *Urban Studies* 12:205–211.

Logan, John R. 2003. Ethnic diversity grows, neighborhood integration lags. In *Redefining urban and suburban America: Evidence from Census 2000, vol. 1*, Bruce Katz and Robert E. Lang, eds., 235–255. Washington, DC: Brookings Institution Press.

Massey, Douglas S., and Nancy A. Denton. 1993. *American apartheid: Segregation and the making of the underclass.* Cambridge, MA: Harvard University Press.

Moving to Opportunity. http://nber.org/~kling/mto/.

Patterson, Orlando. 1997. *The ordeal of integration: Progress and resentment in America's "racial" crisis.* Washington, DC: Civitas/Counterpoint.

Powell, John A., and Marguerite L. Spencer. 2003. Giving them the old "one-two": Gentrification and the k.o. of impoverished urban dwellers of color. *Howard Law Journal* 46:433–490.

Putnam, Robert D. 2000. *Bowling alone: The collapse and revival of American community.* New York: Simon & Schuster.

Sander, Richard H. 1998. Housing segregation and housing integration: The diverging paths of urban America. *University of Miami Law Review* 52:977–1010.

Schelling, Thomas C. 1978. *Micromotives and macrobehavior.* New York: Norton.

Schuck, Peter H. 2003. *Diversity in America: Keeping government at a safe distance.* Cambridge, MA: Belknap Press of Harvard University Press.

Schwab, Robert M., and Wallace E. Oates. 1991. Community composition and the provision of local public goods: A normative analysis. *Journal of Public Economics* 44:217–237.

Span, Henry A. 2001. How the courts should fight exclusionary zoning. *Seton Hall Law Review* 32:1–107.

Stolzenberg, Nomi Maya. 1993. "He drew a circle that shut me out": Assimilation, indoctrination, and the paradox of a liberal education. *Harvard Law Review* 106:581–667.

Tein, Michael R. 1992. Comment: The devaluation of nonwhite community in remedies for subsidized housing discrimination. *University of Pennsylvania Law Review* 140: 1463–1503.

Tiebout, Charles M. 1956. A pure theory of local expenditures. *Journal of Political Economy* 64:416–424.

7

Nonfiscal Residential Zoning

Stephen Calabrese

Dennis Epple

Richard Romano

Zoning restrictions on residential property in higher-income neighborhoods and subdivisions are commonplace in the United States.[1] Minima are set on lot sizes and square footage, building materials are dictated, facades are regulated, and high levels of property maintenance are required.[2] These and other such property regulations are enforced by the police powers of jurisdictions and contractually by homeowners' associations. Zoning restrictions have been shown to facilitate Tiebout-like "fiscal" sorting into jurisdictions by acting as a screening device that deters poorer households from moving into richer jurisdictions with higher tax bases and higher provision of local public goods. Zoning restrictions frequently originate and are imposed in relatively small residential areas *within* jurisdictions, as when applied to a particular subdivision. Given that a subdivision has no fiscal authority and provides little if any public goods, the fiscal explanation for zoning is suspect in such instances. Here we examine a variant of the argument that explains exclusionary zoning restrictions within subdivisions of a jurisdiction.

We assume a positive "peer" externality from having relatively wealthy neighbors. More wealthy neighbors may be associated with enhanced social

We are grateful to conference participants and especially to our discussant Thomas Nechyba and editor William Fischel for their many insightful comments. We also thank the National Science Foundation for financial support and William Strange for his helpful suggestions.

[1] We use the term *zoning* in a general sense to refer to restrictions on residential property that can be thought of as placing a minimum on housing quality.

[2] See Fischel (1985) and Helsley and Strange (1998) for examples and data on residential property regulations.

interaction, greater opportunity for making business connections, better role models and perhaps more desirable friends and classmates for children, less crime due to greater parental policing and political pull, more attractive development and upkeep of residences, and so on. By requiring a binding minimum housing consumption, a subdivision can select richer residents from the jurisdiction, in equilibrium, thus partially internalizing the residential externality.

We feel that an equilibrium model of within-jurisdiction zoning should address the following issues. First, mobility in and out of the subdivision is a crucial element. Hence, our model permits moving to and from the subdivision (within the jurisdiction) following imposition of a zoning restriction. Second, effects on all residents of the jurisdiction are important to analyze. These are of inherent interest, but we also understand the zoning process to be constrained by the interests of residents of the entire jurisdiction. Therefore, we require that, to be enacted, the subdivision's zoning constraint must be approved by the municipal zoning board, with the board representing the majority interest of the entire jurisdiction. The third central element of the environment is the mechanism by which zoning proposals of the subdivision are proposed. We assume that the zoning proposal is collectively developed by property owners in the subdivision, specifically by majority choice. We also discuss the alternative where a profit-maximizing developer instead makes the zoning proposal.

The main result is that a binding zoning restriction can arise in a subdivision of a jurisdiction for realistic parameter values. In our benchmark case, only about 5 percent of the jurisdiction's population resides in the subdivision, yet 98 percent of the residents of the jurisdiction benefit from the subdivision's zoning constraint. The highest segment of income types would live in the subdivision without zoning. A zoning restriction in the subdivision induces migration of the lower end of that income segment from the subdivision to elsewhere in the jurisdiction, with the result that these households become the wealthiest outside the subdivision with an accompanying positive residential externality. Provision of the jurisdiction's local public good also increases as a result of zoning because housing consumption, and thus tax revenues, in the jurisdiction increase (with little or no effect on the property tax rate). Thus, zoning in the subdivision is good for everyone who would reside outside of the subdivision in the absence of zoning, and it benefits almost everyone else as well (as explained later), meeting the requirement for approval by the municipal zoning board.

A perhaps surprising finding is that the equilibrium zoning constraint is severe. More than half the residents of the subdivision are bound by the constraint; the pivotal (median-income) voter in the subdivision binds himself. We also find a lower gross housing price in the subdivision as a consequence of zoning but an aggregate increase in welfare measured by compensating variation.

The seminal paper on fiscal zoning is Hamilton (1975). He makes the point that a zoning restriction can convert a property tax into a head tax, lending support to Tiebout's model of jurisdictional competition and household sorting. The positive theory of fiscal zoning is developed further in Mills and Oates's edited volume (1975)[3] and by Wheaton (1993). Fischel (1985) examines the law and economics of zoning, making the case that zoning is best understood as a *collective* property right.[4] Ladd (1998) provides a fairly recent summary of the research on fiscal zoning. More recent models of fiscal zoning that emphasize collective choice are Fernandez and Rogerson (1997) and Calabrese, Epple, and Romano (2004). As just mentioned, the chapter is differentiated mainly by its examination of zoning within jurisdictions that derive from neighborhood peer externalities.[5]

A smaller literature on "private governments," like homeowners' associations, is related to this chapter (see Helsley 2005 for a survey). The most closely related work on this topic is Helsley and Strange (1998). Individuals take a costly action with a positive externality on members of their group, with an individual's group determined by whether or not they are affiliated with the private government. The private government requires a minimum level of action; this selection device channels those with low-action cost into the private government and others into the outside group. The similarity of our model to theirs is clear if we describe the quality of housing purchase as an action. One difference is that the regulated action in their model constitutes the externality. In our model it only serves to select household types from which the externality derives. A more important difference derives from our examination of regulation of an enclave's housing consumption in the presence of a peer externality. This externality leads to separation even in the absence of regulation.[6] As noted previously, we find a near Pareto improvement from the zoning regulation (in examples), in part because zoning "reduces" stratification relative to the equilibrium with no zoning. In the Helsley and Strange model, the regulated minimum induces separation, implying that those not joining the private government are made worse off.

The Model

The economy consists of one jurisdiction with given property tax rate t. Tax revenues are used to provide households with a local public good g. Having in

---

[3] In addition to the papers in Mills and Oates (1975), other leading papers in the early theoretical development of fiscal zoning are White (1975); Ohls, Weisberg, and White (1974, 1976); and Courant (1976).

[4] Fischel's perspective is consistent with the model of zoning that we examine in this chapter.

[5] See also Henderson and Thisse (1999), who characterize second-degree price discrimination by a developer who sells housing while providing a local public good. The menu of housing and total price combinations offered can be interpreted as a system of prices with zoning restrictions.

[6] We also examine general equilibrium effects on provision of a local public good that everyone consumes.

mind public education, we measure g in dollars per household, but the results apply as well if the local public good is not congested or only partially so. The jurisdiction is divided into two physically separate neighborhoods: the city (C) and the subdivision (S). A residential peer effect, described in more detail later, will be confined to residents within each neighborhood. A natural or synthetic barrier separates the neighborhoods (e.g., a river or railroad track), which we treat as exogenous in either case. Access to the subdivision will be rationed by a competitive housing market. Units of housing are supplied elastically at per unit cost c in the city, and likewise but only up to a maximum (H_S) in the subdivision. Hence, the supply of housing is horizontal in the city and a reverse L in the subdivision. We assume throughout that H_S is sufficiently small that it will all be consumed in the equilibria we study. One can interpret c as the cost of converting a unit of land into a unit of housing, with land scarce in the subdivision but not in the city. This scarcity of housing in the subdivision is crucial to our results but not a strong assumption, although specified in a simple way. The nonscarcity of housing in the city avoids housing price changes there.

Households in the jurisdiction differ by endowed income y, with continuous and differentiable cumulative density function (c.d.f.) $F(y)$, and associated density $f(y)$ that is everywhere positive on its support $[y_{\min}, y_{\max}] \subset (0, \infty)$. The population of households is given and is normalized to measure one.

Households obtain utility from four goods, with CES utility function:

$$U(x, h, \bar{y}_i, g) = [\alpha_x x^\rho + \alpha_h h^\rho + \alpha_{\bar{y}} \bar{y}_i^\rho + \alpha_g g^\rho]^{1/\rho}, \; \rho < 0, \tag{7.1}$$

where x is numeraire consumption, h is housing consumption, g is consumption of the local public good, and $\bar{y}_i, i \in \{C, S\}$, is the mean income of households in neighborhood i. Thus, we assume that higher-income households generate a positive neighborhood externality. This might derive from their greater propensity to consume higher-quality property and other quasi-public goods, from their greater propensity to support neighborhood quality (e.g., via crime prevention), and/or from enhanced social interaction.[7] Such externalities might well be associated with correlates of income rather than income per se. Of course, our assumption is not uncontroversial—for example, snobbery might imply the opposite. In equation 7.1, we assume that $\rho < 0$, implying the elasticity of substitution between any two of the goods ($1/(1 - \rho)$) is less than one. As shown following, this will imply a wealth-stratified equilibrium in the absence of zoning.

The scarce housing (land) in the subdivision is initially owned by outsiders in the main analysis. This assumption has only income effects on the analysis, and we have examined alternatives without effect on the main results. We

---

[7] If public schools operate within neighborhoods, this could provide a source of this externality.

present the results for this case simply because it is a standard assumption and we are able to avoid a specific alternative specification.[8]

Equilibrium unfolds in three stages. In stage one, households make an initial housing purchase in one of the neighborhoods, denoted h_{Ii}, where $i \in \{C, S\}$ henceforth, unless indicated otherwise. Purchasing housing in the subdivision gives the household the right to vote over the zoning constraint there in the second stage. We assume that households can only purchase housing in one of the neighborhoods (justified later). A zoning constraint in the subdivision might be established in the second stage by the following process. Households who purchased housing in the subdivision vote over a minimum housing consumption requirement (denoted h_m), with their majority preference subject to the approval of the municipal zoning board. The municipal zoning board will approve the proposal if and only if it makes a majority of the jurisdiction's households better off, where the alternative is no zoning constraint. We assume no zoning constraint can be established in the remainder of the city, though a natural extension would entail multiple subdivisions with potentially different zoning ordinances. Permitting zoning in all subdivisions might lead to equilibria with homeless households.

In the third stage, households can frictionlessly reoptimize with respect to their housing consumption, including location, and otherwise consume. At this stage tax revenues are collected and spent on the local public good.

Households have rational expectations and thus correctly anticipate continuation equilibrium outcomes. They are atomistic and thus take as given the payoff-relevant variables (i.e., housing prices, peer measures, government provision, and any zoning constraint), with their individual choices having no impact.

Several issues concerning the model and equilibrium process warrant discussion. Given our simple specification of the housing market, it is equivalent to think of the first-stage purchase by households as just of land, with those buying land in the subdivision having the right to vote on zoning there. With the analogous assumption that land can be sold after the determination of zoning and before homes are built, the results would be the same. The presentation is simplified by describing the initial purchase as of housing, since we then need not introduce prices of both land and housing. The related assumption that reoptimization in the third stage is frictionless is no doubt an exaggeration, but with the latter interpretation, it is perhaps less extreme than it appears.

---

[8] Note, too, that initial ownership of land in the city is completely irrelevant, since no land rents will ever arise there.

Given this frictionless reoptimization and the atomism of households, households are indifferent to their initial housing purchases, with a multiplicity of equilibria.[9] We restrict attention to the equilibrium where households' initial purchase is such that they do not change their residence or level of housing consumption. This would be the equilibrium with vanishingly small adjustment costs. Another multiplicity-of-equilibrium issue arises if no zoning constraint is imposed in the subdivision. Again, due to the atomism of households, there is always a nonstratified equilibrium with both neighborhoods having the same peer measure and housing price. Such equilibria are unstable (since the rich would collectively prefer to congregate in the suburb). Hence, we assume a stratified equilibrium arises whenever one exists.

We have assumed collective choice of a zoning constraint in the subdivision and that it must be approved by the municipal board that represents a majority of the jurisdiction's residents. The more common modeling assumption in analysis of new housing developments is that a profit-maximizing developer, who initially owns the land, sets the agenda, and so would make zoning proposals. We believe that there is merit in both approaches, the better characterization depending on the particular dynamics of development. We have also investigated cases where a developer makes zoning proposals but prefers not to zone, with starkly different results. This discrepancy in incentives points to a tension between the developer and the subsequent homeowners. (Later we will examine such a case further and see how the preferences of those who ultimately buy the house prevail in zoning decisions.)

Our assumption that the zoning proposal must be approved by the municipal zoning board, which in turn represents the interest of a majority, is in part to capture the spirit of states' enabling legislation that frequently requires zoning to be "for the purpose of promoting health, safety, or the *general welfare of the community*."[10,11] Those involved in making zoning decisions are also politically accountable. Requiring majority approval is obviously an idealization of the process, but we think this is the most natural way to account for the legal-political limits on zoning actions. In any case, it is of interest to examine the effects of desired zoning by those in a subdivision on the community.

---

[9] This indifference also depends on the fact that the initial equilibrium price of housing will equal the final price of housing, since everyone has rational expectations.

[10] Italics are added. This quote is from Section 1 of the Standard State Zoning Enabling Act written by the U.S. Department of Commerce in 1926. This act served as the guideline for states in developing their own zoning statutes, and, while zoning legislation has evolved, this principle remains standard.

[11] Fischel (1985) makes the case that zoning is a collective right. The argument in this paragraph borrows freely from his analysis.

Theoretical Analysis

Equilibrium in the Third Stage

Let us first analyze equilibrium characteristics of the final stage, which must satisfy individual household optimization with the implied peer measures, housing market clearance in each neighborhood, and government budget balance. At this stage a zoning constraint in the subdivision may have been established, and, again, the property tax rate is given at the outset.

Consider household optimization. Let p_i denote the final net (or supplier) housing price in neighborhood i, p_{Ii} the initial net housing price, and $p_i^t \equiv (1+t)p_i$ and $p_{Ii}^t \equiv (1+t)p_{Ii}$ the associated gross (or consumer) housing prices. While the initial prices will equal the final prices in the full (three-stage) equilibrium, we must allow for out-of-equilibrium values in the later stages. Having observed this, obviously net housing price in the city must equal c in any stage equilibrium, and we employ this at some points. Because we will see that almost every household will have strict preference for their choices (e.g., of residence), we can assume that households with the same income make the same choices. Wealth (w) at the third stage is given by

$$w(y) = y + (p_i - p_{Ii})h_{Ii}. \tag{7.2}$$

The second term in wealth is the capital gain/loss on the initial housing purchase.

Let $h_d(w,p^t)$ denote the ordinary (Marshallian) demand for housing, which, using equation 7.1, is given by

$$h_d(w,p^t) = wz(p^t); \quad z(p^t) = \left[p^t + \left(\frac{\alpha_x}{\alpha_h} \right)^{\frac{1}{1-\rho}} (p^t)^{\frac{1}{1-\rho}} \right]^{-1}. \tag{7.3}$$

If the household chooses to live in the city, then $h = h_d$, and indirect utility is given by

$$V_C(p_C^t, \bar{y}_C; y) = [\alpha_x(w(y) - p_C^t h_d(w(y), p_C^t))^\rho + \alpha_h h_d(w(y), p_C^t)^\rho$$

$$+ \alpha_{\bar{y}}(\bar{y}_C)^\rho + \alpha_g g^\rho]^{1/\rho}. \tag{7.4}$$

If the household chooses to live in the subdivision, then optimal housing consumption is given by

$$h_S(p_S^t, w, h_m) = \text{Max}[h_m, h_d(w, p_S^t)], \tag{7.5}$$

where we use the quasi-concavity of the utility function. The zoning constraint may or may not be binding on households, and equation 7.5 subsumes the case with no zoning constraint where $h_m = 0$. Indirect utility for household living in the subdivision is given by

$$V_S(p_S^t, \bar{y}_S, h_m; y) =$$

$$[\alpha_x(w(y) - p_S^t h_S(p_S^t, w(y), h_m))^\rho + \alpha_h h_S(p_S^t, w(y), h_m)^\rho + \alpha_{\bar{y}}(\bar{y}_S)^\rho + \alpha_g g^\rho]^{1/\rho}. \tag{7.6}$$

Letting $\theta(y)$ denote the probability that household with income y will live in the subdivision, the optimal residential choice is summarized by[12]:

$$\theta(y) \begin{cases} =1 \text{ if } V_S > V_C \\ \in [0,1] \text{ if } V_S = V_C \\ =0 \text{ if } V_S < V_C \end{cases} \tag{7.7}$$

The implied peer measures are given by

$$\bar{y}_C = \int_{y_{min}}^{y_{max}} y(1 - \theta(y)) f(y) dy \Big/ \int_{y_{min}}^{y_{max}} (1 - \theta(y)) f(y) \, dy; \tag{7.8a}$$

and

$$\bar{y}_S = \int_{y_{min}}^{y_{max}} y\theta(y) f(y) dy \Big/ \int_{y_{min}}^{y_{max}} \theta(y) f(y) \, dy. \tag{7.8b}$$

Equations 7.2–7.8 then summarize household maximization.

Since we consider the case where housing is scarce in the subdivision, the market-clearance condition there is

$$\int_{y_{min}}^{y_{max}} h_S(p_S^t, w(y), h_m) \theta(y) f(y) \, dy = H_S, \tag{7.9a}$$

where the LHS is housing demand. Market clearance in the city has $p_C^t = (1 + t)c$ and housing consumption

$$\int_{y_{min}}^{y_{max}} h_d(w(y), p_C^t) (1 - \theta(y)) f(y) \, dy. \tag{7.9b}$$

Equations 7.9a and 7.9b, along with equations 7.2, 7.3, and $p_S^t = (1 + t)p_S$ summarize housing market clearance.

Last, the government budget constraint is given by

$$t \left[p_S H_S + c \int_{y_{min}}^{y_{max}} h_d(w(y), p_C^t) (1 - \theta(y)) f(y) \, dy \right] = g. \tag{7.10}$$

Turning to properties of equilibrium in the third stage, we say that equilibrium is stratified by wealth if, for some threshold wealth w_b, household with wealth $w > (<)$ w_b strictly prefers to live in the subdivision (city). The main result regarding equilibrium in the third stage (hence characterizing the full equilibrium) is as follows:

Proposition 1: If $p_S > c$, then equilibrium with both neighborhoods occupied is wealth stratified. If $p_S = c$ and a zoning constraint in the subdivision strictly binds any residents, then equilibrium with both neighborhoods occupied is wealth stratified.

---

[12] As noted previously, almost every household will have a strict preference in the equilibria we study, so the middle line of equation 7.7 will be largely irrelevant.

Proof of Proposition 1: Taking first the case having $p_S > c$, obviously $p_S^t > p_C^t$. At least one wealth type must be indifferent between residing in the two neighborhoods. If everyone had a strict preference for their neighborhood of residence, either one neighborhood is not occupied or continuity of preferences in wealth would be contradicted. Let w_b denote the wealth of an indifferent household. Let $\Delta(w) = V_S - V_C$ denote the difference in utility if neighborhood S is chosen over neighborhood C. Computing the derivative, using the Envelope Theorem, one obtains:

$$\Delta'(w) = \alpha_x [V_S^{1-\rho} x_S^{\rho-1} - V_C^{1-\rho} x_C^{\rho-1}],$$

where x_i denotes numeraire consumption in neighborhood i. Given that $p_S^t > p_C^t$, housing demand is inelastic (by equation 7.3 and $\rho < 0$) and that housing consumption is no less than $h_d(w, p_S^t)$ in the subdivision, it follows that $x_S < x_C$. Further, since $V_S = V_C$ when $w = w_b$, it follows that $\Delta'(w_b) > 0$. And it follows that the difference Δ continues to increase with w, thus implying wealth stratification. The proof for the case having $p_S = c$ and some household residing in the subdivision strictly bound by the zoning constraint is essentially the same. The minimum-wealth resident in the subdivision must be strictly bound by the zoning constraint, since some residents are strictly bound and demand for housing is normal. Also, that resident must be indifferent to residence, or, by continuity of utility, a lower-wealth type would choose the subdivision, a contradiction. Since the housing prices are the same, demand for housing is the same in each neighborhood, implying $x_S < x_c$ for strictly constrained households living in the subdivision and $x_S = x_c$ for unconstrained ones. Again, using $\Delta'(w) = \alpha_x \left[V_S^{1-\rho} x_S^{\rho-1} - V_C^{1-\rho} x_C^{\rho-1} \right]$ wealth stratification is implied.

Q.E.D.

Stratified equilibrium has the obvious property that $\bar{y}_S > \bar{y}_C$. Otherwise, no one would pay the higher housing price in the subdivision and perhaps be constrained in his consumption of housing. We will see later that in the full (three-stage) equilibrium, wealth will increase with income so that $\bar{y}_S > \bar{y}_C$ will arise. Another approach to demonstrating wealth stratification clarifies the intuition. Suppose first that there is no housing minimum, keeping in mind that the preceding proof applies to such a case. If we draw indifference curves of households in the $(\bar{y}_i, p_i^t)$ plane, we can see that they become steeper as wealth increases:[13] Higher-wealth households are willing to pay more in a higher-housing-price neighborhood for more desirable peers. Hence, a higher price of housing in the subdivision supports the stratification of wealth types. Introducing a minimum housing constraint in the subdivision reinforces this

---

[13] More formally, these indifference curves are defined by $V_i = \text{const.}$, where V_i is of the form in equation 7.4, since we have assumed no housing minimum in the subdivision.

stratification because such a constraint is less consequential to higher-wealth types who demand more housing anyway.

We should note that wealth stratification with no zoning constraint would not arise if $\rho \in [0,1]$, corresponding to cases with elasticity of substitution between goods of at least one. Here, higher-wealth types are not willing to pay a higher housing price for a better neighborhood peer group because they find it easier to substitute more consumption of the numeraire and housing for a better peer group while living in the city. However, it may be that a zoning constraint itself would lead to a stratified equilibrium. We analyze the case with price-inelastic housing demand because it is more consistent with the empirical evidence.

Equilibrium in the Second and Third Stages

The main issue is, of course, whether a binding zoning constraint arises. The zoning constraint is chosen by majority vote of those who purchased housing in the subdivision in the first stage, subject to approval by the municipal zoning board. The possibility of frictionless reoptimization in the third stage, no capital gains or losses in equilibrium, and atomism of households implies that households are indifferent to their housing purchase in the first stage. As already noted, we restrict attention to the equilibrium where households make initial housing purchases corresponding to their final choices, so no reoptimization actually takes place in equilibrium. Since equilibrium will be wealth stratified whether or not a binding zoning constraint is chosen, it is implied that the set of voting households will be all those with income $y \geq y_b$, for y_b satisfying $V_C = V_S$, the latter indirect utilities evaluated at the final equilibrium values.[14]

When voting on h_m, the values that are already established are the initial housing prices p_{Ii}, the initial housing purchases h_{Ii} (corresponding to the final housing purchases), and the given tax rate t. Voters are sophisticated and anticipate all values established in the third stage—in other words, how they vary with h_m. Specifically, they anticipate the continuation equilibrium values of the final net and gross housing prices; everyone's wealth; the residential pattern and peer measures; g; and their own consumption choices, including residence. In short, voters anticipate the third-stage equilibrium as it varies with h_m.

Mathematically, a voter solves[15]

$$\max_{h_m, p_i, p_i', p_C, p_C', \bar{y}_i, \bar{y}_c, \theta(y), g} \left\{ \max[V_C, V_S] \right\}$$
$$\text{s.t. } (2) - (10);$$

(7.11)

---

[14] We assume that households with $y = y_b$ reside in the subdivision, although they are indifferent. Given the continuum of types, this assumption is innocuous.

[15] Because equilibrium will be wealth stratified for any h_m, binding or not, one can alternatively suppress $\theta(y)$ and write the problem in terms of the boundary wealth that arises as h_m varies.

and subject to the municipal-board-approval constraint. Even ignoring the approval constraint, this is a complicated problem, and we cannot prove analytically that voting preferences are sufficiently well behaved to guarantee existence of equilibrium. However, we are able to confirm in our computations existence of voting equilibrium and that the median-income resident of the subdivision is the pivotal voter. We also find the approval constraint is not binding—that is, that a majority in the economy gain from the unconstrained majority choice.

Likewise, we cannot prove analytically that a binding zoning constraint will always be the equilibrium choice. We find computationally that a binding voting constraint is chosen for realistic parameter values. To gain insight as to why the latter occurs, consider what would need to be true otherwise. In equilibrium without zoning, the pivotal voter will anticipate residing in the subdivision, and it would require that $\frac{dV_s}{dh_m}\Big|_{h_m = h_d(y_b, p_s^t)} \leq 0$, where $h_d(y_b, p_s^t)$ is the unconstrained housing demand of the lowest-income household in the subdivision and thus the housing level where a zoning constraint would just become binding.

Using that the pivotal voter would be unconstrained in his own housing choice, we calculate

$$\frac{dV_s}{dh_m}\Bigg|_{h_m = h_d(y_b, p_s^t)} = V_S^{(1-\rho)}\left[-t\alpha_x x^{\rho-1} h_d \frac{dp_S}{dh_m} + \alpha_{\bar{y}} \bar{y}_S^{\rho-1} \frac{d\bar{y}_S}{dh_m} + \alpha_g g^{\rho-1} \frac{dg}{dh_m}\right], (7.12)$$

where the derivatives in the brackets are with respect to the continuation equilibrium values (i.e., satisfying equations 7.2–7.10). It is unlikely that the bracketed term will be nonpositive. Increasing the zoning constraint is likely to drive out the lowest-income households, thus increasing $\bar{y}_s$. It is likely to increase tax revenues because some of those who stay in the subdivision are forced to consume more housing, while those who leave consume more housing in the city (but at a lower price). The likely effect on p_s is less clear, since housing demand in the subdivision might increase or fall. But this term is weighted by the tax rate and so is likely to be relatively small. Once we have quantified these effects in our computational analysis, we will come back to this discussion.

Computational Model and Results

Calibration of the Model

We specify a computational model to examine whether zoning arises in equilibrium. We assume that household income follows the lognormal distribution: $Ln(y) \sim N(\mu, \sigma^2)$. Our calibration is based on mean and median income in the

---

[16] Mean income of those employed is $56,313, and 80 percent are employed, so we obtain an overall mean of $45,050.

that income is lognormally distributed imply $\mu = 10.561$ and $\sigma = .5547$. We set $c = 1$, thus normalizing the net price of housing in the city to equal one. We chose utility function parameters to yield a net-of-tax expenditure share for housing of approximately 20 percent of income and a housing price elasticity of $-.75$. With the normalization $\alpha_x = 1$, these yield $\alpha_h = .2$ and $\rho = .5$. We then chose α_g to yield a property tax rate of the order of magnitude observed in practice. We calibrated to a tax rate $t = .35$, which is the tax rate on annualized implicit rent in our model and implies a tax rate on property value that is realistic on the order of 2.5 to 3.0 percent.[17] The connection between α_g and the tax rate is established by choosing α_g so that the median-income household would in equilibrium choose the realistic tax rate taking residences (hence peer groups), net housing prices, and housing consumption (hence the tax bases) as given. This approach yields $\alpha_g = .033$. In our benchmark calibration, this yields a local government expenditure share of approximately 7.2 percent of income. For our benchmark calibration, we set the weight on neighborhood peer income equal to the weight on government provision: $\alpha_{\bar{y}} = \alpha_g$. Finally, we set land area in the subdivision such that in the benchmark equilibrium the subdivision houses approximately 5 percent of the population. This yields $H_s = 1335$.

Results

Column 1 of table 7.1 presents values in the benchmark zoning equilibrium, with the minimum housing consumption the preferred choice of the median-income household that resides in the subdivision (that income denoted y_{med}). Column 2 reports values in the counterpart equilibrium that would result if zoning is disallowed. Observe first that almost everyone in the jurisdiction is better off with this level of zoning relative to no zoning: The vote favoring allowing this level of zoning is 98 percent! Hence, the unconstrained preference of the median-income household in the subdivision is approved by the zoning board.

Before explaining why almost everyone gains from zoning, consider the extremeness of the zoning constraint. We see in column 1 that the minimum housing requirement ($h_m = \$23,686$) substantially exceeds the preferred housing consumption of the marginal household living in the subdivision ($h_b = \$18,885$ denotes unconstrained housing demand of the y_b household). Perhaps more startling is that the pivotal voter constrains his own housing consumption in equilibrium. Income

---

[17] Observed property tax rates are expressed as a percent of property value. In our model, rates are expressed as a percentage of annual implicit rent. Employing the approach of Poterba (1992), Calabrese and Epple (2005) conclude that tax rates on annualized implicit rents can be converted to rates on property values using a conversion rate on the order of 7 to 9 percent. Thus, our annualized rate of .35 translates to a tax rate on property value on the order of 2.5 to 3 percent, which is the order of magnitude of observed property tax rates.

TABLE 7.1

Welfare Gains from Zoning

	(1)	(2)	(3)	(4)
	Benchmark	No Zoning	H_s Doubled	α_y Doubled
g	3,238	3,222	3,258	3,248
p_s	1.037	1.098	1.000	1.129
y_b	95,559	91,899	73,606	93,520
y_m	119,854	91,952	95,623	118,171
$\bar{y}_C$	40,792	40,351	37,373	40,552
$\bar{y}_S$	123,510	119,553	99,899	121,306
h_m	23,686	17,394	19,440	21,902
h_b	18,884.6	17,434	17,949	17,333
y_{med}	113,907	110,064	90,974	111,766
t	0.350	0.351	0.349	0.350
% Subdiv	0.051	0.059	0.122	0.055
Welfare Chg CV	42.16		59.40	89.02
Vote	98.2%		98.1%	95.9%
H_s	1335	1335	2670	1335
α_y	0.0263	0.0263	0.0263	0.0526

y_m denotes the maximum income of constrained households. The fact that $y_{med} <$ y_m implies the pivotal voter constrains his own consumption, since all those in the subdivision with income below y_m are bound by the zoning constraint. Referring to equation 7.12 and the results in table 7.1, the intuition for this finding is clear. Zoning is seen to improve the peer group in the subdivision (as well as in the city), increase g, and decrease the supplier and thus consumer price of housing in the subdivision. Imposition of the zoning constraint excludes households, increasing the income of the marginal household and increasing the peer measures relative to no zoning. The floor on housing consumption forces up the demand for housing in the subdivision by the constrained set of households, but this is more than offset by those that are induced by zoning to move out of the subdivision. So housing demand in the subdivision declines, as then does the net and gross price of housing. Nevertheless, tax revenues increase as does g because of the increased housing demand in the city (and with virtually no change in the tax rate).[18] Referring, then,

---

[18] In the theoretical model we fixed the tax rate. To examine how strong an assumption this is, we calculated equilibrium without zoning, allowing the median-income household in the jurisdiction to

FIGURE 7.1A   Compensating Variation of Zoned Allocation Relative
to Allocation Without Zoning

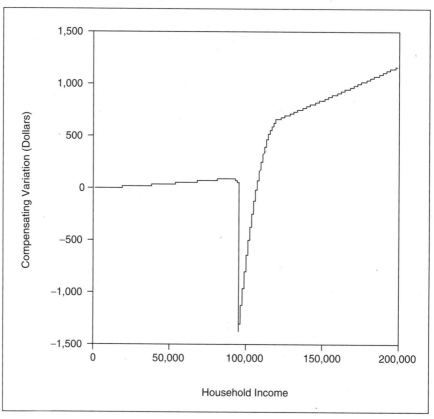

to equation 7.12, the directions of the effects all provide an incentive for the pivotal voter to increase the zoning constraint, until these are offset by the utility
cost of distorting his own housing consumption (the latter effect not yet in force
in equation 7.12). Note that the decrease in the net and gross housing prices in
the subdivision from increasing zoning have a net benefit to residents of the subdivision for given housing consumption: They take a capital loss on their initial
housing purchase, but the consumption cost of housing declines by more.

choose a different tax (under the same assumptions used to calibrate the tax rate discussed earlier). We
find the preferred tax rate of the median-income household is virtually unchanged, and we then report
these results in column 2 of table 7.1. This no-zoning equilibrium is used as well in the welfare calculations. Obviously, given the virtual equality of the tax rates, no conclusions would change with the tax
rate fixed at .35. This endogeneity of the tax rate applies to the other columns as well, with the same lack
of consequence.

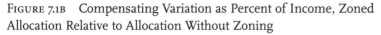

FIGURE 7.1B   Compensating Variation as Percent of Income, Zoned
Allocation Relative to Allocation Without Zoning

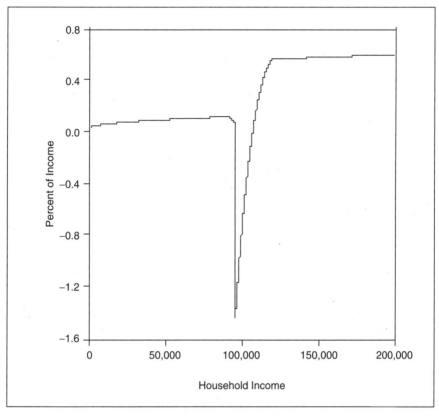

Why does almost everyone gain from zoning? Figure 7.1A and B show the compensating variation (*CV*) as a function of income, in absolute terms (A) and measured as a proportion of income (B) that would be needed if the zoning proposal were rejected. That is, *CV* is the dollar amount that a household would need to be given to get the same utility if zoning were not approved as if it were approved. Those with positive *CV* then gain from approval of the zoning constraint and the reverse for those with negative *CV*. All those who live in the city with zoning are better off, although not by much. Higher *g* and a better peer group in the city under zoning imply that those who would live in the city in either case are better off with zoning (see footnote 18). Those who are excluded by zoning are better off because the better city alternative outweighs the exclusion cost. Of course, the latter may not hold in all cases.

Now consider those who live in the subdivision with zoning. The changes from zoning discussed in the previous paragraph imply those unconstrained in the subdivision with zoning are better off. Those with incomes in the vicinity of the median-income household in the subdivision (and those constrained with higher incomes) obviously prefer zoning as well. The group that is worse off are those who live in the subdivision with zoning but are near the margin of doing so. For them, the utility cost of the zoning constraint is high. But there is also an opportunity cost to them of retaining the zoning constraint, associated with their initial (constrained) housing purchase. We are calculating compensating variation as voters contemplate elimination of the zoning constraint; hence, voters are contemplating a deviation from the *equilibrium with zoning*.[19] Suppose the zoning constraint were not approved (a deviation from equilibrium). Then those who are constrained by the zoning requirement in the subdivision will own more housing than they will consume if the zoning constraint is eliminated. If zoning is eliminated, those households experience a capital gain as they sell housing at the higher housing price that results without zoning. The opportunity cost of not obtaining this capital gain is why the CV curve jumps down at y_b with zoning.[20] But only 2 percent lose out from zoning! While this percentage of losers from zoning in the subdivision will be higher in some cases, note that if those who would reside outside the subdivision without zoning gain, this will be enough for majority approval. This points to our assumption of elastic supply of housing in the city. Increased demand for housing in the city from zoning would lead to higher net and gross housing price there if land is scarce in the city, with a net negative effect on city dwellers. This would also lead to higher tax revenues and g. But the poorest city dwellers would probably then lose out (since everyone is a homeowner in our model).

The per capita welfare change from zoning (CV) is presented in table 7.1. Not surprisingly, this is positive. The efficiency gain that underlies this is a reduction in a residential choice externality in the model. It is well known (see, for example, the discussion in Scotchmer [2002]) that direct (nonfiscal) residential externalities must be priced if unregulated locational choices are to be efficient in their presence. Absent zoning, too many households choose to live in the subdivision. The marginal household that chooses to reside in the suburb gains nothing by doing so but confers a negative externality, as this household lowers the peer measure in both the city and the subdivision.[21] The exclusionary effect of zoning is then associated with a welfare gain.[22]

---

[19] To find equilibrium with zoning, one must ask if zoning would be approved by a majority, given the initial housing choices corresponding to a zoning equilibrium. We are now measuring the welfare effect of this, in a case where zoning is approved, using CV.

[20] All those who choose to live in the subdivision and would sell housing if the zoning constraint were (unexpectedly) not approved would experience such a capital gain. But this effect vanishes as income rises.

[21] The change in housing rents from his choice to live in the subdivision is a transfer.

[22] There are also some fiscal effects, since tax payments differ in the city and suburb. Also, housing consumption in the city is distorted. But these efficiency effects are likely to be quite small.

Robustness

Consider the following robustness issues. First, results are reported in the third and fourth columns of table 7.1 for two key parameter variations. In column 3, we consider the effect of doubling housing supply in the subdivision. In column 4, we consider the effect of doubling the utility weight on the peer variable. The finding of a substantial zoning constraint—that is, one that binds a majority in the subdivision—persists in both cases. As well, the changes in variables relative to the no-zoning allocation are qualitatively the same as in the benchmark case, and again a large majority gain from zoning. Note that the comparison, no-zoning equilibrium changes with each case, and we have not reported these values in table 7.1. We do not mean to suggest that one will generally find a near-Pareto improvement, but our analysis has not been contrived to generate this. Also, there is an aggregate welfare gain as measured by *CV* in both variations.

The preceding results survive an alternative specification of the timing of choices that may better describe reality in some cases. Suppose that, following initial housing purchases, the municipal zoning board decides whether to permit the residents of the subdivision to impose a zoning constraint. If the approval is given, then residents of the subdivision collectively choose the zoning constraint by majority vote, facing no further approval constraint.[23] In any case of the original model where the approval constraint does not alter the subdivision's zoning choice, as in the preceding examples, the same outcome is an equilibrium with this alternative timing. Anticipating that the approval will be given, the housing purchases in the first stage in the original model continue to be equilibrium ones. If the zoning power is not granted, then the outcome would be the same as if the zoning constraint is rejected by the municipal zoning board in the original model. If approval is given in the new model, obviously the outcome is the same. Hence, approval will be given because a majority in the jurisdiction will gain. In the case of homeowners' associations, this may provide a better description of the reality of the process. If, however, the equilibrium in the original model has a zoning constraint that is strictly limited by the need to make a majority better off, the alternative timing would have no zoning. If the zoning power were granted, then the minimum housing would be the unconstrained one, but since this does not benefit a majority in the jurisdiction, that power would not be granted.

Last we discuss the alternative model where a profit-maximizing developer initially owns all the land in the subdivision. Suppose that the developer will sell the land but can first propose a zoning constraint to the municipal zoning board that would, if approved, be a condition of development of the land by

---

[23] As in the preceding model, consumption with frictionless reoptimization occurs last.

those who purchase the land. For the cases we have just examined, the developer would not propose a zoning constraint because it would reduce demand for the land and the price the developer could get.[24] So this suggests a very different outcome.[25]

It also points to a tension between the developer and the purchasers of land. More specifically, following land purchases, the landowners would have a collective incentive to introduce zoning. If, for example, the landowners can form a homeowners' association, then they would want to introduce a zoning constraint—one that the preceding analysis indicates would be approved by the municipal zoning board. What this implies is that if the developer first sells all the land *and there are no frictions*, then the model we have developed is the correct one. However, we do not mean for this extended model, with a developer, to be realistic. If the developer is selling built homes and not just land, surely there are important "frictions." Rather, we interpret this tension between the developer and purchasers to suggest that analyzing their dynamic interaction is an important topic for future research on zoning.

Conclusion

We have presented circumstances where neighborhood peer group effects that are correlated with housing demand can explain zoning restrictions. This zoning is exclusionary, like fiscal zoning, but it has only indirect fiscal effects. In our examples, those who are excluded are actually better off. Those outside the zoned area gain because their peer group improves and public provision increases with no tax rate change. Nearly everyone gains, so the zoning practice is consistent with the "general welfare of the community." Since zoning restrictions frequently apply within jurisdictions, the explanation studied here may be important in understanding the reality of zoning practices.

In our model, a developer has no incentive to zone, while a majority of those living in the subdivision want a zoning constraint. This points to a tension that is an interesting topic for further research.

Our model permits zoning ordinances that can impose restrictions on the use of land after individuals have made their land purchases. Individuals make their purchases correctly anticipating the regulations that will be adopted. Hence, we find that adoption of a zoning ordinance does not induce individuals to make ex post changes in their ownership patterns. For example, zoning does not lead to

---

[24] Henderson and Thisse (2001) also find that developers have no incentive to zone in an oligopolistically competitive model of developers with fiscal zoning.

[25] The situation we describe has one price per unit of land—hence, no price discrimination by the developer. Henderson and Thisse (1999) show that a developer can increase profits with second-degree price discrimination by selling different sizes or qualities of homes at different total prices. This could be effected by more complicated zoning.

ex post exit of households. One might nonetheless doubt whether it is realistic to model zoning ordinances as being adopted after households have purchased land, the concern being that such ordinances would not be enforced by the courts. However, all zoning ordinances are applied to land that someone already owns, and the courts tend to give great deference to localities in their setting of zoning restrictions. Land is often zoned in ways that individual landowners would prefer to change. Thus, our model is not unrealistic in permitting adoption of zoning ordinances on land that has already been purchased. At the same time, it is the case that existing owners of residential properties in existing subdivisions are often exempted (i.e., grandfathered) from changes in zoning restrictions that are imposed on tracts of land that have not yet undergone subdivision. Such grandfathering is potentially important in understanding the effects of zoning.

In our model, zoning would have no impact if there were grandfathering. To see why, consider a household that would be constrained in some way by zoning if it were to move to the subdivision in the third stage. If there were grandfathering, such a household would instead locate in the subdivision in the first period, thereby being grandfathered and avoiding consequences of zoning. An analogous logic implies that a grandfather clause would not deter any household from moving into the subdivision. Thus, any household that would be impacted by zoning would simply circumvent the zoning ordinance by exploiting the grandfathering provision. Hence, for zoning to arise in equilibrium when there is grandfathering, some friction (e.g., information asymmetry) must be present. We have shown that, even without grandfathering incentives, a majority of the subdivision's residents gain from zoning. Moreover, we have shown that the pivotal voter constrains her own consumption. These findings make clear that grandfathering is not needed to explain the presence of zoning. Whether an environment that leads to grandfathering would tend to lead to more or less severe zoning restrictions is, nonetheless, an interesting research question.

One promising avenue for future research might be to extend our model to provide greater scope for consideration of grandfathering. This appears to be most naturally done by extending our analysis to a dynamic setting in which prospective residents of an area arrive at different points in time. This would motivate analysis of policies that early arrivals impose on future arrivals, while possibly exempting (i.e., grandfathering) themselves. Such an analysis should investigate whether grandfathering will be collectively supported and should also include modeling of forward-looking private decisions by early arrivals with respect to their own future residential choices. For example, consider a household that is an early arrival and is relatively poor. Such a household might locate in the subdivision and support a stringent zoning ordinance for future arrivals. This household might also construct a house with an eye toward selling the house to a wealthier future arrival. The household might thereby reap a capital gain by building a house that is tailored to the preferences of a future arrival, a house that the future arrival would be prohibited by the zoning ordinance from building. The relatively poor early household might then relocate outside the subdivision, since such a household would place relatively low value on the high peer quality in the subdivision. As this discussion indicates, grandfathering is not the only potentially important consideration that arises when not all households arrive at once. This chapter provides a potentially valuable point of departure for such an analysis.

REFERENCES

Calabrese, Stephen, and Dennis Epple. 2005. On the political economy of tax limits. Working paper.

Calabrese, Stephen, Dennis Epple, and Richard Romano. 2004. On the political economy of zoning. Working paper.

Courant, Paul N. 1976. On the welfare effects of zoning and housing values. *Journal of Urban Economics* 3:88–94.

Fernandez, Raquel, and Richard Rogerson. 1997. Keeping people out: Income distribution, zoning, and the quality of public education. *International Economic Review* 38:23–42.

Fischel, William A. 1985. *The economics of zoning laws: A property rights approach to American land use controls.* Baltimore: Johns Hopkins University Press.

Hamilton, Bruce. 1975. Zoning and property taxation in a system of local governments. *Urban Studies* 12:205–211.

Helsley, Robert W. 2005. Urban political economics. In *Handbook of regional and urban economics, vol. 4,* J. V. Henderson and J. F. Thisse, eds. Amsterdam: North-Holland.

Helsley, Robert W., and William C. Strange. 1998. Private government. *Journal of Public Economics* 69:281–304.

Henderson, J. Vernon, and Jacques-François Thisse. 1999. On the pricing strategy of a land developer. *Journal of Urban Economics* 45:1–16.

———. 2001. On strategic community development. *Journal of Political Economy* 109:546–569.

Ladd, Helen. 1988. *Local government land use policies in the United States.* Cheltenham, UK: Edward Elgar.

Mills, Edwin S., and Wallace E. Oates, eds. 1975. *Fiscal zoning and land use controls.* Lexington, MA: Heath-Lexington.

Ohls, James C., Richard Weisberg, and Michelle J. White. 1974. The effects of zoning on land value. *Journal of Urban Economics* 1:428–444.

———. 1976. Welfare effects in alternative models of zoning. *Journal of Urban Economics* 3:95–96.

Poterba, James. 1992. Taxation and housing: Old questions, new answers. *American Economic Review, Papers and Proceedings* 82:237–242.

Scotchmer, Suzanne. 2002. Local public goods and club goods. In *Handbook of public economics, vol. 4,* A. J. Auerbach and M. Feldstein, eds., 1997–2042. New York: Elsevier.

Wheaton, William. 1993. Land capitalization, Tiebout mobility, and the role of zoning regulations. *Journal of Urban Economics* 34:102–117.

White, Michelle. 1975. The effect of zoning on the size of metropolitan areas. *Journal of Urban Economics* 5:279–290.

COMMENTARY

Thomas J. Nechyba

Exclusionary zoning is often viewed as an attempt by wealthier jurisdictions to exclude poorer residents because of *fiscal* externalities. Put differently, when tax revenues are raised locally, wealthier residents have an interest in excluding poorer residents (who would contribute disproportionately less in local tax revenue) in order to prevent them from "free-riding" on the tax payments of the wealthy. While excluding low-income households directly is illegal, restricting their access indirectly through the setting of minimum house and lot sizes is more commonly accepted. Such exclusionary zoning is often viewed as quite fundamental to theoretical modeling of local public finance—providing a stabilizing force that might otherwise not permit the existence of stable equilibria in such models.

Peer externalities are a second reason for exclusionary zoning. If, for instance, lower household wealth is correlated with the need for greater public expenditures to achieve the same local public service levels, wealthier households have an additional incentive to segregate and erect barriers to lower-wealth households because the presence of such households increases additional *fiscal needs*. For instance, lower-wealth households may be statistically more likely to commit crimes or may bring negative peer externalities to local public schools, thus requiring increased local public expenditures to offset these negative externalities. This is an empirically important consideration, as there is strong evidence that higher-wealth neighborhoods refuse access to potential lower-wealth residents even when substantial compensation to overcome fiscal externalities is offered. Their motivation is almost certainly derived from a perception of extensive negative peer externalities associated with the presence of lower-wealth households.

This paper introduces the motivation (on the part of high-wealth residents) for this nonfiscal form of exclusionary zoning by defining household preferences not only over private consumption, housing, and local public good levels, but also over average community income. Were average community income not explicitly included in preferences, the model would contain only incentives to exclude lower-income households to the extent to which they bring with them the negative *fiscal* externalities (because of "free-riding" on higher tax payments by higher-income households). (Such incentives play no role in the model here because the public good is assumed to be provided by a higher-level government.) The inclusion of average community income in household preferences therefore represents a "reduced form" way of introducing the concern over a need for increased local public expenditures to maintain public service levels in the presence of lower-income households, or, alternatively, it represents a more direct form of peer externality that cannot be compensated for by increased local public spending (given that public good spending is assumed to be set at a level above the local community level).

This formulation of preferences also implicitly assumes a perfect correlation of peer externalities with household income. In this sense, it becomes observationally similar to the more standard fiscal externality in the usual discussions of exclusionary zoning. This is because both fiscal and nonfiscal externalities arise solely through the channel of household income when nonfiscal externalities are presumed to correlate perfectly with income. At the same time, introducing an imperfect correlation between household income and peer externalities would not substantially change the predictions of the model. Higher-wealth communities would then have an incentive to statistically discriminate against lower-income households through exclusionary zoning (so long as they cannot differentiate between low-income households with different types of peer externalities). The authors therefore wisely choose to use the simplified framework of assuming perfect correlation of peer externalities with income, given that nothing fundamental would change by assuming a more realistic imperfect correlation.

The political economy process by which exclusionary zoning is established in the model is also different from what has previously been considered. Communities that impose exclusionary zoning are viewed as part of a larger urban jurisdiction that itself has to approve of exclusionary zoning imposed in subjurisdictions. This focuses attention on cases in which the larger urban governments could in principle block exclusionary zoning in neighborhoods within the urban area and allows the authors to investigate conditions under which voters in the entire local economy choose to permit exclusionary zoning in some parts of the area. Others who are more intimately familiar with how zoning policies are set in different contexts are more qualified to comment on the degree to which this new view of the political economy underlying exclusionary zoning matches with real world policy making, but it seems quite plausible that this framework is applicable in at least a subset of empirically relevant cases.[1]

The framework also restricts itself to the existence of two communities within the larger urban jurisdiction that is modeled, with one labeled the "city" and the other labeled the "suburb." In the absence of zoning, a single crossing property of the model results in a segregation of the population along income lines into the two districts, with lower-income residents choosing the city and higher-income residents choosing the suburb. Thus, unlike other models of local public finance, the model itself does not *require* the existence of zoning in order for a Tiebout equilibrium to exist. This is a nice feature of the model, because it allows the authors to directly compare an equilibrium without zoning to one in which exclusionary zoning is permitted.[2]

Introducing the possibility of zoning restrictions then shifts the "boundary" between city residents and suburban residents—causing some relatively lower-income households who would reside in the suburbs without zoning to instead live in the city. The assumption of a perfectly elastic housing market in the central city implies that the outward shift in demand for central-city housing does not alter housing prices in the city, while the assumption of a perfectly inelastic housing market in the suburbs implies that the inward demand shift for suburban housing causes a reduction in housing prices in the suburb. But because the residents who shift from the suburb to the city have incomes below the suburban average but above the city average, *average community income rises in both districts when exclusionary zoning is implemented.*

It is then easy to see how such nonfiscal exclusionary zoning (which requires approval by the entire population) is politically popular in the model. Those who reside in the city in the absence of zoning experience no change in housing prices but an increase in average community income (which enters directly

---

[1] The typical model for exclusionary zoning, based on the work of Hamilton (1975, 1976) and extended by Fischel (2001), assumes that local communities are the ultimate authority authorized to impose exclusionary zoning within some statewide legal system and thus are not required to pass a larger voting test that includes voting by nonresidents. This view of zoning has formed the basis for the debate over whether local property taxes represent efficient "Tiebout" benefit taxes or inefficient taxes on mobile capital (Mieszkowski and Zodrow 1989; Fischel, 1992).

[2] Other local public finance models require, explicitly or implicitly, the existence of zoning in order for an equilibrium to exist. This is because of the well-known "musical chairs" phenomenon in which lower-income households "chase" higher-income households in order to free-ride on their higher public good levels by paying disproportionately lower taxes. The authors have a series of papers over two decades that have established a framework in which the introduction of a single crossing property in household tastes eliminates the need for zoning (or other restrictions on housing markets) to overcome the musical chairs problem. An early discussion of this is provided by Rose-Ackerman (1979); Epple, Filimon, and Romer (1993); and Nechyba (1997), with models ultimately assuming either single crossing properties on preferences (as initially modeled by Epple, Filimon, and Romer) or restrictions on housing markets with no restrictions on preferences (as in Nechyba) to establish existence of an equilibrium. This is discussed more extensively in Epple and Nechyba (2004).

into their preferences). Thus, initial city residents are unambiguously better off when the suburb engages in exclusionary zoning. Those who continue to live in the suburbs, on the other hand, experience a reduction of housing prices and an increase in average community income. While some now have to purchase larger houses than they would in the absence of exclusionary zoning, the simultaneous reduction in housing prices and increase in average community income makes most of them better off. This leaves those residents who switch from the suburb to the city who may (or may not) be worse off. But simulations suggest that the introduction of exclusionary zoning by the suburbs results in the vast majority of residents becoming better off—thus, large majorities supporting the move by the suburb toward exclusionary zoning.[3]

The result has clear efficiency implications, with zoning serving as a means for internalizing peer externalities. Ideally, one would want to price such externalities, perhaps through impact or entrance fees that would, however, have to depend on the household characteristics (income) that correlate with the peer externality. Given that such pricing is probably not feasible, the model raises the possibility that the efficiency properties of fiscal exclusionary zoning (as it relates to property taxes) in the previous literature (Fischel 1992) extend to nonfiscal exclusionary zoning that arises from peer externalities.

The authors make a persuasive case that changes in many of the underlying preference parameters of the model are unlikely to overturn their main result. Even the addition of taste heterogeneity (as in Epple and Platt 1998), while adding complexity, is also unlikely to overturn the result. Similarly, adding additional suburban districts to the model would continue to give rise to the same essential forces. For instance, if the model included two rather than one suburb, exclusionary zoning would again result in an increase in average community income in both suburbs as well as the city—the main driving force behind the result. Within the confines of the model's setup, the result therefore seems quite robust.

The bigger question, then, is whether there are fundamentally restrictive assumptions built into the basic setup of the model that, when altered to be more empirically plausible, would introduce sufficient tension to overturn the result of large political support for exclusionary zoning by subdistricts within an urban/suburban economy. Alternatively, we can ask whether additional real world elements to the model might raise severe equity concerns—that is, even if substantial majorities continue to approve of exclusionary zoning, might additional considerations cause concerns about the welfare of severely disadvantaged households?

---

[3] Public good levels are held fixed in the theoretical section and virtually unchanged in the simulations (where voting on public goods is endogenized) when nonfiscal zoning is introduced. Zoning-induced public goods changes therefore play no role in the analysis.

One of the least appealing assumptions in the current setup relates to the assumption regarding housing supply elasticities. The model currently assumes that supply is perfectly elastic in the city and (at the margin) perfectly inelastic in the suburb. When we think of typical urban areas, however, the reverse assumptions would seem more empirically plausible. Central cities are more likely to be land-constrained and more likely to have existing housing stocks that are difficult and expensive to alter. Suburbs, on the other hand, are more likely to have available land suitable for newly constructed housing. An increase in demand for central-city housing from exclusionary zoning in the suburb would then cause an increase in central district housing prices—creating a tension between higher housing costs for current city residents and higher average income. Renters in particular would be adversely affected by increased housing prices while enjoying the benefits of higher average city income. This would create a more ambiguous welfare prediction for central-city residents—and thus would reduce political support for exclusionary zoning. It may still be the case that such exclusionary zoning would receive majority political support, but the case is no longer as clear cut, and the welfare implications are more worrisome.[4]

A second concern arises from the assumption of an *exogenous* number of suburbs in the current model. As long as this number is exogenous, exclusionary zoning in suburban districts continues to have the potential of raising average income in all districts—and thus (under the supply elasticity assumptions of the model) is likely to result in continued high levels of political support for exclusionary zoning. However, if—in the true "Tiebout spirit"—suburban districts can emerge endogenously, I conjecture a much more complicated scenario. Suppose, for instance, that we begin in a model in which, in the absence of exclusionary zoning, there are two districts: the city and one suburb. Now suppose exclusionary zoning is introduced in the suburb, pushing some households with incomes below the suburban average out of the suburb. In the absence of the possibility of another suburban district forming, this population will simply join the city and thereby raise average income in the city. But if this population can form a new suburb, it may well attract some relatively higher-income households from the existing city into its new suburb. This would imply an increase in average income only in the original suburb and a decrease in average income in the central city. Within the newly created suburb, residents who have joined from the city would experience an increase in average income, while those who previously lived in the older suburb would experience a decrease. Those who remain in the city, as well as some of those who originally resided in the older

---

[4] The supply elasticity assumptions in the model also in part create the tension between homeowner and developer preferences that the authors cite.

suburb, would then band together to oppose the introduction of exclusionary zoning in the local economy. It is quite likely that this would result in majority opposition to exclusionary zoning.

Even if political support for exclusionary zoning did emerge under the endogenous community formation just discussed, zoning would introduce an equity concern that does not arise in the current model. In particular, households who remain in the city would become unambiguously worse off because of the decrease in average city income. But these are by definition the poorest residents in the model. This would imply that exclusionary zoning benefits the richest households and hurts the poorest, with somewhat ambiguous predictions for households in the middle.

Similar equity concerns might arise even without the endogenous formation of suburban communities under exclusionary zoning if such zoning is permitted also in the city district. While the migration of relatively high-income households into the district from the suburb that introduces exclusionary zoning implies an increase in average income in the city, the city could further increase average income by imposing its own zoning to drive the poorest residents out of the urban area altogether. Virtually everyone who remains in the area will benefit from this—implying that large majorities would still favor the introduction of exclusionary zoning. But the most vulnerable residents of the city district would be driven out of the area (and the model), leaving them (and the areas they migrate to) almost certainly worse off.

None of this is meant to take away from the considerable achievements in this chapter. The authors have recast a well-established "work horse" model in the local public finance literature to permit a rigorous examination of the political economy issues surrounding exclusionary zoning, adding in the process a new and empirically important nonfiscal dimension to such zoning. The model has some especially appealing features—in particular the possibility of discussing a stable equilibrium in the absence of exclusionary zoning that then facilitates a comparison of a no-zoning equilibrium to one that includes zoning. Other local public finance models are inherently ill suited for this purpose, given that they require some form of zoning to establish the existence of an equilibrium in the first place. Furthermore, the authors present a convincing case that the intuitions emerging from the model are quite robust within the model's setup and thus provide us with a firm basis from which to discuss the likely candidates for additional features that might be fruitfully analyzed in future research in order to explore additional empirically relevant considerations surrounding the political economy of exclusionary zoning. The paper therefore provides a fresh lens to an old question, one that will no doubt receive considerable further attention in the future and may well change the way we think about exclusionary zoning policies.

References

Epple, Dennis, Radu Filimon, and Thomas Romer. 1993. Existence of voting and housing equilibrium in a system of communities with property taxes. *Regional Science and Urban Economics* 23:585–610.

Epple, Dennis, and Thomas Nechyba. 2004. Fiscal decentralization. In *Handbook of regional economics, vol. 4*, J. Vernon Henderson and Jacques-François Thisse, eds. Amsterdam: North-Holland.

Epple, Dennis, and Glenn Platt. 1998. Equilibrium and local redistribution in an urban economy when households differ in both preferences and income. *Journal of Urban Economics* 43:23–51.

Fischel, William. 1992. Property taxation and the Tiebout model: Evidence for the benefit view from zoning and voting. *Journal of Economic Literature* 30:171–177.

———. 2001. Homevoters, municipal corporate governance, and the benefit view of the property tax. *National Tax Journal* 54:157–173.

Hamilton, Bruce. 1975. Zoning and property taxes in a system of local governments. *Urban Studies* 12:205–211.

———. 1976. Capitalization of interjurisdictional differences in local tax prices. *American Economic Review* 66:743–753.

Mieszkowski, Peter, and George Zodrow. 1989. Taxation and the Tiebout model: The differential effects of head taxes, taxes on land rents and property taxes. *Journal of Economic Literature* 27:1098–1146.

Nechyba, Thomas. 1997. Existence of equilibrium and stratification in local and hierarchical public good economies with property taxes and voting. *Economic Theory* 10:277–304.

Rose-Ackerman, Susan. 1979. Market models of local government: Exit, voting and the land market. *Journal of Urban Economics* 6:319–337.

8

Compared to What? Tiebout and the Comparative Merits of Congress and the States in Constitutional Federalism

Roderick M. Hills Jr.

Charles Tiebout's (1956) theory of local government has an ambiguous status in American law schools. On one hand, Tiebout's famous hypothesis features prominently in legal scholarship on local government. Excerpts from "A Pure Theory of Local Expenditures" appear in the leading local government law casebooks, and a simple Westlaw search reveals that Tiebout's name is widely cited by law professors. On the other hand, much of this legal scholarship is relentlessly hostile to Tiebout's theory as a normative proposition, treating it as a whipping boy rather than a foundation for legal interpretation. Tiebout's name and ideas are also invisible in judicial opinions, even in those that reach conclusions suggested by Tiebout's theory. The invisibility in the legal doctrines bears some relationship to the hostility in the legal scholarship.

The Tiebout hypothesis has played a significant role in shaping the scholarly debate over the constitutional doctrine of enumerated powers. A doctrinal area ripe for Tiebout's influence is the doctrine of Congress's enumerated powers under Article I of the Constitution. Could the Tiebout hypothesis be the basis for a general theory of constitutional federalism in the United States?

It would not be an extraordinary stretch of textual materials to infer that the U.S. Constitution's enumeration of powers should be informed by a theory of subsidiarity that, in turn, would be influenced by Tiebout's confidence in competition between subnational jurisdictions. One could argue, for instance, that federal laws did not fall within Congress's Article I, §8 power to regulate commerce "among . . . the several states" unless those laws addressed some failure in the intergovernmental marketplace—for instance, a problem of external costs

239

such as smog drifting across state lines.[1] Such an interpretation of Article I might rule out federal environmental laws when subnational jurisdictions meet Tiebout's criteria for effective regulation, such as when the activities they regulate generate highly local effects. Indeed, some dissenting federal judges have recently attacked federal environmental laws as falling outside Congress's jurisdiction precisely because they address activities that are too localized to generate interstate effects.[2] The Canadian Supreme Court, with no specific textual warrant, has adopted a theory of federal powers along these lines, striking down federal laws that regulate highly localized environmental harms while allowing the central government to regulate activities that generate effects beyond the provinces' capacity to control (*R. V. Crown Zellerbach Ltd.*, 1 S.C.R. 401 [1988]). Why should not the U.S. Supreme Court do the same, inspired by the idea that firms' mobility between subnational jurisdictions ensures that the costs of regulation will not exceed the benefits to the jurisdiction's residents?

The Tiebout hypothesis might enjoy more popularity in legal circles if both economic and legal scholarship focused on comparing the flaws of the spatial economy of subnational governments with the flaws of centralized decision making. Much of the economic literature compares the intergovernmental market with the private marketplace and unsurprisingly finds the former to fall short by this standard. But one might instead urge that Tiebout's system of local government be compared to centralized regulation, which is the realistic alternative to governmental decentralization. It is true that subnational jurisdictions are pervasively plagued by external economies. Congress is plagued by an analogous problem arising from an analogous cause. The problem is excessive uniformity in policy making, and the cause is congressional decentralization through powerful subcommittees and weak, nonprogrammatic political parties. Such a decentralized lawmaking process leads to a system of "universalism" (i.e., "you vote for my pork, and I'll vote for yours"), creating incentives for excessive uniformity possibly more inefficient and distributively unjust than anything attributed to the intergovernmental spatial economy, even assuming that local governments are plagued by pervasive external economies and diseconomies. Economists have rarely, if ever, offered a formal model comparing the costs of universalism in a decentralized legislature with the costs of externalities in a decentralized system of local government.

Such a model would go far to rehabilitate the Tiebout hypothesis as a normative matter—and perhaps a constitutional matter, as well. Compared to a

---

[1] The U.S. Supreme Court's commerce clause doctrine allowing Congress to regulate activities exerting a "substantial effect" on interstate commerce suggests implicitly the notion that Congress should be able to regulate external economies that individual states cannot control. See Regan (1995).

[2] See, for example, *Gibbs v. Babbitt*, 214 F.3d 483 (4th Cir. 2000) (Luttig, J., dissenting) (permitting enforcement of federal law that prohibits killing of an endangered species by farmers seeking to protect livestock against predators).

genuinely competitive market, the actual intergovernmental market leaves much to be desired. But compared to our actual institutions of centralized law-making, our system of spatial economies measures up well on both distributive justice and allocative efficiency. Indeed, Tiebout's reputation is on the rise in legal scholarship precisely because lawyers have become increasingly disappointed with Congress and the federal courts as instruments of both efficiency and social justice. Oddly, both economists and lawyers have generally failed to make the necessary real-world comparison.

In evaluating how well the Tiebout hypothesis has fared in the law, it is also important to distinguish between judicial restraint of Congress and judicial self-restraint. First, courts could use such ideas to justify their imposition of legal restrictions on nonjudicial actors: legislatures, governors, city councils, and so on. Second, courts could use such ideas to justify their own self-restraint. Not surprisingly, courts and legal academics are generally more willing to invoke social science theories for the second purpose. And the Tiebout hypothesis is no exception. No court is likely to use Tiebout's ideas as a justification for judicial restraint of Congress. Those ideas might, however, motivate a court to exercise self-restraint in enforcing dormant commerce clause doctrines that limit states' efforts to attract business through tax subsidies of various sorts.

Initial Success for Tiebout: The Defeat of "Race-to-the-Bottom" Rationales for Federalization

Legal scholars took almost 15 years to absorb Wallace Oates's 1969 revival of the Tiebout hypothesis.[3] By the early 1980s, Tiebout's and Oates's ideas began to percolate into legal scholarship. Glen Robinson, for instance, defended antitrust immunity for cities in 1982 on the ground that intergovernmental competition would adequately constrain their monopolistic behavior. Likewise, Robert Ellickson (1982) argued that cities ought to have autonomy to experiment with voting rulers other than "one person, one vote," on the ground that the mobility of voters gave them a smaller stake in the local political process. Ellickson's reliance on Tiebout was especially notable when contrasted with the distrust of local governments manifested by his landmark article urging stricter judicial controls on suburban zoning, an article that ignored Tiebout entirely (Ellickson 1977). In short, legal scholars discovered a new faith in subfederal jurisdictions at the same time that they began citing Tiebout in earnest in the 1980s.

But Tiebout's theory did not produce any revival of federalism, largely because states seemed too large. It was simply implausible to believe that mobile

---

[3] Oates (1969). Various economists elaborated the conditions under which local governments would make efficient decisions concerning the environment. See, for example, Fischel (1975).

households could freely migrate between competing states in search of the best package of taxes and services. Only corporate law scholars debated the merits of a mobility-based theory of federalism in the literature that emerged from William Cary's (1974) article on corporations' decision about the state in which to incorporate. But this literature shed little light on the critical issues that any mobility-based theory of federalism must confront. Corporate decisions about where to incorporate are only metaphorically concerned with mobility: They are actually costless decisions to choose a particular law to govern the corporate contract. Thus, the corporate law literature never addressed the problem of imperfect interstate mobility. Moreover, the literature focused so heavily on whether managers were the shareholders' faithful agents that it said little about the problem of externalities on constituencies other than management and shareholders.

It was not until 1992 that legal scholarship seriously began to grapple with the problems of external effects and limited mobility that are at the heart of any mobility-based theory of federalism. The target of this scholarship was the theory that, absent federal standards, subnational jurisdictions would inefficiently reduce the stringency of their environmental laws in an effort to attract mobile capital.[4] Richard Revesz (1992) relied heavily on an article by Oates and Schwab (1988) to argue that this "race to the bottom" argument rests on the non sequitur. Strictly speaking, Revesz's argument does not rely on Tiebout's premise of individual mobility. Instead, following Oates's decentralization theorem, Revesz (1992, 1220, n. 25) assumed that individuals were perfectly immobile: In Revesz's argument, individual residents express their preferences for public goods through voice—voting—rather than exit from, or entry into, a jurisdiction. The point of this assumption of voter immobility was to make the model less vulnerable to the accusation that it was relevant only in seminomadic societies like the United States, where restless wanderers regularly uproot themselves in search of better jobs, warmer weather, or more efficient government (Revesz 1992, 1237; Oates 1999, 1124). However, Oates's theory is nevertheless a mobility-based theory because it assumes that owners of capital are fully mobile across jurisdictions. Substitute capital mobility for household mobility, and Tiebout's and Oates's theories seem fundamentally similar. Moreover, like Tiebout, Oates relies on the intuition that governments will provide a more finely articulated picture of citizens' preferences for local public goods than central governments, because local governments will be

---

[4] In *Hodel v. Virginia Surface Mining & Reclamation Ass'n*, 452 U.S. 264, 280 (1981), for instance, the Court stated that nationwide surface mining standards were necessary "to insure that competition in interstate commerce among sellers of coal produced in different states will not be used to undermine the ability of the several states to improve and maintain adequate standards on coal-mining operations within their borders."

more capable of responding to the preferences of heterogeneous subcommunities within the nation than a single national government. For Oates, such subcommunities arise by happenstance; for Tiebout, they arise from household mobility. However, this difference seems much less important to legal scholars like Revesz than the essential point that mobility might limit government power without producing inefficient results.

Revesz did not deny that competition between subnational governments constrains subnational governments' capacity to engage in environmental regulation. He simply denied that such competition could be presumed to decrease social welfare. So long as the benefits and costs of industrial relocation are wholly bestowed on local residents, the local government elected by those residents should make a correct balance of environmental quality and (say) higher wages.[5] If the benefits and costs of both the jurisdiction's regulation and the investment of capital are confined within a single jurisdiction, then the jurisdiction's elected policy makers ought presumptively to balance the two as well as, or better than, any other rival government. If West Virginia wants to sell its scenery for a mess of tax base, then why not let it do so, just so long as the residents experience all of the costs and benefits of the decision?

As a criticism of current federal environmental policy, Revesz's article seems to have bested its critics.[6] However, Revesz's success depended critically on the modesty of his ambitions. He did not stake a general theory of federalism but simply drove a stake through existing federal policy. Revesz accepted jujitsu-style his critics' premises that interjurisdictional competition was likely to be inefficient in many circumstances, either because of interjurisdictional spillovers or because the competing players possessed excessive market power.[7] Instead, Revesz argued that existing federal environmental law was not well suited for addressing such failings of the interjurisdictional market for location. Many of the environmental harms addressed by federal law—for instance, unsafe drinking water—were extremely localized in their effects. Indeed, by measuring environmental compliance through ambient air quality standards, the Clean Air Act actually encouraged jurisdictions to export smoke to other states by requiring factories to install high smokestacks. Such laws were justified solely by the need for regulatory uniformity to prevent interstate competition—uniformity that imposed large welfare losses on those communities with

---

[5] Under the Oates-Schwab version of the argument, the owners pay higher wages to an immobile workforce composed wholly of local voters in return for the right to pollute the local environment.

[6] Even the critics of Tiebout seem to have conceded that Revesz won the argument against the general race-to-the-bottom argument. See, for example, Bratton and McCahery (1997, 219, n. 74) for sources conceding the argument to critics of race-to-the-bottom theory.

[7] Kirsten Engel (1997) rested her critique of decentralized environmental policy largely on the basis of the excessive market power of both industry and state government.

differing tastes for environmental quality (Revesz 1997, 1224–1227). As for the locational advantages of subnational jurisdictions, Revesz argued that these advantages justified federal *ceilings* on subnational regulation, not federal *floors*.

Thus, Revesz was in the enviable position of shooting statutory fish in the narrow barrel of economic analysis. Without saying anything generally on behalf of decentralized policy making, he could note the irrationality of centralized policy making. On this narrow ground, the article was a tour de force.

Some Problems for Tiebout: External Costs and Distributive Justice

In a later article, Revesz (1997) hinted at a more general argument in favor of a "presumption of decentralization." But Revesz's argument has not provided much basis for a more ambitious use of Tiebout in the federalism doctrine. There are two important reasons for this reluctance. First, courts and scholars tend to presume that externalities are ubiquitous and that, therefore, decentralization will tend to be inefficient. Second, legal scholars worry that interjurisdictional competition tends to be distributionally arbitrary, giving special advantages to the owners of mobile capital that are inconsistent with democratic equality. As elaborated following, both the possibility of inefficiency and distributive injustice has undermined the value of the Tiebout hypothesis in the eyes of legal academics.

Three Sources of External Effects: Monopolistic States, Constrained Fiscal Instruments, and Cumbersome Intergovernmental Bargaining

Consider three reasons why one might presume the ubiquity of external effects requiring centralized regulation. For the sake of convenience, we can label these arguments the dilemma of monopoly versus externality, the inability to discriminate against newcomers, and the costliness of intergovernmental bargaining.

First, consider the dilemma of externality versus monopoly. It might be impossible to ensure that subnational governments are small enough to be constrained by mobility of taxpayers yet large enough to encompass the effects of their residents' activities. To minimize spillover effects from underregulation, the boundaries of subnational jurisdictions should coincide with the range of effects generated by the activities that such subnational jurisdictions are charged with regulating—traffic, decibel levels, housing, smoke, and so forth. The smaller the subnational jurisdiction, the more likely that the activities within their jurisdiction will impose spillover costs on nonresidents, justifying intervention from a larger unit of government. However, as one enlarges the subnational government's boundaries to encompass these effects, one increases the likelihood that the demand for access to the government's land will be inelastic, allowing the government to externalize the costs of their operations on to nonresidents who are dependent on the jurisdiction for employment, recreation, or travel.

Thus, a regional megalopolis (call it Gotham) might control sufficient land area to ensure that the costs of its regulation are experienced within the population that elects its policy makers. But Gotham also commands such an enormous landmass that it can externalize the costs of its operations on nonresident commuters who are forced to drive to Gotham for employment or recreation, given the absence of adequate substitutes in the commuter shed for the sites that Gotham has to offer. By contrast, a tiny hamlet (call it Mayberry) cannot impose fiscal externalities on nonresidents: Any commuter tax would simply induce those nonresidents to shop or work in a neighboring and entirely fungible jurisdiction. However, Mayberry is simply too small to contain the effects of most of its residents' activities. Any real estate development sited in Mayberry, for instance, will have enormous effects on the roads in neighboring jurisdictions. The design of local government boundaries, therefore, presents the choice of tax-exporting Brobdingnagians or nuisance-exporting Lilliputians.

As a second obstacle to efficient decentralization, consider the legal inability to discriminate against newcomers. The U.S. Supreme Court has developed an elaborate array of doctrines prohibiting states from discriminating against nonresidents or newly arrived immigrants based on the duration of their residency. Although the textual source of this doctrine varies (including the Privileges and Immunities clauses of Article IV, §2 [*Zobel v. Williams*, 457 U.S. 374 (1982)] and the Fourteenth Amendment [*Saenz v. Roe*, 526 U.S. 489 (1999)]; the Equal Protection clause of the Fourteenth Amendment [*Shapiro v. Thompson*, 394 U.S. 618 (1969)]; and the Commerce Clause of Article I [*Edwards v. California*, 314 U.S. 160 (1941)]), the underlying purpose of all such doctrines is to ensure that states do not undermine our sense of shared national citizenship by discriminating in favor of their long-term residents or against nonresidents.[8]

To create efficient incentives for migration, however, jurisdictions may sometimes need to discriminate against newcomers. As a general matter, Tiebout's theory of efficient interjurisdictional mobility requires that jurisdictions match the costs of services consumed with the amount of taxes paid (Oates 1999, 1125). Otherwise, a state's tax bill would not send a correct signal about the costs of the services consumed, and immigrants will have an incentive to migrate to the state in inefficiently high or low numbers.[9]

For instance, suppose that the marginal cost of supplying services to a new immigrant exceeds the average costs of those services. This situation could arise if

---

[8] For a summary of the various doctrines and their relationship to national unity, see Hills (1999).
[9] For a standard catalogue of such fiscal externalities, see Gordon (1983, 578–580).

the services consumed by the newcomer were subject to increasing marginal congestion costs: Think of roads on which cars move smoothly until the nth driver arrives, at which point they slow down. If the jurisdiction charges the newcomer only the average costs of supplying the service, then the newcomer will ignore the excess marginal cost she imposes on the old-timers. To send the correct signal to the newcomer, therefore, the jurisdiction should charge the newcomer with a fee higher than the average tax bill (Tolley 1974). As another example, consider income support for low-income households. Any state that provides relatively generous assistance and thereby attracts low-income households from less-generous states bestows a beneficial fiscal externality on those states (Wildasin 1991). To force the migrants' state of origin to internalize this benefit, the generous state might discriminate against new migrants in assistance payments, thereby encouraging them to stay home and seek assistance from their stingier state of residence. Moreover, if a state's taxpayers derive some special pleasure from providing income support to their long-time neighbors, then such assistance has the characteristic of a local public good (Pauly 1998). In such a case, discrimination against newcomers would seem to be just as efficient as refusal to pay for parks located in another state.

The U.S. Supreme Court, however, would likely forbid all such discrimination against newcomers in the name of national citizenship. Thus, the Court has held that states may not discriminate against indigent migrants based on the duration of their residency in determining the amount of assistance that such indigents may receive (*Saenz v. Roe*). Likewise, the Court has held that Alaska could not provide higher payments from its mineral funds to old-timers than to newcomers—again in the name of national unity (*Zobel v. Williams*).

Thus, the courts knock out the cornerstone of the Tiebout hypothesis by limiting the fiscal instruments available to subnational jurisdictions in the name of equality. This problem is analogous to an argument made by several economists that Tiebout competition will tend to lead to the underprovision of local public goods if subnational jurisdictions are forced to rely exclusively on the taxation of mobile capital (Zodrow and Mieszkowski 1986; Wilson 1987). The lawyer's short answer to these economists' arguments is that subnational jurisdictions are nowhere compelled to rely solely on such a narrow range of taxes: To the contrary, interjurisdictional competition tends to ensure that each jurisdiction discriminates in favor of mobile capital, converting taxes on such capital into fees, special assessments, or other benefits charges to cover the costs of services required by the owners of such capital.[10] But judicial insistence on nondiscrimination between nonresidents and residents introduces a more realistic problem for Tiebout's spatial economy: Subnational jurisdictions can-

---

[10] This is how Louis Kaplow (1996, 462) explains the wooing of industry with tax abatements. A similar point is made by Arnott and Grieson (1981, 25–37).

not engage in discrimination against newcomers even when such discrimination might create efficient incentives for migration.

In theory, many of these problems could be solved through intergovernmental bargaining. In theory, for instance, subnational jurisdictions could bribe nonresident poor persons to stay home by offering funds to the poor households' subnational government. But the bargaining process would predictably be plagued by transaction costs peculiar to the governmental context.

As Clayton Gillette (2001) has observed, the goals pursued by local government tend to be less homogeneous than the goals of for-profit firms, making the division of the gains from interlocal bargains especially difficult.[11] Moreover, to the extent that an interlocal bargain attempts to control a region-wide spillover effect, it will frequently be necessary for every local government within the region to enter into the bargain, multiplying the cost of negotiating a settlement among dozens of potential holdouts. For these reasons, interlocal bargaining has not been a notable success in resolving city-suburb conflicts over the allocation of tax base or low-income housing.[12]

Are the Advantages of Mobile Capital in Federal Regimes Distributively Unjust?

Even given the three sources of inefficiencies just identified, one might nevertheless conclude that interjurisdictional competition would efficiently set the level of regulation for highly localized environmental harms—for instance, polluted drinking water. But there is a second objection to interjurisdictional competition that may be more influential among lawyers and political scientists: Such competition seems to give disproportionate political power to the owners of mobile capital. As John Donahue (1997) argues, interjurisdictional competition seems to

---

[11] See Gillette (2001, 216–218). Imagine, for instance, that a central city and its suburbs attempt to resolve the issue of commuter taxes and residency requirements for city employees (two issues that raise classic problems of interlocal conflict and external costs). If the suburbanites' demand for jobs with the central city is sufficiently high, then the suburban governments may offer the central city some sort of revenue-sharing in return for access to those city jobs. However, the central city might demand that its employees live in the city for symbolic and patronage-based reasons as well as purely fiscal reasons. It is not obvious how the suburbs could conjure up an offer that would reasonably approximate the monetary value of these nonfiscal goals.

[12] For a detailed account of bargaining between Hartford, Connecticut, and its suburbs over the provision of affordable housing in the region, see Susskind, van der Wansem, and Ciccarelli (2000) and Connerly and Smith (1996, 90). These negotiations took place in a detailed framework provided by state law under Conn. Gen Stat. §8-383, which created the Connecticut Regional Housing Compact Pilot Program. As illustrated by William Fischel's account of intergovernmental bargaining over landfill sites in *The Homevoter Hypothesis*, whether neighboring municipalities can strike a deal is an empirical question, influenced by the degree to which local officials work together formally on countywide commissions or share school districts and state legislative and congressional electoral districts. Such channels for repeated formal or informal interaction among politicians may reduce mutual suspicion to the point where local officials can resolve even the hotly contested issue of landfill siting (Fischel 191–202).

confer "disproportionate solicitude for the more mobile kinds of business," working "an implied transformation in what we mean by governmental accountability" (78). Peter Enrich makes a similar point, urging that interstate competition for mobile capital erodes democratic accountability by deterring states from taxing the owners of mobile capital on the basis of their ability to pay.[13]

These critics of Tiebout's spatial economies, in other words, may be making an argument from distributive justice and not from efficiency. So, that understood, the "race to the bottom" is simply a race to a system of benefits charges in which mobile capital is charged no more than the cost of supplying it with services. This is a "bottom" in the sense that subnational jurisdictions are foreclosed by capital's mobility from pursuing a policy that they are constitutionally entitled to pursue— that is, from redistribution of wealth from the owners of mobile capital to others.

How can an economist (or economically inclined lawyer) respond to such a concern? The normal response is to note that the central government could specialize in redistributing income from the owners of mobile capital to other constituents, while subnational jurisdictions could specialize in the delivery of local public goods (Musgrave and Musgrave 1989). Outside of the international context where there is no central government capable of large-scale redistribution of wealth (Avi-Yonah 2000), this response seems to address the worry that federalism will undermine the welfare state. But this conventional response misses the point. The problem is not that redistribution cannot occur in federal systems but that subnational governments disproportionately target owners of immobile assets—say, vacant land—for such burdens, letting owners of mobile capital off the hook. Thus, one might worry that subnational governments redistribute in morally arbitrary ways. Moreover, subnational jurisdictions that control vital ports, Mediterranean climates, oil wells, unique mountain views, or other assets for which there is inelastic demand will have an advantage over other jurisdictions in the power to redistribute wealth. California will have greater power to redistribute wealth than, say, Rhode Island. Why should it?

Reviving Tiebout: What Are the Comparative Costs of Centralization and Decentralization?

It is not difficult, in short, to come up with reasons why the decentralized provision of governmental services would be inefficient and distributively unjust. But the persuasiveness of these arguments depends on the efficiency of the alternative

---

[13] According to Enrich (1996, 403–404), "If voters place a higher value than would the market on government services or on the redistribution of resources, then achieving a socially optimal outcome may entail imposing some of the attendant costs on businesses (or others) that are neither the beneficiaries of the governmental functions nor the causes of the government's costs."

system, in which such services are provided by the central government. To resolve the dispute, one must compare the pathologies of centralized and decentralized decision making. How might centralization lead to vices similar to the problems of efficiency and distributive justice cited by Tiebout's critics?

Centralization and Excessive Uniformity

So far as efficiency is concerned, the characteristic vice of subnational government is the externalization of costs. The corresponding vice of centralized decision making is said to be excessive uniformity.

Why should one believe that centralized provision of regulation and infrastructure will necessarily be excessively uniform? Consider two problems to which large-scale jurisdictions might be distinctively prone: universalism and nontraceability. "Universalism" is the tendency of each legislator to vote for the favored spending projects of every other legislator in exchange for his support of her favored projects.[14] Legislators adopt this strategy as a sort of insurance policy. They could theoretically obtain more expenditures for their own constituents by cutting rival legislators out of the budget. But legislators who adopt such a strategy run the risk of finding themselves left out of the minimum winning coalition. In such a case, the legislator's constituents would bear the costs of everyone else's projects while getting nothing for themselves—a recipe for an incumbent's losing elections. The legislator who voted against another member's projects would not even secure a reduction in taxation or deficit spending by voting against another member's project. Such a vote would simply write her out of the (otherwise) universalistic coalition, leaving her with nothing to bring home to her constituents, while her share would be divided up among the remaining legislators. Therefore, the risk-averse incumbent legislator spreads the budget thinly across the entire nation, voting for every representative's preferred project just so long as it is small enough to ensure the financing of similar projects by other members of the legislature (Inman and Fitts 1990).

Large-scale jurisdictions also might be prone to the problem of variable traceability, which may lead them to favor an inefficiently high level of expenditures. "Traceability" is the ability of constituents to link a legislative vote on some governmental action to either some cost or some benefit.[15] Constituents' capacity to trace some situation (say, scarcity of housing) to a representative's vote on some governmental action (say, rent control) depends not only on some level of economic sophistication (the constituent must understand the relationship between price controls and supply), but also on some level of political awareness

---

[14] Both the term and the concept described in the preceding sentence are drawn from Barry Weingast (1979).

[15] I borrow the term *traceability* from R. Douglas Arnold (1990).

(the constituent must know how her representative voted on rent control). Both sorts of knowledge vary by issue, political environment, constituent group, and (most importantly for a theory of federalism), jurisdictional size.

In particular, it may sometimes be easier for the public to focus on geographically compact benefits that are focused on a small group of constituents than on diffuse costs spread over a much larger group. This tendency to exaggerate geographically compact benefits is not universal,[16] but it might be especially pronounced for *recurrent* geographically concentrated benefits that are also associated with some program of interest to an attentive interest group. Geographically concentrated benefits might be especially attractive to the extent that they provide credit-taking opportunities to cultivate the personal vote through casework, ribbon-cutting, press conferences announcing a particular project, and so on.[17] Although the legislator's constituents would be upset by higher taxes, they might attribute the taxation levels to Congress as a whole rather than to their own congresspersons. Such "pork"—military bases, for instance—have proven famously irresistible to Congress because the benefits are perceived even by otherwise inattentive publics as part of their normal baseline of entitlement, the loss of which is taken as a harm (Arnold 1990, 140–141).

Both variations in traceability and universalism can lead central governments to adopt excessively uniform policies. Nontraceability causes government to impose uniform taxes (or deficits) across the entire nation, on the theory that the costs of such policies will be less visible than the discrete benefits of local pork that they fund. Universalism causes government to scatter similar packages of infrastructure across congressional districts, oblivious of the relative needs or preferences of these districts for public goods. In the worst-case scenario, the federal government would spend as much on infrastructure in Wyoming as on the New Orleans levees, oblivious to the relative need of the two jurisdictions for the expenditures.

When the supporters of the Tiebout hypothesis argue that decentralization will avoid the pathologies of excessive uniformity, they might have the pathologies of universalism and nontraceability in mind. It is certainly plausible to believe that local governments are less prone to these vices. The switch from a minimum winning coalition to a universal coalition is an effort to address the cost of coalition-building. But these costs ought to decrease as the size and heterogeneity of a population decrease. Likewise, as the population decreases, the costs imposed by government become less diffuse, and it becomes more difficult

---

[16] It is not the case that Congress cannot trim back on geographically compact benefits. See Arnold (1990, 132–141) describing instances in which Congress reduced expenditures on water projects, general revenue sharing, and other geographically constrained benefits in order to bring budgets under control.

[17] The classic account of credit-taking and incumbent advantage is Morris Fiorina (1989).

for legislators to exploit differences in the traceability of such costs and the traceability of more discrete benefits. Put simply, when compared to members of the House of Representatives, state legislators or city council members should be less fearful of voting against a rival's pork and more fearful of maintaining high taxes throughout the state or city.

In short, decentralization of decision making would likely decrease the risk of excessively uniform policies throughout the nation. But decentralization also increases the risk that subnational governments will impose external costs on nonresidents. The decentralization decision ought to depend, in significant part, on a comparison of these two risks.

The difficulty is that little of the scholarship, legal or nonlegal, makes much headway on this comparison. At the risk of oversimplifying, legal scholars assume that centralized governments can easily devolve power to subunits, while economists assume that centralized governments cannot engage in such devolution. On the economic side, the benefits of decentralization are some-times rooted in the assumption that central governments' policies will be rigidly uniform across the entire nation.[18] But this assumption could be unwarranted. In theory, centralized governments could vary policies to suit the preferences of different regions or communities, using special districts, field offices, user fees, and other mechanisms for gauging local demand for services.[19] Rather than devolving powers wholesale to locally elected officials, the central government might instead "delegate" or "deconcentrate" specific tasks to field offices, pre-fects, or even locally elected boards, carefully circumscribing such authority to prevent the local official from off-loading costs on to neighboring districts. (I borrow the terms from Richard Bird [2000].) Although the theory of univer-salism suggests otherwise, the evidence for a universalistic Congress is mixed.[20] It is not obvious that the members of Congress overvalue geographically com-pact benefits and downplay diffuse costs of deficits and taxation.[21] Both univer-salism and the theory of variable traceability depend on empirically contingent assumptions about weak political parties and unstable coalitions smaller than the entire legislature, both of which are conditions that change over time.[22]

---

[18] See, for example, Oates (1999, 1122–1123), who rests a case for decentralization on the assumption that "centralized provision will entail a uniform level of output across all jurisdictions."

[19] Both law professors and economists have observed that the assumption of uniform national provi-sion distorts reality. See, for example, Breton, Cassone, and Fraschini (1998, 27–30) and Rubin and Feeley (1994, 924–925).

[20] Even classic "pork"—military bases, for instance—does not seem to be universally distributed across congressional districts (Stein and Bickers 1994).

[21] For skepticism about the existence of any asymmetry between voters' perception of localized ben-efits and diffuse costs, see Donald Wittman (1989, 1410–1412).

[22] Weingast (1979, 245) roots his formal argument for universalism in the premise that "all minimum winning coalitions are equally likely," a premise that is only weakly supported by the evidence. At certain times, Congress seems to be dominated by universalistic coalitions. But other periods are defined by stronger, more ideologically motivated political parties. See Melissa P. Collie (1988).

On the legal side, law professors frequently make the uncritical assumption that Congress can easily devolve powers that courts assign to them in the first instance. The operating assumption seems to be that judicial abdication to congressional claims for regulatory authority would not lead to excessive centralization because Congress can easily devolve such power downward whenever such devolution would be politically convenient.[23] Even economically inclined law professors sometimes seem to assume that the members of Congress can magically make collective decisions to decentralize power simply because such decisions are collectively beneficial to the incumbents' reelection chances.[24] But some substantial evidence suggests that Congress does not find it easy to vary policy by region. It is notoriously difficult to obtain waivers from federal regulatory policy for a subsection of a nation, in part because all other regions tend to object to the competitive advantage that such a waiver might imply.[25] When federal policy requires different regulatory policies in different regions, these differences seem to be geared toward suppressing interregional competition rather than addressing the peculiar demands of a national subcommunity.[26] The federal government also has found it difficult to impose user fees, even when it offers excludable and geographically discrete services for which such fees would seem to be appropriate as measures of local demand.[27] One explanation for this is that Congress is reluctant to impose costs on service users, who tend to be more organized and vocal than the general public. Moreover, federal agencies gain little revenue advantage from such fees, because the revenue that they obtain can be offset by reductions in their appropriations.[28]

In sum, both the lawyers' optimism and the economists' pessimism about the central government might be rooted in the same oversight: the failure to see that the central legislature and competing subnational governments are both afflicted by a similar collective action problem. In both cases, national or subnational politicians tend to view certain costs as exogenous to their decisions because they

---

[23] See, for example, Larry Kramer (2001, 127), describing the political incentives for decentralization that protect state power.

[24] See, for example, Jonathan Macey (1990).

[25] For an anecdotal account of environmental policy suggesting that national policy making tends to be excessively uniform, see James Krier (1995).

[26] Consider, for instance, the policy of barring significant deterioration of environmental quality anywhere in the nation—a policy that holds rural areas to a higher standard of air quality than nonattainment areas. As Pashigian (1988, 498) has argued, the support for such a policy comes largely from dirtier regions that seek to prevent cleaner regions from gaining a competitive advantage in attracting industry.

[27] See, for example, General Accounting Office (1998) report on forest service fees and John Kingdon (1995, 14) on Domenici's efforts to enact waterway user fees. Of course, the federal government frequently uses excise taxes that are functionally equivalent to user fees, such as gasoline taxes the revenue of which is earmarked for interstate highways.

[28] Gillette and Hopkins (1987, 870) argue that agencies might lobby for fees to maximize their budgets. But agencies cannot make enforceable agreements with Congress to ensure their retention of fee revenue, reducing their incentives to lobby for the power to collect such fees.

cannot bargain with each other to allocate these costs more efficiently. The costs of decentralization are easy to see when local governments, lacking a regional government, impose smoke, low-income households, traffic, or other external costs on each other. But decentralized legislatures like Congress, lacking a strong party system, face a similar problem of collective action: Absent strong political parties that could discipline members for refusing to accept collectively beneficial budget cuts, each legislator lacks an incentive to consider the effects of his or her votes on the national budget. The budget becomes a common-pool resource that each representative overuses (Inman and Fitts 1990). Centralization of policy making in Congress, therefore, merely relocates, rather than eliminates, collective action problems faced by subnational governments.

Centralization and Distributive Injustice

What about distributive justice? Are there reasons to believe that centralized policy making causes distributional inequities at least as great as the advantages that federalism bestows on large states and mobile capital? One might argue in federalism's defense that the inequities of federalism hardly seem like burning injustices. True, California has more bargaining power than Rhode Island, and owners of mobile capital like Morgan Stanley have an advantage over, say, Texaco. As Clayton Gillette (1997, 466–467), one of the few defenders of Tiebout in the legal academy, has argued, we tolerate greater inequities in constitutional law for the sake of efficiency.

Another response is that regulatory uniformity generates distributive inequities of its own. Uniform national policies strip regions preferring laxer regulation of their competitive advantage over regions preferring stricter regulation. Indeed, eliminating this competitive advantage might sometimes be the purpose of centralization of policy.[29] The demand for at least some public goods, such as environmental quality, is normal: It rises with residents' income (Kahn and Matsusaka 1997). For these goods, a policy of enforcing higher regulatory standards throughout the nation will tend to protect voters with higher incomes by ensuring that they can obtain regulatory benefits without sacrificing tax base to competing jurisdictions, the residents of which care less about the relevant regulatory benefits. One might characterize such a strategic use of centralization as distributively regressive.

Such a distributional argument against centralization, however, has a controversial pedigree in the history of American constitutional law that would ensure the argument's rejection by the U.S. Supreme Court as a basis for limiting

---

[29] Peter Pashigian (1988, 498). For a discussion of an analogous way in which voters support uniform statewide taxation levels to prevent low-tax localities from gaining a competitive advantage over high-taxing jurisdictions, see Jacob Vigdor (2004).

the power of Congress. Most famously, the Supreme Court held in 1918 that Congress could not prohibit goods produced with child labor from moving through interstate commerce. In the course of rejecting Congress's power to prohibit "unfair competition" between the states, the Court asserted that "there is no power vested in Congress to require the states to exercise their police power so as to prevent possible unfair competition. Many causes may cooperate to give one state, by reason of local laws or conditions, an economic advantage over others. The commerce clause was not intended to give to Congress a general authority to equalize such conditions" (*Hammer v. Dagenhart*, 247 U.S. 251, 273 [1918]). The strong hint of *Hammer v. Dagenhart* was that states were entitled to the competitive advantages created by their libertarian policies. But the obvious rejoinder to the Court's implicit defense of such an entitlement is that, in a federal regime where labor and capital are mobile, states' redistribution of wealth from one part of their population to another creates a fiscal externality: States with generous redistributive programs end up subsidizing the altruistic inclinations of other states when the low-income households in the latter migrate to the generous state, and the ensuing collective action problem ensures that no states' redistributive inclinations are satisfied. Given the pre–New Deal Court's hostility toward redistributive regulation, the Court's holding in *Hammer* was probably a covert method of eliminating rather than allocating the redistributive function. After the Court accepted the legitimacy of redistribution in the mid-1930s, it promptly overruled *Hammer*.

In short, it is now well established that Congress can create regulatory uniformity to deprive libertarian states of their competitive advantages over other states. Any argument that rejected such a power as a general matter would be dead on arrival in any federal court. The popularity of "race-to-the-bottom" arguments in legal academia may stem from this constitutional consensus. The Court's invocation of such an argument in *Hodel* to justify a federal environmental statute regulating strip mining highlights the futility of arguing against Congress's regulatory redistribution from libertarian regions to regulation-preferring regions.[30]

There may be a more modest argument, however, that could distinguish environmental laws from labor regulations such as minimum wage or maximum hours laws. The purpose of the latter is more obviously redistributive than the former. It is a familiar point that the federal government is the level best suited for the redistribution of wealth. The overruling of *Hammer v. Dagenhart* might be narrowly understood as an effort to secure this redistributive power

---

[30] *Hodel v. Virginia Surface Mining & Reclamation Ass'n*, 452 U.S. 264, 280 (1981) upheld nationwide surface mining standards "to insure that competition in interstate commerce among sellers of coal produced in different states will not be used to undermine the ability of the several states to improve and maintain adequate standards on coal-mining operations within their borders."

for the federal government. But environmental laws are not, at least on their face, intended to redistribute wealth: The apparent purpose of environmental laws is to restore the status quo existing before some polluter engaged in a nuisance-like activity—emitting smoke, for instance. One might argue, therefore, that such laws cannot be justified by a need to eliminate any fiscal externality arising from competition between regions. In order for one to justify federal environmental law as an exercise of the federal government's power to redistribute wealth, one would have to argue that such laws are intended to redistribute wealth from the owners of polluting firms to the rest of society beyond the costs imposed by the firms' pollution. It is certainly possible that the actual purpose of such laws is to extract wealth from firms by threatening them with costly regulations that they will pay to avoid (McChesney 1997). But these are not the terms in which such laws are defended. Moreover, one might argue that courts ought not to attribute such a rent-seeking purpose to federal statutes, given that the redistributive purpose in question seems, at best, morally arbitrary (Macey 1986).

One might argue, therefore, that the redistribution of wealth brought about by federally imposed regulatory uniformity is no justification for federal law unless the law's supporters defended it as a mechanism for redistributing wealth. Absent such a defense, the redistribution appears to be nothing more than morally arbitrary rent-extraction. Is such a distributive consequence any more arbitrary than the benefits bestowed on the owners of mobile capital by interjurisdictional competition? Again, neither lawyers nor economists seem to have made this comparison, although it lies at the heart of the distributive issue between centralization and Tiebout's system of mobility.

In sum, as with the argument over the efficiency of Tiebout's spatial economy, the distributive justice of Tiebout requires a comparative perspective. It is not enough to complain about the inequities of interjurisdictional competition. Instead, one must consider the inequities of uniform national legislation.

Judicial Self-Restraint Versus Judicial Restraint of Congress

The gist of the preceding argument is simply that Congress and subnational jurisdictions both suffer from costs associated with excessive decentralization. Politicians elected by cities' and states' voters impose external costs on their neighbors, but so do congresspersons elected from single-member districts. Mayors and governors find it costly to negotiate intergovernmental bargains to control this costly behavior, but so do congresspersons who lack strong political parties or a centralized governance structure.

What, then, should a conscientious judge do? Judges with Herculean capacities for social science might try to resolve the impasse by figuring out which level of government is likely to perform more inefficiently for different sorts of regulation. The Rehnquist Court's efforts to revive limits on Congress's Commerce Clause powers could be construed as efforts in this vein. However, it is unlikely that the Court will attempt to enforce substantial new limits on Congress's jurisdiction in the name of Tiebout. The difficulty is not simply that judges properly lack self-confidence in their capacity to resolve complex questions of social science. An equally great difficulty is that the U.S. Supreme Court would have to reduce the considerations relevant to the Tiebout hypothesis in rules simple enough for the average federal district judge to grasp and apply in a consistent manner. The Court can hardly instruct lower courts to bar federal legislation whenever such legislation regulates activities that, all things considered, subnational jurisdictions can regulate better than Congress. Federal judges cannot consider all things: They will need some relatively plain instructions classifying activities for them according to crude criteria that do not require expertise in economics to apply. It is unlikely that the facts relevant to the Tiebout hypothesis can be captured in such criteria.

But there is another way in which federal judges might shape constitutional doctrine in response to the Tiebout hypothesis. Rather than attempting to restrain Congress, they could restrain themselves. In particular, they could exercise self-restraint in their enforcement of the "dormant" commerce doctrine.

The "dormant" commerce clause is the legal shorthand for the doctrine authorizing federal courts to strike down subnational taxation or regulation that interferes with interstate commerce. The theory underlying the doctrine is that Article I gives Congress exclusive power to enact certain sorts of regulations of commerce among the several states. States, therefore, can enact such laws only if the Congress authorizes them to do so. Absent such authorization, federal judges take it upon themselves to enjoin such state legislation. The precise scope of the prohibition has been hotly debated since *Gibbons v. Ogden*, 22 U.S. 1 (1824), and the doctrine has a baroque profusion of detailed qualifications and extensions. At the core of the modern doctrine, however, are two principles. First, states may not enact protectionist regulations or taxes that discriminate against goods or services merely because they originate from out of state. Second, under the so-called "market participant" exception, states may enact subsidies that favor the state's own residents over nonresidents. A state law banning or taxing the importing of nonresidents' garbage from a neighboring state into landfills located within the regulating state's territory is unconstitutional under the first rule (*Philadelphia v. New Jersey*, 437 U.S. 617 [1978]). A state law providing that only the state's own residents are eligible for a subsidy to cover the cost of garbage disposal is constitutional under the second rule (*Hughes v. Alexandria Scrap*, 426 U.S. 794 [1976]).

It is easy to see that the distinction between discriminatory taxes (forbidden) and discriminatory subsidies (permitted)[31] is hard to justify, or even define, given that the economic effects of both can be identical. The Court's tentative efforts to explain this distinction, however, bear a striking resemblance to the Tiebout hypothesis. As the name implies, the "market participant" exception rests on an analogy between state governments and private firms. In the Court's words, when states deal in property by spending their own money, they should be able to exercise "the long recognized right of trader or manufacturer, engaged in an entirely private business, freely to exercise his own independent discretion as to parties with whom he will deal" *Reeves, Inc. v. Stake*, 447 U.S. 429, 438–439 (1980). In order to encourage states' taxpayers to bear the cost and risk of investing their tax dollars in publicly provided services, those taxpayers need to get preference in the benefits that flow from the state government's investments (*Reeves* at 444, n. 17). In short, the Court seems to argue that, when state governments are subject to the same regulatory and competitive constraints as private firms, then they ought to enjoy the private firms' prerogatives to reward their shareholders in order to encourage investment. On this analogy, the state government is simply a consumers' cooperative that gives reduced prices and dividends to its members.

The Court's distinction between taxes and subsidies might also be understood as a way to accommodate the real world's departure from the idealized conditions of the Tiebout hypothesis. In Tiebout's world, no subnational jurisdiction possesses any monopoly over any unique site: Land is perfectly fungible, as "there are a large number of communities in which consumer-voters may choose to live," and these consumer-voters are not constrained by considerations of employment (Tiebout 1956, 419). This assumption is obviously untrue at the level of state governments, even if one substitutes owners of mobile capital for consumer-voters. California and New York, for instance, are notorious for aggressively exercising their taxing power (Zimmerman 2004, 139), and one suspects their zeal is stoked by the locational rents that such immense jurisdictions can extract from less than perfectly mobile capital. By prohibiting states from discriminating against nonresident firms in taxation, the Court ensures that firms can gain access to the state's market—that is, its territory and residents—free from the monopolistic power of such huge jurisdictions.

By contrast, firms' demand for access to a state's treasury is likely more elastic than firms' demand for access to the state's territory. For most firms, state subsidies are just one source of funds, a source dwarfed by private equity and

---

[31] Or so the Court has suggested. *New Energy Co. of Ind. v. Limbach*, 486 U.S. 269, 278 (1988) ("direct subsidization of domestic industry does not ordinarily run afoul" of the negative Commerce Clause).

debt. Given the political and legal constraints on state taxation, state subsidies are likely to remain relatively unimportant as a source of private finance. The need for judicial policing of discrimination in subsidies, therefore, is not nearly as pressing as the need for judicially enforced guarantees that a firm can buy and sell within the territory of the state. As the leading commentator on dormant commerce clause jurisprudence has noted, this theory that spending of residents' tax dollars is politically more difficult than taxation or regulation of foreign producers seems to be an important explanation of the "market participant" exception to the dormant commerce clause doctrine (Regan 1986, 1194–1200). The Court's refusal to extend the "market participant" exception to the state's disposition of its natural resources to which states might have "unique access" (*Reeves, Inc. v. Stake*, 447 U.S. 449, 444 [1980]) follows this logic: Where the state is unconstrained by effective competition, the Court should play a stronger role in limiting state discrimination.

The Court's tolerance for discriminatory spending, in short, implicitly recognizes that such spending is sufficiently constrained by interjurisdictional competition. But judicial tolerance for such fiscal discrimination frequently wavers. Take, for instance, the problem of state tax incentives to lure businesses into investing within a state's territory. In *Cuno v. DaimlerChrysler Inc.*, 386 F.3d 738, 743 (6th Cir. 2004), for instance, the U.S. Court of Appeals for the Sixth Circuit recently held that the City of Toledo's use of an investment tax credit to lure DaimlerChrysler into building an auto factory in Toledo was a violation of the dormant commerce clause, because the tax credit "coerc[e]d businesses already subject to the Ohio franchise tax to expand locally rather than out-of-state" (id.). The Sixth Circuit reasoned that corporations doing business in Ohio would reduce its Ohio franchise tax liability by investing in Ohio but not by investing in other states. Thus, Ohio would be effectively imposing higher taxes on firms engaged in out-of-state investment, punishing such firms for their refusal to invest locally.

The U.S. Supreme Court has granted certiorari in *Cuno*, but as of this writing, it has not yet reached a decision on the case. If one adopted a mobility-based theory of federalism, however, one might urge the Court to reverse in *Cuno*. Whatever the merits or demerits of Toledo's tax credit, it seems unlikely that Toledo will be able to extort much . from mobile investors like DaimlerChrysler.[32] The credit can provide no more incentive to relocate to Ohio than the underlying franchise tax. But the amount of this tax is already constrained by the Court's requirement that the tax be nondiscriminatory and

---

[32] In general, as the mobility of taxpayers increases, the ability of the local government to extract more in taxes than it confers on the taxpayer in services, or suffers from the taxpayer in nuisance costs, decreases. See Louis Kaplow (1996, 462).

fairly attributable to the taxpayer's activities within the taxing jurisdiction (*Complete Auto Transit, Inc. v. Brady*, 430 U.S. 274 [1977]).

Moreover, there is little reason to believe that imperfections in subnational government's competition for investment are larger than the imperfections of the federal lawmaking process. It might be reasonable, therefore, for the Court to tolerate all but the most egregiously harmful state practices, on the theory that the risks of federal inefficiency outweigh the risks of state protectionism.

What are the risks of centralization? The greatest danger is excessive uniformity in public finance. Efficient public finance requires the matching of fiscal burdens paid with governmental services received (Breton 1996, 23–24). But a Congress controlled by weak political parties and decentralized leadership structure has only the weakest electoral incentives to match fiscal burdens and governmental benefits. In theory, Congress could use fees, special assessments, and special districts to perform this matching function. In practice, it rarely does. The result is uniform federal taxation and allocation of federal revenue by the political power of the congressional subcommittee chair rather than the fiscal need of the benefited jurisdiction.

If the federal courts erroneously strike down a state subsidy or fee that correctly charges the nonresident business with the actual costs of the services received by that business, then the courts would deter nonfederal finance of public infrastructure and services. In such a case, only Congress could fill the gap. In the context of *Cuno*, this means that Congress would have the responsibility of creating a system of "enterprise zones" to encourage investment in impoverished communities. The Court, therefore, needs to compare evils—the evil of state parochialism with the evil of congressional parochialism. Interjurisdictional competition for mobile capital gives states some incentives, albeit imperfect, to match burdens with services. Of course, gigantic states like California can extract rents for the unique locations that they control. But the capacity of any state to impose costs on nonresident businesses in excess of services supplied is constrained by a combination of voice and exit: the voice of resident voters who are angry at being deprived of cheaper goods and services provided by those nonresident businesses and the ability of mobile nonresident businesses to exit the rent-extracting jurisdiction. The entire dormant commerce clause jurisprudence might be regarded as nothing more than a judicial supplement to these state safeguards of voice and exit. If states were perfectly fungible, then all capital would be mobile, and competition for mobile capital would prevent any state from exporting taxes to nonresidents. If voters were perfectly informed about state politics, then they would not tolerate redistribution of wealth from themselves to resident businesses through protective tariffs. Perfect interstate competition and perfectly informed state voters are, of course, Tiebout-style fictions. But are these fictions any more incredible than the fiction that the Court so frequently pretends to believe: the fiction that Congress perfectly weighs the preferences of everyone that it represents? Much of the legal scholarship urging a more aggressive enforcement of the dormant commerce clause against tax exemptions and tax subsidies ignores this question. Thus, Peter Enrich (1996, 395) argues that state governments cannot be trusted to award tax exemptions to attract business investment because "the costs of tax incentives remain largely invisible in the political process." But the costs of congressional universalism also are not highly salient to the public. If the federal courts are not going to prohibit wasteful federal spending on local infrastructure, then why should the federal courts worry about wasteful state spending to attract business investment? It is no answer to say that state politicians compete with each other to attract business. Federal congresspersons compete with each other to win federal grants. Both the states and Congress, in short, are decentralized institutions, and this decentralization can lead to inefficiency.

Of course, one might respond that the failure of the federal courts to curb Congress's inefficient spending is no reason for the federal courts to ignore state parochialism. A partial check is better than none at all. But this response assumes that the federal courts can get it right—that they can perfectly detect state programs that wastefully redistribute wealth from voters and nonresident businesses to resident businesses. As just noted, dormant commerce clause doctrine is hardly so finely tuned: It is little more than crude prophylactic rules that both under- and overenforce the policy against wasteful redistribution. If courts were to extend the doctrine to ban all tax incentives intended to attract mobile capital, for instance, courts might very well deprive states of the fiscal instruments necessary to match the real costs of supplying services to such capital with the real fiscal burdens that such capital must pay. This loss of nonfederal fiscal flexibility is an invitation for Congress to fill the gap with its own versions of "empowerment zones" or other federal tax relief. Neither Enrich nor any other legal scholar provides any reason to believe that Congress's spending policies will not exceed the states' in shortsighted waste.

In short, the likelihood of congressional inefficiencies cautions judicial restraint in striking down state law. The U.S. Supreme Court has never cited the former as a justification for its cautious attitude toward state subsidies. Nevertheless, comparing Congress to the states, one might applaud the Court's restraint on the enforcement of dormant commerce clause jurisprudence. Actual competition between the states for mobile capital does not follow the idealized conditions laid out by Tiebout's or Wallace Oates's theories. But perhaps this comparison between the real and the ideal misses the point. The real comparison should be between the institutions of centralization—Congress and the federal courts—and those of decentralization. In this competition, it is not clear why the latter do not outperform the former. At least, it is a question that the federal courts should ask before they hamper subnational governments with constitutional doctrines while leaving the national government unconstrained.

REFERENCES

Arnold, R. Douglas. 1990. *The logic of congressional action.* New Haven, CT: Yale University Press.

Arnott, Richard, and Ronald Grieson. 1981. Optimal fiscal policy for a state or local government. *Journal of Urban Economics* 9:23–48.

Avi-Yonah, Reuven. 2000. Globalization, tax competition, and the fiscal crisis of the welfare state. *Harvard Law Review* 113:1573–1676.

Bird, Richard. 2000. Fiscal decentralization and competitive governments. In *Competition and structure: The political economy of collective decisions,* Gianluigi Galeotti, Pierre Salmon, and Ronald Wintrobe, eds., 129–149. New York: Cambridge University Press.

Bratton, William, and Joseph McCahery. 1997. The new economics of jurisdictional competition: Devolutionary federalism in a second-best world. *Georgetown Law Journal* 86:201–278.

Breton, Albert. 1996. *Competitive governments: An economic theory of politics and public finance.* New York: Cambridge University Press.

Breton, Albert, Alberto Cassone, and Angela Fraschini. 1998. Decentralization and subsidiarity: Towards a theoretical reconciliation. *University of Pennsylvania Journal of International Economic Law* 19:21–51.

Cary, William L. 1974. Federalism and corporate law: Reflections upon Delaware. *Yale Law Journal* 83:663–705.

Collie, Melissa P. 1988. The rise of coalition politics: Voting in the U.S. House of Representatives, 1933–1980. *Legislative Studies Quarterly* 13:321–342.

Connerly, Charles E., and Marc T. Smith. 1996. Developing a fair share housing policy for Florida. *Journal of Land Use and Environmental Law* 12:63–102.

Donahue, John. 1997. Tiebout? Or not Tiebout? The market metaphor and America's devolution debate. *Journal of Economic Perspectives* 11:73–82.

Ellickson, Robert C. 1977. Suburban growth controls: An economic and legal analysis. *Yale Law Journal* 86:385–511.

———. 1982. Cities and homeowners associations. *University of Pennsylvania Law Review* 130:1519–1580.

Engel, Kirsten H. 1997. State environmental setting: Is there a "race" and is it "to the bottom"? *Hastings Law Journal* 48:271–398.

Enrich, Peter. 1996. Saving the states from themselves: Commerce Clause constraints on state tax incentives for business. *Harvard Law Review* 110:377–468.

Fiorina, Morris. 1989. *Congress: Keystone of the Washington establishment.* 2nd ed. New Haven, CT: Yale University Press.

Fischel, William A. 1975. Fiscal and environmental considerations in the location of firms in suburban communities. In *Fiscal zoning and land use controls,* Edwin S. Mills and Wallace E. Oates, eds. Lexington, MA: Heath-Lexington.

General Accounting Office. 1998. *Forest Service: Barriers to generating revenues or reducing costs.* Report to Chairman, Committee on the Budget, House of Representatives, No. 98-58.

Gillette, Clayton P. 1997. Business incentives, interstate commerce, and the Commerce Clause. *Minnesota Law Review* 82:447–502.

Gillette, Clayton P., and Thomas Hopkins. 1987. Federal user fees: A legal and economic analysis. *Boston University Law Review* 67:795–874.

Gillette, Clayton P. 2001. Regionalization and interlocal bargains. *New York University Law Review* 76:190–271.

Gordon, Roger. 1983. An optimal taxation approach to fiscal federalism. *Quarterly Journal of Economics* 98:567–586.

Hills, Roderick M., Jr. 1999. Poverty, residency, and federalism: States' duty of impartiality towards newcomers. *Supreme Court Review* 1999:277–335.

Inman, Robert, and Michael Fitts. 1990. Political institutions and fiscal policy: Evidence from the historical record. *Journal of Law, Economics, and Organization* 6:79–132.

Kahn, Matthew, and John G. Matsusaka. 1997. Demand for environmental goods: Evidence from voting patterns on California initiatives. *Journal of Law and Economics* 40:137–173.

Kaplow, Louis. 1996. Fiscal federalism and the deductibility of state and local taxes. *Virginia Law Review* 82:413–492.

Kingdon, John W. 1995. *Agendas, alternatives, and public policies.* 2nd ed. New York: Addison Wesley Longman.

Kramer, Larry. 2001. 2000 Supreme Court foreword: We the Court. *Harvard Law Review* 115:4–168.

Krier, James E. 1995. On the topology of uniform environmental standards in a federal system—and why it matters. *Maryland Law Review* 54:1226–1241.

Macey, Jonathan. 1986. Promoting public-regarding legislation through statutory interpretation: An interest group model. *Columbia Law Review* 86:223–313.

———. 1990. Federal deference to local regulators and the economic theory of regulation: Towards a public choice theory of federalism. *Virginia Law Review* 76:265–291.

McChesney, Fred. 1997. *Money for nothing: Politicians, rent extraction and political extortion.* Cambridge, MA: Harvard University Press.

Musgrave, Richard A., and Peggy B. Musgrave. 1989. *Public finance in theory and practice.* 5th ed. New York: McGraw-Hill.

Oates, Wallace E. 1969. Effects of property taxes and local spending on property values: An empirical study of tax capitalization and the Tiebout hypothesis. *Journal of Political Economy* 77:957–971.

———. 1999. An essay on fiscal federalism. *Journal of Economic Literature* 37:1120–1149.

Oates, Wallace E., and Robert M. Schwab. 1988. Economic competition among jurisdictions: Efficiency enhancing or distortion inducing? *Journal of Public Economics* 35:333–354.

Pashigian, Peter B. 1988. Environmental regulation: Whose self-interests are being protected? In *Chicago studies in political economy,* George Stigler, ed. Chicago: University of Chicago Press.

Pauly, Mark V. 1998. Income redistribution as a local public good. In *The economics of fiscal federalism and local finance,* Wallace E. Oates, ed. Cheltenham, UK, and Northampton, MA: Elgar.

Regan, Donald. 1986. The Supreme Court and state protectionism: Making sense of the Dormant Commerce Clause. *Michigan Law Review* 84:1091–1287.

———. 1995. How to think of the federal commerce power and incidentally re-write *United States v. Lopez. Michigan Law Review* 94:554–614.

Revesz, Richard L. 1992. Rehabilitating interstate competition: Rethinking the "race-to-the-bottom" rationale for federal environmental regulation. *New York University Law Review* 67:1210–1255.

———. 1997. Federalism and environmental regulation: A normative critique. In *The new federalism: Can the states be trusted?* John Ferejohn and Barry Weingast, eds. Washington, DC: Brookings Institution Press.

Robinson, Glen O. 1983. The Sherman Act as a home rule charter: *Community Communications Co. v. City of Boulder. Supreme Court Economic Review* 2:131–164.

Rubin, Edward, and Malcolm Feeley. 1994. Federalism: Some notes on a national neurosis. *UCLA Law Review* 41:903–952.

Stein, Robert, and Kenneth Bickers. 1994. Universalism and the electoral connection: A test and some doubts. *Political Research Quarterly* 47:295–317.

Susskind, Lawrence, Mieke van der Wansem, and Armand Ciccarelli. 2000. *Mediating land use disputes: A handbook for local officials.* Cambridge, MA: Lincoln Institute for Land Policy.

Tiebout, Charles M. 1956. A pure theory of local expenditures. *Journal of Political Economy* 64:416–424.

Tolley, George S. 1974. The welfare economics of city bigness. *Journal of Urban Economics* 81:324–345.

Vigdor, Jacob. 2004. Other people's taxes: Non-resident voters and statewide limitation of local government. *Journal of Law and Economics* 47:453–477.

Weingast, Barry. 1979. A rational choice perspective on congressional norms. *American Political Science Review* 23:245–262.

Wildasin, David. 1991. Income redistribution in a common labor market. *American Economic Review* 81:757–774.

Wilson, John D. 1987. Trade, capital mobility, and tax competition. *Journal of Political Economy* 95:835–856.

Wittman, Donald. 1989. Why democracies produce efficient results. *Journal of Political Economy* 97:1395–1426.

Zimmerman, Joseph F. 2004. *Interstate economic relations.* Albany, NY: SUNY Press.

Zodrow, George, and Peter Mieszkowski. 1986. Pigou, Tiebout, property taxation, and the underprovision of local public goods. *Journal of Public Economics* 19:356–370.

COMMENTARY

The Tendency to Exceed Optimal Jurisdictional Boundaries

CLAYTON P. GILLETTE

Rick Hills provides us with a comprehensive way to think about the appropriate allocation of governmental responsibility in federal systems. Different levels of government present reciprocal risks. Centralized entities may tend to create too much uniformity, threatening the competitive benefits that decentralized governments promise and the higher level of preference satisfaction that is the hallmark of Tiebout's analysis. Decentralized governments, on the other hand, will tend to favor policies that generate local benefits while externalizing costs, threatening spillovers that more centralized decision making can forestall. Calculating the optimal tradeoff between these risks can inform theories of federalism generally. While Hills concentrates on the importance of his analysis for defining the enumerated powers of Congress, similar examinations can inform the proper scope of the Commerce Clause and the Tenth Amendment at the federal level, and proper allocation of governmental authority between state and local governments at the more decentralized level.

It is difficult to argue with Hills's formulation. As is true with all of his scholarship, his argument provides a refreshing perspective on a traditional problem and ties together different strains of analysis in a largely successful effort to find unifying themes. Indeed, one can find at least occasional forays by the Supreme Court that are consistent with, if not wholesale endorsements of, Hills's theory. For instance, the Court's limitation of Tenth Amendment constraints on Congress to those acts that interfere with "traditional" or "integral" local government operations may best be understood as referring to activities that primarily have intrajurisdictional effects, rather than those that produce sufficient externalities to warrant federal intervention.[1]

---

[1] See, for example, *Hodel v. Virginia Surface Mining and Reclamation Ass'n*, 452 U.S. 264, 287–288 (1981).

Moreover, Hills's analysis demonstrates the need to appeal to some external, perhaps legal mechanism for resolving the contest between federal and decentralized authority, since purely extralegal, Tieboutian interjurisdictional competition is unlikely to accomplish that objective. That is the inevitable result of the heroic assumptions that underlie Tiebout's original analysis. Mobility is, in fact, constrained; individuals do not live on dividend income alone; and, perhaps most importantly for current purposes, local activity tends to generate negative spillovers. This does not mean, of course, that Tiebout is irrelevant to local government law. To the contrary, if we believe that the resource allocations that we would obtain in a world characterized by the Tiebout assumptions are desirable, then Tiebout provides us with a guide for evaluating the extent to which legal doctrine compensates for our inability to achieve a world characterized by those assumptions. In this sense, Tiebout theory largely reflects the proper use of the Coase Theorem in legal scholarship. The useful lesson that legal scholars draw from that principle is not that the legal rule doesn't matter where transactions costs are zero, but rather that because transactions costs are positive, the rule of law *does* matter. As a consequence, other things being equal, legal entitlements should be assigned in a manner that minimizes the transactions costs of bargaining away from default rule. Similarly, if we believe that Tieboutian local governments would ideally allocate local government resources, then local government law should compensate for the barriers that preclude realization of those assumptions. Local government law, for instance, should reduce obstacles to mobility, enhance the formation of competing localities, and—perhaps most relevant here—diminish local capacity to generate negative externalities.

For Hills, the failure to achieve the Tieboutian ideal is related primarily to three constraints: the inevitable presence of externalities, the legal inability to discriminate in ways that signal optimal size (by attracting or, more importantly, by discouraging new residents), and the inability to bargain effectively with neighbors. Here, law has not been a panacea, in part because of institutional incompetence (law cannot easily overcome obstacles to division of a potential bargaining surplus); in part because legal doctrine gives pride of place to objectives (national citizenship) that are inconsistent with the kinds of jurisdictional discrimination that would allow jurisdictions to achieve something closer to the Tieboutian optimal size; and in part because, as a practical matter, approximating the Tieboutian ideal requires distributional burdens of questionable appeal. Thus, the quandary of explicitly comparing centralized tendencies for excessive uniformity with decentralized tendencies for externality production remains, and Hills would relegate the striking of that balance to legal institutions.

In all this, it is difficult to argue significantly with Hills. One might be somewhat more sanguine than he is about the extent to which the constraints on interjurisdictional competition can be overcome by current doctrines and practice. For instance, broader use of development impact fees allows some, if imperfect, discrimination against new residents, while multijurisdictional special districts and authorities facilitate interlocal bargaining. The distributional consequences of interjurisdictional competition are similarly reduced, though not eliminated, by effects that limit the "mobility" of mobile capital. For instance, owners of nominally mobile capital, whom Hills suggests can avoid redistributive taxation at the decentralized level, may be relatively immobile as a practical matter. Firms are not locked into jurisdictions only by virtue of their need for "ports, Mediterranean climates, oil wells, [or] other assets." Agglomeration economies will similarly hamper mobility for lawyers, suppliers, bankers, or competitors who benefit from the geographic presence of clients, customers, and other competitors.[2] But these are quibbles, and they do little to undermine Hills's main thrust. Therefore, I concentrate on Hills's argument about what underlies the reciprocal risks that he has identified.

As suggested previously, the choice between excessive uniformity and the production of externalities provides a key dividing line in the allocation of government responsibility. My minor disagreement with Hills, therefore, is not about the suitability of the analysis he proposes. Rather, my skepticism arises from his attributing the cause of these phenomena to structural characteristics that he suggests predominate at different levels of government. Hills's argument is that the root cause of excessive uniformity, at least as practiced by Congress, lies in the universalizing effects of vote trading that induce legislators to impose similar policies on geographical areas with highly divergent needs. Decentralized tendencies to generate externalities, on the other hand, arise as a less nefarious, but no less inefficient, function of small size and the limited availability of interlocal bargaining.

My diagnosis, however, is that both of these phenomena emerge from a common cause. The root cause of the contest between excessive uniformity and the generation of externalities is the shared tendency of government actors at all levels of government to exceed the jurisdiction in which they have a competitive advantage. But that has different meanings for different governments. For centralized legislatures, like Congress, exceeding the ideal jurisdiction means imposing uniform regulations where competition would better provide optimal regulation or where there is little need for uniformity because the externalities of local action are minimal. Nevertheless, Congress can act expansively in these areas, and even trump state and local resistance, by virtue of the Supremacy Clause and narrow interpretation of restraints that arise under Tenth Amendment doctrine or principles of federalism. For states

---

[2] See, for example, Arthur (1994, 103–104), Quigley (1998), Glaeser (1998), and Gillette (2001).

and localities, exceeding the jurisdiction of comparative advantage means pursuing activities that internalize local benefits but that externalize costs to neighbors. Centralized logrolling or small jurisdictional size may exacerbate these effects, but they are not the root causes of the phenomena, nor are they either necessary or sufficient for the results that Hills finds most troublesome. Instead, legislative mechanisms for exceeding jurisdictional boundaries, such as logrolling within the centralized legislature, become symptoms of the phenomenon rather than a cause.

In particular, logrolling need not be universalizing in the sense that Hills uses the term. Logrolling may instead balkanize federal efforts by allowing different legislators to trade support for highly localized benefits. Nor need excessive uniformity involve logrolling. Much of the excessive uniformity we see arises without any need to attract dissenters with offers of trades, because the proposals systematically enhance the authority of federal officials at the expense of voteless, but more appropriate, decentralized officials. Finally, the vote trading that Hills attributes to Congress is not necessarily less nefarious in more decentralized settings. I expand on these observations below and conclude that the conflict Hills describes is more deeply embedded in governance structures than the symptoms suggest.

Uniformity Without Universalism

Consider first the tendency of federal legislators to expand the scope of federal regulatory authority in ways that threaten to produce excessive uniformity. That expansion may arise because all (or a majority of) federal legislators benefit from the extension of their authority. Jurisdictional expansion may provide them access to larger budgets, capacity to influence appointments within the new jurisdiction, or gratitude from constituents who provide electoral support. If no centralized legislator would suffer from having an expanded jurisdiction, then vote trading is unnecessary to bring it about.

Think about the significant growth of federal criminal law in these terms—and as an indicator of a larger phenomenon. That growth has typically been attributed not to logrolls but to a desire of federal legislators generally to take credit for addressing social problems in a manner that earns the appreciation of the electorate (Stuntz 2001). At a time when crime is perceived as a significant social problem, both state and federal legislators presumably would desire to obtain credit for addressing the problem by enacting legislation that was perceived as addressing the issue. Federal legislators could expand the scope of federal jurisdiction because the Supremacy Clause permitted them to trump state law or to establish concurrent jurisdiction (Beale 2002, 2005, 754). Indeed, Hills's concern about traceability supports the proposition. Federal legislators might fear little redress from expanding federal crimes because doing so requires little in the way of programmatic changes that might be directly related to higher taxes. Instead, all Congress has to do is define a crime. Of course, doing so might require higher budgets for the federal judiciary or federal prisons. But those costs lie in the future and will not easily be traced to the broader boundaries of federal criminal law as opposed to a less detectable and debatable cause, such as "rigorous law enforcement."

Here, we have a plausible case of excessive uniformity. Its cause, however, has nothing to do with logrolling. Rather, uniformity is generated by a systemic preference on the part of federal legislators to engage in activity in which they have no comparative advantage but that will tend nevertheless to generate support among constituents. As a result, centralized legislators suffer no constraint on expanding their jurisdiction and applying a one-size-fits-all solution to regions that may have very different attitudes about what constitutes antisocial behavior. The poster child for that propensity might be the conflict between the California Compassionate Use Act and the federal Controlled Substances Act with respect to the medical use of marijuana.[3]

The same motivation underlies the tendency toward excessive centralization that can be found in unfunded mandates. Some unfunded mandates are perfectly appropriate, as where a centralized entity can deter the race to the bottom that could materialize if all decentralized entities avoid obligations that all would undertake if only they could be assured that others will act similarly (Zelinsky 1993; Gillette 1996). In short, centralized government can solve a Prisoners' Dilemma by imposing cooperation on entities that would otherwise defect. Once the centralized government solves that problem, however, it is not necessarily appropriate for it also to pay for the localized activity, unless that activity creates positive spillovers that would cause the local governments to underinvest from the social perspective.

But unfunded mandates may have a more disreputable provenance. Legislators in centralized legislatures may perceive benefits in enacting programs, while simultaneously imposing the related costs on decentralized governments that are obligated to provide funding. The inability of the electorate to match increases in local taxes with the centralized programs permits legislators to take credit for creating the programs without incurring the wrath that attends the necessary tax increases. Thus, unfunded mandates, which typically impose the same programmatic obligations on all affected decentralized governments, may perversely impose uniformity on states and localities that would not have voted to use their scarce tax dollars for these programs. Again, however, the cause is less Hills's universalist logrolling than a general tendency of federal legislators to exceed the scope of their comparative advantage. After all, if the mandated programs do not solve Prisoners' Dilemma problems, there seems little reason to

---

[3] See *Gonzales v. Raich*, 125 S. Ct. 2195 (2005).

require decentralized governments to fund programs that they have presumably decided to eschew. And if the only reason for federal intervention is to guarantee that localities engage in activities that produce benefit spillovers, there seems less reason not to fund the mandate from federal sources.

Nonuniversalizing Logrolling and Decentralized Universalization

None of this is to say that logrolling cannot similarly be universalizing in the way that concerns Hills. But logrolling need not generate uniformity at all. Indeed, common logrolls involve the accumulation in one bill of numerous unrelated measures, each of which satisfies a particular localized constituency and none of which would independently attract a majority of the legislature as a whole. The frequent practice of placing public works projects with highly localized effects in omnibus appropriation bills is perhaps the most obvious example.[4] The presence of "single-subject" requirements for state legislation in state constitutions is perhaps some evidence of a belief that legislation that consists of multiple unrelated items is widespread, and more likely to represent both localized benefits and a negative-sum logroll (Farber and Frickey 1991, 127–128).

Moreover, even to the extent that logrolls generate universalizing effects, there is little reason to believe that the phenomenon is peculiar to the most centralized legislatures. Virtually every state constitution contains at least one provision that appears intended to constrain legislative logrolling. The most common clauses are prohibitions on special legislation, which preclude the legislature from favoring or disfavoring a subset of jurisdictions within the state unless it can demonstrate some rational basis for the discriminatory treatment;[5] the grant of a line-item veto to the executive;[6] and the prohibition on single-subject legislation. Single-subject legislation raises monitoring costs of enforcing logrolls, since legislators who trade votes on unrelated bills will have greater difficulty ensuring that the deal is maintained over multiple votes.[7] The federal Constitution has no counterpart to these provisions, although "special legislation" prohibitions are essentially enforced through an analysis that replicates the inquiries that are made to determine whether federal legislation impermissibly denies equal protection (Vermeule 2001, 411–412).

One might conclude that the presence of these state constitutional clauses reveals that states, in fact, do not suffer from excessive uniformity because the constitutional clauses that states have invoked as a bulwark actually retard

---

[4] The recent debate on and ultimate defunding of the $223 million "bridge to nowhere" in Alaska is the most recent publicly debated example of the practice (Utt 2005).

[5] See, for example, Calif. Const. Art. 4, §16; Georgia Const. Art. 3, §6.

[6] See, for example, Ill. Const. Art. 4, §9; Mich. Const. Art. 5, §19.

[7] See, for example, N.Y. Const. Art. 3, §14; Tex. Const. Art. III, §35.

logrolls that have unfortunate universalizing effects. If that were the case, then Hills could simply propose the adoption of similar safeguards at the federal level. Unfortunately, what little evidence that exists provides weak support for this simple remedy. Empirical studies reveal little support for the proposition that the availability of a gubernatorial line-item veto has much effect on total spending or budget outcomes. Any effect of these provisions appears to apply only under severely limited conditions (Carter and Schap 1990).

Logrolling for Externalities

Finally, the dichotomy between centralized logrolling that produces uniformity and decentralized production of externalities omits a potential relationship between vote trading and negative spillovers in the service of jurisdictional expansion. One would anticipate that logrolling or related universalizing tendencies would likely materialize in local legislatures with significant frequency, simply as a function of the characteristics of the two bodies. Local legislatures consist of a relatively small number of representatives, so repeat play among the parties and the consequent pressures to create consensus are more prevalent than in relatively large, diffuse legislatures. Party politics are less prevalent at the local level, so the ability to discipline those who "compromise" by accommodating colleagues who fail to toe an official line is significantly diluted. But logrolling in this context may be "universalizing" only in the sense that inappropriate extensions of jurisdictional authority at the local level have the consequence of generating externalities. Again, the most productive way to regard Hills's comparison is not as one between a centralized legislature that desires to universalize and a locality that desires to impose externalities. Instead, it is between two levels of government, each of which desires to expand its jurisdiction beyond its realm of comparative advantage. The effect may be the same, but the latter way of putting it avoids the identification of logrolling with the former and unified action with the latter.

To see this, consider how logrolls are likely to play out in decentralized jurisdictions. Hills is likely correct that since localities are more homogeneous than geographically larger jurisdictions, logrolls will be less necessary, since any legislation that benefits one part of the community is more likely to benefit others as well. But it is not clear how much solace can be taken from that characteristic. It may mean that when logrolls do exist, they reflect the kind of imposition of external costs that Hills correctly deems dangerous for decentralization. That is, logrolls may be both necessary and endemic when a representative from one part of the decentralized jurisdiction desires to impose on a neighbor. That legislator's colleagues might disagree for fear of interjurisdictional retaliation but be willing to forgo their concerns where the externalizing legislator promises a vote on a matter of immediate benefit to his or her colleagues' constituents.

Conclusion: Comparisons and Bargains

Hills provides us with an insightful and fruitful paradigm with which to address the complicated task of assigning responsibility among multiple levels of government. He identifies the problems that are likely to materialize as a consequence of misallocation of authority and demonstrates the limited capacity of markets for politics and residents to rectify those misallocations that do arise. In effect, he has provided a worthwhile and workable structure that is more informative than the judiciary's vague and seemingly ad hoc interpretations of those legal doctrines intended to enforce a federalist structure for analyzing the conditions under which centralized or decentralized governments should be charged with the responsibility for either regulation or the production of public goods.

But if the source of the problem that complicates the issue is more general than Hills suggests, then his proposed solutions may also need some reconsideration. If, in fact, both excessive uniformity and the imposition of externalities emanate from the ubiquitous tendency of legislatures to exceed their jurisdiction of comparative advantage, then Hills may be too quick to cede the judiciary's need to police legislative setting of jurisdictional boundaries. Concepts such as the enumerated powers clause and the Tenth Amendment at the centralized level or inquiries into the scope of home rule, local autonomy, and permissible conflicts between state statutes and local ordinances at the decentralized levels may provide doctrinal hooks that can be used to achieve the precarious balance that Hills admonishes us to strike. But doctrines with that level of generality and vagueness cannot be self-executing. If the relevant legislators are incapable of policing themselves, then there might seem little alternative to judicial intervention. Of course, that possibility introduces an additional set of risks related both to the legitimacy of judicial invalidation of legislative acts and to the institutional incompetence of the judiciary to make the empirical inquiries that one might think crucial to comparing the risks of uniformity and externality.

Perhaps that leaves open the availability of extralegal norms and bargains as checking mechanisms on legislative excess. And perhaps that takes us right back to Tiebout and Coase. If local governments, which must be repeat players with their neighbors, fear retaliation from activities that generate externalities, they have some incentive either to restrain themselves or to enter into mutually beneficial treaties against proposals that externalize costs. If state and local governments fear excessive uniformity, they have incentives to enter into compacts among themselves to constrain federal intrusions and to enter into compacts with Congress to allocate authority more explicitly than vague legal doctrines can achieve. As Hills suggests, the costs of interlocal bargaining limits the amount of contracting behavior that can occur among and between governments. But those costs are themselves often a function of the assignment of legal entitlements and the failure of legal doctrine to assign fruitful ways of dividing a bargaining surplus. To the extent that excessive uniformity and the generation of externalities are reciprocal risks, one might imagine that either implicit or explicit bargains between the parties themselves would internalize both the costs and benefits of any solution. As a result, perhaps the relevant parties would be better situated than courts to make the comparison that Hills correctly identifies as the relevant one for the optimal allocation of government authority. If so, then the quandary that Hills has demonstrated may best be escaped by seeking ways to reduce the intergovernmental bargaining costs that currently make the ideal worlds of Tiebout and Coase less accessible.

REFERENCES

Arthur, W. Brian. 1994. *Increasing returns and path dependence in the economy.* Ann Arbor: University of Michigan Press.

Beale, Sara Sun. 2002. The unintended consequences of enhancing gun penalties: Shooting down the commerce clause and arming federal prosecutors. *Duke Law Journal* 51:1641–1681.

———. 2005. The many faces of overcriminalization: From morals and mattress tags to overfederalization. *American University Law Review* 54:747–782.

Carter, John R., and David Schap. 1990. Line-item veto: Where is thy sting? *Journal of Economic Perspectives* 4:103–118.

Farber, Daniel A., and Philip P. Frickey. 1991. *Law and public choice.* Chicago: University of Chicago Press.

Gillette, Clayton P. 1996. Reconstructing local control of school finance: A cautionary note. *Capital University Law Review* 25:37–50.

———. 2001. Regionalization and interlocal bargains. *NYU Law Review* 76:190–271.

Glaeser, Edward L. 1998. Are cities dying? *Journal of Economic Perspectives* 12:139–160.

Quigley, John M. 1998. Urban diversity and economic growth. *Journal of Economic Perspectives* 12:127–138.

Stuntz, William J. 2001. The pathological politics of criminal law. *Michigan Law Review* 100:505–600.

Utt, Richard D. 2005. The bridge to nowhere: A national embarrassment. Heritage Foundation, Web Memo 889, http://www.heritage.org/Research/Budget/wm889.cfm.

Vermeule, Adrian. 2001. Veil of ignorance rules in constitutional law. *Yale Law Journal* 111:399–433.

Zelinsky, Edward. 1993. Unfunded mandates, hidden taxation, and the Tenth Amendment: On public choice, public interest, and public services. *Vanderbilt Law Review* 46:1355–1415.

9

The Law of Demand
in Tiebout Economics

Edward Cartwright

John P. Conley

Myrna Wooders

We consider a general-equilibrium local public goods economy in which agents have two distinguishing characteristics. The first is *crowding type,* which is publicly observable and provides direct costs or benefits to the jurisdiction (coalition or firm) that an agent joins. The second is *taste type,* which is not publicly observable, has no direct effects on others, and is defined over private good, public goods, and the crowding profile of the jurisdiction that the agent joins. The law of demand suggests that as the quantity of a given crowding type (plumbers, lawyers, smart people, tall people, nonsmokers, for example) increases, the compensation that agents of that type receive should decrease. In this chapter, we will see counterexamples, however, that show that some agents of a given crowding type might actually benefit when the proportion of agents with the same crowding type increases. This reversal of the law of demand seems to have to do with an interaction effect between tastes and skills, and seems to relate to the degree of difference between various patterns of tastes—in particular, if tastes are homogeneous, the law of demand holds.

Our research continues the seminal work of Charles Tiebout, in particular his 1956 paper. Tiebout's (1956) central insight was that many types of public goods are subject to crowding and congestion. As a result, it would be impractical and inefficient to provide them at the level of national governments. Instead, services like schools, a police force, and fire protection are produced by local jurisdictions. In choosing where to live, consumers evaluate the bundles of public goods, taxes, and other amenities each jurisdiction offers. In making their locational choices, in effect, they reveal their willingness to pay for public goods. Thus, in this economic environment the preference revelation and free-riding problem pointed out by Samuelson (1954) for the case of pure public goods disappear.

Tiebout's paper stimulated an enormous theoretical literature. Subsequent authors have shown that although efficient Tiebout sorting may not occur in completely general circumstances, adding economic restrictions that are natural in the study of clubs or local public goods provides support for Tiebout's hypothesis. Wooders (1978), for example, shows that when there is only one private good, agents crowd each other anonymously (only the numbers of agents sharing the public goods matters), and all gains to coalition forming are realized in small groups (or coalitions), the core can be decentralized with anonymous prices. On the other hand, Bewley's (1981) early attempt to formalize the Tiebout hypothesis led to largely negative conclusions. Bewley shows that in some cases anonymous decentralization of efficient outcomes is not possible and in other cases anonymous prices may only serve to decentralize inefficient outcomes. Bewley's formalization, however, has not gained wide acceptance. Key concerns are that in his model the numbers of jurisdictions in some cases is fixed, public goods are not subject to congestion, and, most important, small groups are not effective (more on this later).

The local public-goods approach to the provision of congestible public goods centers on agents who make locational choices among competing jurisdictions that offer possibly distinct public good bundles. The main questions concern how the entire population of a large economy can be best sorted into non- overlapping and exhaustive coalitions (jurisdictions, clubs, or firms). There are, however, significant classes of congestible goods that are provided by coalitions not connected to a location. For example, agents join country clubs, fitness clubs, private schools, churches, professional organizations, and so on in order to enjoy both the public goods they provide and the company of the other members. Note that agents can belong to one club, several clubs, or even no clubs. Thus, unlike the local public-goods case, there is no need to require that the outcome be a partition of the agents. Buchanan (1965) is generally credited as being the first to write a formal model of clubs, but the roots can be seen as far back as the early papers on tolls and congested roads by Pigou (1920) and Knight (1924).

Since Buchanan published his seminal paper the club literature has developed in several different directions. In a model with essentially homogeneous agents, Pauly (1967, 1970) explored the issue of optimal club size and the stability of its membership. Wooders (1978) considered anonymous crowding and anonymous prices—prices that do not depend on unobservable characteristics of agents—in a model permitting multiple types. McGuire (1974) and Wooders (1978) address whether club membership will be homogeneous when agents differ in tastes or endowments. Questions of core and equilibrium existence in club economies arose in works such as Pauly (1967, 1970) and Wooders (1978, 1980) and numerous subsequent papers. Wooders (1989) addressed similar questions in a model with nonanonymous crowding. McGuire (1991) and Brueckner (1994) allow complementarities between different types of workers (nonanonymous crowding) and investigate conditions under which optimal jurisdictions will nevertheless be homogeneous. Issues involving the potential costs for excluding unwanted members of an exclusive club are presented by Davis and Whinston (1967), Millward (1970), Nichols, Smolensky, and Tiedman (1971), Oakland (1972), and Kamien, Schwartz, and Roberts (1973). Early explorations of uncertainty in club models include DeVany and Saving (1977) and Hillman and Swan (1979). More recent directions of investigation include multiproduct clubs, variable usage, and intergenerational clubs.

In this chapter we take on a new question: When will a law of demand hold for skills or other "crowding" characteristics in coalition economies and, in particular, in economies with local public goods? For example, will the compensation that gregarious people experience from joining social groups decrease if more people become outgoing? Will smart college applicants receive less college aid if the population at large gets smarter? Will the wage of teachers go down if more teachers are trained? In labor markets there is a strong intuition that the law of demand should hold. The question is, does it continue to hold in Tiebout economies?

The central issue we encounter in addressing this question was already nicely pointed out by Adam Smith (1976):

> The whole of the advantages and disadvantages of the different employments of labor and stock must, in the same neighborhood, be either perfectly equal or continually tending to equality. If in the same neighborhood there was any employment evidently either more or less advantageous than the rest, so many people would crowd into it in one case, and so many would desert it in the other, that its advantages would soon return to the level of other employments. (111)

As Adam Smith recognized, wage differentials are required to equalize the total monetary and nonmonetary advantages and disadvantages among alternative employments. A job with favorable conditions can attract labor at relatively low wages, while a job with unfavorable conditions must offer a compensating wage premium to attract workers. This well-known theory of equalizing differences is suggested to be "the fundamental market equilibrium construct in labor economics" (Rosen 1986) and is an example of the central question in this chapter. Clearly, whether this theory holds in Tiebout economies, clubs with attractive memberships and public-goods offerings can charge more for admission.

The value of a worker's skills is determined by the market values of the products he is able to generate. How conditions of employment are valued, however, depends on the tastes of individual workers. For example, whether indoor or outdoor work is more highly paid depends on the tastes of workers. If there is an abundance of workers who prefer to stay indoors, then outdoor work may fetch a premium. Thus, when we allow for equalizing differences, the tastes of workers become important determinants of labor market equilibrium. We find that getting the most out of an economy's resources requires matching the appropriate type of worker with the appropriate type of firm: The labor market must solve a type of marriage problem of slotting workers into their proper "niches" within and between firms (Rosen 1978, 1986; Bennett and Wooders 1979; Elliot 1990).

It is difficult to address the process of assigning workers to firms in a general equilibrium model, since each commodity, including labor, is treated as a homogeneous good that is allocated to productive uses, without reference to the agents who supplied it. In other words, there is a structural debundling of the tastes and skills of workers inherent in the model. Under these circumstances, and given diminishing marginal productivity of labor, one expects a law of demand to hold. That is, as the quantity supplied of a given skill increases, the price it receives in equilibrium should go down.

We will therefore explore the law of demand in the context of the *crowding types model* introduced in Conley and Wooders (1996, 1997). The advantage of this model in examining law of demand issues is that it sets up a formal distinction between the tastes and crowding effects of agents. Crowding characteristics are publicly observable and generate direct effects on other agents. Crowding characteristics include, for example, gender, whether one is a smoker, skills and abilities, personality characteristics, appearance, and languages spoken. Note that some of these characteristics are exogenously attached to agents (gender), and some are endogenously chosen in response to market and other incentives (skills and professional qualifications). See Conley and Wooders (2001, 2004) for more discussion of the latter. Tastes, on the other hand, are assumed to be private information and in themselves produce no direct effects on other agents.

The key observation underlying the crowding types approach is that an agent is a bundle of tastes and observable characteristics, such as education. These cannot be taken as independent. Thus, it is the joint distribution of tastes and crowding types and not their separate distributions that determines the equilibrium outcome of the economy. Modeling this feature allows us to explore explicitly how the tastes of agents determine the compensating differentials needed to induce agents to join different jurisdictions, firms, or coalitions and in turn to see when a law of demand for skills, for example, will and will not hold in a Tiebout economy.

To do so, we consider a coalitional economy in which small groups are strictly effective. Informally, this means that all per capita gains can be realized in groups that are small relative to the size of the population and that no particular type is scarce (and thus might have monopoly power). In these circumstances the core has the equal-treatment property—that is, all agents of a given type must receive the same utility in any core allocation.

To address whether the law of demand holds, we consider two economies that differ only in that the number of one particular crowding type is larger in one than the other. We show that at a core allocation, the law of demand need not hold. We demonstrate this through a pair of examples; some agents of the relatively more abundant crowding type may benefit. In fact, the average compensation of agents possessing the crowding type that has become more abundant in the population may go either up or down. For example, if there is an increase in the number of plumbers in the world, it might be that plumbers who have a taste for working hot steam tunnels actually benefit from the overall increase. Similarly, while computer programmers in general might oppose the free immigration of programmers from India, it might still be the case that some types of programmers (say, game writers) might actually benefit from this migration.

This failure of the law of demand seems to be due to interactions between tastes and crowding characteristics and especially to how they are bundled. As we will discuss, if all agents have the same tastes, then the law of demand holds.

The Model

We consider economies in which agents are described by two characteristics: their taste types and crowding types. An agent has one of T different taste types, denoted by $t \in 1, \ldots, T \equiv \mathbf{T}$ and one of C different crowding types, denoted by $c \in 1, \ldots, C \equiv \mathbf{C}$. We assume no correlation between c and t.

A group of agents is described by a vector $m = (m_{11}, \ldots, m_{ct}, \ldots, m_{CT})$, where m_{ct} denotes the number of agents with crowding type c and taste type t in the group. The *crowding profile* of a group m is a vector $(m_1, \ldots, m_C)$, where $m_c = \sum_t m_{ct}$. A crowding profile simply lists the numbers of agents of each crowding type in the coalition or economy. An economy is determined by the group of agents $N = (N_{11}, \ldots, N_{ct}, \ldots, N_{CT})$. A *club* $m = (m_{11}, \ldots, m_{ct}, \ldots, m_{CT}) \leq N$ describes a group of agents whose membership collectively produces and consumes a public good. The set of all feasible clubs contained in N is denoted by $\mathbf{N}$.

A *partition* n *of the population* is a set of clubs $\{n^1, \ldots, n^K\}$ satisfying $\sum_k n^k = N$. We will write $n^k \in n$ when a club n^k belongs to the partition n. It will sometimes be useful to refer to an individual agent, denoted by $i \in \{1, \ldots, I\} \equiv \mathbf{I}$, where $I = \sum_{ct} N_{ct}$ is the size of the population. We let $\theta : \mathbf{I} \to \mathbf{C} \times \mathbf{T}$ be a mapping that describes the crowding and taste types of individual agents; thus, $|\{i \in \mathbf{I}, i \in N : \theta(i) = (c,t)\}| = N_{ct}$.

We will say an agent i has *type* (c,t) if $\theta(i) = (c,t)$.

With a slight abuse of notation, if agent i is a member of the club described by m, we shall write $i \in m$, and if i belongs to the economy determined by N, we write $i \in N$.

An economy has one private good x and club goods $y_1, y_2, ..., y_A$ that are provided by clubs exclusively for their own memberships. A vector $y = (y_1, y_2, ..., y_A) \in \mathbf{R}_+^A$ gives club good production. Each agent belongs to exactly one club. Each agent $i \in \mathbf{I}$ of taste type t is endowed with $\omega_t \in \mathbf{R}_+$ of the private good and has a quasi-linear utility function $u_t(x,y,m) = x + h_t(y,m)$, where $i \in m$ and y is the club good production of club m containing agent i. The cost in terms of the private good of producing y club good in a club with membership m is given by a production function $f(y,m)$.

A particular combination of preferences and endowments for players in the economy N and production possibilities available to clubs is referred to as the *structure* of the economy.

We shall assume preferences satisfy *taste anonymity in consumption* (TAC), and production functions satisfy *taste anonymity in production* (TAP), defined as follows:

TAC: For all $m, \hat{m} \in N$, if for all $c \in C$, it holds that $\sum_t m_{ct} = \sum_t \hat{m}_{ct}$, then for all $x \in \mathbf{R}_+$, all $y \in \mathbf{R}_+^A$, and all $t \in T$, it holds that $(x, y, m) \sim_t (x, y, \hat{m})$.

TAP: For all $m, \hat{m} \in N$, if for all $c \in C$, it holds that $\sum_t m_{ct} = \sum_t \hat{m}_{ct}$, then for all $y \in \mathbf{R}_+^A$, it holds that $f(y, m) = f(y, \hat{m})$.

TAC and TAP capture the idea that agents care only about the crowding types and not the taste types of the agents that are in their respective clubs. These conditions can be seen as defining crowding types rather than imposing restrictions on preferences. To illustrate, the cost of production depends on the skill mix of the people in the jurisdiction, but whether or not skilled workers like warm or cool climates is of no relevance. As for consumption, we might care about the age of other people but are indifferent to whether or not they are danger averse.[1] We will assume throughout that all economic structures satisfy both TAC and TAP.

A *feasible state* of the economy $(X,Y,n) \equiv ((x_1,..., x_I),(y_1,...y_K),(n_1,...n_K))$ consists of a partition n of the population, an allocation $X = (x_1,..., x_I)$ of pri-

---

[1] You may well indirectly care about the tastes of agents you live with through the eventual choice of public good y. However, given y, TAC and TAP imply that your welfare does not directly depend on the tastes of other agents.

vate goods to agents, and a club goods production plan for each club, $Y = (y_1, \ldots y_K)$, such that

$$\sum_k \sum_{ct} n_{ct}^k \omega_t - \sum_i x_i - \sum_k f(y^k, n^k) \geq 0.$$

We also say that (x, y) is a *feasible allocation for a club m* if

$$\sum_{c,t} m_{ct} \omega_t - \sum_{i \in m} \overline{x}_i - f(\overline{y}, m) \geq 0.$$

A club $m \in N$ producing a feasible allocation $(\overline{x}, \overline{y})$ *can improve upon* a feasible state (X, Y, n) if for all $i \in m$, $u_t(\overline{x}_i, \overline{y}, m) > u_t(x_i, y_k, n_k)$, where i is of taste type t and, in the original state, $i \in n_k$ and $n_k \in n$. A feasible state of the economy (X, Y, n) is a *core state of the economy* or simply a *core state* if it cannot be improved upon by any group m acting as a coalition.[2] This simply says that a feasible state is in the core if it is not possible for a coalition of agents to break away and, using only resources of its members, provide all of its members with preferred consumption bundles. A utility vector $\hat{u} \in \mathbf{R}^I$ is a *core utility* if, for some core state of the economy, (X, Y, n), $u_i(x_i, y_k, n_k) = \hat{u}_i$.

Since we are restricted to economies with quasi-linear preferences, we can also define the core entirely in terms of vectors of utilities. Given a club $m \in N$, we define $v(m)$ as the maximum total utility that can be achieved by the club; that is,

$$v(m) = \max_{(\overline{x}, \overline{y})} \sum_{i \in m} u_t(\overline{x}_i, \overline{y}, m),$$

where the maximum is taken over the set of feasible allocations for the club m. We define $V(N)$ as the maximum total utility that can be achieved by the entire economy when it can partition into jurisdictions; that is,

$$V(N) = \max \sum_k v(n^k),$$

where $n = (n_1, \ldots, n_K)$ is a partition of N for some K. It is easy to show that a utility vector $\hat{u} \in \mathbf{R}^I$ is a core utility if and only if

$$\sum_{i \in m} \hat{u}_i \geq v(m) \text{ and } \sum_{i \in N} \hat{u}_i = V(N).$$

Our paper makes heavy use of a concept of strict small group effectiveness, SSGE. Before introducing this concept, we discuss the weaker concept of small group effectiveness (SGE), introduced in Wooders (1992, 1994a, b). This concept dictates that *almost* all gains to collective activities can be realized by cooperation

---

[2] Note that we can define the core as the set of feasible states that cannot be improved upon by any club (rather than by a coalition forming perhaps multiple clubs), since there are no benefits to be gained from trade between clubs. This contrasts to works such as Wooders (1989), for example, with multiple private goods.

only within relatively small groups of agents, such as jurisdictions, clubs, communities, or even nations. SGE ensures that in large economies approximate cores treat most-similar players nearly equally, and it is thus important to the competitiveness of economies with many agents. Also, SGE is an apparently mild requirement, closely related to the mild requirement that per capita utilities can be bounded, independent of the numbers of agents in the economy (Wooders 1994a, Theorem 4). Our stronger requirement of SSGE ensures that *all* gains to collective activities can be realized by partitions of the total player set into groups bounded in size with cooperation only within these groups.

This chapter focuses solely on economies in which small groups are strictly effective. An economy satisfies *strict small-group effectiveness*, SSGE, if there exists a positive integer B such that

1. For all core states (X,Y,n) and all $n_k \in n$, it holds that $|n_k| < B$.
2. For all $c \in C$ and all $t \in T$, it holds that either $N_{ct} > B$ or $N_{ct} = 0$.

SSGE is a relatively strong, formalized version of the sixth assumption in Tiebout's paper that there must be an optimal community size. Condition one states that any coalition with more than B agents can be improved upon, while condition two says that this limit of B is small relative to a population that contains at least B agents of each type. As recent literature shows, however, economies satisfying apparently mild conditions can be approximated by those satisfying SSGE (cf. Kovalenkov and Wooders 2003 and references therein).

Equal Treatment

The first result follows immediately from SSGE and shows that any core state must have the *equal treatment property*—that is, any two agents of the same type must be equally well off in any core state.[3]

Theorem 1: Let (X,Y,n) be a core state of an economy satisfying SSGE. For any two individuals $i,\hat{i} \in I$ such that $\theta(i) = \theta(\hat{i}) = (c,t)$, if $i \in n^k$ and $\hat{i} \in n^{\hat{k}}$, then $u_t(x_i,y,n^k) = u_t(\hat{x}_i,\hat{y},n^{\hat{k}})$.

Proof: See Conley and Wooders (1997). One consequence of this result is that with any core state (X,Y,n), we can associate a vector of payoffs $u = (u_{11},\ldots, u_{ct},\ldots,u_{CT}) \in \mathbf{R}^{CT}$, where u_{ct} is the utility of an agent with crowding type c and taste type t. Note that Theorem 1 cannot be directly verified by looking at the observable data. Wages received by agents of a given type could be widely dif-

---

[3] More general versions of this result appear in Wooders (1983, Theorem 3) and in Kovalenkov and Wooders (2001).

ferent, provided the nonobservable nonmonetary compensations of joining a club offset the wage differences. The next result provides a directly observable counterpart to Theorem 1 and is a key feature of the crowding types model.

Theorem 2: Let (X,Y,n) be a core state of an economy satisfying SSGE. Suppose that for some club $n^k \in n$, for some crowding type $c \in C$, and for two taste types $t, t' \in T$, both $n^k_{ct} > 0$ and $n^k_{ct'} > 0$. Then, for all $i, j \in k$ such that $\theta(i) = (c,t)$ and $\theta(j) = (c,\hat{t})$, it holds that

$$\omega_t - x_i = \omega_j - x_i \equiv \rho_c(y^k, n^k).$$

Proof: See Conley and Wooders (1997). Theorem 2 illustrates that in a core state players of the same crowding type will be offered the same "price" (which may be positive or negative) to enter clubs. Thus, there is anonymity in the sense that the prices of club membership for two individuals who have the same crowding type do not depend on tastes.

From now on, given a core state, we will interpret $\rho_c(y,m)$ as the *admission price for players of crowding type c to enter the club m producing y of the club good*. For the special case of production, or coalition production, admission prices will generally be negative and are interpreted as the wages paid by firms to workers.

Core Equivalence

Expanding on the preceding, a *Tiebout price system for crowding type c* associates to each possible club good level and possible club (containing at least one player with crowding type c) an admission price, which applies to all players of crowding type c. Thus, players know the price to join any possible jurisdiction, and we also see that prices are anonymous in the sense that they do not depend on the tastes of agents.[4] A *Tiebout price system* is simply a collection of price systems, one for each type, and is denoted by ρ.

We define a *Tiebout equilibrium* as a feasible state $(X,Y,n) \in F$ and a Tiebout price system ρ such that

1. For all $n^k \in n$, all individuals $i \in n^k$ such that $\theta(i) = (c,t)$, all alternative clubs $m \in N_c$, and for all levels of public good production $y \in R^A_+$,

$$\omega_t - \rho_c(y^k,n^k) + h_t(y^k,n^k) \geq \omega_t - \rho_c(y,m) + h_t(y,m).$$

2. For all potential clubs $m \in N$ and all $y \in R^A_+$,

$$\sum_{c,t} m_{ct}\rho_c(y,m) - f(y,m) \leq 0.$$

---

[4] Formally we also require that for all $m, \hat{m} \in N$, if for all $c \in C$ it holds that $\sum_t m_{ct} = \sum_t \hat{m}_{ct}$, then for all y it holds that $\rho(y,m) = \rho(y,\hat{m})$.

3. For all $n^k \in n$,

$$\sum_{c,t} n_{ct}^k \rho_c(y^k, n^k) - f(y^k, n^k) = 0.$$

It can be seen that a Tiebout equilibrium is a decentralized market equilibrium. Condition 1 states that, given prices to join clubs, every agent is in his preferred club. Condition 2 states that, given the price system, no new club could make positive profits, while existing clubs make zero profit.[5]

Under strict small-group effectiveness, a strong result can be proven about the relationship between the core and Tiebout equilibrium.

Theorem 3: If an economy satisfies SSGE, then the set of states in the core of the economy is equivalent to the set of Tiebout equilibrium states.

Proof: See Conley and Wooders (1997). Theorem 3 confirms that in the crowding types model efficient allocations can be decentralized through an anonymous price system. Thus, when we consider firm formation, all workers can choose among jobs to maximize their utilities, and the resulting outcome will be an efficient stable outcome in which workers and firms are optimally matched.[6] Note that, unlike the situation in private-goods exchange economies, we have equivalence of core and equilibrium outcomes in economies with a finite number of agents. This is due to our assumption of SSGE. There are no new effective clubs that arise when the economy becomes larger. This is in contrast to situations as in Wooders (1997), where, for some results, forever increasing returns to jurisdiction size are allowed.

The crowding types model allows us to consider firm, jurisdiction, or region formation, taking account of both the tastes of workers and their productivity. As such, it gives us a reasonably complete way to model the theory of equalizing differences. The rest of this chapter uses this model to consider the relevance of the law of demand when crowding types and taste types are taken into account.

The Law of Demand

By using comparative statistics exercises for two economies, we can formally develop both positive and negative results regarding the law of demand. These economies have identical technologies and identical populations of all

---

[5] From a firm perspective this does not imply that the firm makes zero profit, but it means that any profit has been redistributed to the workers and owners of that firm.

[6] We note that a major difference between this result and analogous results for differentiated crowding models as in Wooders (1997), for example, is that prices do not depend on the tastes of agents, only on their crowding types. Analogous results for models with anonymous crowding, as in Wooders (1978) and subsequent papers, are special cases of Theorem 3, since anonymous crowding models are crowding types models but with only one crowding type.

agents, except for one particular crowding type c. The second economy has an increased population of crowding type c spread in some arbitrary way across taste types. Thus, for example, the two economies have the same number of plumbers who like football, plumbers who like hockey, plumbers who like baseball, lawyers who like football, lawyers who like baseball, and so on. However, the second economy might have twice as many doctors who like football, one additional doctor who likes hockey, and the same number of doctors who like baseball.

Formally, consider two economies, S and G, with agent sets $S = (S_{11},...,S_{ct},...,S_{CT})$ and $G = (G_{11},...,G_{ct},...,G_{CT})$, where S_{ct} is interpreted as the total number of agents with crowding type c and taste type t in economy S, and where G_{ct} is interpreted as the total number of agents with crowding type c and taste type t in economy G. The most recent, and also the most general, versions of the following result appear in Kovalenkov and Wooders (2005).[7] Because of our assumption of SSGE, the following proof is particularly simple.

Theorem 4: Let S and G be as just stated, and assume both economies satisfy SSGE. Assume also that there are vectors $u^S = (u_{11}^S,...,u_{ct}^S,...,u_{CT}^S) \in \mathbf{R}^{CT}$ and $u^G = (u_{11}^G,...,u_{ct}^G,...,u_{CT}^G) \in \mathbf{R}^{CT}$ representing core payoffs in the equal treatment core of economies S and G, respectively. Then

$$(u^S - u^G) \cdot (S - G) \leq 0.$$

Proof: From the assumption that u^S is the core of the economy S, $u^S \cdot m \geq v(m)$ for all jurisdictions m with $\|m\| \leq B$. We claim that $u^S \cdot G \geq v(G)$. Let n^G be a partition of G into jurisdictions n_k^G satisfying $\|n_k^G\| \leq B$ for each jurisdiction and supporting the core allocation u^G for each n_k^G, it holds that $u^G \cdot n_k^G = v(n_k^G)$ and $u^G \cdot G = \sum_k v(n_k^G)$. Then, $u^S \cdot m \geq v(m)$ for all jurisdictions m implies $u^S \cdot n_k^G \geq v(n_k^G)$ for each k and

$$u^S \cdot G = \sum_k u^S \cdot n_k^G \geq \sum_k v(n_k^G) = v(G).$$

Similarly, $u^G \cdot S \geq v(S)$. Also, since u^S is a core utility for the economy S and u^G is a core utility for the economy G, it holds that $u^S \cdot S = v(S)$ and $u^G \cdot G = v(G)$. We now have

$$0 \geq v(G) - u^S \cdot G + v(S) - u^G \cdot S$$
$$= u^G \cdot G - u^S \cdot G + u^S \cdot S - u^G \cdot S$$
$$= u^G \cdot G - u^S \cdot G + u^S \cdot S - u^G \cdot S$$
$$= (u^S - u^G) \cdot (S - G)$$

---

[7] Kovalenkov and Wooders (forthcoming) provide a discussion of related literature.

The conclusion now follows from some simple algebra.

One immediate consequence of Theorem 4 is that a ceteris paribus increase in the number of players of a particular type (that is, a particular c,t combination) cannot be beneficial to all players of that type.

Corollary 1: Let S and G be as just stated, and assume both economies satisfy SSGE. Assume also that there are vectors $u^S = (u^S_{11},...,u^S_{ct},...,u^S_{CT}) \in \mathbf{R}^{CT}$ and $u^G = (u^G_{11},...,u^G_{ct},...,u^G_{CT}) \in \mathbf{R}^{CT}$ representing core payoffs in the equal treatment core of economies S and G, respectively. Then, given the core vectors u^S and u^G, if $S_{ct} < G_{ct}$ and $S_{c't'} = G_{c't'}$ for all other types (c',t') then it must hold that

$$u^S_{ct} \geq u^G_{ct}.$$

Corollary 1 states that the law of demand applies on a type-by-type basis. The problem with this is that the taste component of a type is not observable. Thus, the data cannot tell us anything about the relative increases for agents of crowding type c of different taste types.

One particular case in which we can obtain a law of demand is when all agents have the same taste types. This case may be important in application to empirical economics.

Corollary 2: Let S and G be as just stated, and assume both economies satisfy SSGE. Assume also that $T = 1$. Then, if $u^S = (u^S_{11},...,u^S_{c1},...,u^S_{C1}) \in \mathbf{R}^C$ and $u^G = (u^G_{11},...,u^G_{c1},...,u^G_{C1}) \in \mathbf{R}^C$ represent core payoffs in the equal treatment core of economies S and G, respectively, it holds that if $S_{c'1} = G_{c'1}$ for all other types $(c',1), c' \neq c$, then it must hold that

$$u^S_{c1} \geq u^G_{c1}.$$

This can easily been seen, since the core vectors given in Theorem 4, $u^S = (u^S_{11},...,u^S_{ct},...,u^S_{CT}) \in \mathbf{R}^{CT}$ and $u^G = (u^G_{11},...,u^G_{ct},...,u^G_{CT}) \in \mathbf{R}^{CT}$, will be in the spaces $\mathbf{R}^C$ (since $T = 1$), and the relationship $(u^S - u^G) \cdot (S - G) \leq 0$ will hold. Another situation where the law of demand will hold is where all agents have the same genetic type and can acquire any crowding type at the same cost (as in Conley and Wooders [1996]). Of course, if there is only one crowding type (that is, if crowding is anonymous), then the law of demand will also hold. While these cases may be important empirically, from a theoretical perspective they are quite narrow.

In view of the observability of crowding types, of particular interest is a ceteris paribus increase in the number of players with a particular crowding type. The following result shows that not all agents of a crowding type can gain from an increase in the numbers of agents with that crowding type.

Corollary 3: If $S_{ct'} \leq G_{ct'}$ for all $t' \in T$ and $S_{c't'} = G_{c't'}$ for all $c' \in C$, $c' \neq c$, and for all $t' \in T$, then $u_{ct}^S \geq u_{ct}^G$ for at least one type t, and, moreover, if $u_{ct'}^S < u_{ct'}^G$ for some type t', then there exists some t such that $u_{ct}^S > u_{ct}^G$.

Proof: There are two cases: (1) $u_{ct}^S = u_{ct}^G$ for all $t \in B$, in which case Corollary 3 is completely trivial. (2) There exists some $t' \in T$ such that $u_{ct}^S > u_{ct}^G$. Given the result that $(u^S - u^G) \cdot (S - G) \leq 0$, if $u_{ct'}^S < u_{ct'}^G$ for some type t', then it must hold that there is at least one other type t for which $u_{ct}^S > u_{ct}^G$; otherwise, we would have a contradiction to the conclusion of Theorem 4.

Corollary 3 states that if the number of agents of any crowding type c increases, while the number of agents of every other crowding type, taste type pair is held constant, if one taste type gains from the increase, then another taste type loses. We cannot, however, say that will happen to average payoffs of the agents with a particular taste type, as the following example illustrates.

Example 1: Suppose that there is only one crowding type and two taste types. Agents with taste type 1, like work agents with taste type 2, gain no utility from work. A pair of agents can work together and produce output worth $10.00. If a type 1 agent works, he experiences a utility increase just from working worth $7.00, while a type 2 agent gains 0 utility from working. An equal-treatment core utility vector assigns payoff of $12.00 worth of utility to a player of type 1 and $5.00 to each player of type 2. If the number of agents of taste type 1 increases, then core utilities on average increase, while the opposite holds if the number of agents of taste type 2 increases. Note that for this example, the core will be non-empty only if there is an even number of agents, but if there are many agents, approximate cores will be nonempty and give most players of type 1 approximately $12.00 and most of type 2 approximately $5.00 (Wooders 1994b). This is a rather trivial example, and it could be made more elaborate without changing the point. What it demonstrates is that given the differences in how agents value different kinds of work situations and so on, the simple proposition that the average payoffs to agents of any given crowding type must decrease as the number of that crowding type increases in the population is false.

Failures of the Law of Demand

Now we demonstrate that the law of demand need not hold for all agents when the crowding type they possess increases. This example considers the case of crowding in consumption. (An example that treats crowding in production is available from the authors upon request.)

Example 2: There are three taste types: people who love music at work (L), people who hate music at work (H), and people who are indifferent about music at work (I). There are three crowding types: people who always whistle at work (W), people who never whistle at work (D), and people who occasionally whistle at work (O). People join together to form partnerships and produce a good—say, a building service. Note that all agents are equally productive in production of the good. An agent's utility from a partnership depends on his tastes and the crowding profile of the partnership. The utility of belonging to a partnership can be detailed as follows:

$$U_H(W,W)=0 \quad U_L(W,W)=4 \quad U_H(O,D)=3 \quad U_L(O,D)=1$$
$$U_H(W,O)=1 \quad U_L(W,O)=3 \quad U_H(D,D)=4 \quad U_L(D,D)=0$$

with all other partnerships giving utility 2. For example, if someone who always whistles at work but who hates music at work joins with someone who occasionally whistles, he receives payoff $U_H(W,O) = 3$. If he joins with someone who never whistles, he receives payoff $U_H(W,D) = 2$.

We contrast two economies where the number of players of each type is either zero or as follows:

Type	WH	WI	OH	OL	DI	DL
Number of type in economy S	6	4	2	4	4	4
Number of type in economy G	6	4	4	6	4	4

Note that the number of players with crowding type O has increased.[8]

Two possible core allocations can be detailed as follows:

1. Economy S: $4 \times (WI, OL)$, $4 \times (WH, DL)$, $2 \times (OH, DI)$, and $2 \times (WH, DI)$
2. Economy G: $4 \times (WI, OL)$, $4 \times (WH, DL)$, $4 \times (OH, DI)$, and $2 \times (WH, OL)$

This economy has the following core payoffs:

Type	WH	WI	OH	OL	DI	DL
Payoff in economy S	2	3	3	2	2	2
Payoff in economy G	1.5	2.5	2	2.5	3	2.5

To see that these represent core states, we detail the relevant parts of the value function. With the following exceptions, the worth of any pair of agents is 4.

---

[8] As stated, the number of players of type OI remains the same at zero. In the two core states given, we could have partnerships (OI, OI), giving core payoffs of 2 to players of type OI. Thus, we could easily consider two economies where the number of players of type OI also increases by 2.

Composition	Total Utility	Composition	Total Utility	Composition	Total Utility
WH, WH	0	WI, OH	3	DL, DL	0
WH, WI	2	DI, OH	5	DI, DL	2
WI, OL	5	DL, OL	2		
WH, OH	2	DI, OL	3		

We observe that agents of type OL receive a higher payoff in economy G despite the increase in agents with crowding type O and type OL. So why, intuitively, are agents of type OL able to gain? Given that agents of type OL love to listen to music, they would naturally want to form a partnership with agents who always whistle (crowding type W), as opposed to those who never whistle (D). Conversely, agents of type OH would naturally want to form a partnership with agents who never whistle (D), as opposed to those who always whistle (W). In economy S it so happens that agents with crowding type W are doing relatively well, and agents with crowding type D are doing relatively poorly. This has the side effect that agents of type OL receive a relatively low payoff, and agents of type OH have a relatively high payoff. In economy G the increased number of agents of type OH sees their "bargaining position" reduced, and consequently their payoffs fall. This feeds through into an increased bargaining power for those agents who never whistle and a decreased bargaining power for those who always whistle. As the bargaining power of whistlers falls, agents of type OL are able to increase their payoff. Basically, there are cross-type influences whereby agents of type OL gain more bargaining power by the increased number of players of type OH than they lose by the increased number of players with their own type, OL.

Conclusion

In this chapter we extended the basic approach pioneered by Tiebout to reexamine the theory of equalizing differences. We do this by drawing a connection between local public goods and the nonwage attributes of jobs. That is, the attributes that necessitate equalizing differences, such as danger, cleanliness, climate, and the range of local amenities, can all be seen as club goods.

Our model allowed us to present a more complete model of equalizing differences in which we can account for the compensating wages between differing taste types, while also modeling the markets for different productivity and skill levels. In doing so, we make assumptions standard to the literature: free mobility, no redistribution between clubs (e.g., no governments), and perfect information on the types of jobs available. We assume that a player's crowding type is observable and that crowding types are independent of taste types, the main innovation of Conley and Wooders (1997). We should acknowledge that there are some contexts in which these assumptions may not be reasonable. For example, it may not be possible to fully observe how smart or honest a potential new employee is, and it may be that smokers (a crowding type) like to smoke (a taste). However, there are many other circumstances in which these assumptions can be justified.

Having introduced the model, we turned to an application of particular interest: whether, following a ceteris paribus increase in the supply of a factor of production, the per-unit return to that factor can increase. The introduction of compensating differentials means that taste types become important parts of the labor market: If one player prefers the attributes of the firm or region, you can afford to pay that person a lower wage. This creates an independence in the money wage that players with the same skills but different tastes can earn, and, as such, the arbitrage to equalize wages that we would expect within the standard market paradigm no longer applies.

From the general perspective of modeling equalizing differences there remains one significant area of further study. Compensating differentials apply to a wide variety of attributes, many of which can be modeled as previously stated; the model can be used to look at regional compensations because of climate, local amenities and scenery, and so on. We have also considered firm and individual specific attributes, which can include cleanliness, vacations, shift work, pension packages, probability of unemployment and danger, and so on. The preceding results, however, do not apply to compensating differentials on the basis of human capital. That is, we have not considered the equalizing variations resulting from the cost and time spent learning a trade or skills. To do so would require us to look at the model from a different perspective. We have been comparing the payoff to players with the same crowding type but different taste type, while modeling human capital would require us to consider the payoffs to players with the same tastes but different crowding type. This chapter shows how to do this, but the issue of human capital neatly fits the model of genetic types introduced in Conley and Wooders (2001). This paper generalizes the crowding types model so that players are endowed with a genetic type and not a crowding type. Players then purchase their crowding types at costs dependent on their genetic type. For example, the genetic type may be the level of intelligence, and people purchase their skill level, with players with a higher intelligence finding it cheaper to purchase a high-skill level. This question naturally fits the issue of human capital and would allow us to present a very interesting discussion of the role education and training play in the process of equalizing differences. One further issue we note for future consideration is the possibility of players belonging to more than one club. That is, a person joins a firm, then chooses the type of region he wants to live in, and finally chooses the type of jurisdiction, meaning that an agent belongs to three distinct coalitions or, alternatively, may belong to two firms. This opens up a whole range of issues as to how the model can be extended and what we can learn from doing so.

In conclusion, we presented a new way to consider two very old economic issues. Using the crowding types model, we have analyzed the process of compensating differentials in the labor market and applied this to question the law of supply. The crowding types model has previously only been used to model public-good economies, but clearly it can have a very interesting role to play in modeling firm formation. This chapter has merely addressed one possible application, but there is a whole range of issues that still remain to be studied.

References

Bennett, Elaine, and Myrna Wooders. 1979. Income distribution and firm formation. *Journal of Comparative Economics* 3:304–317.

Berglas, Eitan. 1976. Distribution of tastes and skills and the provision of local public goods. *Journal of Public Economics* 6:409–423.

Bewley, Truman. 1981. A critique of Tiebout theory of local public expenditure. *Econometrica* 49:713–740.

Brueckner, Jan K. 1994. Tastes, skills, and local public goods. *Journal of Urban Economics* 35:201–220.

Buchanan, James M. 1965. An economic theory of clubs. *Economica* 32:1–14.

Conley, John, and Myrna H. Wooders. 1996. Taste-homogeneity of optimal jurisdictions in a Tiebout economy with crowding types and endogenous educational investment choices. *Recherche Economiche* 50:367–387.

———. 1997. Equivalence of the core and competitive equilibrium in a Tiebout economy with crowding types. *Journal of Urban Economics* 41:421–440.

———. 2001. Tiebout economies with differential genetic types and endogenously chosen crowding characteristics. *Journal of Economic Theory* 98:261–294.

———. 2004. Hedonic independence and taste-homogeneity of optimal jurisdictions in a Tiebout economy with crowding types. *Les Annales d'Economie et de Statistique* 75–76: 197–216.

Davis, Otto A., and Andrew B. Whinston. 1967. On the distinction between public and private goods. *American Economic Review* 57:360–373.

DeSerpa, Allan C. 1977. A theory of discriminatory clubs. *Scottish Journal of Political Economy* 24:33–41.

DeVany, Arthur S., and Thomas R. Saving. 1977. Product quality, uncertainty, and regulation: The trucking industry. *American Economic Review* 67:583–594.

Elliot, Robert F. 1990. *Labour economics: A comparative text.* New York: McGraw-Hill.

Filer, Randall K., Daniel Hamermesh, and Albert Rees. 1996. *The economics of work and pay.* New York: HarperCollins.

Hillman, Arye L., and Peter L. Swan. 1979. Club participation under uncertainty. *Economics Letters* 4:307–312.

Kamien, Milton I., Nancy L. Schwartz, and Donald J. Roberts. 1973. Exclusion, externalities, and public goods. *Journal of Public Economics* 2:217–230.

Knight, Frank H. 1924. Some fallacies in the interpretation of social cost. *Quarterly Journal of Economics* 38:582–606.

Kovalenkov, Alexander, and Myrna Wooders. 2001. Epsilon cores of games with limited side payments: Nonemptiness and equal treatment. *Games and Economic Behavior* 36:193–218.

———. 2003. Approximate cores of games and economies with clubs. *Journal of Economic Theory* 110:87–120.

———. 2005. Laws of scarcity for a finite game: Exact bounds on estimation. *Economic Theory* 26:383–396.

———. Forthcoming. Comparative statics and laws of scarcity for games. In *Rationality and equilibrium: Essays in honor of Marcel K. Richter*, Charalambos Aliprantis, Rosa Matzkin, Daniel McFadden, John Moore, and Nicholas Yannelis, eds. Berlin: Springer.

McGuire, Martin. 1974. Group size, group homogeneity, and the aggregate provision of a pure public good under Cournot behavior. *Public Choice* 18:107–126.

———. 1991. Group composition, collective consumption, and collaborative production. *The American Economic Review* 81:1391–1407.

Millward, Robert. 1970. Exclusion costs, external economies, and market failure. *Oxford Economic Papers* 22:24–38.

Ng, Yew-Kwang, and Robert D. Tollison. 1974. A note on consumption sharing and non-exclusion rules. *Economica* 41:446–450.

Nichols, Donald, Eugene Smolensky, and T. Nicolaus Tideman. 1971. Discrimination by waiting time in merit goods. *American Economic Review* 61:312–323.

Oakland, William H. 1972. Congestion, public goods, and welfare. *Journal of Public Economics* 1:339–357.

Pauly, Mark. 1967. Clubs, commonality, and the core: An integration of game theory and the theory of public goods. *Economica* 34:314–324.

———. 1970. Cores and clubs. *Public Choice* 9:53–65.

Pigou, Arthur C. 1920. *The economics of welfare*. London: Macmillan.

Rosen, Sherwin. 1978. Substitution and division of labour. *Economica* 45:235–250.

———. 1986. The theory of equalising differences. In *Handbook of labor economics, vol. 1*, Orly Ashenfelter and Richard Layard, eds. Amsterdam: Elsevier.

Samuelson, Paul A. 1954. The pure theory of public expenditure. *Review of Economics and Statistics* 36:387–389.

Smith, Adam. 1976. *An inquiry into the nature and causes of the wealth of nations*. Chicago: The University of Chicago Press.

Tiebout, Charles M. 1956. A pure theory of local expenditures. *Journal of Political Economy* 64:416–424.

Tollison, Robert D. 1972. Consumption sharing and non-exclusion rules. *Economica* 39:279–291.

Wooders, Myrna H. 1978. Equilibria, the core, and jurisdiction structures in economies with a local public good. *Journal of Economic Theory* 18:328–348.

———. 1980. The Tiebout hypothesis: Near optimality in local public good economies. *Econometrica* 48:1467–1485.

———. 1983. The epsilon core of a large replica game. *Journal of Mathematical Economics* 11:277–300.

———. 1989. A Tiebout theorem. *Mathematical Social Sciences* 18:33–55.

———. 1992. Inessentiality of large groups and the approximate core property: An equivalence theorem. *Economic Theory* 2:129–147.

———. 1994a. Equivalence of games and markets. *Econometrica* 62:1141–1160.

———. 1994b. Large games and economies with effective small groups. In *Game-theoretic methods in general equilibrium analysis*, Jean-François Mertens and Sylvain Sorin, eds., 145–206. Dordrecht: Kluwer Academic Publishers.

———. 1997. Equivalence of Lindahl equilibria with participation prices and the core. *Economic Theory* 9:113–127.

COMMENTARY

JAN K. BRUECKNER

Chapter 9 carries out an extension of previous work by Conley and Wooders. That work generalized the standard Tiebout model, in which consumers differ only in their tastes for public goods, by assuming that individuals also exhibit different "crowding" characteristics. Some people, for example, may be heavy users of a public facility, so that their presence in a community requires higher public expenditures in order to maintain the quality of public services. Alternatively, in a model where the community's stock of private goods is produced using the labor of its residents (rather than coming from an exogenous endowment), "crowding" can be interpreted in terms of productivity. Rather than being a heavy public-facility user, a high-crowding individual would then be one with low productivity in the workplace. In either case, the presence of high-crowding individuals reduces the resources a community has at its disposal after paying public-sector costs.

The authors review the key results from their prior research on this "crowding types" model and then ask whether the "law of demand" holds within the model, in the following senses. Their first question is whether an increase in the number of individuals of a given type (with given taste and crowding characteristics) reduces the equilibrium utility they enjoy. Their second question is whether the same outcome occurs when, within each taste type, the number of individuals with particular crowding characteristics increases. Do the utilities for the members of the given crowding type decrease across the range of taste types? The answer to the first question is yes: The common utility level of individuals with a given combination of taste and crowding characteristics falls as their number increases. However, the answer to the second question is more limited: Although increasing the representation of a particular crowding type within each taste group must reduce utility for at least one taste type, some taste groups could benefit. Such an outcome, which is roughly analogous to the wage for some members of an occupational group rising instead of falling as the group's size grows, violates the authors' version of the law of demand. They provide several examples that demonstrate the outcome's feasibility.

While the reasons for the failure of the law of demand are not especially clear, changes in jurisdictional structures in response to an increased supply of agents might play a role. In other words, altering the numbers of different types of agents may have complex effects on the way individuals are organized into communities, and these effects may produce unexpected changes in utilities like those demonstrated by the authors.

To understand this point more clearly, it is useful to consider the problem of optimally organizing a set of agents into communities. In the standard Tiebout model, the features of the optimal community structure are well understood. In such a world, all individuals have identical crowding characteristics but differ in their tastes. It is then optimal to house the members of a given taste group in identical homogeneous communities, with the population of each community chosen to strike a balance between losses from crowding and the gains from the sharing of public-sector costs. This arrangement is repeated for each taste group, with the optimal community sizes possibly differing across groups. If the economy is large, individuals left over after partitioning each taste group into communities are of negligible consequence.

Suppose instead that different crowding types exist and that crowding occurs on the production side, with individuals playing different roles in the community production process for private goods. Furthermore, assume for simplicity that there are just two taste types—high and low public-good demanders, denoted H and L—and two "skill" types—1 and 2. In addition, suppose that the economy exhibits constant returns, with CRS in production and public-sector costs proportional to population. These latter assumptions imply that optimal community sizes are indeterminate. Finally, suppose that output per worker in a community is maximized with an equal skill mix in production—in other words, equal numbers of skill type 1 and skill type 2 workers.

How should the population of this economy be organized into communities? The answer depends on the relative sizes of the economy's four taste/skill groups. These groups are H-1, L-1, H-2, and L-2, where the first index refers to the taste type and the second refers to the skill type. Consider first a situation where these four groups are equal in size, each with population 100. In this case, the answer is immediate: The optimum has two taste-homogeneous communities, each of size 200. Since each community has 100 members of each skill type, the skill mix is optimal and the economy's private-good output is as high as possible. In addition, since each community is taste homogeneous, the public-good level can be exactly tailored to suit individual preferences. Note that the indeterminacy of community size allows each taste group to be housed in a single community.

If the taste/skill groups are instead unequal in size, then the simplicity of this solution vanishes. For example, suppose that the sizes of the groups are as follows: H-1 has 150 individuals, L-1 has 50, H-2 has 50, and L-2 has 150. Now taste-homogeneous communities would have nonoptimal skill mixes, with the H community having a 150/50 skill type 1/skill type 2 ratio and the L community having a 50/150 ratio (both communities have size 200). While public-good levels would be tailored to suit community populations, these undesirable skill mixes sacrifice private-good output. In a different arrangement, one community would have size 300, containing 150 H-1 individuals and 150 L-2 individuals, with a second size-100 community having 50 H-2 and 50 L-1 individuals (with constant returns, everyone could equivalently be housed in a single community of size 400). In either case, the community skill mix is correct, but preference diversity requires a compromise in the provision of public goods.

Which of these two arrangements is superior depends on the extent of preference divergence between the H and L groups and on the production loss from a nonoptimal skill mix. But neither of the arrangements may itself be optimal, with the best community structure instead representing an intermediate degree of mixing of tastes and skills. For example, the optimum could have two size-200 communities, with community A having 120 H-1s, 50 H-2s, and 30 L-2s, and community B having 30 H-1s, 50 L-1s, and 120 L-2s. In this situation, each community comes close to the ideal 1:1 skill mix (with a ratio of 120/80 in A and 80/120 in B), but this adjustment is limited in order to maintain some semblance of preference homogeneity.

These principles are further explored in Brueckner (1994), who analyzes a model with just two groups, H-1 and L-2, building on the previous analysis of Berglas (1976). In this setting, the absence of two of the taste/skill combinations precludes the creation of taste-homogeneous communities with the correct skill mix, as in the first example above. As a result, the optimum always involves compromise: Taste-homogeneous communities require a sacrifice of output, and skill-optimized communities require compromise in the provision of public goods, as in the related second example above. Brueckner's analysis shows that the first arrangement is optimal if labor complementarity is weak (reducing the importance of the skill mix) or when preference diversity is substantial.

The previous work of Conley and Wooders has very little to say about the makeup of optimal communities, mainly because few general results are available. Instead, their work is mainly devoted to demonstrating that an optimal community structure, *whatever its features*, is an equilibrium structure in an appropriately decentralized economy. But as suggested above, the issue of community structure may be tied to their negative results on the law of demand. For example, suppose in the last example above that the number of skill type 1 workers increases, with the number of L-1 agents in community B increasing and the number of H-1 agents increasing in both communities. Holding the community structure fixed, this change will depress the productivity of skill type 1 agents in both communities given diminishing returns, tending to reduce their utilities. In addition, taste type H preferences will now carry more weight in the public-good choice in community A, a beneficial effect that may dominate the effect of lower productivity, making the H-1 agents in A better off. Moreover, if the H-1 increase in community B is not too large relative to the L-1 increase, then taste type H preferences receive less weight in the community's public-good choice, reinforcing the negative productivity effect and making H-1 individuals worse off.

With H-1 utilities possibly moving in opposite directions in the two communities, maintenance of a common utility level may thus require reallocation of the H-1 population (and possibly that of other types) across communities. The ultimate effect could be an increase in the common utility level for type H-1 agents. This discussion is, of course, entirely speculative, and a proper treatment would require more information on preferences and production technologies. But the discussion indicates that increases in the supply of agents may generate complex adjustments in community structures that may lead to unexpected outcomes.

REFERENCES

Berglas, Eitan. 1976. Distribution of tastes and skills and the provision of local public goods. *Journal of Public Economics* 6:409–423.

Brueckner, Jan K. 1994. Tastes, skills, and local public goods. *Journal of Urban Economics* 35:201–220.

IO

Tiebout—Stability and Efficiency: The Examples of Australia and South Africa

JEFFREY PETCHEY

PERRY SHAPIRO

In 1954 Paul Samuelson published the conditions necessary for efficient provision of pure public goods. He concluded, pessimistically, that it would be impossible to implement his criteria because individual preferences for public goods are not measurable. Charles Tiebout (1956) responded with a free-market analog in which public goods are provided by community service clubs and community competition results in the spatial segregation of individuals into separate excludable public-good clubs. The speculation is that the invisible hand of perfect competition drives the outcome to an efficient level of public-good provision. The model, as Tiebout originally set it down, envisions coalitions of like-minded people (individuals with similar public-good preferences) congregating in one location to choose a bundle of public goods. The utility of this model is that, if true, individuals reveal their preferences for public goods by selecting a community, and Samuelson's preference revelation problem is solved. The structure proposed by Tiebout has been so compelling that it has found use in much of the literature about intercommunity public-good choices. There is also promise (not yet realized) that a first-welfare theorem for public goods is lurking in the Tiebout-type world.

The Tiebout speculation generated much interest and has influenced a diverse literature. There are, however, some incomplete aspects to the Tiebout conjecture. For example, underlying the presumed efficacy of the competitive community–population mobility world are two critical conditions. The first is that community formation arrangements and agreements on free mobility are

295

stable. The entire Tiebout play takes place within a stable (national) environment, one in which there are no intercommunity externalities. The other is that population and factors of production generally are freely mobile and that such mobility is externality free.

If these conditions are met, there is no need for an overriding central government. Communities (public-good clubs) form, guided only by market forces, and efficiency is achieved through the invisible hand of competition. This idea has played an important role in the literature on federalism. The writings of Albert Breton (1984) show that a federal structure works well with states acting as competitive clubs.

Others working in the federalism field, such as Buchanan and Goetz (1972), recognized that, if there are region-specific economic rents and migration-related fiscal externalities influencing the location decisions made by mobile factors of production, Tiebout-type outcomes may be globally inefficient. The world envisaged in the Tiebout model does not consider the existence of such influences on location decisions. It thus rules out the possibility that mobility and competition can be a source of inefficiency. The possibility of locational distortions reestablishes a potential role for government policy because it raises the question again of inefficient provision of public goods.

This is not a criticism of Tiebout's original article because his setting is more applicable to local governments rather than national regions, such as provinces or states, which are the concern of the Buchanan and Goetz article. Local governments, unlike national regions, can control migration through zoning and therefore can, at least in principle, achieve an optimal local population even in the presence of migration-related externalities (Hamilton 1975).

Nevertheless, Flatters, Henderson, and Mieszkowski (1974) took up the Buchanan and Goetz idea on potential inefficiency at the national region level using a more formal analysis. They adopted a multiregion model with externalities and rents, optimizing regional governments and labor migration to satisfy an equal-utility condition. From this they derived the necessary conditions for a decentralized equilibrium and for a globally efficient outcome achieved by a central planner. The authors compare the two sets of necessary conditions to show that in general the decentralized equilibrium is inefficient—confirming the Buchanan and Goetz results. Therefore, even in a world in which jurisdictions choose local policies to make their citizens as well off as possible, the distribution of productive factors is inefficient.

The next advance in this literature tackled the inefficiency problem in order to find policy instruments that might be used to establish global efficiency in a regional economy with distorted location choices. For example, in an important paper, Boadway and Flatters (1982) use a model similar to the one adopted by Flatters et al. They show that a decentralized (Nash) equilibrium is globally efficient if a central authority mandates an interstate "fiscal equalization" transfer that corrects for the migration effects of location-specific externalities and rents. This idea generated a new literature on the so-called efficiency case for fiscal equalization transfers in decentralized economies, including federations.[1] It has had an important impact on the design of equalization systems in many developed countries, including Canada, Australia, and Japan.[2] Though it changes the basic orientation of Tiebout's original work, which was more about local jurisdictions, this literature was clearly motivated by the Tiebout hypothesis and has become an important strand within the literature on fiscal federalism.

In the world envisaged by Tiebout, the stability of political union between the local jurisdictions is not an issue. But if the Tiebout idea is extended to national regions, the implicit assumption of stability is important. Although many contemporary unions of states, such as the United States, Canada, and Australia, are stable, it has taken a long time for this stability to evolve. For example, it was necessary for the United States to suffer through a prolonged and costly civil war to establish a stable union. Australia spent many years negotiating its federating constitution of 1901, which established the bargains that formed one nation from six separate crown colonies. Even then the country faced serious secessionist threats during the 1930s, which were solved through the implementation of a system of interstate compensatory transfers. It is only within these stable unions that the Tiebout process has a hope of achieving its promised efficiency.

Therefore, Tiebout's original article raises two questions when applied to national regions. The first relates to the efficiency of location choices in the presence of externalities. The second pertains to the need for stability of any union between regions and the implications of instability for Tiebout-type results. In this chapter, we examine both questions in a world of interregional migration and jurisdictional competition between national regions. We use the historical context and experience of two countries: a long-term stable federation—Australia—and a newly emerging, decentralized economy—South Africa. Some of the institutional arrangements and public policies in both countries are designed to counteract the problems that arise in a Tiebout-type world of unregulated competition between national regions. Our discussion starts with the question of stability and then examines interregional location efficiency in the presence of externalities.

---

[1] For a succinct discussion of the efficiency-in-migration case for equalization, see Boadway (2004).

[2] A more recent paper to appear in this field—Boadway, Cuff, and Marchand (2003)—uses a three-stage game setup and shows what instruments must be assigned by the center to the regions and what interstate transfers must be made for a decentralized equilibrium to replicate the globally efficient unitary nation outcome.

Stability

The Tiebout model presents some problems when it is applied to larger regions within a nation, when the assumption is that the union of communities is stable enough to allow free migration and residential choice. The origin of the communities and the political structure under which they are formed has always been considered unimportant. But the cases of Australia and South Africa show that community (i.e., state and province) formation and growth have been central to the political economy of those nations. As a result, policies and institutions designed to maintain stability have been developed.

How does the structure for free movement between communities, so necessary for the Tiebout world, evolve? Communities that participate in a union either must benefit from the union or their participation must be coerced. When they join a union, should they be able to drop out and change unions if better opportunities arise? The movement of individuals in search of the best public-good club[3] is an essential feature of the Tiebout model. Is it desirable that the initial union of communities be permitted to freely shop around for union partners?

While it can be argued that original participants in the U.S. constitutional agreement understood that free disassociation was an option,[4] there was no such illusion in the case of Australia. The constitution that created Australia from the separate crown colonies that spanned the continent ensured a strong central power by concentrating all of the public fiscal ability in the central government. The bargain was consummated with transfers from the prosperous colonies of New South Wales and Victoria to the less prosperous states.

Australia

In 1901 the Australian colonies federated to create one nation with a single federal constitution. Major tax powers were ceded to the new federal government as part of the federation settlement. One concession granted the center the exclusive right to levy excise taxes in Section 90 of the constitution. The founders most likely did this because they were afraid states might use excise taxes to interfere with the intended effects of federal tariff policy (Coper 1988). They were also concerned about the potential for excise tax competition between states to distort free internal trade.[5] The general population had fears about the negative effects of intercolonial rivalry, the impact on federal

---

[3] "Exit" according to Hirshman (1970).

[4] This belief motivated the Nullification Movement championed by Calhoun (1953).

[5] Using a model of interstate excise tax competition and comparing the outcomes with those obtained under the centralized tax (i.e., Section 90 applies), Shapiro and Petchey (1994) conclude that these fears were groundless.

stability, and the need for the states to pursue common interests through cooperation. Whatever the intent, the state excise tax exclusion left the states financially weak. In the now-famous words of Alfred Deakin (1902), one of the key instigators of the Australian union, Section 90 left the states "financially bound to the Chariot wheels of the central Government" (17).

Since federation, both judicial opinions and the financial exigencies of World War II have given the commonwealth an effective tax-power monopoly. The High Court of Australia's interpretation of the meaning of an *excise* tax proved unfavorable for the states. Given the lack of clarity in the constitution about its meaning, the High Court was left to offer its own interpretation. In the first case to be considered, *Peterswald v. Bartley*, 1 CLR 497 (1904), the court adopted an economist's view of an excise—namely, that it was a tax on production. This left the states free, in principle, to impose other consumption-type taxes, including general sales or value-added taxes. But this view was soon abandoned in favor of a more expansive interpretation of *excise*, an interpretation that has effectively kept the states from adopting any consumption tax, including sales taxes (as in the United States) or value-added taxes (Petchey and Wells 2004). Thus, the excise tax exclusion within Section 90, together with the High Court's broad interpretation of *excise*, has excluded the states from the consumption tax base.[6] With sales removed as a source of state revenue, personal income became the primary state-specific tax base. However, during World War II the income tax was ceded exclusively to the federal government as a wartime measure. After the war, this power was never returned to the states.

Thus, the Australian states have no direct access to the income tax or consumption tax bases and rely for their revenue on a relatively small set of potential tax bases, including payroll, land, franchise fees, and a range of other minor tax instruments. At the same time, however, they have the dominant expenditure responsibilities (health, education, transportation infrastructure, provision of energy and water). As a result, there is a large fiscal gap in Australia (excess of revenue over direct expenditures) at the federal level, requiring transfers back to the states in a long-running revenue-sharing arrangement.

In 2000 the federal government introduced a new broad-based, value-added tax: the Goods and Services Tax (GST). All of the revenue from this tax is passed back to the states as unconditional transfers in exchange for a reduction or elimination of existing state taxes (e.g., many of the duties on financial

---

[6] There were, until recently, three exceptions: The states were allowed to levy franchise fees on tobacco, alcohol, and petroleum products. The court justified this by arguing that franchise fees are taxes on the right to conduct business rather than consumption itself (this interpretation relied on the use of the previous year's sales as the fee base). Recently, however, even these loopholes have been closed. Now the commonwealth collects franchise fees, and the revenue is returned to the states using a distribution formula.

institutions are to be abolished). The center argues that this is really a state tax, levied and collected by them on behalf of the states because of the Section 90 excise tax exclusion. But because the federal government has the power to set the rate and decide what to do with the revenue, the tax has only worsened both the size of the fiscal gap and state financial dependence.[7]

Financial dependence, and the resultant large fiscal gap, meant that large transfers had to be made to the states immediately after federation. It was also widely recognized that the net social surplus from the federal union was not spread evenly across the states. Indeed, some states—the so-called small states of Western Australia, Tasmania, and South Australia—had been net losers from the federal union. These states suffered because their economies were based on agriculture and extraction. The dominant economies of New South Wales and Victoria (the richest states in the union) were more industrial and relied on high-tariff protection.[8] As just noted, the power to levy customs duties was handed exclusively to the new federal government with federation, and the smaller agricultural states had to accept the high-tariff policy of the two dominant states. It was then determined that, at least over some transitional period, compensatory transfers would have to be made to these states in the interest of federal stability. Thus, transfers made in the Australian federation in the period immediately following federation had two clear rationales: to close a fiscal gap and to compensate some states. These issues were settled through a series of "transitional arrangements." The return of general revenue, necessitated by the fiscal gap, was guaranteed through Sections 89, 93, and 94 of the constitution to ensure that each state got revenues directly related to the monthly revenue surplus (over expenditure) of the commonwealth. Each state's share of this surplus was determined on an equal per capita basis, which is mildly equalizing in favor of the poorer states. The Braddon Clause (Section 87) was also included to guarantee that the states received three-quarters of all federal revenue from customs and excise duties. Section 96 was the primary measure designed to deal with the issue of compensatory payments. This allowed the federal government to give financial assistance to any state on any terms it saw fit.

By 1910 most of these arrangements had come to an end (May 1971, 6). Just before this time, intense negotiations about longer-term intergovernmental financial arrangements took place. Agreement was reached in 1909, and by 1912 a system was established that gave annual grants to the states on a per capita basis that would replace the transitional arrangements. In addition, special

---

[7] Presently the federal government is threatening to withhold GST grants to the states because they claim that the states have been slow to reduce their existing taxes following introduction of the GST. The states are threatening to withdraw support for some federal/state agreements if the center proceeds with this threat.

[8] This is similar to the Civil War struggle of northern versus southern U.S. states.

compensatory payments continued to be made to Western Australia and Tasmania.

In the 1920s the claim by the smaller, primary-resource states that they needed compensatory transfers intensified as the federal government increased uniform external tariffs. An official inquiry was conducted about the impact of the higher external tariffs on Western Australia's economy, with the conclusion that the state had indeed suffered from the uniform tariff. During this period other sources of grievance for the so-called small states emerged. First, the Navigation Act of 1921 produced considerable conflict by imposing uniform shipping and navigation laws. Second, the center established a system of federal minimum wage laws. The Commonwealth Conciliation and Arbitration Act encouraged states to increase wages to federally determined levels.

In 1924 the federal government established a Royal Commission on the Finances of Western Australia as Affected by the Federation. It recommended that the state be compensated for its losses or "disabilities" from federation. In Tasmania a similar commission was established and among its deliberations noted the following:

> The particular disabilities of Tasmania under Federation merge at all points into the more general disabilities to which weaker states are always liable in any system of federation, unless clear safeguards are taken against them. . . . In particular, it is clear that a state like Tasmania, small both in area and population—even without regard to its insular position—is under a severe handicap in a federation which adopts internal free trade and heavy protection against the rest of the world, along with the other methods of regulating industry. . . . All such regulation is inevitably designed and administered from the point of view of the principal constituent states. Unless this position is fairly met, Federation must be an incomplete success, with certain flourishing and prosperous states dragging their harassed sisters at their heels. . . . (May 1971, 11)

As May also highlights, the growing complaints of the smaller states in the 1920s "reflected a general feeling of discontent over the outcome of federation in the smaller states, a feeling that the smaller states were not participating fully in the nation's development and this was due at least in part to the fact that the large states by virtue of their size were able to dictate the broad trend of federal policies" (8).

Unlike the Western Australian Royal Commission, the Tasmanian Commission did not recommend a system of compensatory payments. However, it did propose a system of differential per capita payments with the aim of "equalizing the more general economic conditions between states." The first clear statement of the concept of equalizing fiscal capacities across states, this was a clear departure from the notion of compensating states directly for the disabilities resulting from federation. The idea can be attributed to the presence of two economists on the Tasmanian Royal Commission: J. F. Giblin and J. B. Brigden. Indeed, Giblin attached a separate report to the Commission's findings, which included an analysis of the economic effects of federation on Tasmania. He concluded that these effects could not be measured and that federation disabilities were not an appropriate basis for determining grants in a federation. Rather, he argued, "relative state fiscal positions" were a more appropriate foundation for a system of state grants.

During this time other inquiries took place, and the system of ad hoc compensatory transfers continued. Rising discontent fed the development of secessionist sentiment in two states, Western Australia and Tasmania, in the late 1920s and early 1930s. By 1931 the center faced a plethora of demands from the small states for special transfers, and the Great Depression placed further pressure on weak state finances. Largely in response to these pressures and the perceived need to place the whole system of intergovernmental transfers onto a consistent and sound footing, the federal government formed the Commonwealth Grants Commission (CGC) in 1933. By 1936 the CGC had developed a set of principles to formalize special (compensation) payments to the states.

On the surface, these principles rejected the notion that states should be compensated for the effects of federation. Indeed, the CGC went out of its way to reject the idea of compensation as the basis for future transfers.[9] Arguments used by the Commission were that (1) compensation for the effects of a Commonwealth Government policy would be inconsistent with the aims of that policy; (2) compensating states for the disabilities they may have suffered from federation posed insurmountable statistical and theoretical difficulties (i.e., federation disabilities cannot be measured); (3) states suffering net disabilities from federal policy may be prosperous in any case and hence require no grant, and, conversely, if a state was in financial difficulties, whether due to federalism or not, it would require assistance regardless of the cause; and (4) federation would be meaningless on a strict bookkeeping basis of costs and benefits; federating states should commit themselves to absorbing both the costs and the benefits.

Instead, the CGC adopted a "needs-based" approach to transfers, an approach that is still the basis of transfers today. The Commission stated the following:

> Special grants are justified when a state through financial stress from any
> cause is unable efficiently to discharge its functions as a member of the

---

[9] At the time the small states and the federal treasury were both arguing for compensation as the basis for Australia's transfer system.

federation and should be determined by the amount of help found necessary to make it possible for that state by reasonable effort to function at a
standard not appreciably below that of other states. (May 1971, 63)

The CGC clearly realized that a needs-based approach to transfers would
also compensate for the disabilities of federation. Recognizing that any federation disabilities would be reflected in the financial position of the states, the
CGC stated the following:

> We recognize also that the Commonwealth cannot afford to see a state
> drifting into a financial breakdown and that grants to set it on its feet may
> be necessary. On these two grounds also the evidence of a state's disability
> should be found in its budgetary conditions. It seems therefore to be
> unavoidable to use as some measure of the disability the financial position
> of the state. (May 1971, 161)

The system based on the needs principle, which was really a proxy for compensating for federation disabilities, was used explicitly in the Australian transfer system until the late 1960s. It eventually evolved into the principle of fiscal-
capacity equalization, as the following comment from the Commonwealth
Grants Commission (1983) shows:

> By 1967 the Commission had begun to interpret its principle as one of fis-
> cal equalization rather than financial need. . . . There was no intrinsic
> philosophical reason for preferring either principle to the other. (80)

In summary, regardless of their official justification today, fiscal-capacity
equalization and the Commonwealth Grants Commission have their origins in
earlier conflicts over the net gains from federation and the perceived need to
secure the stability of the union. The needs-based approach, which underpins
equalization, is clearly a proxy for compensating for the costs of federal union
or, in other words, redistributing the net surplus from the union to ensure that
no state was left worse off after 1901. Thus, the first years of intergovernmental
relations in Australia were dominated by a struggle over compensatory payments and the distribution of the net surplus of federation. The development
of the principle of fiscal equalization, with large interstate transfers, is
Australia's particular response to the need to formalize compensation to those
states that had lost from federation in order to ensure federal unity. National
stability may well have been the main motivation for interstate transfers rather
than the common view that equity underlies Australian equalization.[10]

---

[10] Contrast this with the view of Gramlich (1984), who argued that Australia's insistence on equalization is a manifestation of its "fair go" equity ethos. This demonstrates why economists, even very good
ones like Gramlich, should be wary about venturing into political sociology.

South Africa

Although economic disparities existed among the colonies that made up the Australian union in 1901, they were minuscule compared to the differences among many of the regions of post-apartheid South Africa (that is, post-1994). In stark contrast to Australia, South Africa was characterized from 1948 (when Afrikaners wrested political power from the English-speaking whites) to 1994 by a regime of apartheid under which people were segregated geographically on the basis of race. The stability of the apartheid state was guaranteed not through monetary transfers but through military repression, much as in the former Soviet Union and Yugoslavia, for example. Free migration within South Africa, and between South Africa and the rest of the world, was barred or controlled, at least for many nonwhites.

This required a highly centralized system of government with an all-powerful center and weak regional governance. Taxation and public spending in the apartheid state were highly centralized. No system of semiautonomous communities resembling states or provinces existed, but there were some local governments that depended heavily on the center. General administrative "regions" were created for nonwhites—also strictly controlled by the center. These regions were created more for the control of the spatial allocation of the nonwhite population than for economic reasons. Other instruments introduced during the apartheid era to control the geographic location of nonwhites included the unpopular "pass laws" that limited the movement of people between areas. These were so onerous that they led to industrial unrest, mass arrests, and, indirectly, the development of the African National Congress (ANC) party as a major political opposition force.[11]

During the talks held prior to the move to a democratic system in 1994, the idea of adopting a different governance model was examined—namely, a more decentralized federal state with semi-independent provinces with their own tax and spending powers. Some consideration was also given to the creation of a federation with states or provinces drawn up along racial lines—much like Iraq. However, none of these proposals was implemented, partly because of concerns over the cohesion and stability of a decentralized state.

Instead, the ANC pushed for the new state to be highly centralized with an all-powerful central government in full control of all tax and spending instruments, although barriers to free internal migration were removed (see following). In a limited move toward the decentralization of power, nine provinces were created. However, they do not function as provinces or states would

---

[11] An intriguing description of the means used to control the movement of nonwhites during the apartheid era can be found in Nelson Mandela's book *Long Walk to Freedom* (1994).

function in a truly federal system, since they have no tax powers and no access to capital markets. Instead, they act merely as spending agents of the central government, "responsible" for providing education, health, transportation, housing, and welfare services funded entirely through grants from the center. The South African constitution also established a national institution directly responsible to Parliament, the Financial and Fiscal Commission (FFC), whose main function is to oversee and make recommendations on the efficiency and fairness of the system of grants to the provinces. Though the national government, and in particular the National Treasury, has the ultimate power to determine the size of the transfers to provinces, as well as their distribution between provinces, the constitution requires that the FFC be consulted and its recommendations considered on all matters relating to these grants.

Thus, stability has certainly been an issue in post-apartheid South Africa. The main response has been to create a powerful central government while at the same time attempting to obtain some of the advantages that decentralization offers through the establishment of provinces responsible for allocating expenditures. The provinces are nonetheless tied tightly to the central government financially—even more so than in Australia.[12] The FFC is also a major institution set up to try to ensure that the system created is efficient and fair. In this sense, it can be regarded, at least indirectly, as a key institution within a system that was created with stability concerns in mind. The comparison here with Australia is also instructive: Australia's solution to stability issues was to create a system of explicit compensatory transfers, which was necessary because the Australian states had more autonomy than their South African provincial counterparts, while South Africa's response has been to maintain a strong center. Unlike Australia, South Africa has no system of fiscal equalization or other direct interprovincial transfers, although the grants that do occur to the provinces have some mild implicit interprovincial redistribution built into them. The grants are not made on a simple, equal per capita basis but are based on various poverty indicators. It implies that some redistribution from richer to poorer regions is built into the current system, but this is much less than the interstate redistribution in the Australian system.

South Africa's reliance on a strong central state to maintain stability is now changing because there is no longer the fear of the threats to stability of the years immediately following the post-apartheid state. Rather, it is now recognized that not enough has been done to alleviate poverty through redistribution and higher economic growth. This is mainly because in the 10 years

---

[12] The word *federal* does not apply to South Africa; rather, it is viewed domestically as a decentralized unitary state, and the different governments (national, provincial, and local) are considered "spheres" to nullify the idea that South Africa is in any way a federation.

following the end of apartheid, the concern of the national government has been to entrench macroeconomic stability and reduce the level of national debt inherited from the last years of the apartheid regime. Now that these goals have been achieved, the worry is that poverty rather than political and cultural differences is the future threat to the general social stability of the country. Out of a population of about 40 million, nearly 25 million people live in conditions more consistent with standards in Africa generally: limited or no access to basic services such as education and health, a high incidence of diseases such as AIDS, and unemployment. The other 15 million or so live in conditions more comparable with a developed economy such as the United States or Australia. The effects of poverty on such a scale, and the highly visible gap between the so-called first and third worlds, all within one country, are extremely high crime rates and a large number of increasingly alienated people with no stake in the stability of the economic or social fabric of their country.

Poverty also has a regional dimension in South Africa. Table 10.1 shows estimates of the (per capita) value of the stock of public capital by province for five services: education, health, transport, welfare, and housing. Table 10.1 highlights the interprovincial variation in access to public capital for these basic public services. Comparable figures for a country such as Australia, for example, show a much higher degree of uniformity in public capital per person (Levtchenkova and Petchey 2000). Much of this regional inequity is the result of apartheid, which deliberately gave developed world standards of hospitals, schools, and economic infrastructure to some regions at the expense of others. Also note that these highly aggregated data hide variations within provinces (no official capital stock data at the subprovincial level are available).

Therefore, to alleviate poverty in South Africa, policy makers must deal with regional disparities. Poverty cannot be eradicated overnight, mostly because of limited economic resources. As a result, the national government, and in particular the FFC, is developing a new system of interprovincial transfers that will achieve the progressive reduction of overall levels of poverty and address the interprovincial inequities. The grant scheme will also take explicit account of macroeconomic constraints on available resources and the feedback between higher investment in services that build human capital, such as health and education, and future economic growth.[13]

In summary, like Australia, in South Africa there was a need to ensure the cohesion and stability of the pre- and post-apartheid state. Unlike Australia, this was achieved through a strong central government with financial dominance rather than interregional compensatory payments. But more recently

---

[13] Full details of the poverty-reduction program and the economic modeling work being undertaken can be found in Petchey, MacDonald, and Josie (2005).

TABLE 10.1

Public Capital Stock (per Capita) by Provincial Region (for Education, Health, Transport, Welfare, and Housing), South Africa, 2002

	Real Public Capital Stock (1995 Prices) Rand Million	Population (in thousands)	Real Public Capital Stock, Rand per Capita
Western Cape	6,912.0	4,315.6	1,601.6
Eastern Cape	4,058.1	7,135.9	568.7
Northern Cape	1,742.8	888.6	1,961.3
Free State	3,085.9	2,860.1	1,078.9
Kwa Zulu Natal	17,608.1	9,215.8	1,910.7
North West	6,017.8	3,661.3	1,643.6
Gauteng	12,831.6	8,109.7	1,582.3
Mpumalanga	5,404.7	3,157.9	1,711.5
Limpopo	4,745.2	5,848.2	811.4
All Provinces	62,407	45,193.1	1,380.9

Source: MacDonald, Petchey, and Josie (2005).

concerns over new threats to stability have emerged. This has seen the creation of more targeted and specific policy instruments—namely, a grant scheme that will target poverty on a general national basis but regionally, as well.

Efficiency

Besides being silent on the stability of regional communities, the world envisaged by our extension of Tiebout ignores the potential for distortions to location decisions and, thus, a breakdown in the free-market analog for efficient provision of public goods. These location distortions arise from the underlying features of regional communities, which may extract differential rents from the exploitation of natural resources, and the operation of regional tax and expenditure policies.

It is common that the analyses of location distortions use models with benevolent optimizing regional governments that provide a single local public good (which may be pure or congested) to freely mobile homogeneous citizens who also consume a single private good. Some versions include capital as the migrating factor of production. The equilibrium allocation of mobile factors across regions satisfies various equal payoff rules: for labor, equal per capita utility, and, for capital, equal marginal products or rates of return. The models also adopt simple production technologies in which regional output is a function of the supply of the mobile factor(s) for some fixed supply of a region-specific input such as natural resources (Boadway and Flatters 1982).

Unlike Tiebout's intrametropolitan model, in which no community has significant market power, these models assume a small (usually two for mathematical tractability), fixed number of communities (states). Thus, each state has significant market power, contrary to Tiebout's perfect-competition condition. In addition, the mobile factor is assumed to be homogeneous, though the equilibrium factor returns (e.g., wage rates for labor) can differ across regions. The communities and mobile factors play a simultaneous-move "regional competition game." The benevolent regional governments independently choose their public policies with Nash conjectures (the policy vector may include taxes on fixed and mobile factors and levels of provision of local public goods), and the mobile factors make location choices.[14] The necessary conditions for Nash equilibria are analyzed, and it is shown that each state provides its local public good consistent with the Samuelson rule.[15]

The conditions necessary for Nash equilibria of regional competition games are compared with the conditions required for global efficiency. The latter are found by solving the optimization problem faced by a mythical and benevolent central planner. The planner chooses private- and public-good provision in any one of the states to maximize per capita utility, while keeping per capita utility in the other state(s) fixed, conditional on national feasibility and mobile factor migration constraints.[16]

Two necessary conditions must be satisfied for global optimality. The first is that each jurisdiction supplies local public goods in quantities that equate the sum of marginal rates of substitution with the marginal cost (the Samuelson rule). The second is that mobile factors must be allocated efficiently across jurisdictions. For this to be true, the marginal net benefit of an additional citizen-factor must be the same in all jurisdictions. While jurisdictional supply of public goods will satisfy the Samuelson condition, it is unlikely, unless states are identical, that free migration induces an efficient factor allocation.

What policy instruments might be used to establish efficiency in this Tiebout-type world with free migration? One option, demonstrated in Appendix A, is to use an interstate transfer, which aims to correct for the

---

[14] Alternatively, the games may be sequential with, for example, regional governments moving simultaneously in stage one and labor making its location choices in the second stage (Boadway, Cuff, and Marchand 2004).

[15] A two-state model with these features is set out formally in Part 1 of Appendix A. There, the necessary conditions are derived for a Nash equilibrium of a regional competition game (in the model employed only labor is mobile).

[16] This problem is examined in Part 2 of Appendix A.

distortions to location decisions and establishes an optimal allocation of the mobile factor consistent with the equating at the margin rule. The transfer is a function of the state-specific fiscal and rent externalities. Boadway and Flatters (1988) originally proposed that the transfer should be mandated by a central authority, thus providing a rationale for centrally mandated "equalization" transfers on efficiency grounds. However, Myers (1990) has shown that if the set of instruments available to regions is expanded to include lump-sum transfers, the states will have an incentive to make the optimal transfer themselves (see also Mansoorian and Myers [1993] and the discussion in Wellisch [2000]). States "purchase" the optimal population distribution using the transfer, since this maximizes their (equal) per capita utility. In this case the Nash equilibrium is efficient, as there is incentive-equivalence between regions, induced by the presence of free migration.

Myers opened up a new avenue of inquiry. The inefficiencies of the regional-Tiebout equilibrium are explained by the inadequacy of available policy instruments. With sufficient population homogeneity,[17] if states are allowed to make and accept transfers to and from each other independent of central government mandate, the efficient population distribution is an equilibrium outcome. Appendix B shows that this insight holds true even if the population is not homogeneous. This is done with a second-best notion: policy-option-constrained efficiency.

The constrained strategy set is the set of policy instruments (taxes, transfers, public expenditures, and regulations) that are available to a state. States may be prohibited from using certain policy choices—for instance, those that contravene constitutional prohibitions on tariffs on interstate commerce—even though their use might be welfare improving. If an outcome is policy-option-constrained efficient, no other set of feasible (within the constrained set of choices) policies can improve the welfare of all states without diminishing the welfare of some others. The policy-option-constrained efficient population distribution is the one that is the best that can be achieved with the policy options available. Myers showed that the global optimum is supported as a Nash equilibrium of the (implicit) game played between states if the necessary redistributive policy options are feasible. We show that with sufficient homogeneity, all policy-constrained efficient policies are Nash equilibria in a Tiebout world.

Australia

The requirements for policy-constrained efficiency are unlikely to be met in any modern country, including Australia, with its culturally and ethnically

---

[17] Myers's homogeneity condition is severe: a single type homogeneous population. In Burbidge and Myers (1994) the restrictive condition is relaxed to homogeneous groups, but all states must have the same ordering of group welfare and some of each group in residence in every state.

heterogeneous population. Even if states were given the power to make and receive direct money transfers to and from each other, it is unlikely that they would be made. Although it is true that the more wealthy states (New South Wales, Victoria, and Western Australia) understand the advantage from maintaining the economic strength of the less fortunate states, it is unlikely that there would be the political will within any of those states to undertake unilateral transfers. By the nature of the constitutional compact and the allocation of fiscal powers, it falls to the commonwealth—the Australian national government—to coordinate the desired transfers.

Today in Australia, grants to the states are made using the principle of fiscal-capacity equalization that, as noted before, has its origins in the 1930s and the struggle over compensation payments for the disabilities of federation. The motivation for modern equalization, and its links with the needs-based rationale of the past, can be seen in this statement from the *Commonwealth Budget Paper No. 3* on the aims of equalization in Australia today:

> States should receive funding from the Commonwealth such that, if each made the same effort to raise revenue from its own tax bases and operated at the same level of efficiency, each would have the capacity to provide services at the same standard. (18)

The equalization model allocates a grant to each state, which is equal to its per capita share of the pool of funds plus an estimate of its "revenue need" and its "expenditure need." Generally, states with relatively high costs of providing public services will have positive expenditure needs (and vice versa), where the costs of provision are captured using "cost disabilities." States with relatively strong tax bases will have negative revenue needs (and vice versa), where the strength of tax bases is measured using "revenue disabilities." Hence, a state can receive less than its equal per capita share of the grant pool, or more, depending on the interaction between its expenditure and revenue needs. For example, if a state is estimated to have positive revenue and expenditure needs, its equalization grant will be greater than its equal per capita share of the grant pool. On the other hand, if a state has negative revenue and expenditure needs (or if one need is negative and the other positive, but the net value is negative), it will receive less than its equal per capita share. The model also has a "balanced grant" condition to ensure that the sum of the state-specific grants exactly exhausts the grant pool available for distribution.

Application of the model in Australia results in New South Wales, Victoria, and Western Australia—all relatively high per capita income states—receiving a grant less than their equal per capita share, while the remaining states (Tasmania, South Australia, and Queensland) and territories (Northern Territory and the Australian Capital Territory) receive more than their equal per capita share. The implication is that the equalization model redistributes income across states by way of interstate transfers. Until recently the pattern of interstate transfers resulting from equalization was similar to the one that applied during the pre-CGC period (up to 1933) when grants were driven by the requirement to maintain federal stability and compensate for the disabilities of federation.[18]

How efficient is Australian equalization in terms of the location-efficiency arguments discussed previously? We know from that discussion that two conditions must be satisfied for global efficiency in a Tiebout-style economy: Local public goods must be supplied according to the Samuelson condition, and there must be an efficient interstate equalization transfer to establish an efficient allocation of mobile factors. Consider spatial efficiency first. Petchey and Levtchenkova (2004) have argued that the interstate transfer that occurs under Australian equalization is not the one required for global efficiency (discussed previously). This is because the optimal transfer is a function of relative net benefits between states, while the capacity equalization transfer under equalization is a function of the factors used to estimate expenditure and revenue needs—namely, cost and revenue disabilities.[19] Because the assessment of expenditure and revenue needs includes variables chosen directly by the states, Australian equalization also has the potential to induce strategic behavior by states. States can affect the size of their equalization grants by changing their provision of local public goods. This is an additional source of inefficiency (Petchey and Levtchenkova 2004).

Thus, one can conclude that although Australia has a sophisticated system of equalization, it is not the model required to correct for location distortions due to externalities. This is not surprising, since, as previously argued, Australian equalization has its origins in concerns over federal stability, not location efficiency and efficient local public-good provision. The modern equalization model can be traced to its origins in the 1930s and the federal stability rationale, even if today it is couched more in terms of expenditure and revenue needs.

No one today seriously claims that the Australian union is unstable. Any stability rationale for such transfers has surely gone. What remains, however, is a system that has evolved from stability concerns but that now has built-in design inefficiencies: It establishes the potential for strategic behavior and possibly encourages a suboptimal distribution of capital and labor resources across the

---

[18] The exception here is Western Australia, the state most complicit in the secession movement of the 1930s. Until the late 1990s this state received more than its equal per capita share of the pool (it was subsidized by the richer states). Now the state has become rich due to mineral discoveries and is a net contributor to the other states.

[19] Using a computable general equilibrium model, Dixon, Picton, and Rimmer (2005) argue that the welfare effect of inefficient transfers is relatively small. The Dixon et al. model does not capture the impact of strategic behavior.

country. Reform is justified on efficiency grounds, not to establish a pure Tiebout-type federation of freely migrating factors of production but rather a federal economy with an efficiency-enhancing interstate transfer system.

South Africa

With the collapse of apartheid in 1994, the barricade on mobility for nonwhites was removed. Overnight, people were given the freedom, at least in the legal sense, to move where they wished. Though there is no official data on internal migration, anecdotal evidence suggests that the intervening years have seen considerable within-country mobility. Much of this has been from rural to urban areas as people who work in these economic centers such as Johannesburg have relocated their families. Under apartheid, people living in rural areas but working in mining or urban areas were forced to leave their families at home. There may also have been considerable fiscally induced migration once the apartheid barriers were eliminated, and people migrated to capture higher-quality social and economic infrastructure in some of the urban areas. Many rural areas have no schools, hospitals, or roads, while in the richer urban areas these facilities exist at the standard that would be found in developed economies.

Thus, post-apartheid South Africa is characterized by unfettered Tiebout-style free migration and sorting. Much of this is likely to be efficiency-enhancing as workers move from rural areas with relatively low marginal products to urban jobs with relatively higher marginal products or from low to high marginal product regions (provinces). But anecdotal evidence suggests that much of it is fiscally induced and therefore inefficient. In addition, migration is creating negative externalities as shack settlements continue to grow at the urban fringes, along with crime, pollution, and congestion of public services such as hospitals and schools.

South Africa has no plans to respond to this with any form of interregional transfer system. The only policy instrument being considered that might possibly alleviate fiscally induced migration is the grant scheme being developed by the FFC. It is designed to expand access to basic public services to progressively reduce poverty, both at an aggregate level and at the differential levels of poverty between regions. If basic services can be provided more uniformly across regions, the incentive to migrate for fiscal reasons will be lessened, as will the efficiency costs associated with fiscally induced migration.

Conclusion

There are at least two incomplete aspects to the Tiebout view of public policy when applied at the national regional level. The problems associated with the creation and stability of communities and the externalities associated with mobility are ignored. This chapter explored these issues and examined how two countries, Australia and South Africa, have developed policies and institutional responses to regulate free mobility and facilitate stability.

At its beginning Australia adopted policies that interfered with the free migration of capital and labor. Even though the present, publicly stated intention is to equalize fiscal capacities, we believe the policies are the outgrowth of the stability problems encountered in the early years of federation. Therefore, the current spatial pattern of resources in Australia is not purely the result of free-market Tiebout sorting. Even so, because of the design of the current equalization model, it is likely that the spatial allocation of productive factors is inefficient.

In contrast, since 1994 South Africa has allowed unrestricted capital and labor mobility, and much Tiebout-style sorting has taken place. We suggest that some of this may be fiscally induced, creating externalities, and so is inefficient. Moreover, there is little evidence of a policy response in South Africa, with the exception of current work to develop a new grant scheme for provinces that seeks to reduce poverty and its differential regional incidence. Once implemented, this scheme has the potential to influence location decisions and reduce the inefficiencies associated with fiscally induced migration within South Africa.

APPENDIX A: LOCATION DISTORTIONS AND INTERSTATE TRANSFERS

Part 1

Suppose a federal economy with N citizens who have identical incomes and preferences and $i = 1,2$ states. State i has n_i residents who each supply one unit of labor. The national population (labor supply) is, therefore,

$$N = n_1 + n_2. \tag{A.1}$$

The production process in each state is simple. There are two inputs: The first, immobile and in fixed supply, can be thought of as land, fixed physical capital, or natural resources. We denote the supply of this factor in state i as L_i. The second factor is labor. Since each citizen supplies one unit of labor, n_i is state i's labor supply. As shown following, labor is perfectly mobile between states, and its supply can vary from the perspective of each state. The two factors are combined using a production technology based on constant returns to scale to produce a numeraire good whose price is set at one. The value of a state's production of the numeraire (state output) is represented by

$$y_i = f_i(n_i, L_i), \quad i = 1,2. \tag{A.2}$$

Since the immobile factor is in fixed supply in each state, from now on we define the aggregate output of state i as $y_i = f_i(n_i)$, where $f_i'(n_i) > 0$, $f_i''(n_i) < 0$. Though the states have the same production technologies, we allow them to have different endowments of the fixed factor. Competitive factor markets and profit maximization are assumed, implying that each person in a state receives a wage, w_i, equal to their marginal product. Since citizens of a state are identical, each receives the same wage, but because state-specific supplies of land may differ, interstate wage rates may not be the same. The residents of a state own equal portions of that state's fixed factor, and each receives an equal per capita share of the state's fixed-factor income, or economic rent. Since we have assumed constant returns to scale, and thus that output is exhausted by factor payments, the income of a representative citizen in state i is just the state's average product,

$$\frac{f_i(n_i)}{n_i}, \quad i=1,2. \tag{A.3}$$

Part of the numeraire output in a state is transformed into a pure local public good denoted as q_i, with no interstate spillovers, and the rest is consumed directly by state citizens. Per capita consumption of the numeraire is denoted as x_i (private good consumption). There is implicitly a transformation frontier defined between private and public good consumption that we assume to be linear. The (constant) slope of the frontier is the marginal rate of transformation between the two goods (the marginal cost of x_i over the marginal cost of q_i). Under the assumption of perfect competition it is also equal to the price of the numeraire (one) over the price of the public good (which we also assume to be one). The technology that transforms the numeraire into the private and public good is represented by

$$n_i x_i + q_i = f_i(n_i), \quad i=1,2. \tag{A.4}$$

Each citizen of a state has a quasi-concave, continuous, and differentiable utility function,

$$u(x_i, q_i), \quad i=1,2. \tag{A.5}$$

Citizens are also assumed to be perfectly mobile between states and migrate to satisfy the equal per capita utility rule,

$$u(x_1, q_1) = u(x_2, q_2). \tag{A.6}$$

States choose their public good provision simultaneously with Nash conjectures regarding each other's choice (labor makes its location choice at the same time). Governments are benevolent and choose levels of public good provision to maximize the utility of a representative state citizen, while taking into account feasibility constraints and migration responses. Rewriting the budget constraint for states in terms of (per capita) private good consumption, and substituting the result into the per capita utility functions, the problem of state 1 is

$$\underset{(x_1, q_1)}{\text{Max}} \; u\left(\frac{f_1(n_1) - q_1}{n_1}, q_1\right), \tag{A.7}$$

subject to the labor mobility and labor supply constraints,

(i) $u\left(\dfrac{f_1(n_1) - q_1}{n_1}, q_1\right) = u\left(\dfrac{f_2(n_2) - q_2}{n_2}, q_2\right)$

(ii) $N = n_1 + n_2.$ $\tag{A.8}$

Solving yields the necessary condition for public good provision

$$n_1 MRS^1_{x,q} + \frac{\partial n_1}{\partial q_1}(w_1 - x_1) = 1, \tag{A.9}$$

where $MRS^1_{x,q} = u_q / u_x$ is the marginal rate of substitution between the private and public good in state 1, $(w_1 - x_1)$ is the net benefit from an additional migrant in state 1 (their wage less their per capita consumption), and $\partial n_1 / \partial q_1$ is the migration response term. An expression for the migration response can be found from the two labor constraints and substituted into equation A.9, yielding the Samuelson condition

$$n_1 MRS_{x,q}^1 = 1. \tag{A.10}$$

Solving a similar problem for state 2 yields the Samuelson condition

$$n_2 MRS_{x,q}^2 = 1. \tag{A.11}$$

A Nash equilibrium, assuming one exists, is a strategy set (q_1^*, q_2^*) that satisfies equations A.10 and A.11 simultaneously, as well as the free-migration equilibrium condition (conditional on state policies, citizens will be making location choices to satisfy this equal utility condition). One might expect multiple equilibria and in general q_1^* and q_2^* are not the same. Hence, per capita consumption, wage rates, and public-good provision will differ across states. The two states offer different "packages" of public goods and taxes to their residents, with those residents n_1 residing in state 1 being content with their package, and the n_2 residents of state 2 being happy with theirs.

Part 2

While the Samuelson conditions are satisfied in equilibrium, there is the question of whether the mobile factor is allocated efficiently across jurisdictions. For global efficiency we require that the Samuelson conditions are met and that the mobile factor distribution is efficient. The global efficiency of such an equilibrium is assessed by comparing the necessary conditions with those derived by a (Pareto optimal) central planner. The latter are found by supposing that there is a benevolent central planner who chooses private and public good provision in any one of the states to maximize per capita utility while keeping per capita utility in the other state fixed, subject to national feasibility and labor supply constraints

$$\underset{\substack{(x_1, x_2) \\ q_1, q_2 \\ n_1, n_1)}}{Max}\, u\,(x_1, q_1) \tag{A.12}$$

subject to

(i) $(n_1 x_1 + n_2 x_2) + (p_1 q_1 + p_2 q_2) = f_1(n_1) + f_2(n_2)$

(ii) $u(x_2, q_2) = \bar{u}_2$

(iii) $N = n_1 + n_2$.

The Lagrangian is

$$L = u(x_1, q_1) + \lambda_1 \Big(u(x_2, q_2) - \bar{u}_2\Big) + \phi\Big(\big(f(n_1) + f_2(n_2)\big) - \big(n_1 x_1 + n_2 x_2\big) - \big(p_1 q_1 + p_2 q_2\big)\Big)$$
$$+ \mu\,(N - n_1 - n_2) \tag{A.13}$$

The first-order conditions are:

$$x_1: \quad \frac{\partial L}{\partial x_1} = u_{x_1} - \phi n_1 = 0 \tag{A.14}$$

$$q_1: \quad \frac{\partial L}{\partial q_1} = u_{q_1} - \phi n_1 = 0 \tag{A.15}$$

$$x_2: \quad \frac{\partial L}{\partial x_2} = u_{x_2}\lambda_2 - \phi n_2 = 0 \tag{A.16}$$

$$q_2: \quad \frac{\partial L}{\partial q_2} = u_{q_2}(1+\lambda) - \phi n_2 = 0 \tag{A.17}$$

$$n_1: \quad \frac{\partial L}{\partial n_1} = \phi(w_1 - x_1) - \mu = 0 \tag{A.18}$$

$$n_2: \quad \frac{\partial L}{\partial n_2} = \phi(w_2 - x_2) - \mu = 0 \tag{A.19}$$

The term $(w_1 - x_1)$ in equation A.18 is the net benefit of an additional worker in state 1. If we denote this net benefit as NB_1, we can write $NB_1 = (w_1 - x_1)$. The net benefit consists of a migrant's wage, or marginal product, less their per capita consumption of the private good. Similarly, $NB_2 = (w_2 - x_2)$ in equation A.19 is the net benefit from an additional worker in state 2.

Using equations A.14 and A.17 yields the Samuelson conditions (one for each state):

$$n_1 mrs_{xq}^1 = 1, \quad n_2 mrs_{xq}^2 = 1. \tag{A.20}$$

From equations A.18 and A.19 we get

$$(w_1 - x_1) = (w_2 - x_2) \text{ OR } NB_1 = NB_2. \tag{A.21}$$

Pareto optimality requires that local public goods are provided in each state to satisfy the Samuelson condition and that citizens are allocated across states so that the net marginal benefit from an extra person (worker) is the same in each state (an "equating at the margin rule").

In the Nash equilibrium the Samuelson conditions are satisfied (see Part 1), but what about the equating at the margin rule, equation A.21? Will this be satisfied in a Nash equilibrium to the regional competition game? To answer this question, note first that the net benefit expression for each state can be expressed in terms of externalities and rents. From the budget constraint equation A.4, we can write per capita consumption in state i as

$$x_i = \frac{f_i(n_i) - q_i}{n_i}. \tag{A.22}$$

The total economic rent in state i is

$$R_i = f_i(n_i) - w_i n_i. \tag{A.23}$$

Inserting equation A.22 into the net benefit expression for state 1 (where $i = 1$) yields

$$NB_1 = w_1 - \frac{f_1(n_1) - q_1}{n_1}. \tag{A.24}$$

Rearranging and using the definition of total rent from equation A.23, again where $i = 1$, yields

$$NB_1 = \left(\frac{q_1}{n_1} - \frac{R_1}{n_1} \right). \tag{A.25}$$

Consider the first term on the right-hand side, q_1/n_1. This is the contribution (tax payment) of an additional resident in state 1 to the financing of the public good. Since the public good is pure, this contribution is enjoyed by all existing residents of state 1, and q_1/n_1 can be thought of as a "positive fiscal externality," which is ignored by migrating residents and arises because of the public good. The second term in equation A.25 is the migrant's per capita consumption of the region's economic rent. It can be shown that per capita rent is decreasing in n_1; thus, R_1/n_1 can be thought of as a negative rent externality imposed on region 1 by an additional migrant. Thus, for the net benefit of an additional migrant to be zero in state 1 requires that $q_1/n_1 = R_1/n_1$—namely, the (negative) rent externality is exactly offset by the positive fiscal externality.

A similar analysis applies for state 2,

$$NB_2 = \left(\frac{q_2}{n_2} - \frac{R_2}{n_2} \right) \tag{A.26}$$

and again for the net benefit to be zero requires an exact offset between the fiscal and rent externalities—that is, $q_2/n_2 = R_2/n_2$.

We can now show whether equating at the margin rule is satisfied in a Nash equilibrium to the regional competition game. The net benefit to the federation, defined as NB, from moving a resident from state 2 to 1 is $NB = NB_1 - NB_2$. Using equations A.25 and A.26, this is

$$NB = \left(\frac{q_1}{n_1} - \frac{q_2}{n_2} \right) - \left(\frac{R_1}{n_1} - \frac{R_2}{n_2} \right). \tag{A.27}$$

Consider the two terms in the first brackets. As a migrant shifts from state 2 to 1, a positive fiscal externality is created in state 1, q_1/n_1, while a negative fiscal externality is created in state 2, q_2/n_2. Thus, the first set of parentheses is the difference in positive and negative fiscal externalities caused by the migration of a person from state 2 to 1. Now consider the second pair of parentheses. R_1/n_1 is the negative rent externality created as the migrant arrives in state 1, and R_2/n_2 is the positive rent externality generated in state 2 as the person leaves that region.

If $NB = 0$, then the distribution of the mobile citizens will be efficient, since it is not possible to make at least one state better off without making the other worse off. Of course, if there were no fiscal and rent externalities affecting location decisions, NB would automatically be zero: a Tiebout efficiency result.

To see whether NB is zero in a Nash equilibrium to the regional competition game, we can use equations A.22 and A.23 to rewrite the migration equilibrium condition (equation A.6) in terms of per capita rents, per capita tax contributions, wages, and provision of the local public good,

$$u \left(\frac{R_1}{n_1} + w_1 - \frac{q_1}{n_1}, q_1 \right) = u \left(\frac{R_2}{n_2} + w_2 - \frac{q_2}{n_2}, q_2 \right). \tag{A.28}$$

We know this holds in the Nash equilibrium of Part 2, but there is no reason why per capita rents or per capita tax payments will be the same (there is also nothing in the necessary conditions, equations A.10 and A.11, to ensure this). Thus, except by chance, $NB \neq 0$ in a Nash equilibrium, and the mobile population will be distributed suboptimally across states in the sense that some alternative distribution could make the citizens of one state better off without making those in the other state worse off. The Tiebout conjecture that free migration leads to inefficiency breaks down in this model because of the presence of fiscal and rent externalities that distort location decisions and mean that it is possible to have equilibria where there is some social welfare gain from changing the spatial allocation of mobile factors. Though the Samuelson conditions hold in the Nash equilibrium, public-good provision is inefficient, since equation A.21 does not also hold.

There is an optimal interstate transfer that can be used to establish an efficient population distribution, and this transfer is derived in a number of papers, including the one by Boadway and Flatters (1982). We do not derive the transfer here but note that it is a function of the state-specific fiscal and rent externalities, and state and national populations. Boadway and Flatters (1982) argue that a central authority should mandate the optimal transfer, thus creating a case for "equalization" transfers between states. Myers (1990) shows that if states are able to make direct lump-sum transfers among themselves, they will voluntarily choose the optimal transfer, making the Nash equilibrium efficient. Myers's idea is discussed further in Appendix B and in the main text.

APPENDIX B: POLICY-OPTION-CONSTRAINED EFFICIENCY

The problem can be characterized as follows: Let S_j be the set of feasible policy choices for state j and $S = \{S_1, S_2, \ldots, S_J\}$ be the collection of all feasible policy choices. This notation is chosen to suggest intentionally that the choices of policies can be different for each state.

Suppose there are T types of individuals (any two people are of the same type if they have the same preferences and possess the same wealth and earning capacity). For a Tiebout equilibrium, individuals of the same type must have the same level of welfare in every state; if not, there would be migration between states until type-specific utility is equal for all states. In symbols $U_j^t = U_{-j}^t$ (utility of type t in state j is the same as the utility in all other states) for all t. Suppose, further, that there is at least one person of each type in all states and that each state puts the same weight on the welfare of each type. In this case the state objective (welfare) function is

$$W_j = \sum_{t=1}^{T} \alpha^t U_j^T; \quad \sum_{t=1}^{T} \alpha^t = 1. \tag{B.1}$$

Notice that j does not appear as a subscript to α to indicate that the utility weights are not state-specific.

Let $S^* = \{S_1^*, S_2^*, \ldots, S_J^*\}$ be the set of policy choices that maximize aggregate welfare and define $S_{-j} = \{S_1, S_2, \ldots, S_{j-1}, S_{j+1}, \ldots, S_J\}$ as the set of policy choices for all states except state j.

The welfare of individual types is affected by the policy choices of all states. For instance, distribution of the tax burden and the choice of public expenditures have direct impact on welfare. Furthermore, the policies of other states influence individual locational decisions. Because of this, the welfare of a state depends on its own policy choices as well as the choices of the other states

$$W_j = W_j(s_j, s_{-j}) \text{ for } (s_j, s_{-j}) \varepsilon S. \tag{B.2}$$

Given this, consider the choice of a state when all other states make the constrained efficiency choice: State j will select from among its feasible alternatives, the one that maximizes its own welfare, given the policies of its sister states

$$S_j = \underset{s \in S_j}{\arg \max} \ W(s, s_{-j}^*). \tag{B.3}$$

It is clear that it is in the best interest of state j to choose the constrained efficiency policy for its own. This is so because, by the Tiebout equilibrium condition and the presumption that all states have the same welfare function, each state's welfare is maximized by making the choice that maximizes every state's welfare.

REFERENCES

Boadway, Robin W. 2004. The theory and practice of fiscal equalization. *CESifo Economic Studies* 50:211–254.

Boadway, Robin W., Katherine Cuff, and Maurice Marchand. 2003. Equalization and the decentralization of revenue-raising in a federation. *Journal of Public Economic Theory* 5:201–228.

Boadway, Robin W., and Frank Flatters. 1982. Efficiency and equalization payments in a federal system of government: A synthesis and extension of recent results. *Canadian Journal of Economics* 15:613–633.

Breton, Albert. 1984. Towards a theory of competitive federalism. *European Journal of Political Economy* 3:55–86.

Buchanan, James M. 1990. Europe's constitutional opportunity. In *Europe's constitutional future*. London: Institute of Economic Affairs.

Buchanan, James M., and Charles J. Goetz. 1972. Efficiency limits of fiscal mobility: An assessment of the Tiebout model. *Journal of Public Economics* 1:25–43.

Burbidge, John B., and Gordon M. Myers. 1994. Redistribution within and across the regions of a federation. *Canadian Journal of Economics* 27:620–636.

Calhoun, John C. 1953. *A disquisition on government and selections from the discourse*, C. Gordon Post, ed. Indianapolis: Bobbs Merrill.

Commonwealth Budget Paper No. 3: Federal Financial Relations, 2002–03.

Commonwealth Grants Commission. 1983. *Equality in diversity: Fifty years of the Commonwealth Grants Commission*. Canberra: Australian Government Publishing Service.

Coper, Michael. 1988. *Encounters with the Australian Constitution*. Sydney: CCH Australia.

Deakin, Alfred. 1902. The chariot wheels of the central government. In *The development of Australian fiscal federalism* (1980), Wilfred Prest and Russell Mathews, eds. Canberra: Australian National University Press.

Dixon, Peter B., Mark R. Picton, and Maureen T. Rimmer. 2005. Efficiency effects of changes in commonwealth grants to the states: A CGE analysis. *Australian Economic Papers* 44:82–104.

Financial and Fiscal Commission. 2004. Submission for the division of revenue 2005/06. South Africa.

Flatters, Frank R., J. Vernon Henderson, and Peter Mieszkowski. 1974. Public goods, efficiency and regional fiscal equalization. *Journal of Public Economics* 3:99–122.

Gramlich, Edward. 1984. "A fair go": Fiscal federalism. In *The Australian economy: A view from the north*, Richard Caves and Laurence Krause, eds., 231–275. Washington, DC: Brookings Institution Press.

Hamilton, Bruce. 1975. Zoning and property taxation in a system of local governments. *Urban Studies* 12:205–211.

Hirshman, Albert O. 1970. *Exit, voice and loyalty: Responses to decline in firms, organizations and states*. Cambridge, MA: Harvard University Press.

Levtchenkova, Sofia, and Jeffrey D. Petchey. 2000. Regional capital stock data for Australia. *Australian Economic Review* 33:193–197.

MacDonald, Gordon, Jeffrey D. Petchey, and Jaya Josie. 2005. Allocating spending on public infrastructure in developing economies with regional disparities. Working paper. Curtin University, Perth, Western Australia.

Mandela, Nelson. 1994. *Long walk to freedom: The autobiography of Nelson Mandela*. Boston: Little, Brown.

Mansoorian, Arman, and Gordon M. Myers. 1993. Attachment to home and efficient purchases of population in a fiscal externality economy. *Journal of Public Economics* 52:117–132.

May, Ronald J. 1971. *Financing the small states in Australian federalism*. Melbourne: Oxford University Press.

Myers, Gordon M. 1990. Optimality, free mobility and the regional authority in a federation. *Journal of Public Economics* 43:107–121.

Petchey, Jeffrey D., and Sofia Levtchenkova. 2004. Fiscal capacity equalization and economic efficiency: The case of Australia. Paper presented at conference, Challenges in the Design of Fiscal Equalization and Intergovernmental Transfers. Andrew Young School of Policy Studies, Georgia State University, October 3–5.

Petchey, Jeffrey D., Garry MacDonald, and Jaya Josie. 2005. The progressive realization of access to basic services and poverty reduction in South Africa: A concept paper, Financial and Fiscal Commission, South Africa.

Petchey, Jeffrey D., and Graeme Wells. 2004. Australia's federal experience. In *Fiscal federalism and European economic integration*, Mark Baimbridge and Philip Whyman, eds. London: Routledge.

Samuelson, Paul A. 1954. The pure theory of public expenditures. *Review of Economics and Statistics* 36:387–389.

Shapiro, Perry, and Jeffrey D. Petchey. 1994. Shall become exclusive: An economic analysis of Section 90. *Economic Record* 70:171–182.

Shapiro, Perry, Jeffrey D. Petchey, and Bruce T. Coram. 1996. *Federal stability, secession and uniform tax sharing: An application of the theory of the core to federalism.* Canberra: Federalism Research Center of Australian National University.

Sunstein, Cass. 1991. Constitutionalism and secession. *University of Chicago Law Review* 58:633–670.

Tiebout, Charles M. 1956. A pure theory of local expenditures. *Journal of Political Economy* 64:416–424.

Wellisch, Dietmar. 2000. *Theory of public finance in a federal state.* Cambridge, UK: Cambridge University Press.

COMMENTARY

HAROLD M. HOCHMAN

Which Model Is Tiebout's?

The "Tiebout model" may be considered a description of the location process and locational equilibrium in the urban public sector, and the "Tiebout hypothesis" may be regarded as a proposition about fiscal and spatial outcomes at the local level of a multijurisdictional federal system. To summarize the theory, residents of urban areas, by moving or "voting with their feet," erase Samuelsonian inefficiencies in the provision of local public goods. But this is the tip of the iceberg; over time these location decisions nullify interjurisdictional differences in the fiscal residuals (expenditure benefits less tax burdens, calculated at margins of choice) accruing to citizen-voters in the fiscally independent political jurisdictions that make up modern metropolitan regions. In the long run, democratic process, if it acts as a perfect conduit for citizen preferences (a tall assumption), reinforces the sorting and eliminates nonzero fiscal residuals by adjusting expenditure (service) levels and tax incidence, producing what public finance economists call a Lindahl solution.

Like markets in private goods, this spatial market in public goods, both pure and impure, has nice welfare implications—under the right assumptions. If jurisdictional boundaries are stable and, at the margin, free of fiscal externalities, locational adjustments play much the same role as market prices do in such analogous constructs as the Heckscher-Ohlin factor-price equalization theorem in international trade theory. But if mobility is restricted by, say, housing discrimination in suburbs, leaving core cities with an overload of poor families that lack the wherewithal to pay for the public services they require, or in-migration imposes net fiscal burdens on parallel jurisdictions, the Tiebout process can violate Pareto optimality.

All this is in itself neither good nor bad, absent a distributional welfare judgment. To form a normative judgment about the implications of the Tiebout process, we require further information, for example, about distributional effects and distributional preferences. We also need to know about the magnitudes—not simply the existence of—the welfare triangles that measure any inefficiencies that might ensue. Mathematical formulations are not sufficient. Gathering the information and making the calculations that welfare statements require may seem quixotic, but such evidence is necessary to make an informed judgment.

The Petchey and Shapiro model is an expansive interpretation of Tiebout's theory, the topic of the conference on which this book is based. Expansive interpretation is inevitable because the original text is so parsimonious. In addition to the usual provisos, like full and free access to information, Tiebout efficiency requires that there be many fiscally autonomous jurisdictions from which people can choose their residential locations and that they not only have the mobility (including the means) to choose effectively among them, but also exercise it freely. From a Tiebout perspective the discussion is academic unless people move and do so in response to fiscal incentives. (Some years ago, at a seminar in Italy, when I argued that the Tiebout model and the "theory of clubs" were the linchpins of the modern theory of subnational local public finance, I was assailed as a provincial American by my Italian hosts. In Italy, they told me, there is neither much mobility nor fiscal autonomy at the local and regional levels.) Moreover, the jurisdictions among which citizen-voters move, which act like "clubs," must respond to fiscal residuals by adjusting service provision and tax burdens. This in turn requires that higher-level authorities, within their federal systems, delegate the necessary fiscal autonomy to subordinate jurisdictions. Implicitly, at least, Tiebout's theory internalizes a political model in which governments act on constituent preferences, and tax incidence, ultimately, conforms to the benefit principle.

Temporally, Tiebout's paper antedated important developments in the modern theory of public choice as well as most of urban economics. Accordingly, the theory is incomplete, and I have always suggested that students read Tiebout in parallel with, or as a supplement to, public choice classics of its period like Anthony Downs's (1957) *Economic Theory of Democracy* and James Buchanan and Gordon Tullock's (1962) *The Calculus of Consent*, as well as Buchanan's (1965) "An Economic Theory of Clubs," which Tiebout's paper foreshadowed in some ways.

This has been a somewhat lengthy preamble to my comments about the contribution by Petchey and Shapiro. Stripped of its more formal trappings, their paper discusses the extension of Tiebout's argument to higher (province, region, state) levels in federal systems, pursuing a line of reasoning initiated by Flatters, Henderson, and Mieszkowski (1974). Institutionally, it focuses on the federal systems that emerged in Australia early in the twentieth century and South Africa in the 1990s.

The Application to Australia and South Africa

Though the Petchey-Shapiro paper is conceptually sound and rich in historical detail, its application of Tiebout to regions, as opposed to metropolitan areas, is less than convincing. The issues around which it is organized—the effects of fiscal systems on the stability of the federal structure and the Pareto inefficiencies that result from interjurisdictional migration—are salient, to be sure. But it is difficult, perhaps impossible, to assess their practical significance. Whether they have in fact shaped the existing systems of federal grants (or, in American parlance, revenue-sharing) seems very much open to question, absent a more thorough model of political process than they supply. Most of the cited inter-regional redistribution that has occurred in Australia might be attributed to higher-level distributional judgments or interregional politics. As a real possibility, secession seems to have always been remote. This may likewise be the case in South Africa, though there it is impossible to separate redistribution to the rural poor, grounded in considerations of vertical equity, from compensatory grants intended to slow migration to the more developed areas, which modulate Pareto inefficiencies. Petchey and Shapiro seem, thus, to have had more success with this case.

In the geographically restricted context of a metropolitan area, much of the relevant economic and social environment is invariant across jurisdictions, rendering straightforward the application of the Tiebout logic. In the regional context—ironically, perhaps, because his contemporaries thought of Tiebout as primarily being a "regional" economist—the mesh between economic theory (in which efficiency requires stable governmental arrangements and constraints on the external effects of interjurisdictional movement) and political reality is much looser. It seems more likely that population movement among regions is simply an efficient response to basic economic forces and not an artifact of fiscal incentives, as a meaningful interpretation of the Tiebout hypothesis requires. Even more telling, specifically fiscal (or tax-side) incentives to relocate, if they exist at all, are likely to have been minor. Where fiscal authority is centralized, as Petchey and Shapiro claim it is in Australia and South Africa, and regional or state units have little or no fiscal autonomy, Tiebout-type effects, where they occur, derive from expenditure decisions of the central government. While these effects, but not the process, seem to mimic the Tiebout outcome, the fiscal process implicit in Tiebout is not in evidence.

Methodological Issues

All of this brings up some methodological cautions. It is true that such conceptualizations as the theory of federalism, location theory, the Tiebout model, and the theory of clubs have much in common as both theory and application. But they are decidedly not the same thing, and it is important not to confuse them. For example, the whole idea of federalism is much more general than the realities accommodated by the Tiebout model. Federalism is perfectly comfortable, for example, with a system of parallel, institutionally identical jurisdictions that function quite independently, save for sharing in national public goods. New Hampshire and Vermont, for example, which sit side by side, have distinctive fiscal systems that appear to be grounded in widely differing philosophies about the proper role of government in the economy. New Hampshire, where the conference on which this book is based took place, relies almost entirely on a tax on real property for revenue, while its neighbor, Vermont, employs a conventional fiscal mix. Moreover, federal systems like those in Australia and South Africa are not like that of the United States, because the regional entities lack fiscal autonomy. As a consequence, fiscal incentives for relocation, which drive the Tiebout hypothesis, matter relatively little.

Another methodological issue concerns the initial situation from which regional migration occurs. Petchey and Shapiro seem to assume, at least implicitly, that pre-Tiebout situations are on the ex ante welfare frontier and have true optimality properties. Yet, this initial condition may be inconsistent with global efficiency, which cannot be attained unless individuals can sort themselves into preferred locations. In starting from the welfare frontier, with a calculated optimum of the Lange-Lerner type in mind, Petchey and Shapiro worry about implications of the "unwanted externalities"—one wishes they were more specific about what these actually are—associated with Tiebout-type migration. Migration causes the economy to move from the frontier to somewhere inside it. In this context, location-based redistribution appears to be a centrally imposed instrument for stabilizing regional political arrangements rather than a policy to achieve a welfare optimum.

To put this last comment a bit differently, Petchey and Shapiro take, as a methodological given, the rationality of planners. They then worry that real behavior will make things worse. Perhaps so. It would be better to approach the issues the other way round. In a well-functioning federal system, the optimum is constructed from the preferences of citizens, whom planners serve. The Tiebout process is necessary to achieve an efficient outcome. But it is not sufficient because it does not remedy dissatisfaction with distributional realities. As theories of federalism tell us, these are largely the province of central government, and for the outcome to be satisfactory, it must do its job as well.

REFERENCES

Buchanan, James M. 1965. An economic theory of clubs. *Economica* 32:1–14.

Buchanan, James M., and Gordon Tullock. 1962. *The calculus of consent.* Ann Arbor: University of Michigan Press.

Downs, Anthony. 1957. *An economic theory of democracy.* New York: Harper and Row.

Flatters, Frank, J. Vernon Henderson, and Peter Mieszkowski. 1974. Public goods, efficiency, and regional fiscal equalization. *Journal of Public Economics* 3:99–112.

Contributors

Editor

WILLIAM A. FISCHEL
Department of Economics
Dartmouth College
Hanover, New Hampshire

Authors

JACK BUCKLEY
Teachers College
Columbia University
New York, New York

ERIC J. BRUNNER
Department of Economics
Quinnipiac University
Hamden, Connecticut

STEPHEN CALABRESE
Department of Government and
    International Affairs
University of South Florida
Tampa, Florida

EDWARD CARTWRIGHT
Department of Economics
University of Kent
Canterbury, England

JOHN P. CONLEY
Department of Economics
Vanderbilt University
Nashville, Tennessee

DENNIS EPPLE
Tepper School of Business
Carnegie Mellon University
Pittsburgh, Pennsylvania

LEE ANNE FENNELL
College of Law
University of Illinois
Champaign, Illinois

RODERICK M. HILLS JR.
School of Law
University of Michigan
Ann Arbor, Michigan

WILLIAM H. HOYT
Department of Economics
University of Kentucky
Lexington, Kentucky

WALLACE E. OATES
Department of Economics
University of Maryland
College Park, Maryland

JEFFREY PETCHEY
School of Economics and Finance
Curtin University of Technology
Perth, Australia

RICHARD ROMANO
Department of Economics
University of Florida
Gainesville, Florida

MARK SCHNEIDER
Department of Political Science
Stony Brook University
Stony Brook, New York

PERRY SHAPIRO
Department of Economics
University of California
Santa Barbara, California

JON SONSTELIE
Department of Economics
University of California
Santa Barbara, California

MYRNA WOODERS
Department of Economics
Vanderbilt University
Nashville, Tennessee

Discussants

JAN K. BRUECKNER
Department of Economics
University of California
Irvine, California

ROBERT C. ELLICKSON
Law School
Yale University
New Haven, Connecticut

DAVID FIGLIO
Department of Economics
University of Florida
Gainesville, Florida

CLAYTON P. GILLETTE
School of Law
New York University
New York, New York

HAROLD M. HOCHMAN
Program in Economics
CUNY Graduate Center
New York, New York

ROBERT INMAN
Wharton School
University of Pennsylvania
Philadelphia, Pennsylvania

THERESE McGUIRE
Kellogg School of Management
Northwestern University
Evanston, Illinois

THOMAS J. NECHYBA
Department of Economics
Duke University
Durham, North Carolina

ROBERT M. SCHWAB
Department of Economics
University of Maryland
College Park, Maryland

Index

About the
Lincoln Institute
of Land Policy

The Lincoln Institute of Land Policy is a nonprofit and tax-exempt educational institution founded in 1974 to improve the quality of public debate and decisions in the areas of land policy and land-related taxation. The Institute's goals are to integrate theory and practice to better shape land policy and to provide a nonpartisan forum for discussion of the multidisciplinary forces that influence public policy. Inspired by the work of Henry George as expressed in the book *Progress and Poverty* (1879), the Lincoln Institute introduces his thinking and ideas into the contemporary land and tax policy debate to advance a more equitable and productive society.

The work of the Institute is organized around four topics: valuation and taxation, planning, development, and international studies. We seek to inform decision making through education, research, dissemination of information, and demonstration projects in the United States and internationally. Our programs bring together scholars, practitioners, public officials, policy advisers, and involved citizens in a collegial learning community. The Institute does not take a particular point of view but rather serves as a catalyst to facilitate analysis and discussion of land use and taxation issues—both to make a difference today and to help policy makers plan for tomorrow.

L LINCOLN INSTITUTE
OF LAND POLICY

113 Brattle Street
Cambridge, MA 02138-3400 USA

Phone: 1-617-661-3016 x127 or 1-800-LAND-USE (800-526-3873)
Fax: 1-617-661-7235 or 1-800-LAND-944 (800-526-3944)
E-mail: help@lincolninst.edu
Web: www.lincolninst.edu